Identity, Community, and Pluralism in American Life

Identity, Community, and Pluralism in American Life

Edited by
William C. Fischer
David A. Gerber
Jorge M. Guitart
Maxine S. Seller

New York   Oxford
Oxford University Press
1997

Oxford University Press

Oxford   New York
Athens   Auckland   Bangkok   Bogotá   Bombay   Buenos Aires
Calcutta   Cape Town   Dar es Salaam   Delhi   Florence   Hong Kong
Istanbul   Karachi   Kuala Lumpur   Madras   Madrid   Melbourne
Mexico City   Nairobi   Paris   Singapore   Taipei   Tokyo   Toronto

and associated companies in

Berlin   Ibadan

Library of Congress Cataloging-in-Publication Data

Identity, community, and pluralism in American life / edited by
William C. Fischer . . . [et al.].
    p. cm.
Includes bibliographical references.
ISBN 0-19-509470-0.—ISBN 0-19-509471-9 (pbk.)
    1. Pluralism (Social sciences)—United States. 2. Ethnicity—
United States. 3. United States—Civilization. 4. United States—
Race relations. 5. United States—Ethnic relations. I. Fischer,
William C., 1934–   .
E184.A1I34   1997
305.8'00973—dc20   96-8119

Printing (last digit): 1 3 5 7 9 8 6 4 2

Printed in the United States of America
on acid-free paper

To Susan, Carolyn, Sarah, and Bob
with love and thanks for their patience and support

We would like to acknowledge the indispensable help
we received from Ruth Kelly

Contents

PART IV
PERMISSION TO ENTER AND THE RIGHT TO BELONG

PART V
ENDURING CONFLICTS

Introduction

BY WILLIAM C. FISCHER, WITH THE ASSISTANCE OF
THE CO-EDITORS

THE IDEA BEHIND THE BOOK

Identity, Community, and Pluralism in the United States is the result of the
editors' experiences in recent years teaching undergraduates about the complexities of cultural and personal identity in the history, art, and sociopolitics of the
United States. There has been mounting interest in, along with considerable
controversy about, the nature of diversity in our country—how it should be
understood both as a matter of educational policy and practice and as a broad
question of national governance. There has been little disagreement historically
and in the present that indeed the United States continues to be a nation of
diverse peoples coming from numerous different ethnic and cultural origins. But
there has been disagreement as to how this diversity is to be accommodated and
absorbed into national life. There is confusion as to what this diversity actually
means, what it amounts to, in the experiences of particular groups and in the
lives of particular individuals. Exactly what are the ways in which we are diverse?
What are the characteristics of individual or group identity that we can all agree
to acknowledge? Around what issues of mutual interest and advantage can we
transcend the tensions of diversity and act together for the common national
good?

Some categories of identity that make us different from each other are fairly
obvious, like race, ethnicity, gender, and religion. These are widely accepted and
indeed tend to be carelessly simplified in our understanding. There is a tendency
to classify people within these sharply defined categories rather than to recognize that each category is in itself complex. Most of us, in fact, encompass a
number of categories simultaneously. Their boundaries, in reality, are perme-

able, the separate categories of identity interrelated and blending into each other. For instance, a person might be of German descent, female, and Jewish in religious and cultural practice—each element distinct in itself yet all intricately related. About other distinguishing factors there can also be confusion, such as the varieties of ways we might understand class status, or the increasingly mixed identities, through intermarriage, of people deriving from several or many racial, ethnic, and religious backgrounds. In addition, there is some relative lack of understanding about more recently emergent aspects of distinct identity, such as homosexuality, and about the more increasingly visible population of people with handicapping conditions. The German-American Jewish woman might also be a lesbian and by income a member of the working class, and she might also have a physical disability. How is an individual with such multiple and sometimes competing group identities to come into some stable and productive self-possession? How are we to understand the perspective of that person, without some sense of the proportion of reciprocal and contending influences that in the aggregate define who she is? What are both the commonalities and the differrences by which she might be simultaneously welcomed into the larger community of citizens and to a degree rebuffed by it? The editors have each felt the absence, in their teaching, of a reader that addresses in a comprehensive and civil way this enlarged scope of our national diversity and of the pluralistic society that has evolved out of it. Our goal here is to provide an array of selections that thoughtfully address the multiple and often interrelated aspects of our national identity and the nature of our pluralism. The ultimate purpose is to make a contribution to a literacy of diversity and unity among the students we teach.

Questions of diversity and unity were debated throughout the nineteenth century. Immigration from western and northern Europe, slavery and the emancipation of African Americans, the military defeat and containment of Native Americans, and the growth of other racial minority populations, all changed the original conception of the American people about who they were. At the beginning of the twentieth century, some intellectuals and social reformers had become alarmed at the extent to which waves of immigrants from southern and eastern Europe, and to a lesser extent from Asia, were changing the proportions of our collective identity. The new arrivals were markedly different in appearance and cultural heritage from the predominantly Anglo-American population that had shaped official U.S. culture up to that point. Many of them congregated in poor urban enclaves where their differences provoked notice. Accordingly, policymakers and educators placed a good deal of emphasis on assimilating the foreigners into their homogeneous vision of American society, especially through a system of public education in which common American values and expectations could be imposed. The country as a whole embraced a vision of the national future with people having a common identity, mixing and blending as inconspicuously as possible and sharing a common English language, a common set of democratic ideals, and a common understanding of what it means to be an American. By mid-century, differences among people were deemphasized or suppressed as the forces of economic growth, nationwide consumer markets, and suburbanization shaped a shared vision of material well-being that constituted the American Dream.

The second half of the twentieth century would see a remarkable shift in this relatively uniform sense of the American experience. Beginning in the 1950s and culminating in the Civil Rights movement of the 1960s, African Americans, one of the more culturally distinct and socially excluded groups of people in the country, participated in a concentrated period of urban discontent and insurrection. As they moved to assert their social and political rights, they also focused on retrieving and defining a suppressed history and cultural tradition. They articulated their differentness as a cultural and emotional asset rather than as a racial liability, informing difference with a sense of accomplishment and pride instead of inferiority and embarrassment. At the same time, in the West, Mexican Americans began to rehabilitate their cultural and political status, claiming a distinct Chicano culture different from the culture of the mainstream. By the latter part of the century, impelled also by unexpectedly high rates of Asian and Latino immigration and the rapid expansion of a global economy and international mobility, cultural, racial, and ethnic differences had acquired a more positive currency in the United States. In this context, other grounds for legitimizing difference have also emerged. People of European descent as well as Native Americans have demonstrated a renewed interest in their cultural distinctness, while new identities encompassing sexual orientation, disabilities, veteran status, and old age have evolved into political as well as cultural and social forces in their own right. Woven through all of these dimensions has been the emergent and engaged presence of women in life in the United States: more women in the work force, in the professions, in higher education, in politics, in every conceivable area of employment and social productivity. This has not occurred without considerable debate, contention, and a sense of gendered dislocation, especially for men unaccustomed to the degree of gender equity many women have achieved. Depending on where one is located in the present-day spectrum of diversity and multiple identities, the array of claims based on consciously perceived differences can be both heady and bewildering.

There can be little question that we are challenged, as a matter of significant national interest and continuing social progress, to understand who the varieties of our compatriot citizens are and will be in the future. Increasingly our population profile looks very different than it did in the mid-twentieth century. Simply in racial terms alone, we are changing rapidly and will continue to do so well into the next century. By the year 2020, it is estimated that of a total U.S. population of 265 million, approximately one in three citizens will be a person of color, with Hispanics surpassing African Americans as the largest racial group except for Caucasians of European descent. Even in the late 1990s, looking at our demographics from an urban point of view, in the school systems of the country's twenty-five largest cities students of color are for the first time in the majority. Of the 25 million people who will enter the work force in the last decade of the twentieth century, 85 percent will be women, people of color, and immigrants. The implications are enormous for any person participating in the society of the United States in whatever capacity. At a minimum, in order to make one's way economically and socially, one will be increasingly pressed to possess a functional literacy of that complex diversity.

The average college graduate can expect that the constituents of the marketplace, and increasingly of one's social acquaintances, perhaps even of one's own family by birth or marriage, will reflect the new diversity. Whatever the vocational or professional place one comes to occupy, it is inevitable that today's students will have to interact productively with co-workers, colleagues, customers, bosses, patients, students, and friends who will in some ways be quite different from themselves. The demographic changes in the society at large are having an effect on the collective identity of students attending college. The student body is becoming more diversified, more pluralistic, and this growing complexity is causing many faculty and educational administrators to rethink what they are teaching and how they are teaching it in order to address the changing circumstances. There are more women attending college, more older or "nontraditional" students, greater numbers of students of color, more people with disabilities. This potential enrichment of campus culture is not without its attendant problems, as for the first time in their lives many students and faculty try to accommodate and adjust to emotional dynamics and cultural shifts heretofore unfamiliar. Good sense requires that we become engaged at all levels in teaching and acquiring a literacy of multiple identities. Good sense also requires that we engage in a serious examination of what unites us as well as what divides us. Implicitly and explicitly, the selections in this book ask not only how we are different, but also how we are the same. Regardless of our diversities, we share a common humanity and, as U.S. citizens, a common institutional and legal structure within which we interact. This structure produces a vitalizing public discourse, a shared grammar of rights and justice, into which in varying degrees we are all drawn. If American society is to have coherence, and if we are to be able to speak meaningfully to one another, we must understand our commonalities as well as our differences.

THE USES OF THE BOOK

In all its varieties and dimensions, the subject of American pluralism is enormously complicated and mostly experienced as lacking familiar order and coherence. Although many groups and issues are represented in the anthology, our aim is not to represent or cover all of the possibilities inherent in the topic. In our concern to create coherence, we focus on themes and concepts we think will help students come to some clearer understanding of the multiple issues and experiences associated with our national diversity in the past and in the present. We hope the book will ultimately assist them in cultivating a sound critical judgment as they find their way through the intricate web of American identities they will everywhere encounter.

To this end we have used a variety of materials spanning four centuries of the country's evolution from New World settlement to the present postindustrial age: journals, histories, autobiographies, poetry, fiction, government documents, newspaper articles, popular art and music. So that the student and the instructor can explore additional materials and resources, each chapter provides a selected bibliography of supplementary readings. Readers will also notice that current magazines, newspapers, and television programming supply a constant source of information and speculation about diversity in the United States. Indeed, it might be said that the fact of millions of people watching the same television program constitutes one of our culture's eccentric unifying conditions, did we but better understand how to direct such a shared experience to our common benefit.

For the sake of coherence and pedagogical convenience, we have provided an organizing logic in the way the chapters are sequenced. They move from addressing concepts of American pluralism, to individual experiences of it, to group experiences, thence to a number of recurring issues frequently debated and negotiated in our history that have shaped and are still shaping the discourse of American pluralism. We invite instructors to feel free, however, to depart from this logical progression and to use either the chapters or the materials within them in any topical or chronological order that would best fit the logic of their own course organization. We acknowledge, as well, that the problems and issues raised in the later chapters are evolving, that documents timely at the point of selection might not be current now, and that we intend in such instances only to suggest parameters for continuing and unfolding discussion. We further suggest that the issue or "problem" chapters might be used by students and instructors as models for defining still other issues and questions related to pluralism. It is our hope, finally, that the anthology be experienced as having both particular application and generous flexibility.

Our national identity is fluid and complex, its meaning contested by different interpretations and definitions, ever subject to changing conditions and multiple understandings. It is always in the process of qualification and modification. In this regard, we feel that subsequent versions of the anthology will require and benefit from thoughtful evolution and revision. We welcome both general commentary and specific recommendations from students, faculty colleagues, and other readers. Because the chapters are, for the most part, the result of individual efforts, we ask that communication be addressed to the editor concerned.

William C. Fischer, Department of English, 306 Clemens Hall, SUNY at Buffalo, Buffalo, NY 14260
Introduction (with Gerber, Guitart, Seller), Chapter 2 (with Gerber, Guitart, Seller), Chapter 3 (with Seller), Chapter 4

David A. Gerber, Department of History, 564 Park Hall, SUNY at Buffalo, Buffalo, NY 14260
Chapter 1, Chapter 2 (with Fischer, Guitart, Seller), Chapter 8, Chapter 10

Jorge M. Guitart, Department of Modern Languages & Literatures, 923 Clemens Hall, SUNY at Buffalo, Buffalo, NY 14260
Chapter 2 (with Fischer, Gerber, Seller), Chapter 7, Chapter 9, Chapter 11

Maxine S. Seller, Department of Educational Organization, Administration and Policy, 464 Baldy Hall, SUNY at Buffalo, Buffalo, NY 14260
Chapter 2 (with Fischer, Gerber, Guitart), Chapter 3 (with Fischer), Chapter 5, Chapter 6

Identity, Community, and Pluralism in American Life

Part I

Interpreting History and Experience

1

Metaphorizing American Culture

Most of the countries of western Europe have evolved over many centuries, and the large majority of their people have come gradually to possess a sense of sharing of common historical origins and a common culture. By contrast, only in the last two centuries Americans have come together from many different points of origin. Often in our history, in fact, Americans have seemed more different than alike in the habits and values of daily life. Moreover, whereas in many other countries a common nationality and a common political structure evolved gradually and simultaneously over centuries, in the United States the *state* (in other words, the system of government established by the Constitution) was formed long before Americans could begin to think of themselves as a *nation*, that is, as a people sharing a common identity and culture.

Of course, Americans actually came to have many things in common, especially a shared public life of participation in politics, government, and the economy, and increasingly throughout the twentieth century, a shared popular culture created by consumer products, advertising, and the electronic media (movies, radio, television, videos and video games, and recordings). In private life, however, they have tended to preserve a sense of themselves, an identity, as different, and to want to hold on to identities, habits, and values that, to varying degrees, separate them from one another.

In these large patterns of our historical development, the United States may not resemble western European countries, but it does resemble some other countries, such as Argentina, Brazil, and Canada, founded by Europeans yet far from Europe's shores. But there is a critical difference between our country and even these comparable societies. In probably no other large, developed country have those that came to make up the citizenry had such remarkably diverse origins and come in such substantial numbers that they could form large, viable, often long-lasting groups. As the result of forced and voluntary immigrations and territorial incorporations, Americans have come—and are still coming—from every continent and almost every major cultural group to be found on our planet.

The phenomenon we know as "ethnicity," when combined among individuals with racial, social class, religious, and gender differences, is the source of the most visible and culturally perceptible diversity we encounter in our society. There are other sources, however, especially in the late twentieth century. Age, sexual orientation, disability, and lifestyle itself have become the bases of new forms of group identity. These attributes resemble ethnicity in that they provide people with a common sense of identity, but they are not based on the claim of possession of a distant common ancestry.

This complex pattern of great diversity and significant unity within a single country has made the question "What is an American?" an especially urgent one for Americans throughout our history. Getting an easy answer to the question is defeated by the very diversity of the people the question attempts to find ways to define and to describe. As a result, different, subtler questions have been posed that are less concerned with describing the typical American than with figuring out how our society has been, or should ideally be, organized to accommodate diversity. Related to this issue are other questions that seek to determine the consequences of our forms of social organization and whether those consequences are beneficial or detrimental to American life.

In this chapter we are going to examine three distinct ways of conceptually imaging, or metaphorizing, American society in relation to its diversity. In a classic study of American pluralism, *Assimilation in American Life: The Role of Race, Religion, and National Origins* (1964), sociologist Milton Gordon identified the metaphors *Anglo-conformity, the melting pot,* and *cultural pluralism* as long-standing ways of understanding American pluralism. Each metaphor attempts to describe how America is, or ideally should be, organized, and each contains assumptions, observations, and insights that are valid and plausible and others that do not hold up well under close examination. A factor common to each of them is the casual way commentators evade difficult questions, especially the place of racial minorities in American life. A reading at the end of the chapter suggests that while the experts are trying to imagine how America should or should not be in daily life, social relations between individuals and groups, with great creativity and considerable practical success, produce their own complex patterns of unity and fragmentation amidst diversity.

Anglo-conformity: Thomas Jefferson Writes George Flower, 1817

George Flower (1788–1862) immigrated to the United States in 1817 from England and settled on the Illinois frontier, where he and his family joined other English immigrants to form an agricultural colony around what would eventually be known as the town of Albion. Flower's original intention had been to settle in Virginia, and it was in this connection that he had earlier contacted Thomas Jefferson, a Virginian and one of the most prominent Americans of the era.

This selection is a letter Jefferson wrote to Flower upon learning that Flower and his English associates were going to settle in Illinois. Jefferson lays out some familiar attitudes about immigration held by Americans of his background at the time. They very much wanted to encourage immigration to build up the country. Furthermore, they thought of the United States as a haven for the oppressed of all nations. (At the very least, as Jefferson says in this document, the United States could provide an inspiring model of good government for the world.) Yet they did not feel that all peoples could fit equally well into American society. The more similar in culture immigrants were to native white Americans, the more eagerly Jefferson anticipated their settlement in the United States. Thus, he favored English to German immigrants. The letter gives no indication that he would discourage, let alone stop, German immigration, though he did think it best that Germans not be encouraged to settle together in large numbers, because this would retard their learning the English language and American ways. Jefferson appears, therefore, to be an exponent of Anglo-conformity: when it came to thinking about the qualifications of the ideal immigrant, he favored European cultures most in conformity with his own Anglo-American culture. By implication, Jefferson testifies to his conception of the ideal America: a self-governing, English-speaking, Protestant society of independent and intelligent white farmers and craftsmen. This was the vision of American society that provided one of the central inspirations for Jefferson's generation in its struggle from American independence from Great Britain.

Dear Sir

Your favor of Aug. 12 was yesterday received at this place; and I learn from it with pleasure that you have found a tract of country which will suit you for settlement. To us, your first purchase would have been more gratifying, by adding yourself and your friends to our society; but the overruling consideration, with us as with you, is your own advantage: and as it would doubtless be a great comfort to you to have your ancient neighbors and friends settled around you, I sincerely wish that your proposition to purchase a tract of land in the Illinois on favorable terms, for introducing a colony of English farmers, may encounter no difficulties. . . .

For altho, as to other foreigners, it is thought better to discourage their

Source: George Flower and Flower Family Collections, Chicago Historical Society, Chicago, Illinois.

settling together, in large masses, wherein, as in our German settlements, they preserve for a long time their own languages, habits and principles of government that they should distribute themselves sparsely among the natives for quicker amalgamation, yet English emigrants are without this inconvenience. They differ from us little but in their principles of government; and most of those (merchants excepted) who come here, are sufficiently disposed to adopt ours. . . .

Whatever [the relevant federal land policies] may be, they shall be freely exercised for your advantage: and that, not on the selfish principle of increasing our own population at the expense of other nations; for the additions to that from emigration are but as a drop in a bucket to those by natural procreation; but to consecrate a sanctuary for those whom the misrule of Europe may compel to seek happiness in other climes. This [sanctuary], once known, will produce reaction on the happiness even of those who remain there, by warning their task masters that when the evils of Egyptian oppression become heavier than those of the abandonment of country, another Canaan is open where their subjects will be received as brothers, and secured against like oppressions by a participation in the right of self-government. If additional motives could be wanting with us to the maintenance of this right, they would be found in the animating consideration that a single good government becomes thus a blessing to the whole earth; its welcome to the oppressed restraining within certain limits the measure of their oppressions. But should even this be counteracted by violence on the right of expatriation, the other branch of our example then presents itself for imitation, to rise on their rulers, & do as we have done. You have set to your own country a good example, by shewing them a peaceable mode of reducing their rulers. . . . to the necessity of becoming more wise, more moderate, and more honest; and I sincerely pray that the example may work for the benefit of those who cannot follow it, as it will for your own. . . .

Th Jefferson

Anglo-Conformity: The New York City Public Schools, 1906

Long after Jefferson's death, many white Protestant Americans continued to believe in his vision of an America open to all of Europe's oppressed peoples, but most especially to those whose presence would produce a nation that looked most like the world in which they themselves felt comfortable. That vision grew harder to sustain, however, because the immigrants flocking into the country in the nineteenth and early twentieth centuries were less and less like the original British stock from which Jefferson and the other Founding Fathers originated. Some argued that the immigration of those who were most different from the Anglo-American core

Source: New York Tribune, September 16, 1906.

should be sharply restricted. Others argued that much more deliberate and systematic ways had to be found to instruct immigrants in how to conform to Anglo-American ways. These exponents of assimilation, among whom were many educators and teachers, frequently looked to the public schools as a positive instrument for Americanizing the children of immigrant parents. They also hoped that these children could be the agents for their parents' Americanization. The hard-working, often poor parents could not go to school themselves, but their children might still bring home daily the knowledge of the new American ways the schools taught.

This selection demonstrates the ways in which the public schools of New York City, which has long been one of our principal immigrant receiving centers, came increasingly to institutionalize this Anglo-conformist vision of American culture. The children are taught cleanliness, patriotism, civics, and practical industrial or domestic skills that will help them to make an independent living or take care of a husband and children. American visitors to the school, such as the president of Johns Hopkins University and the *New York Tribune's* reporter, are enthusiastic about Public School No. 23 precisely because of the expectation that the students produced by this curriculum would be fully Americanized, carbon copies of their own white Anglo-Saxon ideal. This expectation was more hope than reality. The children returned from school each day to the world of their families and ethnic groups, and here foreign ways held on tenaciously. Even at school, the children's peer groups, which brought their own standards to school from home and neighborhood, exerted a powerful influence that could at times challenge the authority of teachers. The schools did help to Americanize these children, but the children became Americans of a particular type—ethnics in a pluralistic society that was based on difference as well as similarity.

The training of future citizens is the first duty of the public schools, and the work in that congested quarter of this city on the Lower East Side, which reflects more of the foreign than the American coloring in its population, its language, and its outdoor religious observances, presents features unique in many respects. In this quarter the schools are focal points of civilization, as well as centers of the intellectual life of the neighborhood.

In the streets, even in the playgrounds of the schools, Yiddish east of the Bowery and Italian west of the Bowery often join with the latest slang to form the ordinary language of the youngest pupils. Upstairs in the classrooms, all day long, the teachers are struggling to overcome these habits of expression, and, considering that the child hears English for only five hours out of the twenty-four, the results at the end of the fifth and sixth years of school life are wonderful. But these schools are centers of thought-life in more ways than one. The children who attend them are often the teachers of their parents, and hundreds of Italian and Russian adults in this foreign quarter are being taught daily the rudiments of English through the medium of their children.

This gives some slight idea of the influence of these institutions, but were we to stop there possibly the best work of the school would be lost. The principal and teachers, supported at present by the Health Officer, must deal with the question of cleanliness, not as a mere matter of appearance, but rather as an absolute necessity for the good health of the children. This is sometimes the most difficult task of all. Only by insisting—doubly insisting—on clean hands and faces can the teacher lay the foundation for habits of cleanliness. The next step is to insist on combed hair, then on cleaned shoes or boots, and it is not a rare sight in some schools to see a monitor or teacher placed at the entrance to the assembly room as Inspector-General of faces, hair, and shoes. In no other respect does the influence of the school tell more strongly than in this matter of cleanliness. Visitors who are taken to low primary classes first and then immediately afterwards to the highest grammar grades are astonished at the difference. While in the lowest grades a glance shows how necessary is the eternal vigilance of the teacher, in the higher grades one can see the effect of training and habit. Both boys and girls are equal in appearance—especially the girls—to the pupils of similar grades in any quarter of the city. Of course, many of them were from the beginning carefully attended to at home, but many others, whose mothers and fathers possibly went out to daily work as the youngsters were getting up for the day, acquired their habits through compulsion and insistence.

There are many children in these schools whose parents are really wealthy, conducting good paying businesses and owning the great tenements in the neighborhood. These children are not only finely but even expensively dressed, and in most cases have their private tutors after 3:00 p.m. in music and foreign languages. Even the children of much poorer parents to a great extent take private lessons in instrumental music, the piano for girls, the violin and mandolin among the Italians for boys.

First in interest in this citizenship training is the work in civics and the history of the United States. In addition to the regular class work in these subjects this training includes the recitation of patriotic pieces at the morning assemblies, the singing of patriotic songs, and the daily salute to the flag. As one of the best means of rousing the patriotic sentiment, the principal of one school endeavors to make the special exercise in honor of national holidays, the red-letter days of school life. . . .

In the work in civics it is interesting to note the practical knowledge of politics the children have. Three out of four pupils in the higher grades know the names of the assemblyman, alderman, and senator of the district, not to forget the district leader. They usually speak of these men by their first names. They know about the primary fights for leadership, and it is amusing to hear the heated arguments that take place between the partisans around election time.

On one occasion, the principal was visited by a parent before promotion time. The parent was very anxious about his son's promotion, and the teacher was asked to furnish the boy's record for the term. The record being good the parent was informed that his boy would probably be promoted. The father then handed a sealed envelope to the principal and after profuse thankings started to leave the school. On opening the envelope a two-dollar bill was found inside. When the parent was called back and informed that such action was wrong, he took the bill and seemed greatly surprised. In broken English he informed the principal that this was the first time in New York he had ever asked a favor without expecting to pay for it. From a case like this we can see the value of sending out from a school in this neighborhood the true principles of civic virtue, the duties of citizens, and the responsibilities of the city's officers.

As to work in manual training, No. 23 was one of the first schools in this city selected for the experiment. In a very short time the pupils had become expert in the new subjects, and the school was visited by distinguished educators from all parts of the country looking for information as to the results of this training. Ten years ago President Gilman of Johns Hopkins, after a day spent in the classrooms inspecting this work, wrote to the superintendent in charge: "The trustees of the John F. Slater Fund desire me to thank you especially for taking them through ward school No. 23, where one of the most interesting experiments is in progress in respect to the eye and hand under very disadvantageous circumstances. Not one of us will fail to remember the extraordinary progress shown by the boys of that school." The visitors on that occasion included two university presidents and an ex-President of the United States, Rutherford B. Hayes. Since that time manual training work has grown to be one of the most important considerations in elementary education. In No. 23 every branch of the work is represented and it does serve in many instances as a direct preparation for the future life work of the children. But the training has a practical value even during the school life of the pupils. The boys make many necessary and ornamental articles in woodwork for their homes, such as book-racks, shelves, and china closets, while many of the girls in the upper grades learn to prepare the family dinner or attend to the home sewing. In this way the parents are led directly to appreciate the value of school training.

As for the English work in this quarter, the struggle for the teacher is never ending with the vast majority of the pupils up to the sixth and seventh years. There must be constant drill on enunciation and pronunciation all through the school. The class libraries must be made popular, and, by the way, No. 23 has one of the largest school libraries of the city schools. This is because of the consolidation into one grammar department of four grammar schools of the old Sixth Ward, thereby consolidating four school libraries into one. The books in the class libraries amount to a total of 900, and the circulation of these books for October was 2,519. The children, especially the Jewish children, make use of the public circulating libraries in the vicinity, of which there are several. The use of libraries naturally increases the knowledge of the pupils and develops a liking for good reading, but it does not materially affect the natural mistakes in expression. These must be corrected in school by the teacher. One means especially useful here is found in memorizing selections for class drill. This is followed by recitations at the morning assemblies, usually of patriotic pieces. The speakers at these assemblies are supposed to set models of good English before their fellow pupils and are marked by the principal. The best compete twice a year for medals, and the excellence of the speaking on these occasions is remarkable.

Of the graduates of No. 23, some go to high school or to the City College. The great number are forced to end their scholastic work with elementary school, except for the further training that many of them get in evening high school. Of those boys and girls from this and other East Side schools who are able to complete their courses in the City College or the Normal College, the city may well be proud. Of all the vast sums spent by the municipality none is better expended than that required for the training of those bright, studious, and patriotic graduates of the foreign quarter of this city. And they often, as lawyers, doctors, and teachers in that same locality, give back to the city in useful citizenship all the city has done for them.

The Melting Pot: Israel Zangwill Coins a Phrase, 1908

The use of the term *the melting pot* to describe American society dates from the 1908 production of a play by the same name written by Israel Zangwill (1865–1926), a British Jew. In contrast to those whose vision of America was of a society conforming to the culture of its Anglo-American founders, Zangwill saw American society in the process of mixing all of its inhabitants, whatever their original point of origin, into a new American people with its own identity and culture. Zangwill's vision depends on intermarriage, which stirs many anxieties in people. Some of the most powerful moments in Zangwill's play come precisely when his main character, the Jewish immigrant composer and musician David Quixano, articulates this vision of America. David, whose family was murdered in an anti-Semitic massacre by Czarist troops in Russia, has begun to reconstruct his life in New York City, where he lives with his Uncle Mendel, but he is haunted by memories of the slaughter of his loved ones. He takes hope from his belief that the ancient hatreds of Europe are destined to die in America, because American society breaks down the identities and animosities that sustain them. He is attempting to express this theme in a symphony he is writing. David meets Vera, a social worker, who, it turns out, is the disaffected daughter of the officer responsible for the massacre in which David's family was murdered. The two fall in love. In the first of the two scenes that make up this selection, early in their acquaintance, David articulates the vision of America he is attempting to capture in his music. In the second, just after his symphony has been played for the first time to an appreciative audience in New York harbor, within sight of the Statue of Liberty, he again articulates his vision of the great melting pot, this time an even more inclusive one that includes not only European immigrants but also non-white Americans.

i.

VERA

So your music finds inspiration in America?

DAVID

Yes—in the seething of the Crucible.

Source: Israel Zangwill, *The Melting Pot: Drama in Four Acts* (New York: The Macmillan Company, 1909), pp. 36–38, 198–99.

VERA

The Crucible? I don't understand!

DAVID

Not understand! You, the Spirit of the Settlement!*

[*He rises and crosses to her and leans over the table, facing her.*]

Not understand that America is God's Crucible, the great Melting-Pot where all the races of Europe are melting and re-forming! Here you stand, good folk, think I, when I see them at Ellis Island, here you stand

[*Graphically illustrating it on the table.*]

in your fifty groups, with your fifty languages and histories, and your fifty blood hatreds and rivalries. But you won't be long like that, brothers, for these are the fires of God you've come to—these are the fires of God. A fig for your feuds and vendettas! Germans and Frenchmen, Irishmen and Englishmen, Jews and Russians—into the Crucible with you all! God is making the American.

MENDEL

I should have thought the American was made already—eighty millions of him.

DAVID

Eighty millions!

[*He smiles toward* VERA *in good-humoured derision.*]

Eighty millions! Over a continent! Why, that cockleshell of a Britain has forty millions! No, uncle, the real American has not yet arrived. He is only in the Crucible, I tell you—he will be the fusion of all races, the coming superman. Ah, what a glorious Finale for my symphony—if I can only write it. . . .

ii.
VERA

[*They stand quietly hand in hand.*]

Look! How beautiful the sunset is after the storm!
[DAVID *turns. The sunset, which has begun to grow beautiful just after* VERA's *entrance, has now reached its most magnificent moment; below there are narrow lines of saffron and pale gold, but above the whole sky is one glory of burning flame.*]

DAVID

[*Prophetically exalted by the spectacle.*]

It is the fires of God round His Crucible.

[*He drops her hand and points downward.*]

---

*"Settlement" was the name for neighborhood social centers, staffed by social workers, that catered largely to immigrant working-class families.

There she lies, the great Melting-Pot—listen! Can't you hear the roaring and the bubbling? There gapes her mouth

[*He points east.*]

—the harbour where a thousand mammoth feeders come from the ends of the world to pour in their human freight. Ah, what a stirring and a seething! Celt and Latin, Slav and Teuton, Greek and Syrian,—black and yellow—

VERA

[*Softly, nestling to him.*]

Jew and Gentile—

DAVID

Yes, East and West, and North and South, the palm and the pine, the pole and the equator, the crescent and the cross—how the great Alchemist melts and fuses them with his purging flame! Here shall they all unite to build the Republic of Man and the Kingdom of God. Ah, Vera, what is the glory of Rome and Jerusalem where all nations and races come to worship and look back, compared with the glory of America, where all races and nations come to labour and look forward!

[*He raises his hands in benediction over the shining city.*]

Peace, peace, to all ye unborn millions, fated to fill this giant continent—the God of our *children* give you peace.

The Melting Pot: An Eighteenth-century Interpretation, 1782

While Zangwill might have been the first to use the term *melting pot,* the idea that American society was the product of an amalgamation and mixing of peoples and cultures was hardly a new one. In fact, it had been powerfully articulated in one of the most famous early attempts to describe American society.

J. Hector St. John Crèvecoeur (1735–1813) was a French-born essayist who served with the French army in Canada before settling in Orange County, New York. Between 1769 and 1780 he lived there as a farmer. Crèvecoeur wrote a series of essays, which were published in 1782 under the title *Letters of An American Farmer.* In them, he illustrated the ways in which frontier life in the emerging American nation was creating a new, democratic form of society. America was democratic not only in its political arrangements, but in its culture, which, according to Crèvecoeur, was not based on conformity to patterns imposed by an Anglo-American elite but rather on the daily habits and values of ordinary people. In this selection

Source: J. Hector St. John de Crèvecoeur, *Letters from An American Farmer* (London: Thomas Davies and Lockyer Davis, 1782), pp. 41–45.

from his book of essays, Crèvecoeur describes the process by which newly found material security in America leads immigrants to abandon their old identities and cultures and open themselves to new ones that he sees as uniquely American. The inclusiveness of Crèvecoeur's vision has definite limits: racial minorities apparently have no place in his conception of the new culture and society being born in America. On the other hand, for him it was sufficient to feel hopeful about the future of America because the ancient hatreds between European peoples seemed to vanish in the New World.

. . . . In this great American asylum, the poor of Europe have by some means met together, and in consequence of various causes; to what purpose should they ask one another what countrymen they are? Alas, two thirds of them had no country. Can a wretch who wanders about, who works and starves, whose life is a continual scene of sore affliction or pinching penury—can that man call England or any other kingdom his country? A country that had no bread for him, whose fields procured him no harvest, who met with nothing but the frowns of the rich, the severity of the laws, with jails and punishments, who owned not a single foot of the extensive surface of this planet? No! Urged by a variety of motives, here they came. Everything has tended to regenerate them: new laws, a new mode of living, a new social system; here they are become men: in Europe they were as so many useless plants, wanting vegetative mould and refreshing showers; they withered, and were mowed down by want, hunger, and war; but now, by the power of transplantation, like all other plants they have taken root and flourished! Formerly they were not numbered in any civil lists of their country, except in those of the poor; here they rank as citizens. By what invisible power hath this surprising metamorphosis been performed? By that of the laws and that of their industry. The laws, the indulgent laws, protect them as they arrive, stamping on them the symbol of adoption; they receive ample rewards for their labours; these accumulated rewards procure them lands; those lands confer on them the title of freemen, and to that title every benefit is affixed which men can possibly require. . . .

What attachment can a poor European emigrant have for a country where he had nothing? The knowledge of the language, the love of a few kindred as poor as himself, were the only cords that tied him; his country is now that which gives him his land, bread, protection, and consequence; *Ubi panis ibi patria* is the motto of all emigrants.* What, then, is the American, this new man? He is neither a European nor the descendant of a European; hence that strange mixture of blood, which you will find in no other country. I could point out to you a family whose grandfather was an Englishman, whose wife was Dutch, whose son married a French woman, and whose present four sons have now four wives of different nations. *He* is an American, who, leaving behind him all his ancient prejudices and manners, receives new ones from the new mode of life he has embraced, the new government he obeys, and the new rank he holds. He becomes an American by being received in the broad lap of our great Alma

---

*"Where there is bread, that is my country."

Mater. Here individuals of all nations are melted into a new race of men, whose labours and posterity will one day cause great changes in the world. Americans are the western pilgrims who are carrying along with them that great mass of arts, sciences, vigour, and industry which began long since in the East; they will finish the great circle. The Americans were once scattered all over Europe; here they are incorporated into one of the finest systems of population which has ever appeared, and which will hereafter become distinct by the power of the different climates they inhabit. The American ought therefore to love this country much better than that wherein either he or his forefathers were born. Here the rewards of his industry follow with equal steps the progress of his labour; his labour is founded on the basis of nature, self-interest; can it want a stronger allurement? Wives and children, who before in vain demanded of him a morsel of bread, now, fat and frolicsome, gladly help their father to clear those fields whence exuberant crops are to arise to feed and to clothe them all, without any part being claimed, either by a despotic prince, a rich abbot, or a mighty lord. Here religion demands but little of him: a small voluntary salary to the minister and gratitude to God; can he refuse these? The American is a new man, who acts upon new principles; he must therefore entertain new ideas and form new opinions. From involuntary idleness, servile dependence, penury, and useless labour, he has passed to toils of a very different nature, rewarded by ample subsistence. This is an American. . . .

Cultural Pluralism: Randolph Bourne's Vision of America as a Confederation of Distinct Peoples, 1916

War has often bred a fear of cultural difference in the United States, because of the suspicion that the competing allegiances and identities that exist in a pluralistic society will weaken the ability of the nation to defend itself. This was especially the case during World War I, which the United States entered just at the close of the period of tremendous European immigration that stimulated the writings of commentators like Zangwill about American society. The war pitted against each other many of the countries from which so many immigrants had come. During the war years it was discovered that many American ethnics, whether recently arrived or long resident, had deep feelings about the fate of their European homelands that were then at war. For Anglo-conformists, this was proof that the nation had to redouble its efforts to Americanize the foreigner.

The young essayist Randolph Bourne (1886–1918) derived other lessons from this wartime experience. Bourne not only refused to denounce diversity, but embraced it enthusiastically as an antidote to what he regarded as the mindless passion among many Americans for uniformity and homo-

Source: Randolph Bourne, "Trans-National America," *Atlantic Monthly,* 118 (July 1916), 86–97.

geneity. It was not only the war that caused this passion for conformity, Bourne believed, but the larger forces of modern, urban, and industrial society that seemed to require that people live within narrow and fixed patterns and gear themselves strictly to moneymaking and economic productivity. Bourne offered as an antidote to this dreary world of sameness his own vision of cultural pluralism: a cosmopolitan America in which difference was not feared but highly valued and encouraged.

It took a great deal of intellectual courage to state such beliefs at the time, because there was a general climate of intolerance toward diversity in America during World War I. Nonetheless, Bourne advances certain ideas that are, at the very least, arguable. Bourne believed that at the time only the South, with its distinctive climate, economy, dialect, and race relations, had a unique culture. Is there really no American culture? Is the United States just an agglomeration of ethnicities, composed of people who live within separate cultures and have little in common? Notice that Bourne has a low opinion of the popular culture of daily life, with its consumer and media aspects, that has been a powerful influence in the twentieth century in bringing people together across the lines of ethnicity, religion, race, and social class.

Furthermore, Bourne's prescriptions for encouraging cultural pluralism were controversial in his day and remain so in ours. American law has never encouraged dual citizenship, though many other countries make it easy for their citizens to hold two citizenships simultaneously. Public opinion has not looked favorably on people who come to the United States for a brief time to make money and then return to their homeland without making a commitment to American life and values. That such people often work very hard for low wages and pay taxes to support services they do not and will never use has failed to make much difference in the popular mind.

One major question above all others, however, stands out in evaluating Bourne's ideas: Can a society be built less upon what people have in common than upon a commitment to the preservation of the differences among them? Because of the diversity of the American people throughout our history, this question has been asked continually by Americans. One could almost say that preoccupation with the question is one of the things Americans have and have always had in common.

No reverberatory effect of the great war has caused American public opinion more solicitude than the failure of the "melting-pot." The discovery of diverse nationalistic feelings among our great alien population has come to most people as an intense shock. It has brought out the unpleasant inconsistencies of our traditional beliefs. . . . We have had to listen to publicists who express themselves as stunned by the evidence of vigorous nationalistic and cultural movements in this country among Germans, Scandinavians, Bohemians, and Poles, while in the same breath they insist that the alien shall be forcibly assimilated to that Anglo-Saxon tradition which they unquestioningly label "American."

As the unpleasant truth has come upon us that assimilation in this country was proceeding on lines very different from those we had marked out for it, we found ourselves inclined to blame those who were thwarting our prophecies. The truth became culpable. We blamed the war, we blamed the Germans. And then we discovered with a moral shock that these movements had been making great headway before the war even began. We found that the tendency, reprehensible and paradoxical as it might be, has been for the national clusters of immigrants, as they became more and more firmly established and more and more prosperous, to cultivate more and more assiduously the literatures and cultural traditions of their homelands. Assimilation, in other words, instead of washing out the memories of Europe, made them more and more intensely real. Just as these clusters became more and more objectively American, did they become more and more German or Scandinavian or Bohemian or Polish.

To face the fact that our aliens are already strong enough to take a share in the direction of their own destiny, and that the strong cultural movements represented by the foreign press, schools, and colonies are a challenge to our facile attempts, is not, however, to admit the failure of Americanization. It is not to fear the failure of democracy. It is rather to urge us to an investigation of what Americanism may rightly mean. It is to ask ourselves whether our ideal has been broad or narrow—whether perhaps the time has not come to assert a higher ideal than the "melting-pot." Surely we cannot be certain of our spiritual democracy when, claiming to melt the nations within us to a comprehension of our free and democratic institutions, we fly into panic at the first sign of their own will and tendency. We act as if we wanted Americanization to take place only on our own terms, and not by the consent of the governed. All our elaborate machinery of settlement and school and union, of social and political naturalization, however, will move with friction just in so far as it neglects to take into account this strong and virile insistence that America shall be what the immigrant will have a hand in making it, and not what a ruling class, descendant of those British stocks which were the first permanent immigrants, decide that America shall be made. This is the condition which confronts us, and which demands a clear and general readjustment of our attitude and our ideal.

What we emphatically do not want is that these distinctive qualities should be washed out into a tasteless, colorless fluid of uniformity. Already we have far too much of this insipidity,—masses of people who are cultural half-breeds, neither assimilated Anglo-Saxons nor nationals of another culture. Each national colony in this country seems to retain in its foreign press, its vernacular literature, its schools, its intellectual and patriotic leaders, a central cultural nucleus. From this nucleus the colony extends out by imperceptible gradations to a fringe where national characteristics are all but lost. Our cities are filled with these half-breeds who retain their foreign names but have lost the foreign savor. This does not mean that they have actually been changed into New Englanders or Middle Westerners. It does not mean that they have been really Americanized. It means that, letting slip from them whatever native culture they had, they have substituted for it only the most rudimentary American—the American culture of the cheap newspaper, the "movies," the popular song, the ubiquitous automobile. The unthinking who survey this class call them assimilated, Americanized. The great American public school has done its work. With these people our institutions are safe. We may thrill with dread at the aggressive hyphenate, but this tame flabbiness is accepted as Americanization. The same moulders of opinion whose ideal is to melt the different races into Anglo-Saxon gold hail this poor product as the satisfying result of their alchemy.

Yet a truer cultural sense would have told us that it is not the self-conscious cultural nuclei that sap at our American life, but these fringes. It is not the Jew who sticks proudly to the faith of his fathers and boasts of that venerable culture of his who is dangerous to America, but the Jew who has lost the Jewish fire and become a mere elementary, grasping animal. It is not the Bohemian who supports the Bohemian schools in Chicago whose influence is sinister, but the Bohemian who has made money and has got into ward politics. Just so surely as we tend to disintegrate these nuclei of nationalistic culture do we tend to create hordes of men and women without a spiritual country, cultural outlaws, without taste, without standards but those of the mob. We sentence them to live on the most rudimentary planes of American life. The influences at the centre of the nuclei are centripetal. They make for the intelligence and the social values which mean an enhancement of life. And just because the foreign-born retains this expressiveness is he likely to be a better citizen of the American community. The influences at the fringe, however, are centrifugal, anarchical. They make for detached fragments of peoples. Those who came to find liberty achieve only license. They become the flotsam and jetsam of American life, the downward undertow of our civilization with its leering cheapness and falseness of taste and spiritual outlook, the absence of mind and sincere feeling which we see in our slovenly towns, our vapid moving pictures, our popular novels, and in the vacuous faces of the crowds on the city street. . . .

The war has shown us that not in any magical formula will this purpose be found. No intense nationalism of the European plan can be ours. But do we not begin to see a new and more adventurous ideal? Do we not see how the national colonies in America, deriving power from the deep cultural heart of Europe and yet living here in mutual toleration, freed from the age-long tangles of races, creeds, and dynasties, may work out a federated ideal? America is transplanted Europe, but a Europe that has not been disintegrated and scattered in the transplanting as in some Dispersion. Its colonies live here inextricably mingled, yet not homogeneous. They merge but they do not fuse.

America is a unique sociological fabric, and it bespeaks poverty of imagination not to be thrilled at the incalculable potentialities of so novel a union of men. To seek no other goal than the weary old nationalism,—belligerent, exclusive, inbreeding, the poison of which we are witnessing now in Europe,—is to make patriotism a hollow sham, and to declare that, in spite of our boastings, America must ever be a follower and not a leader of nations.

If we come to find this point of view plausible, we shall have to give up the search for our native "American" culture. With the exception of the South, . . . there is no distinctively American culture. It is apparently our lot rather to be a federation of cultures. This we have been for half a century, and the war has made it ever more evident that this is what we are destined to remain. This will not mean, however, that there are not expressions of indigenous genius that could not have sprung from any other soil. Music, poetry, philosophy, have been singularly fertile and new. Strangely enough, American genius has flared forth just in those directions which are least understood *[sic]* of the people. If the American note is bigness, action, the objective as contrasted with the reflective life, where is the epic expression of this spirit? Our drama and our fiction, the peculiar fields for the expression of action and objectivity, are somehow exactly the fields of the spirit which remain poor and mediocre. American materialism is in some way inhibited from getting into impressive artistic form its own energy with which it bursts. Nor is it any better in architecture, the least romantic and subjective of all the arts. We are inarticulate of the very values which we profess to idealize. But in the finer forms—music, verse, the essay, philosophy—the American genius puts forth work equal to any of its contemporaries. Just in so far as our American genius has expressed the pioneer spirit, the adventurous, forward-looking drive of a colonial empire, is it representative of that whole America of the many races and peoples, and not of any partial or traditional enthusiasm. And only as that pioneer note is sounded can we really speak of the American culture. As long as we thought of Americanism in terms of the 'melting-pot,' our American cultural tradition lay in the past. It was something to which the new Americans were to be moulded. In the light of our changing ideal of Americanism, we must perpetrate the paradox that our American cultural tradition lies in the future. It will be what we all together make out of this incomparable opportunity of attacking the future with a new key. . . .

The failure of the melting-pot, far from closing the great American democratic experiment, means that it has only just begun. Whatever American nationalism turns out to be, we see already that it will have a color richer and more exciting than our ideal has hitherto encompassed. In a world which has dreamed of internationalism, we find that we have all unawares been building up the first international nation. The voices which have cried for a tight and jealous nationalism of the European pattern are failing. From that ideal, however valiantly and disinterestedly it has been set for us, time and tendency have moved us further and further away. What we have achieved has been rather a cosmopolitan federation of national colonies, of foreign cultures, from whom the sting of devastating competition has been removed. America is already the world-federation in miniature, the continent where for the first time in history has been achieved that miracle of hope, the peaceful living side by side, with character substantially preserved, of the most heterogeneous peoples under the sun. Nowhere else has such contiguity been anything but the breeder of misery. Here, notwithstanding our tragic failures of adjustment, the outlines are already too clear not to give us a new vision and a new orientation of the American mind in the world. . . .

In this effort we may have to accept some form of that dual citizenship which meets with so much articulate horror among us. Dual citizenship we may have to recognize as the rudimentary form of that international citizenship to which, if our words mean anything, we aspire. We have assumed unquestioningly that mere participation in the political life of the United States must cut the new citizen off from all sympathy with his old allegiance. Anything but a bodily transfer of devotion from one sovereignty to another has been viewed as a sort of moral treason against the Republic. We have insisted that the immigrant whom we welcomed escaping from the very exclusive nationalism of his European home shall forthwith adopt a nationalism just as exclusive, just as narrow, and even less legitimate because it is founded on no warm traditions of his own. Yet a nation like France is said to permit a formal and legal dual citizenship even at the present time. Though a citizen of hers may pretend to cast off his allegiance in favor of some other sovereignty, he is still subject to her laws when he returns. Once a citizen, always a citizen, no matter how many new citizenships he may embrace. And such a dual citizenship seems to [me] sound and right. For it recognizes that, although the Frenchman may accept the formal institutional framework of his new country and indeed become intensely loyal to it, yet his Frenchness he will never lose. What makes up the fabric of his soul will always be of this Frenchness, so that unless he becomes utterly degenerate he will always to some degree dwell still in his native environment. . . .

Along with dual citizenship we shall have to accept, I think, that free and mobile passage of the immigrant between America and his native land again which now arouses so much prejudice among us. We shall have to accept the immigrant's return for the same reason that we consider justified our own flitting about the earth. To stigmatize the alien who works in America for a few years and returns to his own land, only perhaps to seek American fortune again, is to think in narrow nationalistic terms. It is to ignore the cosmopolitan significance of this migration. It is to ignore the fact that the returning immigrant is often a missionary to an inferior civilization.

This migratory habit has been especially common with the unskilled laborers who have been pouring into the United States in the last dozen years from every country in southeastern Europe. Many of them return to spend their earnings in their own country or to serve their country in war. But they return with an entirely new critical outlook, and a sense of the superiority of American organization to the primitive living around them. This continued passage to and fro has already raised the material standard of living in many regions of these backward countries. For these regions are thus endowed with exactly what they need, the capital for the exploitation of their natural resources, and the spirit of enterprise. America is thus educating these laggard peoples from the very bottom of society up, awakening vast masses to a new-born hope for the future. In the migratory Greek, therefore, we have not the parasitic alien, the doubtful American asset, but a symbol of that cosmopolitan interchange which is coming, in spite of all war and national exclusiveness.

Only America, by reason of the unique liberty of opportunity and traditional isolation for which she seems to stand, can lead in this cosmopolitan enterprise. Only the American—and in this category I include the migratory alien who has lived with us and caught the pioneer spirit and a sense of new social vistas—has the chance to become that citizen of the world. America is coming to be, not a nationality but a trans-nationality, a weaving back and forth, with the other lands, of many threads of all sizes and colors. Any movement which attempts to thwart this weaving, or to dye the fabric any one color, or disentangle the threads of the strands, is false to this cosmopolitan vision. I do not mean that we shall necessarily glut ourselves with the raw product of humanity. It would be folly to absorb the nations faster than we could weave them. We have no duty either to admit or reject. It is purely a question of expediency. What concerns us is the fact that the strands are here. We must have a policy and an ideal for an actual situation. Our question is, What shall we do with our America? How are we likely to get the more creative America—by confining our imaginations to the ideal of the melting-pot, or broadening them to some such cosmopolitan conception as I have been vaguely sketching? . . .

Living with Diversity: Our Daily Experiences, 1994

Anglo-conformity, the melting pot, and cultural pluralism are all ways of imagining what America *should* be or, in all its complexity, is in the process of becoming. How Americans actually live has been and remains another matter. In reality, each idea can be found to contribute to our understanding of the way American pluralism has been formed. In this selection, we see how New York City public schools in the 1990s are meeting the challenge of the current massive wave of immigration. The reporter might use the term *melting pot,* but she is sensitive to the full range of circumstances that shape the response of the contemporary school to the needs of immigrant young people. The school she writes about *is* a melting pot in the sense that she seems to use the term—different peoples meet there—but also in the more subtle sense in which the students are creating a code of behavior among themselves to bring a mutually understood order to their interactions. Moreover, as is evident in the references to popular music, makeup, and clothing styles, American popular culture creates a source of unity among them. But the school also embodies a sort of benign Anglo-conformity: its purpose, after all, is to teach English and prepare the students to support themselves in the competitive world of American capitalism. In this, it is not much different than Public School No. 23 in 1906, though its methods seem, by our standards, more responsive to the students' emotional needs and more respectful of the differences among them. Finally the school is also a place where cultural pluralism develops, though it is not precisely Bourne's "transnational" vision. When individual students of a similar background, who were previously unknown to one another, discover that the language and national origins of their parents provide a practical bond between them, they are discovering the value of ethnic identity. On that basis, they take tentative steps toward creating a common ethnic life for themselves, even as their attendance at public school propels them into the pluralistic mainstream of American life.

This example provides us with an illustration of the complexity of American life as we actually live it. We often live at once in several different worlds, which, far from being sharply separated, have unclear boundaries and blend subtly together. Like these students, individual Americans are

Source: Charisse Jones, "Melting Pot Still Bubbles at I.S. 237: Myriad Accents Fill the Halls at Diverse School in Flushing," *The New York Times* (June 12, 1994).

often involved in endless informal negotiations between these worlds in their efforts to create order and meaning in their lives. In this sense, being an American amidst such diversity requires a good deal of creativity and self-reflection.

In parts of her India, it would not have been proper, this friendship between a young man and a young woman, says Nitu Singh. But here, in the United States, she believes it is necessary.

She is 16, and in less than two years has graduated quickly from one level to the next in the school's English-as-a-second-language program. He, Jatinder Singh, 15, has been here two months, and speaks no English. Their bond is the Ponjabi language, and their shared understanding of what it is like to be new in a foreign country.

"He needs help, so I help him," she said. "I treat him like my brother."

The school that has brought Nitu and Jatinder together, Intermediate School 237, the Rachel L. Carson School, at a quiet intersection in Flushing, Queens, is a modern brick building that is among the most diverse schools in New York City. Its students fill the hallways with the accents of El Salvador, Taiwan and Pakistan, and go home to households where mothers scold and comfort them in Spanish, Mandarin and Urdu.

It is not new, this coming together of myriad nationalities under a schoolhouse roof. For more than a hundred years, New York City schools have been a portal for immigrant children, and today the tide of foreign-born students entering the system is as great as that at the turn of the century, historians say. Last school year alone, more than 65,000 children from 188 countries entered the public school system, pushing the city's enrollment to nearly one million.

To wander the halls of I.S. 237 is to see the baby steps and giant strides of young people wrestling with assimilation and ethnic pride, of change and acceptance. It is to watch one youngster from the Punjab teach another to use a lock. Or to watch a young woman from Iran give up her traditional headdress.

A hundred years ago, schools prohibited students from speaking any language but English in the classroom or schoolyard. Now, the effort is to ease the transition and preserve some of the past for children moving between cultures.

"A lot of them are terrified," said Rosiland Tseng, who has been a guidance counselor at I.S. 237 for six years. "They're also very confused about the system, like changing the classrooms. They don't understand."

At the school, one approach has been a buddy system that pairs newcomers with immigrants who have been here longer.

The buddies are often in the same classes, their interdependence evolving into friendship.

Opening a Universe

Nitu helped Jatinder decipher the mystery of a combination lock on his locker, showing him as many as fifteen times how to unlock it until he got it right. She explained to him that here children are fed in a cafeteria, instead of bringing their own food from home.

In a classroom recently, Nitu sat next to Jatinder quietly helping him piece together a puzzle of the United States. She smiles when he utters the states' names correctly, and provides friendship when he feels different and alone.

The children of I.S. 237 come from more than 60 countries. Nearly half of its 1,300 students were born outside the United States, and among them more than 50 languages and dialects are spoken, school officials said.

There is much they must get used to. No longer must they bow or stand when a teacher enters the room. And in New York City, the teacher cannot hit you for being rude.

Often the students' awkwardness is rooted in ordinary adolescence. But other times it is the legacy of immigrant experience.

One boy from Ecuador stood whenever he read aloud, only to be laughed back down by classmates. A girl from Taiwan has the baby fat of a child but the worries of a woman as she struggles to care for a younger sister and find a niche in this unfamiliar place.

The Start Is Bumpy

The first days are the hardest, the children say, filled with the noise of a language not understood, the strangeness of customs never before encountered.

"I felt excluded from the group," Lisa Hou, 14, remembered, "because you look different, because you don't dress the way they do. I wanted to be a part of them. Back home I never had this kind of problem."

That was nearly four years ago, when she first came from Taiwan. Now she says fitting in no longer matters. "I don't really care. I can't change the way I look."

But minutes earlier, as she tried to describe the taunts she had endured, her words got lost in tears.

Many immigrant children are initiated into the youthful mores of American culture the painful way, compelled to get hip in a hurry to stop the insults that come from sporting no-name sneakers and speaking English with a heavy accent.

A year and a half ago, Salima Nabizada each morning would put on the head covering worn by Muslim women in Iran, and go to school. But on a recent Wednesday afternoon, the 13-year-old was the all-American girl, a black hair band where her hijab used to be.

Inside a guidance counselor's office, dressed in a T-shirt and jeans, she explained why the head covering disappeared. For six months, she wore it, and more times than she can remember, other children ripped it from her head.

Dreaded Each Day

"I would feel like everybody was looking at me," she said of the dread that filled her stomach each school day. "I wore it, and they took it off. And so I went home and told my mother I don't want to wear it anymore. I can't. It's so hard."

Cultural adaptation, and the pain that often comes with it, have always been part of the immigrant experience, said Dr. Stephan F. Brumberg, a historian and author of "Going To America, Going to School" (Praeger). Another is conflict between children and parents.

"There are the problems that arise between generations," he said, "parents who come of age in one cultural, linguistic setting who are raising children in a different one. It's an unavoidable tension, and it's something that people who emigrate probably don't really foresee; that they're going to raise aliens."

Eli Pantazis, 15, was raised in a Greek village in Albania, where her parents worked as farmers, and no one had a private telephone. Women did not wear makeup until they were married. Eli did not know a word of English. She had never heard of Michael Jackson.

Now, less than three years after leaving Albania, she keeps a tube of plum-colored lipstick stashed in her back pack. Her favorite artist is Michael Jackson's sister, Janet. And she can no longer remember a word of Albanian.

Not Done on Purpose

"I don't understand that language anymore," she said, blonde hair framing her oval face. "I was born there, I went to school there and now I forgot. My parents think I'm doing it on purpose, that I know but don't want to speak it. But I don't remember."

She still speaks Greek with her parents, but breaks into English more and more. . . .

She is often the family's translator, one of several burdens many immigrant children assume.

For Lisa Hou, interpreting letters from credit card companies and making calls to her parents' bank are just two of the tasks she has taken on. She also does the family's laundry, prepares her sister's breakfast and helps her sibling with homework after school.

"Back home, I just did my homework, and then I could go out," said Lisa. "But here I feel I have to go home first to make sure everything is all right."

Often it is the school's guidance counselors who must try to bridge the widening gulf between children and parents. Mrs. Tseng said that some immigrant children feel overwhelmed by the academic expectations their parents hold for them, as well as the clash of cultures. Parents may also be confused about how to deal with their children, but feel it is improper to ask others for advice, especially school officials, whom they were often taught in their homelands to obey and fear.

Must Get Involved

"The parents often feel they're not supposed to be active in the schools because the school authorities know best," she said. "They don't understand that's part of the process, to get involved."

Programs are also in place for the children, who, once the newness has passed, still often face reminders that they are not originally from here.

The most vivid reminder is language. Luis Figueroa, 14, born in Peru, has lived in the United States for six years. He speaks English with ease, and wears the teen-age uniform: sweatshirt, blue jeans and sneakers.

Still, there are moments he'll be sitting in class, and it will happen. "You read a book," he said, "and you always see a word that you don't know."

I.S. 237 has three teachers in its English-as-a-second-language (ESL) program. There is also a Korean and Chinese bilingual teacher, and 10 paraprofessionals working with special education students who speak languages as diverse as Persian, from Iran, and Pashto, from Afghanistan and Pakistan.

Oscar Cohen, principal of I.S. 237 for 18 years, said that a few of the immigrant students are illiterate in their native languages as well as English, making instruction even more difficult.

In the early 1980's, some staff were intimidated by the task, he said. "People would say, 'What do you want me to do? They can't read or write English. I'm an English teacher.' And I would say, 'You're a teacher. You teach.'"

A Major Shift

It was only two decades ago that New York City's bilingual program was introduced. Seventy years before that, schools were strictly English-only. Intensive English courses nicknamed "steamer classes" were often offered in immigrant neighborhoods at the turn of the century, said Dr. Brumberg.

But by World War I, immigration slowed to a trickle, and such special programs disappeared, he said.

SUGGESTIONS FOR FURTHER READING

Philip Gleason, *Speaking of Diversity: Language and Ethnicity in Twentieth Century America*. Baltimore: Johns Hopkins University Press, 1992.

Milton Gordon, *Assimilation in American Life*. New York: Oxford University Press, 1964.

John Higham, *Send These to Me: Immigrants in Urban America* Rev. ed. Baltimore: Johns Hopkins University Press, 1984.

Horace Kallen, *Cultural Pluralism and the American Idea*. Philadelphia: University of Pennsylvania Press, 1956.

Arthur Mann, *The One and the Many: Reflections on the American Identity*. Chicago: University of Chicago Press, 1979.

2

The Presence of the Past

The readings in this chapter show the wide variety of experiences by which different groups of Americans came to find themselves in the United States.

The United States has often been called "a nation of immigrants." It is certainly true that many of the family stories by which large numbers of Americans have come to understand themselves are about the difficulties of life in an "Old World," far away on the other side of an ocean, and the fateful decision to leave that troubled place for a freer and more prosperous life in America. While this was the experience of tens of millions of our ancestors, *voluntary* immigration from abroad is only one of the several ways by which people came to enter American life. Some groups were forcefully incorporated into the American population. The slave trade brought millions of Africans to American shores. Native Americans and nineteenth-century Mexicans came to be incorporated as a result of various combinations of military conquest and treaties that altered national boundaries.

The voluntary nature of immigration itself is a complex matter. The word *refugee* is used here to apply to people whose leaving one place for another is largely *involuntary,* a result of oppression, exploitation, even the possibility of physical annihilation. Some immigrants, it seems, were more pushed out of their homelands than pulled by the prospect of a good life in America. Often voluntary and involuntary factors mixed together, however, even in the experience of the same group. American laws, too, influenced whether some people were even allowed to come to the United States as immigrants.

The fact that we do not have a common origin, but many different pasts, makes defining what it means to be "American" much more difficult. But, as we are going to find out in later chapters, the effort to come to such a definition is so characteristically American that it is one of the things that Americans have actually come to share with one another.

Voluntary Immigrants

THE QUEST FOR A BETTER LIFE: A NORWEGIAN IMMIGRANT LETTER OF 1835

In the era before instant electronic communications and mass circulation newspapers, personal letters often served to inform people about current events and economic opportunities as well as about strictly private matters. Much of the massive voluntary immigration of over 35 million Europeans to the United States between the 1820s and the 1920s was stimulated by personal letters written by recent immigrants to the kinfolk and friends they had left behind in the Old World. This was certainly the case in mid-nineteenth-century Norway, where the letters of immigrants were circulated throughout farm villages and small towns by those to whom they were sent. In this way, the common people of Norway, then suffering from dislocating changes in peasant agriculture that made daily existence precarious, learned about the possibilities of a better life in the New World.

One letter that was widely circulated throughout rural Norway was written by Gjert G. Hovland, a farmer who immigrated to the United States in 1831 and settled alongside a number of other Norwegian immigrants in Monroe County in northwestern New York State. This letter, written to a Norwegian friend who remained behind in Hovland's old village, is like most immigrant letters. It combines news of family life with discussion of the yield of his farm and the price of a cow and with commentary about American government, laws, and social institutions. Hovland is probably overly optimistic about the prosperity and ease of American life, particularly in areas like northwestern New York, which was just emerging from frontier conditions. But such optimism must be placed in the context of his bitter memories of Norway, which he felt to be a closed society without fairness, opportunity, and democratic freedoms for ordinary people. Though some who were influenced by Hovland's soaring optimism to come to America were likely to be disillusioned, his positive view of American life no doubt spurred many others to high hopes that caused them to persevere under difficult conditions. These hopes and that perseverance do a great deal to account for the fact that the small country of Norway contributed a higher proportion of its population to immigration to the United States than any other country in Europe except Ireland. In this way the Norwegian-American population, one of the first ethnic groups to form as immigration

Source: Theodore C. Blegen, "A Typical 'America Letter,'" *Mississippi Valley Historical Review,* 9 (June 1922), 68–74.

increased in the early nineteenth century, came together, and another component was added to the many that would comprise the American people.

To Torjuls Asbjeldsen, Marland, Ullensuang Sogn, Kingservigs, Prarstegjuld, Norway:
I must take this opportunity to let you know that we are in the best of health, and that we—both my wife and I—find ourselves exceedingly well satisfied. Our son attends the English[-language] school, and talks English as well as the native-born. Nothing has made me more happy and contented than the fact that we left Norway and journeyed to this country. We have gained more since our arrival here than I did during all the time that I lived in Norway, and I have every prospect of earning a livelihood here for myself and my family—even if my family were larger—so long as God gives me good health.

Such excellent plans have been developed here that, even though one be infirm, no one need suffer want. Competent men are elected whose duty it is to see that no needy persons, either in the cities or in the country, shall have to beg for their living. If a man dies and is survived by a widow and children who are unable to support themselves—as is often the case—they have the privilege of petitioning these officials. To each one will then be given every year as much as is needed of clothes and food, and no discrimination will be shown between the native-born and those from foreign countries. These things I have learned through daily observation, and I do not believe there can be better laws and arrangements for the benefit and happiness of the common man in the whole world. I have talked with a sensible person who has traveled in many countries, who has lived here twenty-six years, and has full knowledge of the matter; both of him and of other reliable persons I have made inquiries, for I wish to let everyone learn the truth.

When assemblies are held to elect officials who are to serve the country, the vote of the common man carries just as much authority and influence as does that of the rich and powerful man. Neither in the matter of clothes nor in seats* are distinctions to be observed, whether one be a farmer or a clerk. The freedom which the one enjoys is just as good as that of the other. So long as he comports himself honestly he will be subjected to no interference. Everybody has the liberty to travel about in the country, wherever he wishes, without any passports or papers. Everyone is permitted to engage in whatever business he finds most desirable, in trade or commerce, by land or by water. But if anyone is found guilty of crime, he will be prosecuted and severely punished for it.

No duties are levied upon goods which are produced in the country and brought to the city by water or by land. In case of death, no registration** is required; the survivor, after paying the debts, is free to dispose of the property for himself and his family just as he desires. There is no one here who snatches it away, like a beast of prey, wanting only to live by the sweat of others and to make himself the heir to the money of others. No, everyone must work for his living here, and it makes no difference whether he is of low or of high estate. It would heartily please me if I could learn that everyone of you who are in need and have

*In assigning seats in church.
**Death taxes levied on a deceased person's possessions.

little chance of gaining support for yourselves and your families would make up your mind to leave Norway and to come to America, for, even if many more were to come, there would still be room here for all. For all those who are willing to work there is no lack of employment and business here. It is possible for all to live in comfort and without suffering want. I do not believe that any of those who suffer under the oppression of others and who must rear their children under straightened circumstances could do better than to help the latter to come to America. But alas, many persons, even though they want to come, lack the necessary means, and many others are so stupid as to believe that it is best to live in the country where they have been brought up even if they have nothing but hard bread to satisfy their hunger. It is as if they should say that those who move to a better land, where there is plenty, commit a wrong. But I can find no place where our Creator has forbidden one to seek one's food in an honorable manner. I should like to talk to many persons in Norway for a little while, but we do not wish to live in Norway. We lived there altogether too long. Nor have I talked with any immigrant in this country who wished to return.

We left our home in Norway on June 24, 1831. Sailing from Gottenborg on July 30, we landed in America September 18, and by October 4 we had reached this place in the interior where we now live. The day after my arrival I began to work for an American. In December I went and bought myself fifty acres of land. I put up a house which we moved into in the month of March, 1832. I then set to work with the greatest will and pleasure, for the land was covered with trees. In the fall I planted about one barrel of wheat and in the spring of 1833 we planted about half a bushel of Indian corn and three bushels of potatoes (the latter in May). The next fall we harvested fifteen barrels of wheat, six barrels of Indian corn, and fourteen barrels of potatoes. Wheat, which is grown almost everywhere, is used for one's daily food. It costs from three to four dollars a barrel, corn costs from one and one-half to two dollars a barrel, and potatoes fifty cents a barrel. Oats are a dollar a barrel, being used not for human food, but for the cattle and horses. We purchased a cow in April of the first year that we were here for eighteen dollars, from which we milked six *kander* (Norwegian measure) a day and sometimes more . . .

A hired man engaged for a whole year receives from eight to twelve dollars per month in addition to board, washing, and lodging. A servant girl receives one dollar a week, or fifty dollars a year, besides board, washing, and lodging, and is not required to do heavy or outside work, but only work within the house. A laborer engaged to work the soil receives from one-half to one dollar a day and free board. . . .

Six families of the Norwegians who had settled in this place sold their farms last summer and moved farther west in the country to a place which is called *Ellenaais.** We and another Norwegian family have also sold our farms and

*Hovland here refers to the migration, in 1834, of Norwegians from the New York settlement to the Fox river valley in *Illinois*. The leader of this movement was Cleng Peerson, who in 1833 had visited Illinois and selected the site for the settlement. The Fox river settlement was the first Norwegian settlement in the west, and it became a nucleus from which settlement radiated in Illinois, Wisconsin, and Iowa.

intend to journey, this May, to that state, where land can be bought at a better price, and where it is easier for one to get started. The supply of trees there is only sufficient to meet one's actual needs. Cattle can be fed there at little cost, for one can cut as much hay there as one needs. There is an untold amount of land which the United States own and which is reserved by an established law at a set price for the one who first buys it from the government. It is called public land, and is sold for $1.25 per acre. Land thus bought and paid for is held in allodial possession for the purchaser and his heirs.* Whether native-born or foreign, one is free to do with it whatever one pleases.

This is a very beautiful and fertile country. Prosperity and contentment are to be seen almost everywhere one goes. Practically everything that one needs can be sown or planted here; it grows splendidly and yields in many-fold measure, without the use of manure.

Excellent order and good laws exist here, and the country is governed by wise authorities.

I sold my land last summer, in July, 1834, and by the transaction earned in cash the sum of five hundred dollars. I have now decided to buy one hundred and sixty acres, an amount which can be paid for with two hundred dollars. The eight Norwegian families still in this neighborhood desire to sell their land as soon as they can, and to move west, for they prefer to live near each other, although many of the natives are just as good people.**

In America one associates with good and kindly people. Everyone has the freedom to practice that teaching and religion which he himself favors. Nor are there any taxes to be paid here, except for the land one owns, and not even that tax is large. . . . For the fifty acres which I have sold I paid annually one dollar in taxes. I must let you know that on the piece of land which we sold there were more trees than I could count of the kind that produces sugar, and these trees were common everywhere. We did not take more than we needed for our own use each year. Usually it is in March that one does this work, when the sap begins to spring up in the trees; with a small iron one chops a dent in the tree, placing under it a piece of hollowed-out wood as a trough. From out of the tree there come forth from two to three pails of sweet sap a day, and this sap produces sugar, syrup, ale and vinegar.

There is much more of which I could write to you, but I will close for this time, with hearty greetings from my wife and son and myself to you, my relatives and acquaintances. Let us be happy in heart and consecrated in spirit so that when the race has been run, when the pilgrim's staff has been laid down, we may be worthy of hearing the glorious words: "Blessed of my Father, come ye and inherit the kingdom and the righteousness prepared for you." Wherever we may wander in this earthly sphere, let us seek Him who is the true light and life, and follow His voice which calls to our hearts, no matter where we go or stand.

---

*Settlement and a down payment on public land constituted the basis of a right to remain there until the purchase was completed, even if that purchase required many years.

**Hovland himself went to Illinois in 1835 and lived in the Fox river valley settlement until his death in 1870.

Live well in the sight of God: that is my wish as your friend. Greetings to Knud Oppendal and Johannes Hovland and to all who inquire about me.

April 22, 1835

Gjert Gregoriussen Hovland

ECONOMIC IMMIGRANTS FROM NINETEENTH-CENTURY CHINA: "A CHINAMAN'S CHANCE"

Between 1840 and 1900 about 300,000 Chinese, mainly young male laborers, came to the United States, usually on borrowed money, to work in the mines, on the railroads, or in fishing, agriculture, and service industries. Like the Norwegians, the Chinese emigrated to escape poverty in their homeland. As a nonwhite, "heathen" minority, however, their experience was very different.

Early Chinese immigrants were welcomed in the labor-hungry West and supposedly were protected by the "most favored nation" privileges in the Burlingame Treaty of 1868. However, by the 1870s, recession and heightened economic competition combined with racism to produce a flood of anti-Chinese literature and political demagoguery. Discriminatory state laws drove the Chinese out of mining and other occupations, forbade them to own land or to testify against whites, and put their children in segregated schools. In 1882 Congress passed the Chinese Exclusion Act, the first national legislation to restrict immigration on the basis of race or national origin. By limiting immigration to small numbers of students, merchants, or clergymen, categories that were almost entirely male, the law had the effect of discriminating on the basis of gender as well.

Between 1870 and 1900 there were anti-Chinese riots in sixty-six communities in nine western states and territories, including the Rock Springs, Wyoming, riot described by Chinese survivors in the petition that follows. The immediate cause of the Rock Springs riot was the Chinese workers' refusal to join a proposed strike. Because most planned to return to their families in China as soon as they had accumulated some money, the Chinese were reluctant to sacrifice current wages for uncertain future benefits. Despite petitions such as this one, which was addressed to the Chinese consul at New York City, the perpetrators of the Rock Springs riot, or of any other anti-Chinese riot, were never punished, nor were the Chinese ever compensated for loss of life or property. The expression "a Chinaman's chance" entered the American lexicon, meaning "no chance at all." Given this history, it is not surprising that early Chinese Americans formed tightly knit, inward-looking communities, expecting nothing positive from white America.

Source: Memorial of Chinese Laborers Resident at Rock Springs, Wyoming Territory, to the Chinese Consul at New York (1885) as reproduced in Chang-Tsu Wu, ed., *"Chink!": A Documentary History of Anti-Chinese Prejudice in America* (New York: World Publishing Company, 1972), pp. 152–59.

We, the undersigned, have been in Rock Springs, Wyoming Territory, for periods ranging from one to fifteen years, for the purpose of working on the railroads and in the coal mines.

Up to the time of the recent troubles we had worked along with the white men, and had not had the least ill feeling against them. The officers of the companies employing us treated us and the white man kindly, placing both races on the same footing and paying the same wages.

Several times we had been approached by the white men and requested to join them in asking the companies for an increase in the wages of all, both Chinese and white men. We inquired of them what we should do if the companies refused to grant an increase. They answered that if the companies would not increase our wages we should all strike, then the companies would be obliged to increase our wages. To this we dissented, wherefore we excited their animosity against us.

During the past two years there has been in existence in "Whitemen's Town," Rock Springs, an organization composed of white miners, whose object was to bring about the expulsion of all Chinese from the Territory. To them or to their object we have paid no attention. About the month of August of this year notices were posted up, all the way from Evanston to Rock Springs, demanding the expulsion of the Chinese, &e. On the evening of September 1, 1885, the bell of the building in which said organization meets rang for a meeting. It was rumored on that night that threats had been made against the Chinese.

On the morning of September 2, a little past seven o'clock, more than ten white men, some in ordinary dress and others in mining suits, ran into Coal Pit No. 6, loudly declaring that the Chinese should not be permitted to work there. The Chinese present reasoned with them in a few words, but were attacked with murderous weapons, and three of their number wounded. The white foreman of the coal pit, hearing of the disturbance, ordered all to stop work for the time being.

After the work had stopped, all the white men in and near Coal Pit No. 6 began to assemble by the dozen. They carried firearms, and marched to Rock Springs by way of the railroad from Coal Pit No. 6, and crossing the railroad bridge, went directly to "Whitemen's Town." All this took place before 10:00 a.m. We now heard the bell ringing for a meeting at the white men's organization building. Not long after, all the white men came out of that building, most of them assembling in the barrooms, the crowds meanwhile growing larger and larger.

About two o'clock in the afternoon a mob, divided into two gangs, came toward "Chinatown," one gang coming by way of the plank bridge, and the other by way of the railroad bridge. . . . One squad of them guarded the plank bridge in order to cut off the retreat of the Chinese.

Not long after, it was everywhere reported that a Chinese named Leo Dye Bah, who lived in the western part of "Chinatown," was killed by a bullet, and that another named Yip Ah Marn, resident in the eastern end of the town, was likewise killed. The Chinese now, to save their lives, fled in confusion in every direction. . . .

Whenever the mob met a Chinese they stopped him and, pointing a weapon at him, asked him if he had any revolver, and then approaching him they searched his person, robbing him of his watch or any gold or silver that he might have about him, before letting him go. Some of the rioters would let a Chinese go after depriving him of all his gold and silver, while another Chinese would be beaten with the butt ends of the weapons before being let go. Some of the rioters, when they could not stop a Chinese, would shoot him dead on the spot, and then search and rob him. . . . Some, who took no part either in beating or robbing the Chinese, stood by, shouting loudly and laughing and clapping their hands.

There was a gang of women that stood at the "Chinatown" end of the plank bridge and cheered; among the women, two of them each fired successive shots at the Chinese.

The Chinese who were the first to flee mostly dispersed themselves at the back hills, on the opposite bank of the creek, and among the opposite hills. They were scattered far and near, high and low, in about one hundred places. Some were standing, or sitting, or lying hid on the grass, or stooping down on the low grounds. Every one of them was praying to Heaven or groaning with pain. They had been eyewitnesses to the shooting in "Chinatown," and had seen the whites, male and female, old and young, which were carried across to "White-men's Town."

Some of the rioters went off toward the railroad of Coal Pit No. 6, others set fire to the Chinese houses. Between 4:00 p.m. and a little past 9:00 p.m. all the camp houses belonging to the coal company and the Chinese huts had been burned down completely. . . . All the Chinese houses burned numbered seventy-nine.

Some of the Chinese were killed at the bank of Bitter Creek, some near the railroad bridge, and some in "Chinatown." After having been killed, the dead bodies of some were carried to the burning buildings and thrown into the flames. Some of the Chinese who had hid themselves in the houses were killed and their bodies burned; some, who on account of sickness could not run, were burned alive in the houses. One Chinese was killed in "Whitemen's Town" in a laundry house, and his house demolished. The whole number of Chinese killed was twenty-eight and those wounded fifteen.

The money that the Chinese lost was that which in their hurry they were unable to take with them, and consequently were obliged to leave in their houses, or that which was taken from their persons. The goods, clothing, or household effects remaining in their houses were either plundered or burned. . . .

On the fifth of September all the Chinese that had fled assembled at Evanston; the native citizens there threatened day and night to burn and kill the Chinese. Fortunately, United States troops had been ordered to come and protect them, and quiet was restored. On the ninth of September the United States government instructed the troops to escort the Chinese back to Rock Springs. When they arrived there they saw only a burnt tract of ground to mark the sites of their former habitations. Some of the dead bodies had been buried by the company, while others, mangled and decomposed, were strewn on the ground and were being eaten by dogs and hogs. Some of the bodies were not found until they were dug out of the ruins of the buildings. Some had been burned beyond recognition. It was a sad and painful sight to see the son crying for the father, the brother for the brother, the uncle for the nephew, and friend for friend.

We never thought that the subjects of a nation entitled by treaty to the rights and privileges of the most favored nation could, in a country so highly civilized like this, so unexpectedly suffer the cruelty and wrong of being unjustly put to death, or of being wounded and left without the means of cure, or [of] being abandoned to poverty, hunger, and cold, and without the means to betake themselves elsewhere.

To the great President of the United States, who, hearing of the riot, sent troops to protect our lives, we are most sincerely thankful.

In behalf of those killed or wounded, or of those deprived of their property, we pray that the examining commission will ask our minister to sympathize, and to endeavor to secure the punishment of the murderers, the relief of the wounded, and compensation for those despoiled of their property, so that the living and the relatives of the dead will be grateful, and never forget his kindness for generations.

Hereinabove we have made a brief recital of the facts of this riot, and pray your honor will take them into your kind consideration.

(Here follow the signatures of 559 Chinese laborers, resident at Rock Springs, Wyoming Territory.)

WOULD-BE IMMIGRANTS:
CHINESE POETS ON ANGEL ISLAND

The Chinese Exclusion Act of 1882 was renewed repeatedly until it was superseded by the rigid anti-Asian regulations of the National Origins Quota Act of 1924. Still, impoverished and adventurous Chinese continued to try to enter the country. According to the law, if a Chinese man residing in the United States fathered a child during a visit to China and recorded the birth on the appropriate official papers, the child could immigrate to the United States. Using this loophole, adult "paper sons" (and occasionally "paper daughters") sought entry. Some were, in fact, the children of resident Chinese. Others purchased "slots" and memorized the details of their supposed father's house, village, and family background in order to immigrate.

On Angel Island in the San Francisco harbor, Asian immigrants were examined by physicians and interrogated by immigration officials. This was a frightening ordeal for all immigrants, but especially for "paper" sons and daughters. Determined to minimize the number admitted, legal or illegal, officials detained Chinese immigrants for months, subjecting them to re-

Source: Jim Mark Lai, Genny Kim, and Judy Yung, eds., *Island: Poetry and History of Chinese Immigrants on Angel Island 1910–1940,* published by Hoc Doi, A Project of the Chinese Culture Foundation of San Francisco, 1980, p. 84.

peated, detailed interrogations. Any inconsistency in replies resulted in further detention or deportation. Imprisoned in dreary barracks for indeterminant periods, the Chinese expressed their loneliness and frustration, their hopes, and their anger by writing or carving hundreds of poems on the walls. Two of these poems are reproduced here.

For what reason must I sit in jail?
It is only because my country is weak and
      my family poor.
My parents wait at the door but there is no
      news.
My wife and child wrap themselves in quilt,
      sighing with loneliness.
Even if my petition is approved and I can
      enter the country,
When can I return to the Mountains of Tang [China]
      with a full load?
From ancient times, those who venture out
      usually become worthless.
How many people ever return from battles?

Leaving behind my writing brush and
      removing my sword, I came to America.
Who was to know two streams of tears would
      flow upon arriving here?
If there comes a day when I will have
      attained my ambition and become
      successful,
I will certainly behead the barbarians [Americans] and
      spare not a single blade of grass.

Refugees

ORAL HISTORY OF FANNIE SHAMITZ FRIEDMAN: "THERE WAS NOTHING TO COME HOME TO"

From the colonial years to the present, many groups have come to the United States to escape political or religious oppression. The document that follows provides insight into the experiences of one such group, Russian Jews.

Over two million Jews, a third of the entire Russian Jewish population,

Source: United States Department of the Interior National Park Service Ellis Island Oral History Project, *Voices from Ellis Island: An Oral History of American Immigration.* A Project of the Statue of Liberty–Ellis Island Foundation. Interviewee: Fannie Friedman (#093). Interviewer: Debby Dane. Interview date, November 22, 1985.

immigrated to the United States in the late nineteenth and early twentieth centuries. In the decaying Russian Empire, the Czarist government systematically impoverished and terrorized its Jewish population by crowding them into limited geographic areas, denying them opportunities for education and employment, and organizing murderous pogroms (riots) against them. The result was massive emigration. Although the Czar was overthrown in 1917, the devastating consequences of World War I, the Communist Revolution, and the civil wars that followed led to more poverty, more pogroms, and more emigration. In the oral history that follows, Fannie Shamitz Friedman tells interviewer Debbie Dane about her childhood as a Jew in Czarist and revolutionary Russia and her immigration to the United States at age 15, shortly after World War I. Fannie grew up, in effect, in a one-parent family; her father had come to the United States before the war.

The situations that drove various groups of refugees—such as the Hungarians in 1956, the Cubans in the 1960s, Southeast Asians in the 1970s—varied, as did the reception the refugees met in the United states, the resources they brought with them, and the opportunities they found. Like the Shamitz family, most Jewish immigrants to turn-of-the-century America looked forward to their new lives with cautious optimism. In the United States they encountered social and economic discrimination and anti-Semitic quotas restricting their admission to many universities and professional schools. However, they also found religious and political freedom, free public education (including, in New York City, free colleges), and an expanding urban economy that provided opportunities for employment and, in the next generation, social mobility. Despite their poverty, many, like Fannie Shamitz, came with "cultural capital"—education and saleable skills—and had the support of Americanized friends and relatives and an already established Jewish community. Refugees without these advantages found entry into American life more difficult.

Like the Shamitz family, most Jewish immigrants at the turn of the century were both economic immigrants and refugees from oppression. While immigrants who came solely for economic reasons often returned to their homelands, refugees were much less likely to do so. As Fannie Shamitz Friedman put it, "There was nothing to come home to."

Ms. Dane: . . . Mrs. Friedman, if you would tell me what town you were born in. . . .

Mrs. Friedman: The town was Chechelniek. . . .

Ms. Dane: . . . Was it a big town, a little town? . . .

Mrs. Friedman: It was a small town. The . . . Jewish population, was about four hundred. And then, around the town lived the peasants. They all had gardens and they used to come once a week to sell their wares, chickens, potatoes, onions. And we were the last house from the top, downhill, and my father was a blacksmith, and my mother was a seamstress. She used to sew for the peasant women. . . . And my father was shoeing horses and making wagons. . . . By now we're nine children. The oldest, my oldest brother, went to Kishinev, and he worked as a clerk in the store because there were so many children we just didn't have room for all of them. So my mother . . . had a sister there, so she sent them [there]. Another brother went to work as a tailor and he lived, slept there, too. For two years, ten dollars a year. And another sister also worked. But my mother decided that, when it came to me and my brother next to me that she wants we would get an education. At that time, I mean, do you want to know . . . ?

Ms. DANE: Yes.

MRS. FRIEDMAN: At that time, they did not accept Jewish children to the . . . Russian schools. . . . very limited, unless either you know somebody or you were triple A. Not only A, but . . . . (She laughs) So the intelligentsia in Chechelniek, the people who could afford to go to big cities and study . . . , decided to open up a school for poor children. . . . And so there we learned Russian, arithmetic. I think I started when I was eight years old, and my brother next to me was ten . . . . we also studied Hebrew. Not Yiddish, but Hebrew. . . . We went to this school for a few years. Then . . . the school stopped existing for some reason. During the [Russian] Revolution and the War and all that, people moved. So . . . [my mother] got a woman who finished high school, that she should teach me. Because she wanted I should be educated. . . . [During the Russian Revolution, the Communists set up schools in the confiscated palaces of the deposed local nobility.]

MRS. FRIEDMAN: . . . they hung up in the middle of the square a big sign, "Everybody come to the palaces to register children from six to fourteen or fifteen," you know. So we all went, and we came into those palaces. . . . some of them, the walls were all glass. . . . It was very far for me to walk, you know. In wintertime I didn't have any shoes, so one of my brothers had to stay home so I could go to school. (She laughs.) . . . I was the only one from the family who went. . . . I could write Russian and talk Russian and [do] arithmetic . . . .

Ms. DANE: And were they [the teachers at the palace school] Russian, gentiles. . .?

MRS. FRIEDMAN: Gentiles, all gentiles . . . . Besides Russian and geography and history, they started to teach us German and French. It was just accepted that you have to have all these languages besides the Russian.

Ms. DANE: When the Revolution came and they opened the school, was it exciting? Were you happy that the Revolution had come . . . ?

MRS. FRIEDMAN: Oh, yes. We were. [But] first of all, there was a lot of groups fighting amongst themselves against the Communists, against the Bolsheviks. And . . . in the middle they were killing Jews . . . . We used to hide in the basement, you know, or up in the attic, when all these other people came. Once there was a pogrom [riot] in our town and we had to run . . . . We didn't go to sleep, we used to sit, one of us, at the window, to see whether those people [who] were making pogroms, are coming. Because we knew all around they were there and they were killing Jews. . . . so everybody woke up and we ran to the nearest village. You know, a lot of the people in the village knew us because they used to come to my father for shoeing their horses. But somebody came before and told them that the Jews are coming to kill them . . . . So they were going to shoot [the Jews] when they came near, but they saw all the children. So they took us into a school. The men separate, and the women and children separate. And we didn't know whether they were killing the men or whatever.

Ms. DANE: Were you terrified?

MRS. FRIEDMAN: Oh, sure. We cried and I said to my mother, "Ma, we are such good people. Why are they killing us?" She says, "What God does, you don't ask no questions." She was [a] very religious woman. And they sent the wagon of peasants to see whether it's true that there is a pogrom in Chechelniek, and they went and they said, "Yes. They killed ninety people." And among them four of my teachers. My Jewish teachers. Not the ones from the palace.

Ms. DANE: Oh, but the peasants helped you.

MRS. FRIEDMAN: . . . they gave us wagons to come back. And we were lucky that our house was not destroyed or not burned because it was at the end [of the street] and it was a very small hut. We didn't have any food . . . . So two days later, after the pogrom, my mother took a sack and she went to the peasants, and everybody gave her a piece of bread . . . . It was difficult. We really didn't have nothing to eat. Then they started to bring in potatoes. So we ate potatoes three times a day.

Ms. DANE: Do you eat potatoes today?

MRS. FRIEDMAN: Yeah. But . . . when you're young, well . . . . You just live through it, and you played and you read books, and you went to the library, after they left. But then, the Bolsheviks came in, you know. The Red Army . . . . When they came in they took our blacksmith shop and they started to fix their wagons, and shoe the horses. So my mother said to this guy who was in the propaganda [department], she says, "You claim that you're going to help the poor people. [But] look what you're doing to us" . . . .

Ms. DANE: When your father left . . . . What year [was it]?

MRS. FRIEDMAN: 1912. . . . he had a sister who came [to the United States] in 1905. She was already here, married, and her husband worked in the shipyards. And my father wasn't making much of a living, you know. And, well, the sister wrote him a lot of letters telling him that he could make money and bring over the family and they'll get an education and all that. And so he went, and she sent him money to come. And I remember taking him to . . . a railroad station about two miles away . . . . My mother carried my youngest brother in her arms and the whole family went. And they [her father and others] took next to nothing. They didn't have anything to take. (She laughs.)

Ms. DANE: . . . Did you have an image of what America was like?

MRS. FRIEDMAN: Well, people said that everybody gets rich there. But I was skeptical about it, really. Because my father said that he worked very hard, to save the money before he stopped writing. And my brother also said that there's no money. And everybody works very hard. And we understood that. We were not stupid . . . but we knew it's free and there was no pogroms, and this they let us know. And all children go to school. And that was good enough for us.

[Soon after the end of World War I the Shamitz family escaped first to Roumania then to the United States. Fannie was 15. Although their final destination was Boston, the family landed at Ellis Island, New York, for medical inspections.]

Ms. DANE: Were you afraid [on Ellis Island], or aware, that you might get sent back to Europe?

MRS. FRIEDMAN: Yeah, we were. Because they did send back people . . . . My mother . . . worried more than I did. And [on Ellis Island] we went to a concert. They had all these long benches. We all sat there, we, for the first time in our lives, . . . saw somebody in a concert singing to us music, and everybody looked so happy . . . . And then they announced with the loudspeaker, "The family Shamitz" and we all got up and we ran. You know, they were walking in front of us and showed us, and my father was already standing there. And we all came into the office, where they let people get together, and we kissed and hugged . . . .

Ms. DANE: Did . . . you ever hear the word greenhorn?

MRS. FRIEDMAN: Oh, sure . . . so I'm a greenhorn. I was proud. I know so many languages. I just don't know English. And the first thing my aunt taught me is to say, "How do you do?" . . . Everybody was teaching every few words. Then when we came to the school, the teacher was just saying, "This is a table, this is a chair, I speak." . . . and we learned, because we were so eager.

[Because the family was poor, Fannie had to leave school to work in a skirt factory. Her aunt found her the job.]

Ms. DANE: Were you sad to have to leave school?

MRS. FRIEDMAN: Oh, yes. But then, night school was good, too. I met so many boys there. (She laughs.) They also spoke the same language that I did . . . . I wasn't worried about much . . . . I wanted to work, and my brother, this American that was already here and making a lot of money, he says, "You're making ten, twelve dollars a week," he says. "Five dollars put in the bank." He took me to a bank, and I signed my name . . . ."

Ms. DANE: When you first got here, did you ever miss home? Did you wish that you'd never come?

MRS. FRIEDMAN: Never. Never. There was nothing to come home to.

Ms. DANE: And another question now . . . . citizenship. Did you, how and when and why?

MRS. FRIEDMAN: Oh, I was very determined to become a citizen. So, as soon as I was the age, and I was five years here, we lived in Brooklyn at that time, I was already married. And . . . , I wanted to become a citizen. I wanted to vote. So, I read the book, I didn't fail, and I went. And I had two witnesses who were my friends. I met them in school. And . . . they asked me such easy questions. And the judge was very encouraging . . . . And even my mother wanted to become a citizen and she, she and four women got together and they paid the teacher fifty cents each he should teach them how to become a citizen.

From African to African American

OLAUDAH EQUIANO: "THE MANNERS AND CUSTOMS OF MY COUNTRY HAD BEEN IMPLANTED IN ME WITH GREAT CARE . . ."

Coerced into immigrant status, African slaves had a starkly different experience from that of Europeans, Asians, and others who make up the heterogeneous population of the United States. Two factors further conspired to alienate the African. First, predominantly Protestant slaveholders in the United States, more so than in other more culturally tolerant variations of slavery in the Americas, attempted a policy of eradicating surviving vestiges of African culture. Second, the distribution of slaves mostly into small groups on farms rather than into large plantation populations discouraged the survival of cohesive African community. To be sure, some aspects of an African past were preserved in the expressive styles of gesture, speech, music, and dance passed from generation to generation. As a rule, however, slaves did not have among themselves, as did other immigrants to the New World, the immediate comfort of practicing with impunity the shared traditions of their homeland. With the legal suppression of the African slave trade by Congress in 1808, those few Africans subsequently smuggled in as contraband provided only a tenuous link to a cultural past. Among the well over one hundred written narratives produced by fugitive-slave autobiographers in the United States in the mid-nineteenth century, none has the emotional advantage of being written from a perspective of precise ancestral origins. Indeed, because successive generations of slaves were forced into a shadow world of ignorance and illiteracy, they were often deprived of any extensive knowledge about their own family history within the United States.

It is the rare slave narrator who is able to recall the direct personal experience of an African past, of unviolated family origins in a preslavery homeland. The Anglo-African Olaudah Equiano does provide us with one such early instance. Although held on a Virginia plantation for a brief interval, Equiano spent most of his slave experience in the British West Indies, and later as a free man he would claim England as his home. In excerpts from *The Interesting Narrative of the Life of Olaudah Equiano,* first published in 1789, we can see clearly the intact boyhood experience that precedes the emotional shock and disorientation of his transition into British-American slavery at age 11. Advantaged in his formative years by a culturally supportive African environment, Equiano evinces a degree of self-possession that derives from his cohesive African Ibo identity. He is able to devote an entire first chapter to a rich description of his Ibo homeland, including a secure upbringing by a prominent father and attentive mother.

Source: Olaudah Equiano, *The Interesting Narrative of the Life of Olaudah Equiano, or Gustavus Vassa, the African. Written by Himself* (Leeds: Printed for Cradock and Joy, London; and W. H. Blackburn, Darlington, and sold by all booksellers, 1814).

That part of Africa, known by the name of Guinea, to which the trade of slaves is carried on, extends along the coast about 3,400 miles, from Senegal to Angola, and includes a variety of kingdoms. Of these the most considerable is the kingdom of Benin, both as to extent and wealth, the richness and culture of the soil, the power of its king, and the number and warlike disposition of its inhabitants. It is situated nearly under the line, and extends along the coast about 170 miles, but runs back into the interior of Africa to a distance hitherto, I believe, unexplored by any traveller; and seems only terminated at length by the empire of Abyssinia, near 1,500 miles from its beginning. This kingdom is divided into many provinces or districts; in one of the most remote and fertile of which, named Essaka, situated in a charming fruitful vale, I was born, in the year 1745. The distance of this province from the capital of Benin and the sea coast must be very considerable: for I had never heard of white men or Europeans, nor of the sea; and our subjection to the king of Benin was little more than nominal. Every transaction of the government, as far as my slender observation extended, was conducted by the chiefs or elders of the place. The manners and government of a people who have little commerce with other countries, are generally very simple; and the history of what passes in one family or village, may serve as a specimen of the whole nation. My father was one of those elders or chiefs of whom I have spoken, and was styled Embrenche; a term, as I remember, importing the highest distinction, and signifying in our language "a mark of grandeur." This mark is conferred on the person entitled to it by cutting the skin across at the top of the forehead, and drawing it down to the eyebrows; and applying a warm hand to it, while in this situation, and rubbing it until it shrinks up into a thick wale across the lower part of the forehead. Most of the judges and senators were thus marked; my father had long borne this badge: I had seen it conferred on one of my brothers, and I also was destined to receive it by my parents.

• • • • •

. . . The West India planters prefer the slaves of Benin or Eboe, to those of any part of Guinea, for their hardiness, intelligence, integrity and zeal.—Those benefits are felt by us in the general healthiness of the people, and in their vigour and activity; I might have added, too, to their comeliness. Deformity is indeed unknown amongst us. I mean that of shape. Numbers of the natives of Eboe, now in London, might be brought in support of this assertion: for, in regard to complexion, ideas of beauty are wholly relative. I remember while in Africa to have seen three negro children, who were tawny, and another quite white, who were universally regarded as deformed by myself and the natives in general, as far as related to their complexions. Our women too, were, in my eyes at least, uncommonly graceful, alert, and modest to a degree of bashfulness; nor do I remember to have ever heard of an instance of incontinence amongst them before marriage. They are also remarkably cheerful. Indeed cheerfulness and affability are two of the leading characteristics of our nation.

• • • • •

We practised circumcision like the Jews, and made offerings and feasts on that occasion in the same manner as they did. Like them also, our children were named from some event, some circumstance, or fancied foreboding at the time of their birth. I was named Olaudah, which, in our language, signifies "vicissitude or fortunate," also, "one favoured, and having a loud voice and well spoken." I remember we never polluted the name of the object of our adoration; on the contrary, it was always mentioned with the greatest reverence; and we are totally unacquainted with swearing, and all those terms of abuse and reproach which find their way so readily and copiously into the language of more civilized people. The only expressions of that kind I remember were, "May you rot!" or "may you swell!" or "may a beast take you!"

I have before remarked that the natives of this part of Africa are extremely cleanly. This necessary habit of decency was with us a part of religion, and therefore we had many purifications and washings; indeed almost as many, and used on the same occasions, if my recollection does not fail me, as the Jews. Those that touched the dead, at anytime, were obliged to wash and purify themselves before they could enter a dwelling-house, or touch any person or any thing we eat. I was so fond of my mother I could not keep from her, or avoid touching her at some of those periods, in consequence of which I was obliged to be kept out with her, in a little house made for that purpose, till offering was made, and then we were purified.

· · · · ·

I. I hope the reader will not think I have trespassed on his patience, in introducing myself to him with some account of the manners and customs of my country. They had been implanted in me with great care, and made an impression on my mind, which time could not erase, and which all the adversity and variety of fortune I have since experienced, served only to rivet and record; for, whether the love of one's country be real or imaginary, a lesson of reason or an instinct of nature, I still look back with pleasure on the first scenes of my life, though that pleasure has been for the most part mingled with sorrow.

· · · · ·

The first object that saluted my eyes when I arrived on the coast was the sea, and a slave ship, which was then riding at anchor, and waiting for its cargo. These filled me with astonishment, that was soon converted into terror, which I am yet at a loss to describe, and much more the then feelings of my mind when I was carried on board. I was immediately handled and tossed up to see if I was sound, by some of the crew; and I was now persuaded that I had got into a world of bad spirits, and that they were going to kill me. Their complexions too, differing so much from ours, their long hair, and the language they spoke, which was very different from any I had ever heard, united to confirm me in this belief. Indeed such were the horrors of my views and fears at the moment, that if ten thousand worlds had been my own, I would have freely parted with them all to have exchanged my condition with the meanest slave in my own country. When I looked round the ship too, and saw a large furnace or copper boiling and a multitude of black people, of every description, chained together, every one of their countenances expressing dejection and sorrow, I no longer doubted of my fate; and, quite overpowered with horror and anguish, I fell motionless on the deck, and fainted. When I recovered a little, I found some black people about me, who I believed were some of those who brought me on board, and had been receiving their pay: they talked to me in order to cheer me, but all in vain. I asked them if we were not to be eaten by those white men with horrible looks, red faces, and long hair. They told me I was not: and one of the crew brought me a small portion of spirituous liquor in a wine glass; but, being afraid of him, I would not take it out of his hand. One of the blacks therefore took it from him and gave it to me, and I took a little down my palate, which, instead of reviving me, as they thought it would, threw me into the greatest consternation at the strange feeling it produced, having never tasted any such liquor before.

• • • • •

II. During our passage I first saw flying fishes, which surprised me very much: they used frequently to fly across the ship, and many of them fell on the deck. I also now first saw the use of the quadrant. I had often with astonishment seen the mariners make observations with it, and I could not think what it meant. They at last took notice of my surprise: and one of them, willing to increase it, as well as to gratify my curiosity, made me one day look through it. The clouds appeared to me to be land, which disappeared as they passed along. This heightened my wonder; and I was now more persuaded than ever that I was in another world, and that every thing about me was magic. At last we came in sight of the island of Barbadoes, at which the whites on board gave a great shout, and made many signs of joy to us. We did not know what to think of this, but as the vessel drew nearer we plainly saw the harbour, and other ships of different kinds and sizes; and we soon anchored amongst them off Bridge Town. Many merchants and planters now came on board, though it was in the evening. They put us in separate parcels, and examined us attentively. They also made us jump, and pointed to the land, signifying we were to go there. We thought by this we should be beaten by these ugly men, as they appeared to us; and, when soon after we were all put down under the deck again, there was much dread and trembling among us, and nothing but bitter cries to be heard all the night from these apprehensions, insomuch that at last the white people got some old slaves from the land to pacify us. They told us we were not to be eaten, but to work, and were soon to go on land, where we should see many of our country people. This report eased us much; and, sure enough, soon after we landed, there came to us Africans of all languages.

We were conducted immediately to the merchant's yard, where we were all pent up together like so many sheep in a fold, without regard to sex or age. As every object was new to me, every thing I saw filled me with surprise. What struck me first was that the houses were built with bricks in stories, and were in every other respect different from those I had seen in Africa; but I was still more astonished at seeing people on horseback. I did not know what this could mean; and indeed I thought these people full of nothing but magical arts. While I was in this astonishment one of my fellow prisoners spoke to a countryman of his about the horses, who said they were the same kind they had in their country. I understood them, though they were from a distant part of Africa, and I thought it odd I had not seen any horses there; but afterwards, when I came to converse with different Africans, I found they had many horses amongst them, and much larger than those I then saw.

• • • • •

I stayed in this island for a few days; I believe it could not be above a fortnight; when I and some few more slaves, who from very much fretting were not saleable among the rest, were shipped off in a sloop for North America. On the passage we were better treated than when coming from Africa, and we had plenty of rice and fat pork. We were landed up a river a good way from the sea, about Virginia county, where we saw few of our native Africans, and not one soul who could talk to me. I was a few weeks weeding grass and gathering stones in a plantation; and at last all my companions were distributed different ways, and only myself was left. I was now exceedingly miserable, and thought myself worse off than any of the rest of my companions; for they could talk to each other, but I had no person to speak to that I could understand. In this state I was constantly grieving and pining, and wishing for death rather than any thing else. While I was in this plantation the gentleman to whom I supposed the estate belonged being unwell, I was one day sent for to his dwelling-house to fan him. When I came into the room where he was, I was very much affrighted at some things I saw, and the more so, as I had seen a black woman slave as I came through the house, who was cooking the dinner, and the poor creature was cruelly loaded with various kinds of iron machines; she had one particularly on her head, which locked her mouth so fast that she could scarcely speak, and could not eat or drink. I much astonished and shocked at this contrivance, which I afterwards learned was called the iron muzzle. Soon after I had a fan put into my hand, to fan the gentleman while he slept; and so I did indeed with great fear. While he was fast asleep I indulged myself a great deal in looking about the room, which to me appeared very fine and curious. The first object that engaged my attention was a watch, which hung on the chimney, and was going. I was quite surprised at the noise it made, and was afraid it would tell the gentleman any thing I might do amiss: and when I immediately after observed a picture hanging in the room, which appeared constantly to look at me, I was still more affrighted, having never seen such things as these before. At one time I thought it was something relative to magic; and not seeing it move, I thought it might be some way the whites had to keep their great men when they died, and offer them libations, as we used to do to our friendly spirits. In this state of anxiety I remained till my master awoke, when I was dismissed out of the room, to my no small satisfaction and relief; for I thought that these people were all made up of wonders. In this place I was called Jacob; but on board the African Snow I was called Michael.

FREDERICK DOUGLASS: "I DO NOT RECOLLECT OF EVER SEEING MY MOTHER BY THE LIGHT OF DAY"

Unlike the pastoral setting that fostered Equiano, the childhood described by Frederick Douglass resonates with a sense of corrosive violence. African-ness is an unmentioned absence, his racial identity a stigma. The vexations of this deprivation are nowhere made clearer than in the opening chapter of the *Narrative of the Life of Frederick Douglass* (1845), given here in its entirety. In Douglass' recollection of disrupted and evasive parental origins we have a classic instance of the extent to which slavery painfully complicated both personal and cultural identity for the African American. The language and behavior of the overseer and master are given to us as utterly corrupted, compared with the pristine speech habits and stable village mores of Equiano's Africa. In conspicuous contrast, the circumstances of Douglass' immediate origins are tenuous. He is removed from his mother in infancy and irrevocably distanced from his father who, excruciatingly, is also his owner and master. The forced interracial relationship between masters and slave women, between the Anglo-American father and the African-American mother who produced Douglass, was a common circumstance of slavery, as Douglass emphasizes. Its consequence was to make Douglass and many other slaves both African and American—of mixed racial identity. More painfully, Douglass clearly does not want to claim that alien paternity, angrily denouncing it as the cruelest sexual and economic depredation of slavery. In siring racially mixed children who become valued slave property, the slavemaster gratified both his lust and his desire for profit. Equiano's gateway to hell is his abrupt initiation into the alien horrors of non-African slavery. Douglass' rite of passage is to watch the sexual jealousy of the master played out in the bloody punishment dealt to his Aunt Hester—a relationship sexually similar to the one that the master had manipulated with Douglass' mother. For Douglass there is no strengthening African past, only the appalling personal and cultural complications of his troubled origins as a slave in the United States.

I was born in Tuckahoe, near Hillsborough, and about twelve miles from Easton, in Talbot county, Maryland. I have no accurate knowledge of my age, never having seen any authentic record containing it. By far the larger part of the slaves know as little of their ages as horses know of theirs, and it is the wish of most masters within my knowledge to keep their slaves thus ignorant. I do not remember to have ever met a slave who could tell of his birthday. They seldom come nearer to it than planting-time, harvest-time, cherry-time, spring-time, or fall-time. A want of information concerning my own was a source of unhappiness to me even during childhood. The white children could tell their ages. I could not tell why I ought to be deprived of the same privilege. I was not allowed to make any inquiries of my master concerning it. He deemed all such

Source: Frederick Douglass, *Narrative of the Life of Frederick Douglass, an American Slave. Written by Himself* (Boston: published at the Anti-slavery Office, No. 25 Cornhill, 1845), pp. 255–59.

inquiries on the part of a slave improper and impertinent, and evidence of a restless spirit. the nearest estimate I can give makes me now between twenty-seven and twenty-eight years of age. I come to this, from hearing my master say, some time during 1835, I was about seventeen years old.

My mother was named Harriet Bailey. She was the daughter of Isaac and Betsey Bailey, both colored, and quite dark. My mother was of a darker complexion than either my grandmother or grandfather.

My father was a white man. He was admitted to be such by all I ever heard speak of my parentage. The opinion was also whispered that my master was my father; but of the correctness of this opinion, I know nothing; the means of knowing was withheld from me. My mother and I were separated when I was but an infant—before I knew her as my mother. It is a common custom, in the part of Maryland from which I ran away, to part children from their mothers at a very early age. Frequently, before the child has reached its twelfth month, its mother is taken from it, and hired out on some farm a considerable distance off, and the child is placed under the care of an old woman, too old for field labor. For what this separation is done, I do not know, unless it be to hinder the development of the child's affection toward its mother, and to blunt and destroy the natural affection of the mother for the child. This is the inevitable result.

I never saw my mother, to know her as such, more than four or five times in my life; and each of these times was very short in duration, and at night. She was hired by a Mr. Stewart, who lived about twelve miles from my home. She made her journeys to see me in the night, travelling the whole distance on foot, after the performance of her day's work. She was a field hand, and a whipping is the penalty of not being in the field at sunrise, unless a slave has special permission from his or her master to the contrary—a permission which they seldom get, and one that gives to him that gives it the proud name of being a kind master. I do not recollect of ever seeing my mother by the light of day. She was with me in the night. She would lie down with me, and get me to sleep, but long before I waked she was gone. Very little communication ever took place between us. Death soon ended what little we could have while she lived, and with it her hardships and suffering. She died when I was about seven years old, on one of my master's farms, near Lee's Mill. I was not allowed to be present during her illness, at her death, or burial. She was gone long before I knew any thing about it. Never having enjoyed, to any considerable extent, her soothing presence, her tender and watchful care, I received the tidings of her death with much the same emotions I should have probably felt at the death of a stranger.

Called thus suddenly away, she left me without the slightest intimation of who my father was. The whisper that my master was my father, may or may not be true; and, true or false, it is of but little consequence to my purpose whilst the fact remains, in all its glaring odiousness, that slaveholders have ordained, and by law established, that the children of slave women shall in all cases follow the condition of their mothers, and this is done too obviously to administer to their own lusts, and make a gratification of their wicked desires profitable as well as pleasurable; for by this cunning arrangement, the slaveholder, in cases not a few, sustains to his slaves the double relation of master and father.

I know of such cases; and it is worthy of remark that such slaves invariably suffer greater hardships, and have more to contend with, than others. They are, in the first place, a constant offence to their mistress. She is ever disposed to find fault with them; they can seldom do any thing to please her; she is never better pleased than when she sees them under the lash, especially when she suspects her husband of showing to his mulatto children favors which he withholds from his black slaves. The master is frequently compelled to sell this class of his slaves, out of deference to the feelings of his white wife; and, cruel as the deed may strike any one to be, for a man to sell his own children to human flesh-mongers, it is often the dictate of humanity for him to do so; for, unless he does this, he must not only whip them himself, but must stand by and see one white son tie up his brother, of but few shades darker complexion than himself, and ply the gory lash to his naked back; and if he lisp one word of disapproval, it is set down to his parental partiality, and only makes a bad matter worse, both for himself and the slave whom he would protect and defend.

Every year brings with it multitudes of this class of slaves. It was doubtless in consequence of a knowledge of this fact, that one great statesman of the south predicted the downfall of slavery by the inevitable laws of population. Whether this prophecy is ever fulfilled or not, it is nevertheless plain that a very different-looking class of people are springing up at the south, and are now held in slavery, from those originally brought to this country from Africa; and if their increase will do no other good, it will do away the force of the argument, that God cursed Ham, and therefore American slavery is right. If the lineal descendants of Ham are alone to be scripturally enslaved, it is certain that slavery at the south must soon become unscriptural; for thousands are ushered into the world, annually, who, like myself, owe their existence to white fathers, and those fathers most frequently their own masters.

I have had two masters. My first master's name was Anthony. I do not remember his first name. He was generally called Captain Anthony—a title which, I presume, he acquired by sailing a craft on the Chesapeake Bay. He was not considered a rich slaveholder. He owned two or three farms, and about thirty slaves. His farms and slaves were under the care of an overseer. The overseer's name was Plummer. Mr. Plummer was a miserable drunkard, a profane swearer, and a savage monster. He always went armed with a cowskin and a heavy cudgel. I have known him to cut and slash the women's heads so horribly, that even master would be enraged at his cruelty, and would threaten to whip him if he did not mind himself. It required extraordinary barbarity on the part of an overseer to affect him. He was a cruel man, hardened by a long life of slaveholding. He would at times seem to take great pleasure in whipping a slave. I have often been awakened at the dawn of day by the most heart-rending shrieks of an own aunt of mine, whom he used to tie up to a joist, and whip upon her naked back till she was literally covered with blood. No words, no tears, no prayers, from his gory victim, seemed to move his iron heart from its bloody purpose. The louder she screamed, the harder he whipped; and where the blood ran fastest, there he whipped longest. He would whip her to make her scream, and whip her to make her hush; and not until overcome by fatigue, would he cease to swing the blood-clotted cowskin. I remember the first time I ever witnessed this horrible exhibition. I was quite a child, but I well remember it. I never shall forget it whilst I remember any thing. It was the first of a long series of such outrages, of which I was doomed to be a witness and a participant. It struck me with awful force. It was the blood-stained gate, the entrance to the hell of slavery, through which I was about to pass. It was a most terrible spectacle. I wish I could commit to paper the feelings with which I beheld it.

This occurrence took place very soon after I went to live with my old master, and under the following circumstances. Aunt Hester went out one night,—where or for what I do not know,—and happened to be absent when my master desired her presence. He had ordered her not to go out evenings, and warned her that she must never let him catch her in company with a young man, who was paying attention to her, belonging to Colonel Lloyd. The young man's name was Ned Roberts, generally called Lloyd's Ned. Why master was so careful of her, may be safely left to conjecture. She was a woman of noble form, and of graceful proportions, having very few equals, and fewer superiors, in personal appearance, among the colored or white women of our neighborhood.

Aunt Hester had not only disobeyed his orders in going out, but had been found in company with Lloyd's Ned; which circumstance, I found, from what he said while whipping her, was the chief offence. Had he been a man of pure morals himself, he might have been thought interested in protecting the innocence of my aunt; but those who knew him will not suspect him of any such virtue. Before he commenced whipping Aunt Hester, he took her into the kitchen, and stripped her from neck to waist, leaving her neck, shoulders, and back, entirely naked. He then told her to cross her hands, calling her at the same time a d———d b———h. After crossing her hands, he tied them with a strong rope, and led her to a stool under a large hook in the joist, put in for the purpose. He made her get upon the stool, and tied her hands to the hook. She now stood fair for his infernal purpose. Her arms were stretched up at their full length, so that she stood upon the ends of her toes. He then said to her, "Now, you d———d b———h, I'll learn you how to disobey my orders!" and after rolling up his sleeves, he commenced to lay on the heavy cowskin, and soon the warm, red blood (amid heart-rending shrieks from her, and horrid oaths from him) came dripping to the floor. I was so terrified and horror-stricken at the sight, that I hid myself in a closet, and dared not venture out till long after the bloody transaction was over. I expected it would be my turn next. It was all new to me. I had never seen anything like it before. I had always lived with my grandmother on the outskirts of the plantation, where she was put to raise the children of the younger women. I had therefore been, until now, out of the way of the bloody scenes that often occurred on the plantation.

Finding Meaning in Tradition:
Red Jacket's Testimony

The process by which American Indians lost their ancestral lands unfolded over the course of three centuries. It began in the seventeenth century on the east coast of what would become the United States and slowly worked its way westward. As late as the 1880s and 1890s, the U.S. Army was still engaged in warfare against southwestern and Great Plains Indian peoples,

Source: William Red Fox, *The Memoirs of Chief Red Fox* (New York: McGraw Hill, 1971).

who were resisting those who wished—often in violation of previously negotiated treaties—to take their lands.

The military defeat of the Indians who resisted the European and American onslaught, their loss of ancestral lands, and their removal sometimes to areas, later called reservations, very far from those lands, eventuated in the collapse of their traditional ways of life. They could not hunt as they once had, for their hunting had involved migrating seasonally across vast expanses of land in search of game. Their religions were disrupted by a breakdown in traditional relations with nature and between the generations and by the activities of Christian missionaries. Reservation schools threatened to replace the wisdom of parents and tribal elders. Deliberate efforts to disrupt and destroy Indian cultures and force Indians to assimilate white American ways increased in the decades after the Civil War.

Believing the old ways could never be restored, some Indians embraced European-American culture and sought ways to assimilate into American life. Even the great Apache warrior Geronimo (Goyathlay), who had fought both the Mexican and American armies for years before his defeat in 1886, became a Christian toward the end of his life.

Though defeated militarily, however, many other Indians resisted such assimilation to the extent it was possible to do so. These traditionalists often attempted to strengthen the old beliefs, and frequently to find ways to blend them with European-American culture. One of these traditionalists was the Seneca chief Red Jacket (Sagoyewatha), who was born in central New York State in 1758 and died in 1830. The Senecas were members of the Iroquois Confederation. A skilled orator and negotiator, Red Jacket managed to achieve peace with both the United States and the British. He hoped that without powerful enemies his people might remain independent. He was bitterly opposed to the encroachment of white settlers on the Seneca's ancestral lands and of European ways, especially Christianity, among his people. But he was not able to stop either development.

In this selection, Red Jacket effectively responds to the efforts of a Christian missionary at a meeting in 1805 to lure his people away from their own religion. His speech on that occasion shows his considerable power as a debater. He uses logic, irony, flattery, ridicule, and sarcasm to weaken his white American opponents, who, it was said, left the meeting in bad temper, probably feeling confused as well as defeated. The twentieth-century Native-American leader, William Red Fox, who was educated in American schools and graduated from college, tells us in his autobiography, in which he reprinted Red Jacket's speech, that he always carried a copy of it with him in his briefcase. He took pride in showing it to those who expressed surprise at his own affection for and defense of traditional Indian culture.

"Friend and brother, it was the will of the Great Spirit that we should meet together this day. He orders all things, and he has given us a fine day for our council. He has taken his garment from before the sun, and caused it to shine with brightness upon us; our eyes are opened, and we see clearly; our ears are unstopped, and we have been able to hear distinctly the words that you have spoken; for all these favors we thank the Great Spirit and Him only. . . .

"Brother, listen to what we say. There was a time when our forefathers owned this great land. Their seats extended from the rising to the setting sun. The Great Spirit had made it for use by the Indians. He had created the buffalo, the deer, and other animals for food. He made the bear and the beaver, and the skins served for clothing. He had scattered them over the country, and taught us how to take them. He had caused the earth to produce corn for bread.

"All this he had done for his Red children because he loved them. If we had any disputes about hunting grounds they were generally settled without the shedding of blood.

"But an evil day came upon us; your forefathers crossed the great waters, and landed on this island. Their numbers were small; they found friends, not enemies; they told us they had fled from their own country for fear of wicked men, and came here to enjoy their religion. They asked for a small seat; we took pity upon them, granted their request, and they sat down among us. We gave them corn and meat: they gave us poison in return.

"The White people had now found our country, tidings were carried back, and more came among us; yet we did not fear them. We took them to be friends; they called us brothers, we believed them, and gave them a larger seat. At length their numbers had greatly increased, and they wanted more land, they wanted our country. Our eyes were opened and our minds became uneasy. Wars took place; Indians were hired to fight against Indians; and many of our people were destroyed. They also brought strong liquor among us.

"Brother, our seats were once large, and yours were very small. You now have become a great people, and we scarcely have a place left to spread our blankets. You have our country, but you are not satisfied, you want to force your religion upon us.

"Brother, continue to listen. You say that you are sent to instruct us how to worship the Great Spirit agreeably to His mind, and if we do not take hold of the religion which you White people teach, we shall be unhappy hereafter; you say you are right and we are lost. How do you know this to be true? We understand that your religion is written in a book. If it was intended for us as well as for you, why has not the Great Spirit given it to us, and not only to us, but why did He not give us, and our forefathers, the knowledge of that book, with the means of understanding it rightly? We know only what you tell us. How shall we know to believe, being so often deceived by the White people?

"Brother, you say there is but one way to worship and serve the Great Spirit. If there be but one religion, why do you White people differ so much about it? Why not all agree as you can read the book? . . .

"Brother, the Great Spirit has made all of us, but he has made a great difference between his White and Red children. He has given us a different complexion and different customs. To you he has given the arts: to these he has not opened our eyes. We know these things to be true. Since He has made so great a difference between us in other things, why may we not conclude that He has given us a different religion according to our understanding? The Great Spirit does right. He knows what is best for His children. We are satisfied.

"Brother, you now have heard our answer to your talk. As we are going to part, we will take you by the hand, and hope the Great Spirit will protect you on your journey, and return you safe to your friends."

The Conquered Mexicans of the Southwest: Letter from the Santa Fe Jail, Reies Lopez Tijerina

A considerable portion of what is now the United States was acquired as a result of military conquest, at first by British colonists and later by Americans once the nation was formed. In a well-known case in our history, white Americans vanquished all American-Indian groups and occupied their lands, after negotiating treaties with those groups. The history of the transactions between the whites and the native peoples is a sorry one of broken treaties and unfulfilled promises. Another case of territorial acquisition that resulted from military conquest is that involving the American Southwest and California. History there, too, is marred by the broken word of whites, and negative consequences of it extend from the last century to our own.

On June 5, 1967, a Mexican-American activist named Reies Lopez Tijerina (pronounced ti-heh-RI-na) raided the courthouse at Tierra Amarilla, a town in New Mexico, for the purpose of making a citizen's arrest of the state district attorney. Tijerina was charged with kidnapping and assault to commit murder, but a jury found him innocent. Later that month he was arrested and charged with destruction of federal property and assaulting two officials. He was tried and convicted of the assault charges and given a jail term. His followers charged that Tijerina's frequent brushes with the authorities were the result of a conspiracy on the part of public officials and law enforcement agencies to remove him from the public eye. In August 1969, while in jail awaiting trial, Tijerina wrote an open letter, part of which is reprinted here. He addressed it partly to those he called Indo-Hispanos, meaning not only the Mexican Americans of Mexican-Indian descent but all Hispanic Americans of Indian descent.

Tijerina's protest is better understood within the broad historical framework of the Southwest. In the 1820s the Mexican government started allowing Americans to settle in Texas, then a sparsely populated province of Mexico. In 1836 the Americans in Texas rebelled successfully against Mexico and formed an independent republic, which Mexico did not recognize. Texas was admitted to the United States in late 1845. This led to the armed conflict between Mexico and the United States known as the Mexican War (1846–1848). By the 1848 Treaty of Guadalupe Hidalgo that put an end to hostilities, Mexico renounced its claim to Texas and for $15 million ceded to the United States more than 40 percent of its territory, which included present-day California, Arizona, Nevada, and Utah and parts of New Mexico, Colorado, and Wyoming. The treaty guaranteed land and cultural rights to the Mexicans that chose to stay. But soon U.S. expansionism created in the newly acquired regions a cultural clash between the Protestant white Americans and the Roman Catholic Mexicans, most of whom were of mixed Spanish-Indian ancestry and thus considered nonwhite by the Americans. Spanish language and culture became devalued. The Mexicans became second-class citizens. In addition, many Mexican landowners lost title to

Source: *El Grito del Norte* (Espanola, New Mexico: September 26, 1969).

their land through legal manipulations by unscrupulous American lawyers, and their subsequent claims were largely ignored.

From my cell block in this jail I am writing these reflections. I write them to my people, the Indo-Hispanos, to my friends among the Anglos, to the agents of the federal government, the state of New Mexico, the Southwest, and the entire Indo-Hispano world—"Latin America."

I write to you as one of the clearest victims of the madness and racism in the hearts of our present-day politicians and rulers.

At this time, August 17, I have been in jail for 65 days—since June 11, 1969, when my appeal bond from another case was revoked by a federal judge. I am here today because I resisted an assassination attempt led by an agent of the federal government—an agent of all those who do not want anybody to speak out for the poor, all those who do not want Reies Lopez Tijerina to stand in their way as they continue to rob the poor people, all those many rich people from outside the state with their summer homes and ranches here whose pursuit of happiness depends on thievery, all those who have robbed the people of their land and culture for 120 years. . . .

What is my real crime? As I and the poor people see it, especially the Indo-Hispanos, my only crime is UPHOLDING OUR RIGHTS AS PROTECTED BY THE TREATY OF GUADALUPE HIDALGO which ended the so-called Mexican-American War of 1846–48. My only crime is demanding the respect and protection of our property, which has been confiscated illegally by the federal government. Ever since the treaty was signed in 1848, our people have been asking every elected president of the United States for a redress of grievances. Like the Black people, we too have been criminally ignored. Our right to the Spanish land grant *pueblos* [townships] is the real reason why I am in prison at this moment.

Our cause and our claim and our methods are legitimate. Yet even after a jury in a court of law acquitted me last December, they still call me a violent man. But the right to make a citizens arrest, as I attempted to make that day on Evans, is not a violent right. On the contrary, it is law and order—unless the arrested person resists or flees to avoid prosecution. No honest citizen should avoid a citizen's arrest.

This truth is denied by the conspirators against the poor and by the press which they control. There are also the Silent Contributors. The Jewish people accused the Pope of Rome for keeping silent while Hitler and his machine persecuted the Jews in Germany and other countries. I support the Jews in their right to accuse those who contributed to Hitler's acts by their SILENCE. By the same token, I denounce those in New Mexico who have never opened their mouths at any time to defend or support the thousands who have been killed, robbed, raped of their culture. I don't know of any church or Establishment organization or group of elite intellectuals that has stood up for the Treaty of Guadalupe-Hidalgo. We condemn the silence of these groups and individuals and I am sure that, like the Jewish people, the poor of New Mexico are keeping a record of the Silence which contributes to the criminal conspiracy against the Indo-Hispano in New Mexico.

As I sit in my jail cell in Santa Fe, capitol of New Mexico, I pray that all the poor people will unite to bring justice to New Mexico. My cell block has no day light, no ventilation of any kind, no light of any kind. After 9 P.M., we are left in a dungeon of total darkness. Visiting rules allow only 15 minutes per week on Thursdays from 1 to 4 P.M. so that parents who work cannot visit their sons in jail. Yesterday a 22-year-old boy cut his throat. Today, Aug. 17, two young boys cut their wrists with razor blades and were taken unconscious to the hospital. My cell is dirty and there is nothing to clean it with. The whole cell block is hot and suffocating. All my prison mates complain and show a daily state of anger. But these uncomfortable conditions do not bother me, for I have a divine dream to give me strength: the happiness of my people.

I pray to God that all the Indo-Hispano people will awake to the need for unity, and to our heavenly and constitutional responsibility for fighting peace- fully to win our rights. Already the rest of the Indo-Hispano world—Latin America—knows of our struggle. It is too late to keep the story of our land struggle from reaching the ears of the Indo-Hispano world. All the universities of Latin America knew about our problems when Rockefeller went there last summer. Will Latin America ignore our cry from here in New Mexico and the Southwest? Times have changed and the spirit of the blood is no longer limited by national or continental boundaries.

The Indo-Hispano world will never trust the United States as long as this government occupies our land illegally. The honest policy of the United States will have to begin at home, before [American diplomats] can go to Latin Ameri- ca again to sell good relations and friendship. Our property, freedom and culture must be respected in New Mexico, in the whole Southwest, before the Anglo can expect to be trusted in South America, Mexico and Canada.

This government must show its good faith to the Indo-Hispano in respect to the Treaty of Guadalupe-Hidalgo and the land question by forming a presi- dential committee to investigate and hold open hearings on the land question in the northern part of New Mexico. We challenge our own government to bring forth and put all the facts on the conference table. We have the evidence to prove our claims to property as well as to the cultural rights of which we have been deprived. WE ARE RIGHT—and therefore ready and willing to discuss our problems and rights under the Treaty with the Anglo federal government in New Mexico or Washington, D.C., directly or through agents.

This government must also reform the whole educational structure in the Southwest before it is too late. It should begin in the northern part of New Mexico, where 80% of the population are Indo-Hispanos, as a pilot center. If it works here, then a plan can be developed based on that experience in the rest of the state and wherever the Indo-Hispano population requires it.

Because I know WE ARE RIGHT, I have no regrets as I sit in my jail cell. I feel very, very proud and happy to be in jail for the reason that I am. June 8 in Coyote could have been my last day on earth. My life was spared by God, and to be honored by that miracle at Coyote will keep me happy for many years to come. I am sure that not one of my prison days is lost. Not one day has been in vain. While others are free, building their personal empires, I am in jail for defending and fighting for the rights of my people. Only my Indo-Hispano people have influenced me to be what I am. I am what I am, for my brothers.

SUGGESTIONS FOR FURTHER READING

Rudolpho Acuna, *Occupied America: A History of Chicanos.* 2d ed. New York: Harper & Row, 1981.

Thomas J. Archdeacon, *Becoming American: An Ethnic History.* New York: The Free Press, 1983.

Dee Alexander Brown, *Bury My Heart at Wounded Knee: An Indian History of the American West.* New York: H. Holt, 1991.

W. E. B. Du Bois, *The Souls of Black Folk.* New York: Vintage Books/Library of America, 1990.

Sucheng Chan, ed., *Hmong Means Free: Life in Laos and America.* Philadelphia: Temple University Press, 1994.

Thomas Dublin, *Immigrant Voices: New Lives in America 1773–1986.* Urbana: University of Illinois Press, 1993.

Maxine Schwartz Seller, ed., *Immigrant Women.* Rev. 2d ed. Albany: State University of New York Press, 1994.

Ronald Takaki, *Strangers from a Different Shore: A History of Asian Americans.* Boston: Little Brown, 1989.

Part II

Defining Self, Defining Others

3

On Being Different and "Undifferent" in the United States

This chapter presents first-person accounts by six people who do not feel a sense of belonging to the "majority." Their stories tell of an outsider's struggle, against a variety of odds, to live in a country where welcome is by no means assured. From a mainstream point of view, the experience of growing up in the United States has been one of adjusting to a pattern of social expectations and cultural values that reinforce our collective identity as Americans. Those belonging to groups or categories viewed as standing outside that collective identity, by virtue of their appearance, class, sexual orientation, religion, ethnicity, or any combination of these, are made to feel different from the mainstream. The experience of meeting the presumptions of the majority culture can be painfully complicated, especially for people with multiple and perhaps conflicting identities. For many, a beckoning common American identity can be experienced as intimidating and indeed unachievable.

The opening selection is a chapter from the autobiography of an ex-slave whose girlhood was spent in North Carolina in the middle of the nineteenth century. It is the story of a woman who would very much like to be viewed as "undifferent" from other women in the most basic moral sense but whose differentness, as an African-American female and a slave, makes that impossible. Next is an account by a Sioux Indian who passed his boyhood in the northeast in the latter part of the nineteenth century. Although culturally and racially different, he had educational avenues open to him that were denied the slave and that led, as he believed, to a more expedient and productive affiliation with both the mainstream culture and his Indian heritage. Nor did he face, as a male Indian, the particular barriers of moral and sexual disadvantage that were brought to bear against the African-American woman.

In a short story about a young Hispanic girl, on the other hand, the Chicana author is not concerned with the disadvantage of cultural differences, but rather with their abiding and resilient strengths, especially as experienced from a female perspective. And even Caucasian men wrestle with acute perceptions and experiences of their racial and class differences, as is the case with an accomplished Oklahoma poet. He takes the measure of his own impoverished red-neck origins from the complex racialized reactions of black prisoners who fail to see through his tentatively acquired middle-class disguise. Another selection presents the extraordinary complications of cultural and familial conflict experienced by a gay Korean-American man as he attempts to negotiate his homosexual orientation with parents whose values and traditions prevent them from acknowledging their son's sexual identity. Multiple and unacknowledged identities are also the profound concern of a light-skinned African-American woman who traces the evolution of her consciousness through a series of significant events and personal encounters.

In each of the narratives, no matter what the mark of cultural difference, we encounter people trying to resolve their personal identities at various stages of their lives. Even as they wrestle with their sometimes intractable surroundings, they also struggle toward an expanding and stabilizing cognitive familiarity with the self. However "different" they and others might imagine themselves to be, their stories are about discovering and mastering the intricate ways they might survive and belong in the pluralistic culture of American life.

Harriet Jacobs: The Sexual and Moral Hazards of Growing Up a Female Slave

In 1861, Harriet A. Jacobs (c. 1813–1897), using the pseudonym Linda Brent, published the autobiography of her experiences as a slave under the title *Incidents in the Life of a Slave Girl*. It is estimated that over one hundred ex-slaves like Jacobs were able to acquire sufficient literacy to record their experiences by their own hand, while many hundreds more had their stories written down by others. Although a great number of such accounts, commonly referred to as slave narratives, had been published by the beginning of the Civil War, mostly written by men like Frederick Douglass (see Chapter 2), Jacobs' narrative stood out for its frank portrayal of the sexual abuse typically endured by slave women at the hands of their masters. In Chapter 10 of her autobiography, pointedly entitled "A Perilous Passage in the Slave Girl's Life," she describes the culminating moment when, at age 15, she deliberately chooses to form a voluntary sexual partnership with a sympathetic neighboring gentleman, Mr. Samuel T. Sawyer (named Mr. Sands in the narrative) in order to avoid the more repugnant sexual liaison that her slave master would force upon her. At the time, Jacobs was a slave in the

Source: Harriet Jacobs, *Incidents in the Life of a Slave Girl*, ed. L. Maria Child (Boston: Published for the Author, 1861), pp. 82–89.

home of Dr. James Norcom (named Dr. Flint in the narrative), a prominent citizen in the small town of Edenton, North Carolina, who for several years had without success been trying to coerce her into becoming his mistress. Before being sold to Dr. Norcom, she had been raised by a benevolent slave mistress who exposed her to a relatively genteel lifestyle and taught her to read and write. She had acquired a further sense of self-protection and worth as a woman from her grandmother, who, although a slave, was held in unusually high esteem by the people of Edenton and was able to achieve a modest degree of financial independence.

The stringency of nineteenth-century public morality made it difficult for Jacobs or anyone else to discuss openly the topic of sexuality, so that she was hard pressed to find appropriate ways of talking about the licentious advances of her master. It was especially humiliating for her to confess the degree to which she felt she had contributed to her own moral downfall. This is one of the reasons she did not publish the book under her own name nor refer to others in the narrative by their rightful names. Her prose clearly reflects the values associated with the culture's high expectations of women, particularly the commonplace expectation that any self-respecting woman would, above all else, cherish her purity. Although it is understandable that slave women were in no position to resist the sexual advances of their slave masters, she is nevertheless acutely ashamed of her inability to live up to conventional standards of virtue. As a result, she is placed in a most painful predicament. On the one hand she intensely wants to view herself as possessing the same integrity as women in society at large, indeed has been raised to have the same aspirations and desires as Caucasian women living outside the boundaries of slavery. On the other, she is an African-American woman living within slavery and thus having neither the fundamental right of self-possession nor any of the social freedoms accorded to slave owners. The chapter from her narrative records for us the way she experiences, as the result of her racial and social status, the excruciating conflict of being forced to be sexually and morally different. Her powerlessness as a slave woman makes it impossible for her to sustain a level of conduct that accords with the moral requirements of the society in general, although her own allegiance to morality and virtue cannot be in doubt.

Following the compromise she so painfully records here, the subsequent events of Harriet Jacobs' life are heroic. Ultimately bearing two children by Mr. Sawyer (Mr. Sands), she foils the intentions of Dr. Norcom (Dr. Flint) while at the same time incurring his everlasting wrath. Faced with an unbearable set of conditions in her master's service, she finally escapes, first by spending seven agonizing years literally hidden away in a cramped crawl space over the porch of her grandmother's modest dwelling and then making her way north in 1842 where she is ultimately reunited with her two children in New York City. Employed as a domestic servant and nursemaid until the Civil War, she gathered the strength and courage to write out her personal experiences, encouraged by friends she had made in the Abolition Movement. She insisted, as a nineteenth-century African-American woman, on remaining different in choosing never to marry, in-

stead devoting her energies to the abolition of slavery and, after the Civil
War, to raising money in support of relief work in the South.

After my lover went away, Dr. Flint contrived a new plan. He seemed to
have an idea that my fear of my mistress was his greatest obstacle. In the blandest
of tones, he told me that he was going to build a small house for me, in a
secluded place, four miles away from the town. I shuddered; but I was constrained to listen, while he talked of his intention to give me a home of my own,
and to make a lady of me. Hitherto, I had escaped my dreaded fate, by being in
the midst of people. My grandmother had already had high words with my
master about me. She had told him pretty plainly what she thought of his
character, and there was considerable gossip in the neighborhood about our
affairs, to which the open-mouthed jealousy of Mrs. Flint contributed not a
little. When my master said he was going to build a house for me, and that he
could do it with little trouble and expense, I was in hopes something would
happen to frustrate his scheme; but I soon heard that the house was actually
begun. I vowed before my Maker that I would never enter it. I had rather toil on
the plantation from dawn till dark; I had rather live and die in jail, than drag on,
from day to day, through such a living death. I was determined that the master,
whom I so hated and loathed, who had blighted the prospects of my youth, and
made my life a desert, should not, after my long struggle with him, succeed at
last in trampling his victim under his feet. I would do any thing, every thing, for
the sake of defeating him. What *could* I do? I thought and thought, till I became
desperate, and made a plunge into the abyss.

And now, reader, I come to a period in my unhappy life, which I would
gladly forget if I could. The remembrance fills me with sorrow and shame. It
pains me to tell you of it; but I have promised to tell you the truth, and I will do
it honestly, let it cost me what it may. I will not try to screen myself behind the
plea of compulsion from a master; for it was not so. Neither can I plead ignorance or thoughtlessness. For years, my master had done his utmost to pollute
my mind with foul images, and to destroy the pure principles inculcated by my
grandmother, and the good mistress of my childhood. The influences of slavery
had had the same effect on me that they had on other young girls; they had made
me prematurely knowing, concerning the evil ways of the world. I knew what I
did, and I did it with deliberate calculation.

But, O, ye happy women, whose purity has been sheltered from childhood,
who have been free to choose the objects of your affection, whose homes are
protected by law, do not judge the poor desolate slave girl too severely! If
slavery had been abolished, I, also, could have married the man of my choice; I
could have had a home shielded by the laws; and I should have been spared the
painful task of confessing what I am now about to relate; but all my prospects
had been blighted by slavery. I wanted to keep myself pure; and, under the most
adverse circumstances, I tried hard to preserve my self-respect; but I was struggling alone in the powerful grasp of the demon Slavery; and the monster proved
too strong for me. I felt as if I was forsaken by God and man; as if all my efforts
must be frustrated; and I became reckless in my despair.

I have told you that Dr. Flint's persecutions and his wife's jealousy had given rise to some gossip in the neighborhood. Among others, it chanced that a white unmarried gentleman had obtained some knowledge of the circumstances in which I was placed. He knew my grandmother, and often spoke to me in the street. He became interested for me, and asked questions about my master, which I answered in part. He expressed a great deal of sympathy, and a wish to aid me. He constantly sought opportunities to see me, and wrote to me frequently. I was a poor slave girl, only fifteen years old.

So much attention from a superior person was, of course, flattering; for human nature is the same in all. I also felt grateful for his sympathy, and encouraged by his kind words. It seemed to me a great thing to have such a friend. By degrees, a more tender feeling crept into my heart. He was an educated and eloquent gentleman; too eloquent, alas, for the poor slave girl who trusted in him. Of course I saw whither all this was tending. I knew the impassable gulf between us; but to be an object of interest to a man who is not married, and who is not her master, is agreeable to the pride and feelings of a slave, if her miserable situation has left her any pride or sentiment. It seems less degrading to give one's self, than to submit to compulsion. There is something akin to freedom in having a lover who has no control over you, except that which he gains by kindness and attachment. A master may treat you as rudely as he pleases, and you dare not speak; moreover, the wrong does not seem so great with an unmarried man, as with one who has a wife to be made unhappy. There may be sophistry in all this; but the condition of a slave confuses all principles of morality, and, in fact, renders the practice of them impossible.

When I found that my master had actually begun to build the lonely cottage, other feelings mixed with those I have described. Revenge, and calculations of interest, were added to flattered vanity and sincere gratitude for kindness. I knew nothing would enrage Dr. Flint so much as to know that I favored another; and it was something to triumph over my tyrant even in that small way. I thought he would revenge himself by selling me, and I was sure my friend, Mr. Sands, would buy me. He was a man of more generosity and feeling than my master, and I thought my freedom could be easily obtained from him. The crisis of my fate now came so near that I was desperate. I shuddered to think of being the mother of children that should be owned by my old tyrant. I knew that as soon as a new fancy took him, his victims were sold far off to get rid of them; especially if they had children. I had seen several women sold, with his babies at the breast. He never allowed his offspring by slaves to remain long in sight of himself and his wife. Of a man who was not my master I could ask to have my children well supported; and in this case, I felt confident I should obtain the boon. I also felt quite sure that they would be made free. With all these thoughts revolving in my mind, and seeing no other way of escaping the doom I so much dreaded, I made a headlong plunge. Pity me, and pardon me, O virtuous reader! You never knew what it is to be a slave; to be entirely unprotected by law or custom; to have the laws reduce you to the condition of a chattel, entirely subject to the will of another. You never exhausted your ingenuity in avoiding the snares, and eluding the power of a hated tyrant; you never shuddered at the sound of his footsteps, and trembled within hearing of his voice. I know I did wrong. No one can feel it more sensibly than I do. The painful and humiliating memory will haunt me to my dying day. Still, in looking back, calmly, on the events of my life, I feel that the slave woman ought not to be judged by the same standard as others.

The months passed on. I had many unhappy hours. I secretly mourned over the sorrow I was bringing on my grandmother, who had so tried to shield me from harm. I knew that I was the greatest comfort of her old age, and that it was a source of pride to her that I had not degraded myself, like most of the slaves. I wanted to confess to her that I was no longer worthy of her love; but I could not utter the dreaded words.

As for Dr. Flint, I had a feeling of satisfaction and triumph in the thought of telling *him*. From time to time he told me of his intended arrangements, and I was silent. At last, he came and told me the cottage was completed, and ordered me to go to it. I told him I would never enter it. He said, "I have heard enough of such talk as that. You shall go, if you are carried by force; and you shall remain there."

I replied, "I will never go there. In a few months I shall be a mother."

He stood and looked at me in dumb amazement, and left the house without a word. I thought I should be happy in my triumph over him. But now that the truth was out, and my relatives would hear of it, I felt wretched. Humble as were their circumstances, they had pride in my good character. Now, how could I look them in the face? My self-respect was gone! I had resolved that I would be virtuous, though I was a slave. I had said, "Let the storm beat! I will brave it till I die." And now, how humiliated I felt!

I went to my grandmother. My lips moved to make confession, but the words stuck in my throat. I sat down in the shade of a tree at her door and began to sew. I think she saw something unusual was the matter with me. The mother of slaves is very watchful. She knows there is no security for her children. After they have entered their teens she lives in daily expectation of trouble. This leads to many questions. If the girl is of a sensitive nature, timidity keeps her from answering truthfully, and this well-meant course has a tendency to drive her from maternal counsels.

Presently, in came my mistress, like a mad woman, and accused me concerning her husband. My grandmother, whose suspicions had been previously awakened, believed what she said. She exclaimed, "O Linda! has it come to this? I had rather see you dead than to see you as you now are. You are a disgrace to your dead mother." She tore from my fingers my mother's wedding ring and her silver thimble. "Go away!" she exclaimed, "and never come to my house, again." Her reproaches fell so hot and heavy, that they left me no chance to answer. Bitter tears, such as the eyes never shed but once, were my only answer. I rose from my seat, but fell back again, sobbing. She did not speak to me; but the tears were running down her furrowed cheeks, and they scorched me like fire. She had always been so kind to me! *So* kind! How I longed to throw myself at her feet, and tell her all the truth! But she had ordered me to go, and never to come there again. After a few minutes, I mustered strength, and started to obey her. With what feelings did I now close that little gate, which I used to open with such an eager hand in my childhood! It closed upon me with a sound I never heard before.

Where could I go? I was afraid to return to my master's. I walked on recklessly, not caring where I went, or what would become of me. When I had gone four or five miles, fatigue compelled me to stop. I sat down on the stump of an old tree. The stars were shining through the boughs above me. How they mocked me, with their bright, calm light! The hours passed by, and as I sat there alone a chilliness and deadly sickness came over me. I sank on the ground. My mind was full of horrid thoughts. I prayed to die; but the prayer was not answered. At last, with great effort I roused myself, and walked some distance further, to the house of a woman who had been a friend of my mother. When I told her why I was there, she spoke soothingly to me; but I could not be comforted. I thought I could bear my shame if I could only be reconciled to my grandmother. I longed to open my heart to her. I thought if she could know the real state of the case, and all I had been bearing for years, she would perhaps judge me less harshly. My friend advised me to send for her. I did so; but days of agonizing suspense passed before she came. Had she utterly forsaken me? No. She came at last. I knelt before her, and told her the things that had poisoned my life; how long I had been persecuted; that I saw no way of escape; and in an hour of extremity I had become desperate. She listened in silence. I told her I would bear any thing and do any thing, if in time I had hopes of obtaining her forgiveness. I begged of her to pity me, for my dead mother's sake. And she did pity me. She did not say, "I forgive you;" but she looked at me lovingly, with her eyes full of tears. She laid her old hand gently on my head, and murmured, "Poor child! Poor child!"

Ohiyesa: An Indian Brave Confronts Civilization

North American Indians have a uniquely neutral relationship to the geographic boundaries of Canada, the United States, and Mexico as defined by European-American settlers. Indian cultures did not, and in many respects still do not, acknowledge the sovereign national and cultural entities those boundaries represent for non-Indians. Although Charles A. Eastman (1858–1839), whose Indian name was Ohiyesa (meaning "Winner," a name conferred after his tribe's victory in a lacrosse match), crossed borders in his childhood, he initially remained within a seamless Indian culture indiffferent to American and Canadian national distinctions. He was born of the Wahpeton tribe of the Sioux Nation in the Minnesota Territory. When he was 4 the people of his tribe exiled themselves into northwestern Canada, vigorously pursued across the Missouri River by General Sibley hard upon the 1862 Sioux insurrection in Minnesota. At this time he was separated from his father, Many Lightnings, who was presumed to have been killed in the uprising. For the ensuing ten years of his boyhood, Ohiyesa was initiated into the hunting traditions of an Indian brave in the Manitoba wilderness. This distinct Sioux identity and cultural protection would dramatically break down when, at age 15, he returned to the Dakota

Source: Charles A. Eastman (Ohiyesa), *From the Deep Woods to Civilization: Chapters in the Autobiography of an Indian* (Boston: Little, Brown, and Company, 1916), pp. 15–30.

homestead of his father, who had unexpectedly survived the uprising. In the interval of their separation, to the son's great surprise, the father had converted to Christianity and become firmly persuaded that the survival of the Indian people depended entirely on their acceptance of the white man's civilized ways.

Although young Ohiyesa was at first resistant to the alien agricultural and Christian lifestyle Many Lightnings had adopted, he was grudgingly convinced by what he felt was his father's thoughtful understanding of the advantages it entailed. The title of Eastman's 1916 autobiography, *From the Deep Woods to Civilization,* encapsulates the cultural transition that subsequently challenged him. In Chapter 2, "My First School Days," we are given a moving sense of that transition as Eastman describes the struggle to adjust from a markedly different culture of origin to a sudden immersion in the white man's ways. For the Indian boy, the deep woods meant living in a natural setting where he could move freely, pursue an active physical lifestyle, and cultivate the virtues of personal reserve and communal respect defined by the Sioux culture. It was a world given definition and meaning by the spoken word, a world where natural signs were "read" for what they disclosed about the immediate conditions of the outdoor life of hunting and survival in the wilderness. Now he was being asked to accept a way called civilization where people farmed the land instead of hunting on it, where education was a sedentary experience that emphasized a particular kind of mental agility, where a strange English "sign language" prevailed instead of the familiar Sioux oral tradition, and where expression and self-assertion were clearly valued over the courtesy of reticence.

Eastman's account of first going to mission school and trying to negotiate these bewildering cultural and social shifts remarkably depicts what it is like to grow up radically different and suddenly be faced with becoming undifferent according to someone else's terms. One helpful strategy of initial acculturation, as Eastman records the experience, is the way familiar Indian phrases and meanings are transformed into metaphors that help him define and understand the new lifestyle and its values. Indian culture provides a convincing eloquence by which the reluctant son is encouraged to set out along an unknown path of discovery: "When you see a new trail, or a footprint that you do not know, follow it to the point of knowing." The father makes of this a significant analogy. The idea of going to school and embarking on a new "way of knowledge" becomes comprehensible when Many Lightnings familiarizes it as being like "our old way in hunting." The writing tradition and its books were, for the father, the white man's "bow and arrows." Convinced by these analogies, Ohiyesa (later renaming himself Charles Eastman after his non-Indian maternal grandfather, Captain Seth Eastman) follows an educational trail that would lead to graduation from Dartmouth College in 1887 and a medical degree from Boston University in 1890. Eastman would then complete an extraordinary circle of transformation from Indian brave to trained physician by returning to work among his people.

The man who had built the cabin—it was his first house, and therefore he was proud of it—was tall and manly looking. He stood in front of his pioneer home with a resolute face.

He had been accustomed to the buffalo-skin teepee all his life, until he opposed the white man and was defeated and made a prisoner of war at Davenport, Iowa. It was because of his meditations during those four years in a military prison that he had severed himself from his tribe and taken up a homestead. He declared that he would never join in another Indian outbreak, but would work with his hands for the rest of his life.

"I have hunted every day," he said, "for the support of my family. I sometimes chase the deer all day. One must work and work hard, whether chasing the deer or planting corn. After all, the corn-planting is the surer provision."

These were my father's new views, and in this radical change of life he had persuaded a few other families to join him. They formed a little colony at Flandreau, on the Big Sioux River.

To be sure, his beginnings in civilization had not been attended with all the success that he had hoped for. One year the crops had been devoured by grasshoppers, and another year ruined by drought. But he was still satisfied that there was no alternative for the Indian. He was now anxious to have his boys learn the English language and something about books, for he could see that these were the "bow and arrows" of the white man.

"Oh-hee-ye-sa!" called my father, and I obeyed the call. "It is time for you to go to school, my son," he said, with the usual air of decision. We had spoken of the matter more than once, yet it seemed hard when it came to the actual undertaking.

I remember quite well how I felt as I stood there with eyes fixed upon the ground.

"And what am I to do at the school?" I asked finally, with much embarrassment.

"You will be taught the language of the white man, and also how to count your money and tell the prices of your horses and of your furs. The white teacher will first teach you the signs by which you can make out the words on their books. They call them A, B, C, and so forth. Old as I am, I have learned some of them."

The matter having been thus far explained, I was soon on my way to the little mission school, two miles distant over the prairie. There was no clear idea in my mind as to what I had to do, but as I galloped along the road I turned over and over what my father had said, and the more I thought of it the less I was satisfied. Finally I said aloud:

"Why do we need a sign language, when we can both hear and talk?" And unconsciously I pulled on the lariat and the pony came to a stop. I suppose I was half curious and half in dread about this "learning white men's ways." Meanwhile the pony had begun to graze.

While thus absorbed in thought, I was suddenly startled by the yells of two other Indian boys and the noise of their ponies' hoofs. I pulled the pony's head up just as the two strangers also pulled up and stopped their panting ponies at my side. They stared at me for a minute, while I looked at them out of the corners of my eyes.

"Where are you going? Are you going to our school?" volunteered one of the boys at last.

To this I replied timidly: "My father told me to go to a place where the white men's ways are taught, and to learn the sign language."

That's good—we are going there too! Come on Red Feather, let's try another race! I think, if we had not stopped, my pony would have outrun yours. Will you race with us?" he continued, addressing me; and we all started our ponies at full speed.

I soon saw that the two strange boys were riding erect and soldier-like. "That must be because they have been taught to be like the white man," I thought. I allowed my pony a free start and leaned forward until the animal drew deep breaths, then I slid back and laid my head against the pony's shoulder, at the same time raising my quirt, and he leaped forward with a will! I yelled as I passed the other boys, and pulled up when I reached the crossing. The others stopped, too, and surveyed pony and rider from head to foot, as if they had never seen us before.

"You have a fast pony. Did you bring him back with you from Canada?" Red Feather asked. "I think you are the son of Many Lightnings, whom he brought home the other day," the boy added.

"Yes, this is my own pony. My uncle in Canada always used him to chase the buffalo, and he has ridden him in many battles." I spoke with considerable pride.

"Well, as there are no more buffalo to chase now, your pony will have to pull the plow like the rest. But if you ride him to school, you can join in the races. On the holy days the young men race horses, too." Red Feather and White Fish spoke both together, while I listened attentively, for everything was strange to me.

"What do you mean by the 'holy days'?" I asked.

"Well, that's another of the white people's customs. Every seventh day they call a 'holy day,' and on that day they go to a 'Holy House,' where they pray to their Great Mystery. They also say that no one should work on that day."

This definition of Sunday and churchgoing set me to thinking again, for I never knew before that there was any difference in the days.

"But how do you count the days, and how do you know what day to begin with?" I inquired.

"Oh, that's easy! The white men have everything in their books. They know how many days in a year, and they have even divided the day itself into so many equal parts; in fact, they have divided them again and again until they know how many times one can breathe in a day," said White Fish, with the air of a learned man.

"That's impossible," I thought, so I shook my head.

By this time we had reached the second crossing of the river, on whose bank stood the little mission school. Thirty or forty Indian children stood about, curiously watching the newcomer as we came up the steep bank. I realized for the first time that I was an object of curiosity, and it was not a pleasant feeling.

On the other hand, I was considerably interested in the strange appearance of these school-children.

They all had on some apology for white man's clothing, but their pantaloons belonged neither to the order *short* nor to the *long*. Their coats, some of them, met only halfway by the help of long strings. Others were lapped over in front, and held on by a string of some sort fastened round the body. Some of their hats were brimless and others without crowns, while most were fantastically painted. The hair of all the boys was cut short, and, in spite of the evidences of great effort to keep it down, it stood erect like porcupine quills. I thought, as I stood on one side and took a careful observation of the motley gathering, that if I had to look like these boys in order to obtain something of the white man's learning, it was time for me to rebel.

The boys played ball and various other games, but I tied my pony to a tree and then walked up to the schoolhouse and stood there as still as if I had been glued to the wall. Presently the teacher came out and rang a bell, and all the children went in, but I waited for some time before entering, and then slid inside and took the seat nearest the door. I felt singularly out of place, and for the twentieth time wished my father had not sent me.

When the teacher spoke to me, I had not the slightest idea what he meant, so I did not trouble myself to make any demonstration, for fear of giving offense. Finally he asked in broken Sioux: "What is your name?" Evidently he had not been among the Indians long, or he would not have asked that question. It takes a tactician and a diplomat to get an Indian to tell his name! The poor man was compelled to give up the attempt and resume his seat on the platform.

He then gave some unintelligible directions, and, to my great surprise, the pupils in turn held their books open and talked the talk of a strange people. Afterward the teacher made some curious signs upon a blackboard on the wall, and seemed to ask the children to read them. To me they did not compare in interest with my bird's track and fish-fin studies on the sands. I was something like a wild cub caught overnight, and appearing in the corral next morning with the lambs. I had seen nothing thus far to prove to me the good of civilization.

Meanwhile the children grew more familiar, and whispered references were made to the "new boy's" personal appearance. At last he was called "Baby" by one of the big boys; but this was not meant for him to hear, so he did not care to hear. He rose silently and walked out. He did not dare to do or say anything in departing. The boys watched him as he led his pony to the river to drink and then jumped upon his back and started for home at a good pace. They cheered as he started over the hills: "Hoo-oo! hoo-oo! there goes the long-haired boy!"

When I was well out of sight of the school, I pulled in my pony and made him walk slowly home.

"Will going to that place make a man brave and strong?" I asked myself. "I must tell my father that I cannot stay here. I must go back to my uncle in Canada, who taught me to hunt and shoot and to be a brave man. They might as well try to make a buffalo build houses like a beaver as to teach me to be a white man," I thought.

It was growing late when at last I appeared at the cabin. "Why, what is the matter?" quoth my old grandmother, who had taken especial pride in me as a promising young hunter. Really, my face had assumed a look of distress and mental pressure that frightened the superstitious old woman. She held her peace, however, until my father returned.

"Ah," she said then, "I never fully believed in these new manners! The Great Mystery cannot make a mistake. I say it is against our religion to change the customs that have been practiced by our people ages back—so far back that no one can remember it. Many of the school-children have died, you have told me. It is not strange. You have offended Him, because you have made these children change the ways he has given us. I must know more about this matter before I give my consent." Grandmother had opened her mind in unmistakable terms, and the whole family was listening to her in silence.

Then my hard-headed father broke the pause. "Here is one Sioux who will sacrifice everything to win the wisdom of the white man! We have now entered upon this life, and there is no going back. Besides, one would be like a hobbled pony without learning to live like those among whom we must live."

During father's speech my eyes had been fixed upon the burning logs that stood on end in the huge mud chimney in a corner of the cabin. I didn't want to go to that place again; but father's logic was too strong for me, and the next morning I had my long hair cut, and started in to school in earnest.

I obeyed my father's wishes, and went regularly to the little day-school, but as yet my mind was in darkness. What has all this talk of books to do with hunting, or even with planting corn? I thought. The subject occupied my thoughts more and more, doubtless owing to my father's decided position on the matter; while, on the other hand, my grandmother's view of this new life was not encouraging.

I took the situation seriously enough, and I remember I went with it where all my people go when they want light—into the thick woods. I needed counsel, and human counsel did not satisfy me. I had been taught to seek the "Great Mystery" in silence, in the deep forest or on the height of the mountain. There were no mountains here, so I retired into the woods. I knew nothing of the white man's religion; I only followed the teaching of my ancestors.

When I came back, my heart was strong. I desired to follow the new trail to the end. I knew that, like the little brook, it must lead to larger and larger ones until it became a resistless river, and I shivered to think of it. But again I recalled the teachings of my people, and determined to imitate their undaunted bravery and stoic resignation. However, I was far from having realized the long, tedious years of study and confinement before I could begin to achieve what I had planned.

"You must not fear to work with your hands," said my father, "but if you are able to think strongly and well, that will be a quiver full of arrows for you, my son. All of the white man's children must go to school, but those who study best and longest need not work with their hands after that, for they can work with their minds. You may plow the five acres next to the river, and see if you can make a straight furrow as well as a straight shot."

I set to work with the heavy breaking-plow and yoke of oxen, but I am sorry to admit that the work was poorly done. "It will be better for you to go away to a higher school," advised my father.

It appears remarkable to me now that my father, thorough Indian as he was, should have had such deep and sound conceptions of a true civilization. But there is the contrast—my father's mother! whose faith in her people's philosophy and training could not be superseded by any other allegiance.

To her such a life as we lead to-day would be no less than sacrilege. "It is not a true life," she often said. "It is a sham. I cannot bear to see my boy live a made-up life!"

Ah, grandmother! you had forgotten one of the first principles of your own teaching, namely: "When you see a new trail, or a footprint that you do not know, follow it to the point of knowing."

"All I want to say to you," the old grandmother seems to answer, "is this: Do not get lost on this new trail."

"I find," said my father to me, "that the white man has a well-grounded religion, and teaches his children the same virtues that our people taught to theirs. The Great Mystery has shown to the red and white man alike the good and evil, from which to choose. I think the way of the white man is better than ours, because he is able to preserve on paper the things he does not want to forget. He records everything—the sayings of his wise men, the laws enacted by his counselors."

I began to be really interested in this curious scheme of living that my father was gradually unfolding to me out of his limited experience.

"The way of knowledge," he continued, "is like our old way in hunting. You begin with a mere trail—a footprint. If you follow that faithfully, it may lead you to a clearer trail—a track—a road. Later on there will be many tracks, crossing and diverging one from the other. Then you must be careful, for success lies in the choice of the right road. You must be doubly careful, for traps will be laid for you, of which the most dangerous is the spirit-water, that causes a man to forget his self-respect," he added, unwittingly giving to his aged mother material for her argument against civilization.

The general effect upon me of these discussions, which were logical enough on the whole, although almost entirely from the outside, was that I became convinced that my father was right.

My grandmother had to yield at last, and it was settled that I was to go to school at Santee agency, Nebraska, where Dr. Alfred L. Riggs was then fairly started in the work of his great mission school, which has turned out some of the best educated Sioux Indians. It was at that time the Mecca of the Sioux country; even though Sitting Bull and Crazy Horse were still at large, harassing soldiers and emigrants alike, and General Custer had just been placed in military command of the Dakota Territory.

Helena Maria Viramontes: The Chicana Legacy

There has long been a sizable population in the United States of mixed Spanish-Mexican and Indian descent, people who now identify themselves as Chicano. As a result of military conquest and annexation stemming from the war with Mexico (1846–1848), a modest number of Mexicans inhabiting California, Texas, Arizona, New Mexico, and other northern regions of the Republic of Mexico became, at an instant, Mexican Americans. With this sudden change in national borders they found themselves living in the southwest territories of the United States, their numbers since vastly increased by high rates of immigration from Mexico. This group, conservatively estimated at well over 15 million at present, is one of the fastest growing in the country. In another twenty-five years it is projected to be the largest minority population, even surpassing African Americans in total numbers. Following the Chicano Movement of the 1960s, chiefly sparked by Cesar Chavez's organization of the United Farm Workers, people of mixed Mexican and Indian heritage—sometimes literally referring to themselves as *mestizo,* meaning "mixed"—more deliberately began to look back to their origins and start defining themselves as a cohesive and distinct culture within the United States. In a country with an historical predilection for casting people into simple and unrealistic racial and ethnic categories, this self-conscious insistence on claiming a complex identity with multiple origins far more accurately reflects the American cultural reality.

Writer Helena Maria Viramontes is one of a significant number of Chicano artists who have emerged over the last twenty-five years to represent that distinctness in her fiction. She is a prize-winning author, literary editor of *XismeArte Magazine,* and past coordinator of the Los Angeles Latino Writers Association. She is also one among a growing number of women, of Chicanas, who are as much concerned with distinguishing their experience from that of the men in their lives, the Chicanos, as they are concerned with the consequent difficulties of their minority status in the United States. Her story is particularly concerned with the tensions and healing intimacies between a young teenage girl and her grandmother. The selection is the title story from her collection *The Moths and Other Stories* published in 1985. It catches a moment of intense emotional realization for a troubled 14-year-old upon the death of her maternal grandmother, her *Abuelita,* Mama Luna. Told in the first person, we experience the fictional narrative as an autobiographical moment, drawn into the conflicts of the young Chicana's life and the particular resources and strengths of her Abuelita. Although the focus is on the personal perceptions of the unnamed narrator, the reader can also infer the distinguishing elements that differentiate her culture from that of the mainstream of the United States. Chicano experience derives heavily from the Roman Catholic, male-centered, and Spanish-speaking elements that characterize Mexican culture. These are all present in the story, highlighted by the girl's resentment of her acquiescent

Source: Helena Maria Verimontes, "The Moths," in *Growing Up Chicano,* ed. Tiffany Ana Lopez (New York: Avon Books, 1993), pp. 117–24.

mother and her resistance to an authoritarian father who imposes strict religious expectations upon the women in the family.

In this constraining context, however, is the expansive presence of a sustaining kinship between the girl and her Abuelita, a bond that is expressed through a striking sense of cultural familiarity with death that is passed on quite inevitably to Viramontes' young protagonist. Although the girl is not religious in the conventional sense, she is heir to a ritual healing tradition that provides the means for a moment of extraordinary emotional consummation. In a culture where respect for elders has long been upheld, the grandmother is able to prepare the girl for the transition into maturity. As cultural custodian, she passes on a sustaining mythology by which the troubled granddaughter can survive her familial conflicts and experience an emotional rite of passage. The moth is central to the mythology, both as a healing element in the grandmother's salve at the beginning and as a natural way of explaining death—"the moths that lay within the soul"—remembered by the girl at the end of the story. In the striking image of the flood of moths released as the girl devotedly administers to her grandmother's body, Viramontes employs a creative strategy common to the Chicano and Latin sensibility. She blends the starkly realistic aspects of life with a restorative magical element, a distinguishing characteristic often found in the works of South American and Mexican writers.

I was fourteen years old when Abuelita requested my help. And it seemed only fair. Abuelita had pulled me through the rages of scarlet fever by placing, removing and replacing potato slices on the temples of my forehead; she had seen me through several whippings, an arm broken by a dare jump off Tío Enrique's toolshed, puberty, and my first lie. Really, I told Amá, it was only fair.

Not that I was her favorite granddaughter or anything special. I wasn't even pretty or nice like my older sisters and I just couldn't do the girl things they could do. My hands were too big to handle the fineries of crocheting or embroidery and I always pricked my fingers or knotted my colored threads time and time again while my sisters laughed and called me bull hands with their cute waterlike voices. So I began keeping a piece of jagged brick in my sock to bash my sisters or anyone who called me bull hands. Once, while we all sat in the bedroom, I hit Teresa on the forehead, right above her eyebrow and she ran to Amá with her mouth open, her hand over her eye while blood seeped between her fingers. I was used to the whippings by then.

I wasn't respectful either. I even went so far as to doubt the power of Abuelita's slices, the slices she said absorbed my fever. "You're still alive, aren't you?" Abuelita snapped back, her pasty gray eye beaming at me and burning holes in my suspicions. Regretful that I had let secret questions drop out of my mouth, I couldn't look into her eyes. My hands began to fan out, grow like a liar's nose until they hung by my side like low weights. Abuelita made a balm out of dried moth wings and Vicks and rubbed my hands, shaped them back to size and it was the strangest feeling. Like bones melting. Like sun shining through the darkness of your eyelids. I didn't mind helping Abuelita after that, so Amá would always send me over to her.

In the early afternoon Amá would push her hair back, hand me my sweater and shoes, and tell me to go to Mama Luna's. This was to avoid another fight and another whipping, I knew. I would deliver one last shot on Marisela's arm and jump out of our house, the slam of the screen door burying her cries of anger, and I'd gladly go help Abuelita plant her wild lilies or jasmine or heliotrope or cilantro or hierbabuena in red Hills Brothers coffee cans. Abuelita would wait for me at the top step of her porch holding a hammer and nail and empty coffee cans. And although we hardly spoke, hardly looked at each other as we worked over root transplants, I always felt her gray eye on me. It made me feel, in a strange sort of way, safe and guarded and not alone. Like God was supposed to make you feel.

On Abuelita's porch, I would puncture holes in the bottom of the coffee cans with a nail and a precise hit of a hammer. This completed, my job was to fill them with red clay mud from beneath her rose bushes, packing it softly, then making a perfect hole, four fingers round, to nest a sprouting avocado pit, or the spidery sweet potatoes that Abuelita rooted in mayonnaise jars with toothpicks and daily water, or prickly chayotes that produced vines that twisted and wound all over her porch pillars, crawling to the roof, up and over the roof, and down the other side, making her small brick house look like it was cradled within the vines that grew pear-shaped squashes ready for the pick, ready to be steamed with onions and cheese and butter. The roots would burst out of the rusted coffee cans and search for a place to connect. I would then feed the seedlings with water.

But this was a different kind of help, Amá said, because Abuelita was dying. Looking into her gray eye, then into her brown one, the doctor said it was just a matter of days. And so it seemed only fair that these hands she had melted and formed found use in rubbing her caving body with alcohol and marihuana, rubbing her arms and legs, turning her face to the window so that she could watch the Bird of Paradise blooming or smell the scent of clove in the air. I toweled her face frequently and held her hand for hours. Her gray wiry hair hung over the mattress. Since I could remember, she'd kept her long hair in braids. Her mouth was vacant and when she slept, her eyelids never closed all the way. Up close, you could see her gray eye beaming out the window, staring hard as if to remember everything. I never kissed her. I left the window open when I went to the market.

Across the street from Jay's Market there was a chapel. I never knew its denomination, but I went in just the same to search for candles. I sat down on one of the pews because there were none. After I cleaned my fingernails, I looked up at the high ceiling. I had forgotten the vastness of these places, the coolness of the marble pillars and the frozen statues with blank eyes. I was alone. I knew why I had never returned.

That was one of Apá's biggest complaints. He would pound his hands on the table, rocking the sugar dish or spilling a cup of coffee and scream that if I didn't go to mass every Sunday to save my goddamn sinning soul, then I had no reason to go out of the house, period. Punto final. He would grab my arm and dig his nails into me to make sure I understood the importance of catechism. Did he make himself clear? Then he strategically directed his anger at Amá for her lousy ways of bringing up daughters, being disrespectful and unbelieving, and my older sisters would pull me aside and tell me if I didn't get to mass right this minute, they were all going to kick the holy shit out of me. Why am I so selfish? Can't you see what it's doing to Amá, you idiot? So I would wash my feet and stuff them in my black Easter shoes that shone with Vaseline, grab a missal and veil, and wave good-bye to Amá.

I would walk slowly down Lorena to First to Evergreen, counting the cracks on the cement. On Evergreen I would turn left and walk to Abuelita's. I liked her porch because it was shielded by the vines of the chayotes and I could get a good look at the people and car traffic on Evergreen without them knowing. I would jump up the porch steps, knock on the screen door as I wiped my feet and call Abuelita? mi Abuelita? As I opened the door and stuck my head in, I would catch the gagging scent of toasting chile on the placa. When I entered the sala, she would greet me from the kitchen, wringing her hands in her apron. I'd sit at the corner of the table to keep from being in her way. The chiles made my eyes water. Am I crying? No, Mama Luna, I'm sure not crying. I don't like going to mass, but my eyes watered anyway, the tears dropping on the tablecloth like candle wax. Abuelita lifted the burnt chiles from the fire and sprinkled water on them until the skins began to separate. Placing them in front of me, she turned to check the menudo. I peeled the skins off and put the flimsy, limp-looking green and yellow chiles in the molcajete and began to crush and crush and twist and crush the heart out of the tomato, the clove of garlic, the stupid chiles that made me cry, crushed them until they turned into liquid under my bull hand. With a wooden spoon, I scraped hard to destroy the guilt, and my tears were gone. I put the bowl of chile next to a vase filled with freshly cut roses. Abuelita touched my hand and pointed to the bowl of menudo that steamed in front of me. I spooned some chile into the menudo and rolled a corn tortilla thin with the palms of my hands. As I ate, a fine Sunday breeze entered the kitchen and a rose petal calmly feathered down to the table.

I left the chapel without blessing myself and walked to Jay's. Most of the time Jay didn't have much of anything. The tomatoes were always soft and the cans of Campbell soups had rusted spots on them. There was dust on the tops of cereal boxes. I picked up what I needed: rubbing alcohol, five cans of chicken broth, a big bottle of Pine Sol. At first Jay got mad because I thought I had forgotten the money. But it was there all the time, in my back pocket.

When I returned from the market, I heard Amá crying in Abuelita's kitchen. She looked up at me with puffy eyes. I placed the bags of groceries on the table and began putting the cans of soup away. Amá sobbed quietly. I never kissed her. After a while, I patted her on the back for comfort. Finally: "¿Y mi Amá?" she asked in a whisper, then choked again and cried into her apron.

Abuelita fell off the bed twice yesterday, I said, knowing that I shouldn't have said it and wondering why I wanted to say it because it only made Amá cry harder. I guess I became angry and just so tired of the quarrels and beatings and unanswered prayers and my hands just there hanging helplessly by my side. Amá looked at me again, confused, angry, and her eyes were filled with sorrow. I went outside and sat on the porch swing and watched the people pass. I sat there until she left. I dozed off repeating the words to myself like rosary prayers: when do you stop giving when do you start giving when do you . . . and when my hands fell from my lap, I awoke to catch them. The sun was setting, an orange glow, and I knew Abuelita was hungry.

There comes a time when the sun is defiant. Just about the time when moods change, inevitable seasons of a day, transitions from one color to another, that hour or minute or second when the sun is finally defeated, finally sinks into the realization that it cannot with all its power to heal or burn, exist forever, there comes an illumination where the sun and earth meet, a final burst of burning red orange fury reminding us that although endings are inevitable, they are necessary for rebirths, and when that time came, just when I switched on the light in the kitchen to open Abuelita's can of soup, it was probably then that she died.

The room smelled of Pine Sol and vomit and Abuelita had defecated the remains of her cancerous stomach. She had turned to the window and tried to speak, but her mouth remained open and speechless. I heard you, Abuelita, I said, stroking her cheek, I heard you. I opened the windows of the house and let the soup simmer and overboil on the stove. I turned the stove off and poured the soup down the sink. From the cabinet I got a tin basin, filled it with lukewarm water and carried it carefully to the room. I went to the linen closet and took out some modest bleached white towels. With the sacredness of a priest preparing his vestments, I unfolded the towels one by one on my shoulders. I removed the sheets and blankets from her bed and peeled off her thick flannel nightgown. I toweled her puzzled face, stretching out the wrinkles, removing the coils of her neck, toweled her shoulders and breasts. Then I changed the water. I returned to towel the creases of her stretch-marked stomach, her sporadic vaginal hairs, and her sagging thighs. I removed the lint from between her toes and noticed a mapped birthmark on the fold of her buttock. The scars on her back which were as thin as the life lines on the palms of her hands made me realize how little I really knew of Abuelita. I covered her with a thin blanket and went into the bathroom. I washed my hands, and turned on the tub faucets and watched the water pour into the tub with vitality and steam. When it was full, I turned off the water and undressed. Then, I went to get Abuelita.

She was not as heavy as I thought and when I carried her in my arms, her body fell into a V, and yet my legs were tired, shaky, and I felt as if the distance between the bedroom and bathroom was miles and years away. Amá, where are you?

I stepped into the bathtub one leg first, then the other. I bent my knees slowly to descend into the water slowly so I wouldn't scald her skin. There, there, Abuelita, I said, cradling her, smoothing her as we descended, I heard you. Her hair fell back and spread across the water like eagle's wings. The water in the tub overflowed and poured onto the tile of the floor. Then the moths came. Small, gray ones that came from her soul and out through her mouth fluttering to light, circling the single dull light bulb of the bathroom. Dying is lonely and I wanted to go to where the moths were, stay with her and plant chayotes whose vines would crawl up her fingers and into the clouds; I wanted to rest my head on her chest with her stroking my hair, telling me about the moths that lay within the soul and slowly eat the spirit up; I wanted to return to the waters of the womb with her so that we would never be alone again. I wanted. I wanted my Amá. I removed a few strands of hair from Abuelita's face and held her small light head within the hollow of my neck. The bathroom was filled with moths, and for the first time in a long time I cried, rocking us, crying for her, for me, for Amá, the sobs emerging from the depths of anguish, the misery of feeling halfborn, sobbing until finally the sobs rippled into circles and circles of sadness and relief. There, there, I said to Abuelita, rocking us gently, there, there.

Lloyd Van Brundt: The Racial Measure of the Poor White's Failure

Lloyd Van Brunt's essay, "About Men: Whites Without Money," engages two contending identities—class and race—that his particular personal experience encompasses. Journalist, editor, and author of seven books of poetry, Van Brunt was born in Tulsa, Oklahoma, in 1936 to poor teenage parents. Abandoned by his father and orphaned by his mother's death at the age of 8, he was raised in orphanages and homes as a foster child. The vexing heritage he claims and struggles to understand is that of the poor white male, a figure scorned by society in a litany of derisive labels: Okie, red-neck, cracker, white trash, welfare cheat. This identity is in abrupt conflict with the commonly accepted ideal of the American Dream, the successful man, one who makes money, who produces something tangible that symbolizes his earning power, and whose appearance verifies that achievement and status. Van Brunt has, on the surface, made the transition from failure to success. Yet underneath it all he feels like an interloper, disguised in the garb of success but not feeling the sense of self-possession that ought to accompany his achievements.

Instructively, Van Brunt focuses his lingering sense of humiliation and failure through a racial lens. In an ironically reversed racial vision, he begins to most completely understand the devastation of his poor-white identity as he perceives it in contention with the scornful judgments of black prison inmates. The profoundest measure of his failure, of the humiliation he cannot shake, is their utter disdain of white trash, especially as represented by the woefully inadequate white male prisoners in their midst. Just as African Americans are frustrated again and again by the futility of explaining to prejudiced whites the full sense of the injustice they feel, so does Van Brunt feel inadequate to the challenge of truthfully representing to the African-American male the deep sense of the injustice he has experienced as a poor white boy. The inmates fully appreciate the symbols of his success—the books of poetry, the fine clothes. They cannot detect that it is only a masquerade, that Van Brunt is merely passing as a confidently established white man. In a society where being black is so frequently experi-

Source: Lloyd Van Brundt, "About Men: Whites Without Money," *The New York Times Magazine,* Sunday, March 27, 1994, p. 38.

enced as a liability, the prisoners' racially informed rejection of the failed white male is a painful reckoning the author cannot fully resolve. The essay articulates a strong sense of the inconclusiveness and frustration Van Brunt experiences in trying to bring together the fractious class and racial components of his identity.

Poor whites in this country—whether they're called woodchucks in certain parts of New England, lunch pails in the industrial Midwest or rednecks and crackers in the southern reaches of Appalachia—are often made fun of and referred to as "welfare cheats," since many of them survive on public assistance of one kind or another.

Unlike blacks and other racial minorities, poor and mostly rural whites have few defenders, no articulated cause (although a very small proportion may belong to certain ideological groups). And they have been made to feel deeply ashamed of themselves—as I was. This shame, this feeling of worthlessness, is one of the vilest and most self-destructive emotions to be endured. To be poor in a country that places a premium on wealth is in itself shameful. To be white and poor is unforgivable.

Discussing this issue with a black novelist friend of mine recently, I was surprised at his reaction to my assertion that prejudice against poor whites was still prejudice. I had mentioned Tonya Harding's case, how most of the press had "trashed" her for her "lowlife" life style. My friend had little sympathy for Harding: "Come on. You've never walked into a restaurant and had people raise their eyebrows and frown at you—and neither has she. That's prejudice, or at least the tip of the iceberg of it. We're talking apples and oranges here. What poor whites suffer from mostly is envy of power. They don't have any."

What my friend was too polite to tell me, what would have made conversation awkward between us, was that poor whites are also this country's most bigoted citizens. That's why I call them the Polish-joke class, the one group everybody feels free to belittle, knowing that no politically correct boundaries will be violated. It's mostly poor whites who join the Klan or become skinheads, who tattoo themselves with swastikas. They're angry, and ashamed of their origins. That rage projects itself against minorities. In turn the poor members of minority groups despise and look down on poor whites, especially the men. The unspoken assumption here is that if they had been born white there wouldn't have been anything they couldn't have done.

That attitude was first brought home to me when I worked in several Pennsylvania prisons in the late 70's, teaching creative-writing workshops. Most of my students were either African-American or Hispanic. The most hated members of the groups were the white prisoners. The other men's contempt for these white failures was endless.

I wore a suit and tie and handmade shoes and had long ago lost my Okie accent; I grew up mostly in Oklahoma orphanages. When asked where I was from, I lied and told the men I was a native of Manhattan—New York City; so that placed me in a special category of white men. At least I was successful—or so they had been led to believe.

But the "honkies" in the joints were just honkies—alkies and bums and punks—losers who weren't even good thieves or robbers, many convicted for low-status crimes like child molestation or cashing stolen welfare checks. The real men, the bank robbers and armored-car hijackers, were almost all members of minorities. "We're talkin' white trash here, my man," I was told. "That's for real." His friends agreed. "White trash." That said it all.

I wished then I could have told them the truth about my background, that I had been born "white trash" in Oklahoma. How that fact had been spelled out to me again and again by matrons at the orphanages and, on one occasion, by a schoolteacher who called me a "welfare cheat" in front of a whole class of staring kids. I was so embarrassed, so mortified, that I ran off and was nearly sent to a state reformatory.

I was sure the men would think me a phony if I told them I could have ended up in the joint—one of the despised white failures. If it hadn't been for the right people at the right time encouraging me, I might never have got through a childhood that featured a father who abandoned my mother and me, a mother who died when I was 8 and years and years in orphanages and foster homes where I was abused. As I escorted the men back to their cell blocks, I thought of trying to explain these things—but it wouldn't have worked.

They admired my London-tailored suits, my Turnbull & Asser shirts and ties and silk handkerchiefs that were oh-so-carefully folded and arranged. They admired *success,* wanted to be next to it, associated with it. "Feel these threads," a prisoner once said to me. He put his hand on my shoulder as if to rub an ache out. "Fine, fine." They could never have suspected that for two decades I had kept about $10,000 in debt with credit cards, trying to make myself look like an English gentleman.

These men, I realized, had a considerable investment in me. To them I was a big shot, not a little-known writer who taught creative writing for a living—and one who had had considerable misgivings about teaching in prisons. They had leafed through my four books of poetry and wanted me to be a *celebrity,* one whose signature on the certificates they would receive on completing the workshop would mean something, could be bragged about, could be shown to the parole board. A honky in disguise? Forget it!

Yet no matter how expensive my apparel, I could never have the self-assurance that goes with such clothes. That quality was not for sale. One had to be brought up in a certain way—as many of the students I worked with in a Maryland prep school had. One had to have the easy assumptions of one's class. Teaching in that private school, I was astounded by my students' sense of privilege. They acted as though they owned the space they walked around in. Not all of them were happy or satisfied or had great parents, but most of them had this aura of self-assurance. They seemed sure that no matter what happened they would be protected—as a matter of course.

My novelist friend was right. I had envied these children of the upper middle class—not for the wealth they might inherit (a couple of them already drove $50,000 sports cars, which made *all* the teachers cat-tongued) but for their indefinable feeling of well-being. I knew that no matter how far I ran from my origins, I could never possess their sense of owning the earth—not even a piece of it. For after 10 years of psychotherapy, I still have to remind myself not to walk around in my fine clothes with head down, eyes averted, as if trying to hide some shameful secret, some deep and unreachable sense of worthlessness. That is the legacy of America's poor whites, their only inheritance.

James Jaewhan Lee: "I am learning how to confront elephants. . ."

In this essay originally published in a Korean-American newspaper, James Jaewhan Lee describes the complexities of living at the intersection of two identities, Korean American and gay. He writes about his family with genuine love, but recognizes that his ethnic background includes cultural legacies that, while useful to his parents, are destructive to him. One such legacy is that of Han, "unforgiving guilt." Another is silence, the refusal of his family to confront what they see as unpleasant realities, including his homosexuality. "There's an elephant in the house. . . . Just ignore it and it will go away."

Of course, neither guilt nor silence is exclusive to Korean-American culture. Similarly, Lee's perceived need to break free of some aspects of his ethnic background is shared by the members of many subcultures, especially by the younger generations. Lee's relationship to his Korean-American identity is complicated by the fact that he is gay. Some Asian (and other) immigrants deny the existence of homosexuality within their communities, blaming the appearance of this sexual orientation in the second generation on assimilation and "Americanization." Others do not take their children's same-sex orientation seriously, assuming that it is a passing phase and urging them to marry. Although this may not be the case with Lee, many "minority" lesbians and gays find themselves isolated. Their ethnic and racial communities reject their homosexuality, while "mainstream" gay and lesbian communities do not support their ethnicity.

So much to say. So many stories and realizations. Not too long ago, I was interviewed for the San Francisco edition of the *Korea Times*—because I happen to work for the Gay Asian Pacific Alliance Community HIV Project (GCHP). Now this opportunity to write for KoreAm Journal—the coordinator of this special Lesbian and Gay issue referred to me by one of the two Gay Korean American men I know here in San Francisco. Is there actually an awakening happening in the Korean American communities?

Being Gay. Family. First-generation/second-generation "split." Coming out. HIV/AIDS. Sex. Heterosexism. Racism. Interracial relationships. Rice Queens. Potato Queens. First Boyfriend. Should I try to write about it all? Will this be the last chance to write for a KoreAm audience? Or will the editors realize the need to include Queer voices on a regular basis?

I am writing this in the Castro Hibachi (no Korean restaurants in the Castro, yet) after having seen Pasolini's *Oedipus Rex* (talk about a dysfunctional

Source: James Jaewhan Lee, "Silent Han Elephants," *KoreAm Journal*, August 1993, p. 9.

and guild-ridden family) at the Castro Theater. I live near Dolores Park (no, not the half-Latina, half-Korean drag queen, but the city park between the Mission and the Castro) with a friend of Brazilian origin who is a dancer, and whom I met through the Immigration Working Group of ACT UP.

Family. I can't even remember the last time my two sisters and I sat around the kitchen table making *mandu* for a family gathering. My presence at the annual family Christmas in Los Angeles has been spotty over the last seven years since I came out. At age 31, I think I am almost ready to "reclaim" my family. Okay, so it looks like I am going to write about FAMILY—with much of which many of you will no doubt be familiar.

Dad arrived in 1952, studied at Modesto Junior College, then U.C. Berkeley, then San Francisco State where he met Mom, who had arrived in 1953 (I think). They must have met in 1958 or '59. They were married in 1959 at the Korean Methodist Church in San Francisco's Chinatown. *Kun-noona* lives with her husband (Caucasian) and their two daughters in Boston. *Chagun-noona* lives with her husband (also Caucasian) not too far from the house in which we all grew up since I was ten, and where Mom and Dad still live in South San Francisco.

Monkey/Aquarius/dad, Rooster/Leo/mom, Rat/Aquarius/sister, Cow/Aries/sister, Tiger/Aries/me.

I have been "out" to the family since just before Thanksgiving in November 1985. I thought that not being out was the main block in building meaningful relationships with family and friends—I was very wrong. Not being upfront about my sexuality was just a symptom of a much larger learned problematic behavior made up of the following concepts:

1. (Words to this concept I just learned from a wonderful Filipina friend who has Korean friends, and who has experienced the mostly AIDS related deaths of about 18 friends in the last nine months) *Han*—unforgiving guilt. Or as the Dong-A dictionary states—a grudge; rancor; spite; a lamentation; a regret; grief.
2. "Elephant? What elephant? There's no elephant in the house. You must be imagining it. Just ignore it and it will go away."
3. Silence.

Remember, the parents "lived" through Japanese occupation, the Korean War and immigration to *Mikuk*. Their skills in these "ways" of surviving are flawless. Flawlessness is a powerful teacher. But I have come to realize, through coming out, being affected by HIV/AIDS, and starting psychotherapy (yes, that big taboo) that my circumstances call for different "ways."

When I was living in New York, trying to be a dancer/dance educator, I met a man who was HIV positive. In seven months he went from fairly healthy to dead. This is when a huge dose of *han* entered my consciousness. Could I have done more to help him? Could I have done things differently? What went wrong?

Perhaps these same thoughts went through Mom and Dad's minds when I came out; I don't know; we've never talked about it since.

During the seven months that I knew this human being, who died of AIDS at age 33, I never once called a hotline or asked anyone for advice. I thought I knew how to cope. I lectured him about his diet, his smoking, drinking, neglecting his cat. Did I ever just have fun with him? Did I ever ask him, sincerely, how he was feeling? Did I ever stop my ego long enough to let him be, and let him just have fun being with me? Did I ever stop to think that it was okay to admit to myself that I was out of my depth and needed help?

I remember we, the family, used to have fun driving to church picnics. Dad loved to sing, and loved to listen to musicals. *Oklahoma, The Sound of Music, Camelot* (our all-time favorite; my sisters and I probably know all the lyrics). We used to sing-a-long in the car. We probably learned to sing *Arirang* in our big blue push button transmission Dodge. For all the fun we had singing on the road, at picnics, feeding Wonder bread to the ducks in Golden Gate Park, going to Disneyland with our cousins and aunts and uncles, making *mandu,* and getting money for bowing to the elders on New Year's Day, we had huge "elephants," practically woolly mammoths, lurking about our house. Of course, we never dared seek help outside the walls of our pink house in Daly City, followed by the pink house in South San Francisco, to keep those "elephants" from crushing whatever trust and friendship could have existed between parent and child, siblings, husband and wife. *See no evil, speak no evil, hear no evil. Silence.* According to Webster's: forbearance from speech or noise; muteness; absence of sound or noise—stillness; absence of mention—oblivion, obscurity, secrecy; to restrain from expression—suppress.

Silence has been a survival behavior for me—defense against racism, lookism, heterosexism—inherited from family practices, passed down from generations of Korean ancestors, and learned as a U.S.-born Gay Korean male. The many uses of secrecy have, in many instances, helped me through difficult situations, just as silence, as a tool, probably helped my ancestors. Lately, though, I have come to realize that this tool called silence, called discretion, called privacy and rugged independence, is a double-edged sword that can slash me and hinder growth as easily as it can cut through problems. A history of being silent failed me when I was confronted with a human life put in jeopardy by HIV.

> Knowing ignorance is strength
> Ignoring knowledge is sickness.
> If one is sick of sickness,
> then one is not sick.
> The sage is not sick because he is sick of sickness.
> Therefore he is not sick.
> *from The Tao Te Ching*

I have decided that *han* is something I no longer need in my life—I try to catch myself when I feel that I am falling into *that* abyss. I am learning how to confront "elephants," to accept my limitations, and to ask for help. The existence of GAPA, the Gay Asian Pacific Alliance, is crucial in my learning that not only can I not, but I don't have to do everything; there are men in the community who, by doing what they do best, make it possible for me to stop trying to be *everything* to everybody.

> All I have is a voice
> To undo the folded lie,
> The romantic lie in the brain
> Of the sensual man-in-the-street
> And the lie of Authority
> Whose buildings grope the sky;
> There is no such thing as the State
> And no one exists alone;
> Hunger allows no choice
> To the Citizen or the police;
> we must love one another or die.
> *from September 1, 1939, W. H. Auden*

Taiwanese film director Ang Lee has made a movie called *The Wedding Banquet*. It is the story of a Gay first-generation Taiwanese American man, his Caucasian lover, a green-card marriage, a phony wedding banquet for the parents' sake and the realization of truths. It is the first time I have seen a film and not had to do mental gymnastics to identify with the characters or the story. The day such a film is made about Korean Americans, the richness and complexities of our lives, the joys and the sorrows, I will know that we of Korean descent are well on the road to bidding farewell to our *silent han elephants*. Come out; let's start telling our stories.

Judy Scales-Trent: "On Being Black and White, Different and the Same"

This reading consists of notes from the journal of Judy Scales-Trent, who describes herself as a white black woman. Currently a faculty member in the law school of a large northeastern university, Professor Scales-Trent grew up in North Carolina in a close-knit, well-educated, middle-class African-American family. Like many black families in a nation with a long history of miscegenation, her family includes individuals of different shades of brown as well as some, like herself, who look white. Professor Scales-Trent describes her search for a comfortable, whole, and inclusive identity in a society that treats racial (and other) categories as absolutes, with no place for ambiguities or multiple allegiances. She describes the difficulties of having a racial identity that is not visible; to whom should she "come out" as black—and when? She also describes the experience, common in a mobile American society, of leaving the warmth of her family and community of origin where identity problems scarcely exist ("leaving the reservation," as she puts it), for a less secure but wider world.

Source: Judy Scales-Trent, "Commonalities: On Being Black and White, Different and the Same," *Yale Journal of Law and Feminism*, Vol. 2 (1990), 305–24.

Professor Scales-Trent focuses on race, but her journal also deals with gender and social class. She notes, for example, that she has been protected from some of the bitterness of racism not only because of her appearance, but because she is a woman and because her father was able to give her financial security and an excellent education. Her journal illustrates the fact that individuals from the same racial or ethnic group may have very different experiences, depending on their place in the gender, social class, and other hierarchies within the group. Her journal also illustrates the fact that individuals from one group often have much in common with individuals from other groups, especially those of the same gender and social class. Scales-Trent begins her journal feeling isolated by the problems of being a white black woman. She ends the journal by seeing similarities between her experiences and those of others.

Author's Note

Many in my family are various shades of brown, as is common in most black families. Many others of us, however, look white. I wrote these journal notes, and this essay, as a way of coming to terms with the dilemma of being black and looking white in a society which does not handle anomalies very well.

It is only recently that I have realized that the work that I do is deeply connected with my struggle to live within this dilemma. I am a lawyer and a professor of law. I write about the intersection of race and sex in American law, focusing on the status of black women in the law, that is, on the group which stands at the intersection of the race category and the sex category. I used to define my work in that way. Now that I have written this essay, I see my work differently. In this essay, I struggle to combine two statuses which our society says cannot be combined: black cannot be white, and white cannot be black. In my earlier work on race and sex, I argued that it did not make sense to try to maintain two distinct categories of race and sex in the law, when that separation ignored the very real existence of black women. There again, I argued that the categories seen as so pure, were not pure; that the boundaries thought impermeable were not impermeable. Looking at all of my work, I now understand that I have been working at the intersection of race and sex because I exist at the intersection of race and color, and because I understand, in a very profound way, that in order for me to exist, I must transgress boundaries.

I think this makes people profoundly uncomfortable. Categories make the world appear understandable and safe. Nonetheless, in this essay I ask you to experience my vision of the world—a world where the categories do not clarify, but confuse; a world where one must question the very existence of those categories in order to survive.

Journal Entries: November 1978–December 1981

November 1978

He sang out:

What did I do
to be so black and blue?

And I wept:

> What did I do
> to be so black,
> so white?

November 26, 1978

I wish I had a name to make my home in, to hide inside of. Maybe we should bring back the name "mulatto." For a woman, the French would say "mulâtresse." An identity. A group to belong to. You say "mulatto," and it conjures up meaning: a person despised by dark-skinned brothers and sisters.

("who does she think she is? she think she white, man."

"Hey, you think you better than me, huh?!")

Cast out, cast out, always cast out from the only home, the only safe place, the only refuge in a terrifying, vicious land. Cast out, and alone.

No home. No home.

No place to belong.

No place to rest a frightened and lonely heart.

No place to hide.

White people would let me in, of course. They think that I belong with them. They smile at me. They welcome me. They think I'm their sister.

("Did you see the way that nigger drives? We shouldn't give them licenses!")

They think I'm on their team. And so I'm always waiting, waiting for them to say it. Please don't say it. Don't do that to me. Jesus God, cabbie, can't I even go across town in a cab without having my whole identity called into question? Always wary. Always fighting their silent thoughts, their safe assumptions. Fighting for control of whom I am.

That's who I am. Cast out of my house.

And fighting for control.

And crying.

Missing the safe warmth of my childhood, a colored girl growing up in the protection of a strong family in the segregated South. Surrounded by their love and their strength and their definition of me and of themselves. We moved to New York City when I was very young. One of my warmest memories is of travelling back to North Carolina from New York every summer on the Jim Crow train. We children belonged to all the black adults on the train. Everyone talked and shared food . . . fried chicken and white bread, pimiento cheese sandwiches, deviled eggs: our shoe-box lunch.

Yes, I can see that. What I'm missing is the protection of the family.

But I lost something more when I grew up and moved out of the segregated South, out of the safety of my childhood home. Because the Jim Crow laws gave me an identity and protection I couldn't give myself.

Suddenly, the world was opened to me: streets, movies, schools, restaurants. I put one foot into the world of white-Jewish-liberal-intellectuals when I was in the fifth grade, and I've been straddling two worlds ever since.

What do you do if you're rejected by one world,

("Oh, let's have Judy sit at the table with the white couple when they get here. She acts so white.")

and are constantly rejecting the other. I am perceived by some as white, by some as black, by yet others, as a black person but "really white," so (a) you can trust her and (b) you can't trust her.

And yet I'm me all the time.

Jerked back and forth by other people's needs and fears 'til it gets hard for me to figure out who I am in all this.

I'm glad I've started this writing.

These are the notes of a white black woman.

("Mommy, which water fountain should I drink out of, white or colored?")

December 1, 1979
Sometimes I feel like I'm black, passing for white.
Sometimes I feel like I'm white, passing for black.
On a good day, I just live my life.

December 2, 1979
I went to hear a chamber music recital last night at the Kennedy Center. This is the kind of music that filled my childhood . . . chamber music at the WQXR studio, symphony music at Tanglewood or Lewisohn Stadium, the Saturday afternoon opera on the radio when we were not allowed to make a sound in the apartment.

White music.

We were also exposed to black music—spirituals, "boogie-woogie," and the "classical" black composers and musicians. But our father disapproved of the rhythm and blues records we brought home when we were teenagers. As an adult, I have spent a long time getting in touch with other kinds of black music. Bill introduced me to jazz. And I was almost thirty when I first heard the blues. I couldn't get over it then, and I still can't. It speaks so directly to me and for me. It pierces my heart with pain or joy, sometimes both. And gospel music I have loved since I was a child. I loved it when the men's choir at St. Catherine's AME Zion church went on summer vacation and took their tacky cantatas with them. For that's when the gospel choir came. And the church jumped and shook, and the music made you feel.

It is hard, but very important, to fit the black and white music pieces comfortably into who I am. I need to be able to accept the black and the white heritage with their own validity.

That is all true, and important. But getting a little too intellectual. A way of avoiding the anxiety of last night's chamber recital. For you see, color makes it all more complicated. The concert hall seats maybe eight hundred, a thousand people. It was almost full. And I didn't see anyone who was not white. I felt very anxious and frightened. I was losing control of my identity as a black person: it was slipping away. Wasn't this proof that I was white? By their perception, didn't I fit in just perfectly? and wasn't it obvious that I wouldn't have been there if I weren't white? (1. All people who go to hear chamber music are white. 2. I go to chamber music recitals. 3. Therefore, I am white.) But at intermission, I saw about half a dozen black people. The pendulum tilted back to center and I was steadied.

I must gain better control over who I am. I must learn to live squarely, steadily and surely in the middle of ambiguity, centered strongly in my own No-Name. I must define the No-Name and make it my home.

December 15, 1979

More and more, lately, I have been thinking of dating white men. I have been thinking I could now date white men. I just returned from a visit at Julie's house. One of their friends stopped by. I was attracted by his looks, his openness and enthusiasm, his excitement in learning. Sexy.

I think it would be difficult. But with some help, I could do my part. I think this means something good in terms of my defining and accepting who I am, a white black woman. My definition of who I am is much less at risk.

And it also feels sad, terribly sad. For I am, after all, a black woman, deep down where it counts, and where it hurts.

December 19, 1979

I remember having a startling thought several months ago. Someone gave me a standard line about how she had always wished she were tall. I started my standard response of how I wished I were short—when I suddenly realized that that just wasn't true. I liked being tall and looking good tall.

Then last week I saw "Death and the King's Horsemen," a play by the Nigerian playwright Wole Soyinka. I was watching the beautiful dark-skinned women dancing and started my standard thought of how I wished my skin were that color. But that thought was immediately replaced by: "That's not true. I like the way I look. I look just fine."

I was startled. Pleased.

Hopeful that the thought will return.

There is so much yet I have to tell you about.

About the silence, the lifelong silence of my family. Was it such a terrible secret that we dare not talk about it? what was the secret? and what would happen if we did reveal it?

And about the guilt of a survivor, always protected by a white-skin disguise.

> Is it a disguise?
> How am I to take the good things that come my way?
> would that cabbie have stopped if he had known?
> would the doctor be civil if . . . ?
> would the clerk have been so helpful?
> would the real estate agent have rented me the apartment?

How can I say "no, don't be nice to me; I'm black?"

How can I try to keep from passing when all I'm trying to do is catch a fucking cab?

There is no way around it. I am passing all the time as I walk through the world. I can only correct the perceptions of those persons I deal with on a more than casual basis. And I feel like a fraud. And I hate it. I hate myself for not being able to solve the dilemma. And I hate black people and white people for putting me out there.

Catching a cab is just as hard for a white black person as for a black black person. Or maybe not.

Maybe it has to be made hard to punish myself for my clever disguise.

I heap ashes upon my head and beg for forgiveness.

Sackcloth and ashes.

If I am forgiven,

perhaps I will be allowed back into the fold.

Will someone forgive me?

January 24, 1981

I am beginning to understand what they have done to us. The anger. All of the anger we can't show. And all of the men depressed. And the women, abandoned, un-cherished, un-beautiful. . . .

What will become of us? How can we save ourselves and each other? How do we raise the children? How do we protect the children? (another body found in Atlanta today). Tell me, how do I raise a black-man child? why am I raising a free child who knows what he is feeling? Maybe black men need to be depressed to stay alive. Feelings released create energy and potency: what can a black man do with those?

I am free to feel my aliveness, to stretch as far as I can—because I'm a woman, because I look white. Today, as Pat was getting off the elevator, a white man grabbed her and pushed her back, saying, "No nigger is going to get off this elevator before *me!*" I am spared that craziness by looking white. I am not pushed, abused, humiliated on a daily basis. I have my own craziness from being white/black, but I am not damaged the same way. I get to meet the test of what is called "beautiful" because I look white.

And so I can be valued as a woman by black men. Because I am not so damaged by the racism that I hate them. Because, coming from a white/black family, my father was allowed to make a good living and give us so much—financial security, protection, an open door to the world. Because I can feel beautiful.

It is, I think, the ultimate betrayal, the ultimate irony. The crazy way that racism worked has allowed me to be free and potent. And it has kept the men I love locked in. And impotent. They are enraged at me for being able to take such joy in life and to feel the strength of being whole.

I feel enormous guilt at my whole-ness, at feeling potent, at my joy in life. Luckily, there is a built-in price I will have to pay. Being alone. I can't go back to being less than I am: I want to stand on my toes and reach my arms up as high as I can. But I haven't yet found a black man who can stand watching me do that.

I weep for their need.

But I weep for me also.

• • • • •

Reflections: July 1989

This is how the exploration started, with notes in a journal. It was time for exploring old wounds, a time for growth. I was newly divorced, a single parent head-of-household. And newly come to the world of therapy. It was a time for working on unfinished business. It was a time of rapid, often forced learning. I had been pushed out of one world—not a happy one, but a known one, and therefore, a safe one. And this must have pressed on the bruise of aloneness, of feeling pushed out and homeless because of being a white black woman.

I say unwanted, "forced learning," but clearly it was learning that I wanted, because I went out looking for it. It was a time when I began to open up to the world in a new way, and began to be able to see all the resources and gifts the world made available to me. I began to see that although perhaps I did not see on the table the food that I wanted, there was enough on the table for me not to starve. And, as time went on, I began to see that indeed there was a feast on the table, and that it only took opening up to the feast, reaching out to the richness of life.

It was about this time that I began to hear echoes of my song in the songs of others, that I began to realize that I was not out in the world, a stranger and alone.

It was then that I began to see the many similarities between my feelings of sadness and strangeness and what others felt. How then could I be so sad when I was so much less alone. I was finally able to hear the stories and songs of my sisters, and I heard them say:

> We are like you.
> You are our sister.
> We are with you.
> You are not alone.
> We feel the same pain.
> We sing the same songs.

Let me tell you who spoke to me, and what I heard. Let me tell you how they answered my call. Let me tell you how we are the same in our differences.

• • • • •

Listen to the song of my Indian sister Janet Campbell:

Desmet, Idaho, March 1969

> At my father's wake
>   The old people
>   Knew me,
>   Though I
>   Knew them not,
> And spoke to me
> In our tribe's
> Ancient tongue,
> Ignoring
> The fact
> That I

Don't speak
The language,
And so,
I listened
As if I understood
What it was all about,
And,
Oh,
How it
Stirred me
To hear again
That strange,
  Softly
  Flowing
Native Tongue,
So
Familiar to
My childhood ear.

How this song moved me! I heard then, and hear now, a deep and moving love for her people, a profound memory from childhood of belonging and being safe in the embrace of her family and her people. But I also hear a sadness at the not-belonging-anymore. The loss of her father, the loss of her language, the loss of her home.

I remember summers spent with our grandparents, aunts, uncles and cousins in North Carolina. We played all day long, as we roamed from family home to family home, enjoying the freedom from the city streets, enjoying the sunshine. We ran through the grape arbor quickly, in hopes that the bees would not be able to catch us. We wriggled our bare feet in the grass, as we played "Simon Says" until it was too dark to see anymore. And then, the wonderful dusky evenings, when we sat on the front porch with our mother and grandparents, swinging and fanning, trying to keep cool. Sometimes my grandmother would let me water the petunias in the urns on the front steps (did they like that night watering?) But most of all, I remember it as a quiet, coming-together time. And I remember, like Janet Campbell, the murmurings of the grown-ups as they talked about whatever they talked about. I don't remember what they said. But I do remember the dark and quiet stealing over us all on the porch, enveloping us in quiet and safety. And I remember being embraced and comforted by their murmurings, sounds which lulled us to quiet and to rest.

Now I return to the South to visit my parents. And once again, as I go with them into the black southern community—the church, the bridge club meetings, the college convocation—I am transported back to my childhood, to the safe embrace of family and community and church.

("Lord, child, I can sure see your Aunt Estelle in your face. I would know you anywhere!")

"And, Oh, How it Stir[s] me To hear That strange, Softly Flowing Native Tongue So Familiar to My Childhood ear." And yet, and yet, I too have left home. And I hear the sounds of the language, but I am no longer of the language. One day, in church with my parents, I wept from the beauty and from sadness. Because although I was reminded of coming to church as a child, when I was safe in the embrace of my family, my church, my community, and my God, it was an embrace which I now returned to only rarely, and then, as an outsider. It was a borrowed embrace. And I wept at the loss of leaving home.

This is, of course, a loss all of us know. And we all try to recapture or re-create that embrace as best we know how as we grow older and leave home. But there is something about moving from the southern black community to the northern white community that adds to the sense of loss, of homelessness.

It makes me think of a story I heard about Dr. M., a resident in psychiatry. When I first met her, I felt her warmth and kindness. I noticed her quiet competence, and her quite visible pregnancy! I saw her as a woman filled with life. When I mentioned her to a friend who was also a psychiatrist, he said, almost in passing, that he had not realized that she was an Indian until one evening, when they were both on duty at the emergency psychiatric clinic of a local hospital. At that time, an elderly Indian man was brought in for emergency treatment. I don't think he said why the man was there. What struck him was Dr. M.'s statement that this man had left the reservation. And that reservation Indians are particularly cruel to those who leave the reservation. I was imme-diately stunned by the thought that Dr. M. was talking not only about this man, but about herself. Had she also "left the reservation"? She was clearly successful in a white world. How much had she paid for that success? And it was clear also that she was talking about me. For there are so many reservations: geographical ones, cultural ones, and reservations of the mind. When one leaves to explore, to live in another world, are you leaving the reservation? How do those feel who don't leave the reservation? Do they want to leave? are they afraid to move into a hostile world? are they mad because the world off the reservation is more welcoming to me, a white black person? There is no doubt that the members of the white community in my northern home are more welcoming to me than the members of the black community. How painful that has been. And I can't tell if it is because I am so bi-lingual and bi-cultural that they are not clear that I am black. Or because I have left the reservation and must be made to pay for it. But I am clear that I miss the sweet language of my childhood. And I miss my home. My Indian sisters have helped me see that more clearly.

•   •   •   •   •

It is not all mournful work. Some of the lessons I have learned have been through rowdy laughter. I have had funny teachers. Let me tell you about Dianna. We worked at the appellate division together. And one of the strange things about that office is that it was comprised of about twenty attorneys all in various stages of avoiding writing a brief. One day, when I was in the "walk-the-hall" stage of avoidance, I dropped into Dianna's office and started complaining about the general run of men about town, and the general level of confusion and poverty in my life. "What I need," I said to her, "is to find a prosperous, slightly boring dentist to settle down with." "Oh, I know just what you mean," she declared emphatically. "And if you find one, ask him if he has a sister!" We burst out laughing. And that's how I learned that Dianna was a lesbian.

It wasn't until years later that I realized that gay people, like me, are faced with the problem of "coming out" to people. Dianna has to decide when she should come out to someone, and how. She has to worry about how that person will respond. And as long as she keeps meeting new people, she will have to keep dealing with those issues of self-identification and exposure. These are issues I deal with also: when do I tell someone that I am black? and how? and how will they respond? And if I don't tell people (the apartment rental agent, the cab driver), aren't I "passing"? But Lord knows there's no reason for me to get into self-revelation with someone who's paid to drive me from home to the car shop.

"And why?" I think. "Why should my lesbian sisters have to come out to people? why are they not allowed to keep their sexual life private? why do they have to say: 'this is who I am. I hope you can deal with it. Even if you can't, I need for you to know who I am. I am a member of a despised group. If we are to know each other, you must know this.'" As I write the words, I know why they must come out. They must be clear about who they are, and one way to do this is to force other people to see who they are. As I do. This is also why I "come out." And, with them, I brace myself for the flinch, the startled look, the anxious intake of breath, the wary eye. I come out to white people to say to them: "Beware. I am Other. Proceed with caution." And I come out to black people (how painful it is to have to do it . . .) to say: "I am family. You are safe with me. I am you." But, of course, if you have to *say* that you are black, if your skin doesn't say it for you, then how safe are you, really? how can you be family? And again, I brace myself for not so much the startled look (black people are used to white black people), but for the wary eye. For I am still Other. Coming out only proclaims how I am different, not that I am the same.

I think sometimes how similar are the problems my lesbian sisters and I pose when we come out. Does the person who hears me come out have to confront the notion of black being white? Does the person who hears my lesbian sister come out have to confront the notion of female being male (that is, if one who loves women is a male)? How unsettling it must be to have someone announce to you that black is white, that female is male. . . .

My lesbian sisters have shown me that I am not the only one who has to struggle with coming out. Their courage gives me courage.

•   •   •   •   •

The last story I want to tell you is one that I am really not proud of. I like to think it would not have happened if we hadn't been so tired and jet-lagged. But we were. There were eighteen of us coming from all parts of the country for a two day board meeting in Oakland. We were a group of feminist lawyers and activists, a group very self-consciously created to represent as many different kinds of women as possible. In general, we enjoyed getting together enough to travel thousands of miles for a grueling two day session. It was a group of women who are smart, considerate, funny, and committed to women's issues. Our first meeting was scheduled for Friday night at eight o'clock. We decided to hold the meeting at a restaurant near the hotel.

Now you must remember that for some of us, meeting at eight in the evening was in reality meeting at eleven in the evening, after an exhausting day of travel. Nonetheless, we were all energized by being together, and off we went to search for a restaurant with a table large enough to accommodate us. What a relief it was to find one, only a few blocks away. There were about a dozen of us there, and we were seated around a large round table. Menus came out, along with pots of tea and cups for sipping tea. We started to relax, to look with relish at the menu, to talk about what we would order and how we would share the food. And it was then that Dai broke into the over-tired, energetic talking and said, with a flat voice, "I think we should all consider leaving this restaurant." Dai travels through the world in a wheelchair. And it appeared that this restaurant *was* wheelchair-accessible, but only if you didn't mind going through the back door, past bags of smelly garbage, and through a dirty corridor. Dai was visibly wounded by that process, and although she was by now seated at the table with us, she thought we should leave in protest. There was a long silence. And I don't remember exactly what happened next. But what I do remember is that, at first, no one wanted to leave. There was the suggestion that perhaps we could go ahead and eat, and write a letter of complaint to the management later. Dai was bitter, and angry at us. "You wouldn't stay here if there were an entrance for blacks only." I remember being torn by her analogy. Was she right? But surely not: the only reason she couldn't come in the front door was because she couldn't maneuver her wheelchair up the stairs, a physical, not political, problem. Not a problem of status and degradation. But what I remember most clearly was being angry at her for having to deal with her anger when all I wanted to do was to enjoy my all-too-late dinner after an all-too-long day.

Eventually, of course, we left the restaurant. Two of the group stayed behind to explain to the manager why we left. Another was given the task of writing the owner about his non-compliance with relevant regulations on accessibility. We decided to check the restaurant for compliance before including it in our material for conference attendees that spring. But what struck me the most was that instant when I recalled a conversation with another black woman academic returning from a conference composed predominantly of white feminists, one of whom stated that she was tired of dealing with the anger of black women. We were outraged by their "fatigue." But that evening in Oakland, I saw that I could be, no, *was,* like those white women who were tired of dealing with my anger. For I did not want to deal with Dai's anger. And because I was not in the wheelchair, I was the one who was empowered. I was the one who could listen or not, pay attention to her anger or not, understand or refuse to understand, let my hunger for my own comfort get in the way of recognizing her pain. Dai showed me that in some ways, and to some people, anybody who is not in a wheelchair, be they black, Chinese, Indian, gay, is the insider. And she is the outsider, beating on the door, crying for inclusion. Wanting to be seen, wanting to be known.

I have learned many things from my sisters about being different and being the same. Sometimes, like that time, I did not want to learn the lesson. But it was an important lesson. I learned that sometimes I am the one who gets to wave "the magic wand . . . of exclusion and inclusion." I am like Dai, who feels her difference and her exclusion so keenly. But I am also the non-disabled one. And thus, I am the insider. I am like my white sister too.

There are many more stories I could tell, for once I was able to see the commonalities I see them everywhere. And yet there are more questions, so many more unanswered questions.

I have been wondering why difference is so hard to accept. I have been wondering why difference makes us all so anxious that we create categories, and then expend enormous amounts of energy to make sure people fit in them, and stay in them. And I have been wondering why the system of dualism is so important: what is there about a continuum that is unsatisfying? frightening? Why must life—and we—be seen in either "black" or "white," with no shades in between? For it is this system of rigid dualism that fosters so much anxiety when people don't fit into the categories neatly, when people "transgress boundaries."

And why is it that we look so hard for sameness, when we are, each and every one of us, so different from each other?

And why is it that we find it so hard to find sameness, when we are, in so many ways, so much the same?

But this is the work of another paper. For now, it must suffice that I have come a little way along this path. I have been engaged in my own struggle with being different, and I have found, along the way, the sameness, the connectedness I needed. I have been able to see the commonalities. And have found a home.

SUGGESTIONS FOR FURTHER READING

William L. Andrews, *To Tell a Free Story: The First Century of Afro-American Autobiography 1760–1865*. Urbana: University of Illinois Press, 1988.

Gloria Anzaldua, *Borderlands/La Frontera: The New Mestiza*. San Francisco: Aunt Lute Books, 1987.

Christie Balka and Andy Rose, *Twice Blessed: On Being Lesbian, Gay, and Jewish*. Boston: Beacon Press, 1989.

Charles A. Eastman, *Indian Boyhood*. New York: Phillips & Co., 1902.

Lise Funderburg, *Black, White, Other: Biracial Americans Talk About Race and Identity*. New York: William Morrow & Company, 1994.

Hettie Cohen Jones, *How I Became Hettie Jones*. New York: Dutton, 1990.

Nancy Mairs, "On Being Crippled." In *Plain Text: Essays by Nancy Mairs*. Tucson: University of Arizona Press, 1986, pp. 9–20.

Nary C. Waters, *Ethnic Options: Choosing Identity in America*. Berkeley: University of California Press, 1990.

4

Representations of Prejudice and Ethnocentricity

When the first European voyagers arrived in the western hemisphere, they attempted from the very beginning, as did their descendants in the United States, to depict and define populations of people who appeared to them as physically and culturally different. This was particularly true of the indigenous populations that Christopher Columbus named Indians, mistakenly thinking he had arrived in the East Indies, and subsequently of Africans forced across the Atlantic into slavery. Many of these differences eventually came to be understood in racial terms. The ensuing chapter focuses on some influential modes of representation shaped by the fears, desires, and prejudices of early voyagers and settlers as well as later generations of U.S. citizens. Using historical and personal documents, literary texts, and materials from the theater and popular art, it especially looks at several of the ways both informal and official culture collaborated to produce racialized images of Native Americans and nineteenth-century African Americans. The chapter concludes with a piece that addresses the experience of discrimination, an experience that is the inevitable consequence of this extended tradition of representation simultaneously inventive and manipulative.

Crucial to an understanding of how racial and ethnic groups have been variously represented in the United States is the fact that such populations were, for the most part, not themselves able to participate in the representation process. Although this condition would change over time, especially in the latter half of the nineteenth century and increasingly throughout the twentieth, initially Native Americans and enslaved Africans had little access to literacy and writing, or to printing presses and publishing houses. Indeed, one of the persistent images imposed on them was that of their inherent incapacity to be literate, to write authoritatively, to create serious art, and to function as intellectual and moral beings at the level—so it was alleged—of their civilized and cerebral European-American counterparts. They were relatively powerless to control or influence the written descriptions and the pictures that depicted them. The overall result was an ever-increasing accumulation of misinformed and often deliberately harmful images that projected physical deviance, social chaos, mental incompetence, and moral disorder. Indians and African Americans were, for the most part and frequently with devastating effect, represented the way others saw them, indeed needed to see them, and not the way they knew themselves to be. Racial and ethnic groups have not been the only ones affected by this phenomenon. Generations of Americans of every identity have been heir to a tradition of misinformed representations about the character and habits of people judged to be conspicuously different from others by appearance or cultural lifestyle.

Although in recent times the idea of race has been discredited as a scientific and intellectual concept, there is no question that racialized perceptions and behaviors continue to occupy a central place in our ideas, attitudes, anxieties, and constructions of identity. Certainly we have become a more permeable society in which racial and ethnic boundaries are increasingly dissolved by social mobility, economic fluidity, and intermarriage. Yet collectively we still tend to cling to the simple and comforting distinctions that racial categories seem to afford us. To one degree or another, we have all been acculturated in this way, and thus we are placed in the position of having to unlearn deeply ingrained perceptions about other people that we might eventually discover by experience to be inaccurate. Gaining insight into some of the intricate processes by which such simplistic constructions have been imagined, expressed, promulgated, and perpetuated might help us to unpack some of the burdensome baggage of prejudice and ethnocentricity.

Inventing the Indian: The Account of Amerigo Vespucci

In their contacts with Africa and the Orient, Europeans had already had the experience of differentiating themselves from other categories of people by the time they came into contact with the indigenous inhabitants of the New World. As they did with Asians and Africans, they attempted to measure and represent Indians according to the expectations and values of their own national cultures and interests. Two basic strategies emerged that can be understood as common to all ethnocentric modes of representation. First, *los indios,* as Columbus named them, were depicted as an undifferentiated group, as a collective entity, despite the fact that they comprised multiple cultures, societies, and languages. Second, from this simple idea sprang a cluster of images and traits that were developed as a static and unyielding

Source: Amerigo Vespucci, "Letter of Amerigo Vespucci to Pier Soderini of the Republic of Florence," in *First Four Voyages of Amerigo Vespucci,* Reprinted in facsimile and translated from the rare original edition published in Florence, 1505–6 (London: Bernard Quaritch, 1893), pp. 6–13.

representation of this grouping of people. To the great detriment of the Indians, these images and qualities were in tension with the values and strengths that Europeans in the New World identified with themselves and their own cultural tradition.

Two early influential documents were associated with Italian navigator Amerigo Vespucci (1451–1512), who sailed in 1499 from Cadiz and explored the gulf coast of Mexico. They are the *Mundus Novus* and the *Four Voyages,* both published in 1504 and containing extensive descriptions of the Indian way of life that purport to be Vespucci's observations. Later scholarship has called the authenticity of these two works into question, suggesting that in large part they were forgeries written by political opportunists hoping to capitalize on Vespucci's experiences. They contain numerous inconsistencies and the sensational effects of exaggeration. This in no way diminishes their importance for our purposes, however, as in their quasi-fictional status they even more pointedly reflect the nature of European ethnocentric fantasies in regard to the Indians in the Americas. Most significantly, the two works were widely distributed and became historically influential in establishing the dominant concepts and images associated with the Indians in subsequent writings by the French and the English.

The selection is from the *Four Voyages,* in the form of a letter addressed to one of Vespucci's friends, Pier Soderini, who would later head the city-state of Florence. By powerful implication it defines European superiority against native customers and manners, stressing the absence of any rational social order and the excesses of irrational behavior. The writer can discern no laws, no appointed leaders, no marital fidelity, no religious practice nor worship, no system of commerce nor reasonable evaluation of wealth—all in all a complete lack of coherent governance. The writer makes much, on the other hand, of the widespread presence of nudity, lewdness, licentiousness, and extreme cruelty. In such an ethnography, Indians are perceived to be savage as opposed to civilized, more physically deviant than aesthetically pleasing, emotional rather than rational, depraved heathens as opposed to morally developed Christians. These simplistic depictions would vividly inform the minds and imaginations of New World settlers and be accepted by them as authentic and true.

Although some attractive characteristics were also associated with the idea of the Indian, the negative ones prevailed and endured. They would become justifications for the hostile attitudes and antagonistic behaviors of subsequent colonizers in Virginia and New England who strenuously subdued both the land and its inhabitants. In the ensuing three centuries in the United States, the process of invention and deprecation contributed its share to the disastrous destiny of extermination, resettlement, exclusion, and poverty experienced by Indians.

What we learned of their manners and customs was that they go about entirely naked, the men as well as the women, all shamefully exposed as when they issued from their mother's womb. They are of medium stature, very well proportioned, and with skin of a reddish color almost like a lion's mane, and I believe if they were clothed they would be as white as we. They do not have any hair on their body except the hair on their head, which is long and black. This is especially so of the women, whom it makes handsome. Their appearance is not very good-looking because they have broad faces, making them look like Tartars. They let no hair grow on their eyebrows, nor on their eyelids, nor any place else except the hair on their heads, for they consider hairiness to be a filthy thing. They are very light-footed when they walk and run, the men as well as the women, and the women think nothing of running a league or two, as we saw them do many times. They also have another advantage over us Christians: they are expert swimmers beyond all belief, the women moreso than the men. We have seen them swim two leagues out to sea with nothing to rest upon.

Their weapons are very well made bows and arrows, except they have no iron or other hard metal for making the tips. Instead of iron they use the teeth of animals or fish, or a spike of hard wood with the point tempered by fire. They are sure marksmen, for they hit whatever they aim at, and in some instances the women use these bows. They have other weapons such as fire-hardened spears as well as wooden clubs with beautifully carved knobs. They carry on warfare against people who use a different language, behaving cruelly, without granting life to anyone except to save him for a greater suffering. When they go to war they take their women with them, not so they can fight but to follow behind carrying supplies. Many times have we seen a women carry on her back for thirty or forty leagues a load which no man could bear. They are not accustomed to have any captain, nor do they go forth in any orderly formation, for every man is in charge of himself. They do not go to war for love of conquest, nor to extend their frontiers, but because of some ancient antagonism which arose between them in the past. When asked why they made war, they could give no other reason than to avenge the death of their ancestors or of their parents. These people have neither King nor Lord, obeying no one and living only by a personal liberty. The way they are stirred up to go to war is that when their enemies have slain or captured any of them, the oldest kinsman rises up and goes about haranguing the people to avenge his relatives. By this provocation of feeling are they moved to fight.

They have no judicial system, nor do they punish wrong-doers. Nor does the father or mother chastise their children, and rarely did we see them dispute among themselves. Their conversation appears to be simple, yet they are cunning and acute in matters they consider important. They speak seldom and in low tones, articulating [in their own language] speech sounds similar to ours by using the palate, or the teeth, or the lips. Many are the varieties of their speech, so that for every hundred leagues' distance we found a change of language, one group not being able to understand the other.

The manner of their living is very barbarous, for they eat at no fixed time and as often as they want. And it does not matter very much that the urge may come at midnight or during the day, for they eat at all hours. They take their meal on the ground without a table-cloth or any other cover, for they eat their meats either from earthen bowls made for the purpose or from the halves of gourds. They sleep in cotton netting suspended in the air, and although this manner of sleeping may seem uncomfortable, I say that it is sweet to sleep this way and that we slept better in them than in our quilts. They are a people of neat appearance and clean of body because they wash themselves constantly. When, begging your pardon to say it, they have a bowel movement they do their best not to be observed. And as cleanly and modest as they are in this respect, they are filthy and shameless when urinating. Indeed, even as they stand speaking to us, they let forth their nastiness without turning around or showing any shame.

There is no custom of marriage among them. Each man takes as many women as he pleases, and when he desires to give them up he does so without any imputation of wrong-doing to himself or of disgrace to the women. In this regard, the woman has as much freedom as the man. They are not very jealous of each other, and they are excessively licentious, the women much more so than the men, so that out of decency I omit telling you the arts they practice to gratify their inordinate lust. They are very fertile women, and they do not shirk any work during their pregnancies. Their childbearing labors are so light that, in a single day after giving birth, they are up and about and go everywhere, even to wash themselves in the rivers, being as healthy as fishes.

They are so harsh and devoid of affection that if they are angry with their husbands they immediately pretend to kill the embryo in their womb. They act it out, and in doing so they actually kill an infinite number of creatures by that means. They are elegant women and very well proportioned, their bodies showing no ill-shapen part or limb. They are of ample stature and go about entirely naked, and of their private parts one cannot see, but can only imagine, the most shameful portion, their thighs covering most of it, except that part which nature does not conceal, which is, speaking modestly, the genitals. In sum, they take no more shame in their shameful parts than we do in our nose and mouth. It is rare to see fallen breasts on a woman, or her belly fallen from too much childbearing, or other wrinkles, for they appear never to have given birth. They showed a great desire to have connections with us Christians.

Among these people we did not learn that they had any laws, nor could they be called Moors nor Jews. Indeed they are worse than pagans, because we never saw them offer any sacrifices, nor observe that they had a house of prayer. Their manner of living I judge to be Epicurean. They live in communal dwellings, the houses built like huts, but strongly made, constructed with very large trees, and covered over with palm leaves, secure against storms and winds. In some places they are of so great breadth and length that in one single house we found there were 600 souls. We even saw a village with only thirteen houses where there were four thousand souls. Every eight or ten years they change the location of their houses. When we asked why they did this, they said it was because of the dirt floor, which from its filthiness was already unhealthy and corrupted, and that it bred aches in their bodies, which seemed to us a good reason.

Their riches consist of birds' plumes of many colors, or of beads which they make from fishbones, or of white or green stones which they put in their cheeks and in their lips and ears, and of many other things which we in no wise value. They do not do any trading, nor do they buy or sell. In sum, they live and are content with what nature gives them. The wealth that we enjoy in our own Europe and elsewhere, such as gold, jewels, pearls, and other riches, they hold as nothing. And although they have such riches in their own lands, they do not labor to obtain them, nor do they value them. They are liberal in giving, for it is rarely they deny you anything, while at the same time they are free in asking when they show themselves to be your friends. The greatest sign of friendship which they show you is that they give you their wives and their daughters, and a father and a mother deem themselves highly honored when they bring you a daughter, even if she is a young virgin, if you sleep with her. And in this regard they use every expression of friendship.

When they die, they use several kinds of funeral rites. Some they bury with water and victuals at their heads, thinking the dead will thus have something to eat. They do not have lighted ceremonies with candles nor lamentations. In some places they use the most barbarous and inhuman rite, which is that when a suffering or infirm person is, as it were, at the last stage of death, his kinsmen carry him into a large forest and attach one of those hammocks of theirs, in which they sleep, to two trees, and then put him in it, and dance around him for a whole day. And when the night comes on, they place water and other food at his pillow, so that he may be able to subsist for four or six days. And then they leave him alone and return to the village. And if the sick man helps himself, and eats, and drinks, and survives he returns to the village and is received with ceremony. But few are they who escape. Without receiving any further visit they die, and that place becomes their tomb. And they have many other customs which, to avoid wordiness, I do not relate.

They have many ways of treating their illnesses that are so different from ours that we marvelled how any one survived. For instance, many times I saw a man sick with fever, and when it grew worse they bathed him from head to foot with a large quantity of cold water. Then they lit a grand fire around him, making him turn and turn again every two hours, until they tired him and left him to sleep, and many were thus cured. Along with this they make much use of dieting, for they remain three days without eating food. And they also use blood-letting, but not from the arm, only from the thighs and the loins and the calf of the leg. Also they provoke vomiting with herbs which are placed in the mouth, and they use many other remedies which would take too long to relate. Their phlegm and blood are much weakened because the food consists chiefly of roots and herbs, and fruits and fish. And for their ordinary use and feeding they have a tree root from which they make tolerably good flour, and they call it Iuca, while others call it Cazabi and still others Ignami. They eat little flesh except human flesh, for your Magnificence must know that herein they are so inhuman that they outdo even the way of the beasts. For they eat all of their enemies whom they kill or capture, females as well as males, with so much savagery that merely to describe it seems a horrible thing. And even how much more horrible to see it, as infinite times and in many places it was my fortune to see it. And they were surprised to hear us say that we did not eat our enemies. And this your Magnificence may take for certain, that their other barbarous customs are such that expression is too weak for portraying the reality.

The English Construction of the New England Savage: Three Portrayals

This sequence of three representations of the Indian begins with a selection from William Bradford (1590–1657), who came to the New World aboard the Mayflower in 1620. He was a central figure in the founding and governance of Plymouth Colony. He was also its principal historian, starting his record, entitled *History of Plymouth Plantation,* in about 1630 and completing it in 1651. In 1609, well before coming to New England and to escape religious persecution, he had emigrated to Amsterdam with a group of Separatists, so called because they wished to separate themselves from those Puritans who chose to remain within the Church of England. The selection is from the early part of his history, giving a view of America from the vantage point of a beleaguered exile living in Holland. It describes the apprehensions of the Separatists as they contemplated the daunting prospect of leaving that place to settle in a wilderness where they could freely pursue the practice of their religion. In the context of their own displacement, Bradford's account conveys a vivid sense of how easy it is to demonize an alien and unfamiliar group of people. Among the many obvious dangers anticipated—the desperate hazards of the ocean crossing and settling in uncharted territory—the imagining of the particular terrors identified with the Indian struck a chilling note. Bradford's account is useful for its demonstration of the extent to which earlier characterizations of the Indian, like Vespucci's, clearly contributed to a predominant image of unfettered savagery, indeed of cannibalism. Bradford's perspective, uninformed by any direct experience, is one chiefly influenced by previous constructions of the Indian as the antithesis of the civilized European. In the controlling images of his history, we see the degree to which the English, before setting foot on Plymouth Rock, are predisposed to understand the Indian as a terrifying antagonist. Such portrayals would conveniently merge with the imperatives of survival in the New World wilderness to guide the settlers' attitudes and behaviors in their actual relationships with Indians.

In 1643 a promotional pamphlet was printed in England entitled "New England's First Fruits." Unlike the Bradford account, this document is shaped by actual experiences with Indians. Its main purpose was to extol the attractions and accomplishments of the settlement at Boston. It was designed especially to solicit funds for the support of Harvard College, which had been established in 1636, and to recruit more people to the young Massachusetts Bay Colony. The second part of the tract is devoted to a description of the college, its curriculum, and the bountiful natural resources of the region. The first part, subtitled "In Respect to the Indians," is an intensely worded appeal regarding the opportunity for dedicated Puritans to bring the Indians to a knowledge of the Englishman's Christian God. Although authorship is not attributed, the section on the Indians is believed to be the work of Henry Dunster, a young minister who had been appointed second president of Harvard College in 1640. The first part of the selection given here is the opening paragraph of the tract. Its strategy,

based on actual relationships with the Indian, is contrived to meet theologi-
cal expectations. Rather than deploying the idea and images of the intractable brute savage, the writer imagines and constructs the Indian as the
personification of the damned soul, yet susceptible to the word of God and
conversion to Christianity. The force of religious rhetoric and feeling derives from the Doctrine of Natural Depravity, a pivotal guiding vision in
Puritan theology that understood all humankind as naturally depraved and
consigned to eternal damnation, except a select few to be spared by God on
the Day of Judgment. Already well entrenched in prior accounts as an
uncivilized wilderness people, the Indian is additionally positioned as the
resonant symbol of evil incarnate that Puritans could associate directly with
the work of the Devil. On religious grounds, it powerfully rationalizes a
sense of natural antipathy, of moral disgust, of deeply felt prejudice. The
Indian is here narrowly depicted as a morally unformed heathen, devoid of
Christian grace. Thus he becomes an occasion for the English to enact
certain principles of religious faith that could enhance their stature in the
eyes of their own God. Also included is a passage describing the piety and
death of Sagamore John, a member of the Massachusetts tribe of the Algon-
quians, one of the numerous triumphs of conversion claimed by the pamphlet. Successful conversion activity among the Indians, bringing them to
God, is presented as one of New England's first singular religious harvests,
among its "first fruits." That the pamphlet is in part a solicitation for
Harvard suggests the extent to which a prejudicial imagination is intertwined with the fundamentals of education and religion.

The third portrayal is from the *Journal* of the Puritan John Winthrop
(1588–1649), first governor of the Massachusetts Bay Colony established
in 1630. It is best understood from the standpoint of the Puritan vision of
this world: that every event and experience could be interpreted as an
allegory that revealed the will of God to his people. Such a view attached
spiritual significance to what might appear to be the most mundane and
ordinary experiences. Referring to himself in the third person, Winthrop
describes in the journal entry for October 11, 1631, how he got lost one
night and was forced to take shelter in the hut of Sagamore John, the same
referred to in "New England's First Fruits" and known by all to be a
courteous and friendly Indian. Winthrop would have understood the experience to symbolize a test of his Christian faith. He has strayed from the
familiar path, has momentarily lost his moral bearings, and is being tempted
by the Devil—the presence of the Indian. He is spiritually armed, however,
to meet the challenge: he possesses a compass to provide moral direction, a
match to keep him enlightened, snakeweed to protect him from the serpent,
and psalms to fortify his watchfulness. The final twist occurs when he
momentarily succumbs, permitting himself to take refuge in the hut from
the rain. It is at this point that he invokes the figure of the Indian woman—
the sudden appearance of the "squaw" (originally from the Massachusetts
Indian term *squas,* meaning "wife")—as the extreme symbol of his seduc-
tion. Here Winthrop has taken advantage of the Indian as the established
equivalent of evil, grafting onto that construction the implication of the

sexualized female savage, a wilderness Eve relentlessly at hand to provide the ultimate temptation. He will not share his shelter with her in a gesture of charity. Instead he would seem to bar her out in a determined demonstration of his spiritual fortitude. The Indian is prejudicially imagined so as to serve the purpose of validating Winthrop's own spiritual well-being, not as another human being with equivalent personal and moral claims.

HISTORY OF PLYMOUTH PLANTATION

The place they had thoughts on was some of the vast and unpeopled countries of America, which are fruitful and fit for habitation; being devoid of all civil inhabitants; where there are only savage and brutish men, who range up and down, little different from the wild beasts of the region. This proposition [of immigrating from Holland to America] being made public, and coming to the attention of all; it raised many variable opinions amongst men, and caused many fears, and doubts amongst themselves. Some, by the reasons and hopes they conceived, labored to stir up and encourage the rest to undertake and carry out the venture; while others, out of fear, objected to it, and sought to divert people from it; alleging many things that were neither unreasonable nor improbable. For example, that it was an ambitious plan, and subject to many inconceivable perils and dangers; such as, besides the casualties of the seas (which none can be free of), the length of the voyage being such that the weak bodies of women and other persons worn out with age and toil (as many of them were) could never be able to endure. And yet if they should endure, the miseries of the land, which they should be exposed to, would be too hard to bear; and likely some, or all of them together, would be consumed and utterly ruined. For there they should be liable to famine, and nakedness, and be deprived of many things. The change of air, diet, and drinking of water, would infect their bodies with sore sicknesses and grievous diseases. And also those who should escape or overcome these difficulties, should yet be in continual danger of the savage people; who are cruel, barbarous, and most treacherous, being most furious in their rage, and merciless where they conquer; not being content only to kill and take away life, but delight to torment men in the most bloody manner that may be; flaying some alive with the shells of fishes, cutting off the limbs and joints of others piecemeal and, broiling them on the coals, eat the collops of their flesh in their sight whilst they live; with other cruelties horrible to be related. And surely this could not but move the very bowels of men to grate within them, and make the weak to quake and tremble. It was further objected that it would require greater sums of money to furnish such a voyage (and outfit it with necessities) than their depleted estates would amount to; and yet they must also look to be supported with supplies as are presently transported abroad. Also many precedents of ill success and lamentable miseries befallen others in similar situations were easy to

Source: William Bradford, "History of Plymouth Plantation," in *The Puritans: A Sourcebook of Their Writings*, eds. Perry Miller and Thomas H. Johnson (New York: Harper Torchbooks, 1963), Vol. I, pp. 96–98.

be found, and not forgotten to be alleged. Besides their own experience, in their former troubles and hardships in their removal into Holland; and how hard a thing it was for them to live in that strange place, though it was a neighbor country, and a civil and rich commonwealth.

NEW ENGLAND'S FIRST FRUITS: "IN RESPECT OF THE INDIANS, &C"

Because the Lord has not shown himself to be lacking where the needs of his Servants are concerned, since he has not frustrated the plan of our Transplanting [from England to New England]; so neither is He lacking in giving some light to those poor Indians who have ever sat in hellish darkness, adoring the Devil himself as their GOD: but hath given us some testimony of His gracious acceptance of our poor endeavors towards them, and of our groans to Himself for mercy upon those miserable Souls (the very ruins of mankind) there amongst us; our very bowels yearning within us to see them go down to Hell in swarms without remedy.

Wherefore we judge it is our duty no longer to conceal, but to declare (to the praise of His own free grace) what first Fruits he hath begun to gather in amongst them, as a sure pledge (we are confident) of a greater Harvest in His own time. And wonder not that we mention no more instances at present: but consider, First, their infinite distance from Christianity, having never been prepared thereunto by any Civility at all. Secondly, the difficulty of their Language to us, and ours to them; there being no Rules to learn either by. Thirdly, the diversity of their own Language to it self; every part of that Country having its own Dialect, differing much from the other; all which make their coming into the Gospel the more slow. But what God hath done for some of them, we will declare.

•   •   •   •   •

Sagamore John, a Prince of the Massachusetts Indians, was from our very first landing more courteous, ingenious, and to the English more loving than others of them; he desired to learn and speak our Language, and loved to imitate us in our behavior and apparel and began to hearken after our God and His ways; saying, "Much good men, much good God," and being convinced that our condition and ways were better far than theirs, did resolve and promise to leave the Indians, and come live with us; but yet kept down by fear of the scoffs of the Indians, he had not power to make good his purpose; yet went on not without some trouble of mind, and secret plucks of Conscience, as the sequel declares: for being struck with death, he fearfully cried out of himself that he had not come to live with us in order to have known our God better. "But now," said he, "that I must die, the God of the English is much angry with me, and will destroy me; ah, I was afraid of the scoffs of those wicked Indians; yet my Child

Source: "In Respect of the Indians, &c.," from *New England's First Fruits,* in Samuel Eliot Morrison, *The Founding of Harvard College* (Cambridge, Mass.: Harvard University Press, 1935), Appendix D, pp. 421–23.

shall live with the English, and learn to know their God when I am dead; I'll give him to Mr. Wilson, he is a much good man, and much loved me": so he sent for Mr. Wilson to come to him, and committed his only Child to his care, and so died.

FROM JOHN WINTHROP'S *JOURNAL*

October 11, 1631. The governor, being at his farmhouse at Mystic, walked out after supper, and took a gun with him, supposing he might see a wolf (for they came daily about the house, and killed swine and calves, etc.). A half mile from the house it grew suddenly dark, so that in returning home he mistook his path, and went on till he came to a little house of Sagamore John, which stood empty. There he stayed, and having a piece of match in his pocket (for he always carried about him match and a compass, and in summer time snake-weed), he made a good fire near the house, and lay down upon some old mats which he found there, and so spent the night, sometimes walking by the fire, sometimes singing psalms, and sometimes getting wood, but could not sleep. It was (through God's mercy) a warm night; but a little before day it began to rain, and, having no cloak, he managed to climb up into the house. In the morning, there came thither an Indian squaw, but perceiving her before she had opened the door, he barred her out; yet she stayed there a great while trying to get in, and at last she went away, and he returned safe home, his servants having been much perplexed for him, and having walked about, and shot off guns, and hallooed in the night, but he heard them not.

Prejudice Masked as Humor: Harriet Stowe Jumps Jim Crow

In 1828, Thomas Dartmouth Rice (1806–1860), an obscure actor from New York City, invented a stage character named Jim Crow, an event that marked the beginning of blackface minstrelsy in the United States. In this extremely popular form of vernacular theatre, white actors blackened their faces with burnt cork and performed exaggerated impersonations of African Americans. The chief strategy was that of burlesque humor. As with representations of the Indian, every attempt was made to dramatize the difference between culturally superior Caucasians and Africans incapable of civilized behavior and accomplishment. Rice's stage creation was apparently the result of his having observed a slave working in a livery stable perform an impromptu song and dance routine. Rice was intrigued. He blackened his face, imitated the slave's raggedy appearance, and presented his own version of the performance in a theatre in Louisville, Kentucky, where he was working at the time. He titled the song and accompanying dance "Jim Crow."

Source: John Winthrop, *The History of New England from 1630 to 1649*, ed. James Savage (Boston: Little, Brown and Company, revised edition 1853), Vol. I, pp. 74–75.

Rice's routine concluded with an intricate leaping and turning motion that became a signature of the performance, generally known as jumping Jim Crow. An instant success, it remained a national sensation throughout the 1830s and 1840s, becoming familiar to people of all classes and walks of life. Composer Stephen Collins Foster, who wrote numerous songs expressly for the minstrel stage, jumped Jim Crow as a young child in impromptu theatricals, as did many other citizens in the privacy of their own home.

Rice's reductive and humorous caricature was generally accepted as an accurate portrait. One New York reviewer enthusiastically confirmed the fidelity of the impersonation, calling it "the best representation of our American negro that we ever saw. . . . It was *the* negro, par excellence. Long live *James Crow,* Esquire!" Such indiscriminate appreciation served only to confirm in the mind's eye of the public a hopeless confusion between comic entertainment and ethnic reality. Themselves excluded from the public stage, African Americans were powerless to correct the image. The cover illustration and music shown here are from a version published in New York in the early 1830s at the beginning of Rice's popularity. Also provided is the text for an additional page of the forty-four choruses Rice had conceived up to that point. The tattered clothing, darkly obscured features, and bodily contortions were the hallmarks of the stage figure. The visual image, the dialect lyrics, and the dance permeated the collective American imagination. It is an inevitable irony that Rice's naive theatrical invention would lend its name to the rash of legislation in the South at the turn of the century that legalized racial segregation. These were the infamous "Jim Crow laws" that implemented comprehensive social discrimination against African Americans and that were not successfully challenged and repealed until the 1954 *Brown v. Board of Education* case.

Rice's popular portrait readily found its way into one of the most widely read and influential literary works of the mid-nineteenth century. Harriet Beecher Stowe (1811–1896) published her famous abolitionist novel, *Uncle Tom's Cabin,* in 1852. It was the first novel in the United States to feature an African American, the slave Tom, as its major protagonist and hero. An instant best-seller, it was quickly translated into numerous other languages. The portraiture of its major characters—especially Tom, Little Eva, Topsy, and Simon Legree—have vigorously survived the currency of the novel itself, thriving even today as part of our general cultural legacy. The novel's enormous popularity and influence would also include the perpetuation of unflattering racial portraits.

Stowe's intention was to depict the ills of slavery in the most realistic terms possible, to represent the slaves themselves in a most sympathetic light. And indeed the novel did exert effective pressure in advancing the antislavery cause. Yet in constructing the identity of the African American, Stowe was energized by some of the virulent prejudices abroad in the popular culture. Consequently, her novel, in all the legitimacy of its moral persuasion, became a literary conduit for those racial prejudices at the level of official culture.

The moment of collaboration between Stowe and Rice occurs in the opening chapter when the novel introduces the reader to the first appear-

ance of an African American. Encumbered by debt, Colonel Shelby is negotiating the sale of his faithful slave Uncle Tom. Dan Haley, the slave trader,
wants other slaves to be included in the bargain, at which opportune moment a slave child named Harry enters the room. The brief episode that
follows is essentially informed by Rice's "Jim Crow" and the racially com-
promising theatrical performance associated with it. Given Rice's widespread fame, the reader of the time would have been well conditioned to
respond to the racial cues and images Stowe had borrowed from him.
Although racially identified as a quadroon (one-quarter African, three-
quarters Caucasian), Harry is very light skinned and functions in the role of
an actor doing "darky impersonations." White in appearance but "black" in
fact, he plays without blackface, acting out three brief vignettes of slave
characters that would be familiar to the reader as dark-skinned, comic variations of a Jim Crow minstrel burletta. Stowe deliberately capitalizes on the
connection, having the slavemaster greet the child by the nickname "Jim
Crow." She demonstrates her familiarity with Rice's performance by having
the boy respond with a song and dance routine incorporating the particular
gestures and "comic evolutions" that would be entirely familiar as jumping
Jim Crow. The burlesque of Uncle Cudjoe with the rheumatism echoes the
limping eccentricity that Rice incorporated into his choreography, a trait
often mentioned in descriptions of his performance. In the final scenario
where Harry pokes fun at Elder Robbins leading a psalm, Stowe, under the
influence of the Jim Crow mystique, strikes an awkward note that bears on
the subsequent appearance of Uncle Tom himself, a deeply religious man
who also leads services among the slaves.

Of these implications it is certain that Stowe herself meant no conscious
racial harm beyond seizing a light-hearted moment to entertain the reader.
Yet one must contemplate the way this curiously digressive introduction to
the African American in the novel might have affected the reader's perceptions of the more seriously drawn characters like Uncle Tom. When describing Topsy later on in the novel, Stowe would have Augustine St. Clare refer
to the girl as "rather a funny specimen in the Jim Crow line." That Stowe
has incorporated and transmitted some of the most dynamic racial ideas and
images of the popular culture, despite the high moral mission of the novel
itself, there can be little doubt. By Stowe's time, African Americans had
become so firmly established as figures of ridicule and contempt that not
even advocates on behalf of Abolition and the slave's well-being could
escape the pernicious influence of such representations.

Source: Sheet music cover for T. D. Rice's "Jim Crow," published by E. Riley, New York, nd (c1833). Bequest of Evert Jansen Wendell, Harvard Theatre Collection, The Houghton Library.

JIM CROW.

NEW-YORK.
Published by E. RILEY, 29 Chatham Street.

Come lis_ten all you galls and boys I's jist from Tuckyhoe, I'm goin to sing a lit_tle song, My name's Jim Crow, Weel about and turn about and do jis so, Ebry time I weel about and jump Jim Crow.

<table>
<tr><td>

I
Oh I'm a roarer on de Fiddle,
  And down in old Virginny,
They say I play de skyentific
  Like Massa Pagannini.

III
I went down to de riber,
  I did'nt mean to stay,
But dere I see so many galls,
  I could'nt get away.

</td><td>

II
I git 'pon a flat boat,
  I cotch de Uncle Sam,
Den I went to see de place
  Wher dey kill'd Packenham.

IV
An den I go to Orleans
  An feel so full of fight
Dey put me in de Calaboose,
  An keep me dare all night.

</td></tr>
</table>

(2.)

Source: Music sheet for T. D. Rice's "Jim Crow," published by E. Riley, New York, nd (c1833).
Bequest of Evert Jansen Wendell, Harvard Theatre Collection, The Houghton Library.

VI

When I got out I hit a man,
  His name I now forget,
But dere was nothing left
  'Sept a little grease spot.

VII

I wip my weight in wildcats
  I eat an Alligator,
And tear up more ground
  Dan kifer *50* load of tater

VIII

I sit upon a Hornet's nest,
  I dance upon my head,
I tie a Wiper round my neck
  And den I goes to bed.

IX

Dere's Possum up de gumtree,
  An Raccoon in de hollow,
Wake Snakes for June bug's
  Stole my half a dollar.

X

A ring tail'd monkey,
  An a rib nose Babboon,
Went out de odder day
  To spend de arternoon.

XI

Oh de way dey bake de hoecake
  In old Virginny neber tire,
Dey put de doe upon de foot,
  An hole it to de fire.

XII

O by trade I am a carpenter,
  But be it understood,
De way I get my liben is,
  By sawing de tick oh wood,

XIII

I'm a full blooded niggar,
  Ob de real ole stock,
An wid my head and shoulder
  I can split a horse block,

XIV

I struck a Jarsey niggar,
  In de street de oder day,
An I hope I neber stir,
  If he didn't turn gray.

XV

I'm berry much afraid of late,
  Dis jumping will be no good
For while de Crow are dancing,
  De Wites will saw de wood.

XVI

But if dey get honest,
  By sawing wood like slaves
Der'es an end to de business,
  Ob our friend Massa Hays.

XVII

I met a Philadelphia niggar
  Dress'd up quite nice & clean
But de way he 'bused de Yorkers
  I thought was berry mean.

XVIII

So I knocked down dis Sambo,
  And shut up his light,
For I'm jist about as sassy,
  As if I was half white.

XIX

But he soon jumped up again,
  An 'gan for me to feel,
Says I go away you niggar,
  Or I'll skin you like an eel.

XX

I'm so glad dat I'm a niggar,
  An dont you wish you was too
For den you'd gain popularity,
  By jumping Jim Crow.

XXI

Now my brodder niggars,
  I do not think it right,
Dat you should laugh at dem
  Who happen to be white.

XXII

Kase it dar misfortune,
  An dey'd spend ebery dollar,
If dey only could be,
  Gentlemen ob colour.

XXIII

It almost break my heart,
  To see dem envy me,
An from my soul I wish dem,
  Full as black as we.

XXIV

What stuf it is in dem,
  To make de Debbil black
I'll prove dat he is white,
  In de twinkling of a crack.

XXV

For you see loved brodders,
  As true as he hab a tail,
It is his berry wickedness,
  What makee him turn pale.

XXVI

I went to Hoboken,
  To hab a promenade,
An dar I see de pretty gals,
  Drinking de Lemonade.

XXVII

Dat sour and dat sweet,
  Is berry good by gum,
But de best of lemonade is,
  Made by adding rum.

XXVIII

At de Swan cottage,
  Is de place I tink,
Whar dey make dis 'licious,
  An 'toxicating drink.

XXIX

Some go to Weehawk,
  An some to Brooklyn hight
But dey better stay at home,
  If dey want to see de sight.

XXX

To go to de museum,
  I'm sure it is dare duty,
If for noting else,
  Jist to see de sleeping beauty

XXXI

An dare is daddy Lambert,
  An a skeleton on he hunkie,
An likeness of Broadway dandy
  In a glass case of monkies.

XXXII

De Broadway bells,
  When dey carry full sail,
Around dem wear a funny ting,
  Just like a fox tail.

XXXIII

When you hear de name of it,
  I sure it make you roar,
Why I ax'd 'em what it was,
  And dey said it was a boar.

XXXIV

De great Nullification,
  And fuss in de South,
Is now before Congress,
  To be tried by word ob mouth

XXXV

Dey hab had no blows yet,
  And I hope dey nebber will,
For its berry cruel in bredren,
  One anoders blood to spill.

XXXVI

Wid Jackson at de head,
  Dey soon de ting may settle
For ole Hickory is a man,
  Dat's tarnal full ob mettle.

XXXVII

Should dey get to fighting,
  Perhaps de blacks will rise,
For deir wish for freedom,
  Is shining in deir eyes.

XXXVIII

An if de blacks should get free,
  I guess dey'll fee some bigger,
An I shall concider it,
  A bold stroke for de niggar.

XXXIX

I'm for freedom,
  An for Union altogether,
Aldough I'm a black man,
  De white is calld my broder.

XL

I'm for union to a gal,
  An dis is a stubborn fact,
But if I marry an dont like it,
  I'll nullify de act.

XLI

I'm tired of being a single man
  An I'm 'tarmined to get a wife,
For what I think de happiest,
  Is de swee married life.

XLII

Its berry common 'mong de white
  To marry and get divorced
But dat I'll nebber do
  Unless I'm really forced

XLIII

I think I see myself in Broadway
  Wid my wife upon my arm,
An to follow up de fashion,
  Dere sure can be no harm.

XLIV

An I caution all white dandies,
  Not to come in my way,
For if dey insult me,
  Dey'll in de gutter lay.

(Jim Crow, 2.)

FROM HARRIET BEECHER STOWE, UNCLE TOM'S CABIN

Here the door opened, and a small quadroon boy, between four and five years of age, entered the room. There was something in his appearance remarkably beautiful and engaging. His black hair, fine as floss silk, hung in glossy curls about his round, dimpled face, while a pair of large dark eyes, full of fire and softness, looked out from beneath the rich, long lashes, as he peered curiously into the apartment. A gay robe of scarlet and yellow plaid, carefully made and neatly fitted, set off to advantage the dark and rich style of his beauty; and a certain comic air of assurance, blended with bashfulness, showed that he had been not unused to being petted and noticed by his master.

"Hulloa, Jim Crow!" said Mr. Shelby, whistling, and snapping a bunch of raisins towards him, "pick that up, now!"

The child scampered, with all his little strength, after the prize, while his master laughed.

"Come here, Jim Crow," said he. The child came up, and the master patted the curly head, and chucked him under the chin.

"Now, Jim, show this gentleman how you can dance and sing." The boy commenced one of those wild, grotesque songs common among the negroes, in a rich, clear voice, accompanying his singing with many comic evolutions of the hands, feet, and whole body, all in perfect time to the music.

"Bravo!" said Haley, throwing him a quarter of an orange.

"Now, Jim, walk like old Uncle Cudjoe, when he has the rheumatism," said his master.

Instantly the flexible limbs of the child assumed the appearance of deformity and distortion, as, with his back humped up, and his master's stick in his hand, he hobbled about the room, his childish face drawn into a doleful pucker, and spitting from right to left, in imitation of an old man.

Both gentlemen laughed uproariously.

"Now, Jim," said his master, "show us how old Elder Robbins leads the psalm." The boy drew his chubby face down to a formidable length, and commenced toning a psalm tune through his nose, with imperturbable gravity.

"Hurrah! bravo! what a youn 'un!" said Haley; "that chap's a case, I'll promise. Tell you what," said he, suddenly clapping his hand on Mr. Shelby's shoulder, "fling in that chap, and I'll settle the business—I will. Come now, if that ain't doing the thing up about the rightest!"

The Perpetuation of Racial Humor:
Mark Twain and E. W. Kemble

In *Life on the Mississippi,* which appeared the year before *Adventures of Huckleberry Finn* (1884), Mark Twain (1835–1910) counts among his boyhood heroes the black-face minstrel player. In his creation of Miss Watson's Jim,

Source: Harriet Beecher Stowe, *Uncle Tom's Cabin* (Boston: John P. Jewett & Company, 1852), Vol. I, pp. 15–17.

the slave who is Huck Finn's devoted companion throughout their adventures, we can see distinct traces of the burlesque minstrel tradition. Jim—after "Jim Crow?"—is first introduced to the reader in the opening section of Chapter 2, subtitled "The Boys Escape Jim." The overall effect is similar to Harry's Jim Crow theatricals in Stowe's novel. In the initial appearance of the African American in both works, the irresistible impulse of the white author, following the influence of the dominant popular culture, was to trivialize the slave as a figure of shallow burlesque entertainment. Huck's intrepid friend Tom Sawyer is particularly insistent on producing amusement at Jim's expense, while Twain underscores the role by exaggerating Jim's naive and incredulous responses to Tom's trickery. Twain's introductory gesture casts Jim in the recognizable stage role of the amusingly confused darky (or coon, as people commonly referred to the type) devoid of rational understanding and easily spooked by witches and ghosts—a recurrent racial motif in the novel. Jim's successively elaborate accounts of his bewitchment to spellbound "nigger" audiences further evoke minstrel overtones. In the few lines that Jim speaks in his own voice, readers would recognize the stage dialect. Detecting the stealthy approach of the two boys, the first words he utters are, "Who dah?"

Edward Windsor Kemble (1861–1933) provided 174 illustrations for the first publication of *Huckleberry Finn*. Kemble's introductory drawing of Jim for Chapter 2 shares some of the characteristics of the cover illustration for the music "Jim Crow." Both represent figures in exaggerated pose, tattered attire, and faces darkened to the extent that individual features are indistinct. In "Illustrating Huck Finn" (1930), written thirty-one years later, Kemble describes hiring a young boy, Cort Morris, to model all of the characters in the novel. Entirely independent of Twain's literary approach, Kemble's artistic invention of Jim also occurred within the blackface minstrel context. Kemble makes it clear that Cort delighted in acting like a minstrel player when posing for sketches of Jim. Even though Cort, like Stowe's Harry, is not actually in blackface, the characteristics of the blackface tradition were tangibly present to Kemble's imagination as he drew Jim.

In his account, Kemble tells how the experience with Cort Morris posing for Jim would be a defining moment, launching him on a forty-five-year career specializing in Negro drawings. Almost every historical and critical commentary suggests that Kemble's Negro illustrations were sympathetic and charming. Indeed, some of his work was rendered in an accurate realistic style, some in a somewhat subdued sentimental style. His most notable accomplishments, however, were a series of elaborately published book collections of coon cartoons. They were an energetic artistic extension of the Jim Crow tradition, a style featuring simplistic racialized qualities of animalism, violently explosive gestures, the absence of civility, and the substitution of impulsive behavior for rational order. The identities constructed from the aggregate of these projected traits betray a subsurface of racial prejudice thinly disguised as dismissive humor. Kemble, whose perspective is typical of the time, would have vigorously claimed that he intended no harm. After all, popular art, literature, theater, and music at the turn of the century were flooded with similar coon images. The three cartoon sequences presented here are from *A Coon Alphabet* published in 1898. Although Kemble's motivation was commercial, the strategy of presenting racial humor in the guise of an alphabet primer for young children suggests how constructions of prejudice could be provocatively associated with processes of basic education. This racial pedagogy falls in the same category of children's acculturation as the story of "Little Black Sambo" or the nonsense rime "Eenie, meenie, minee, moe, catch a nigger by the toe. . . ." The extended intertwining of the creative origins of Jim, whom Twain ultimately intended as the type of a folk hero, and Kemble's later more egregious cartoon art suggests the subtle continuum of the ideas and images of prejudice in our cultural dynamics.

FROM TWAIN'S ADVENTURES OF HUCKLEBERRY FINN

We went tip-toeing along a path amongst the trees back towards the end of the widow's garden, stooping down so as the branches wouldn't scrape our heads. When we was passing by the kitchen I fell over a root and made a noise. We scrouched down and laid still. Miss Watson's big nigger, named Jim, was setting in the kitchen door; we could see him pretty clear, because there was a light behind him. He got up and stretched his neck out about a minute, listening. Then he says:

"Who dah?"

He listened some more; then he come tip-toeing down and stood right between us; we could a touched him, nearly. Well, likely it was minutes and minutes that there warn't a sound, and we all there so close together. There was a place on my ankle that got to itching; but I dasn't scratch it; and then my ear begun to itch; and next my back, right between my shoulders. Seemed like I'd die if I couldn't scratch. Well, I've noticed that thing plenty of times since. If you are with the quality, or at a funeral, or trying to go to sleep when you ain't sleepy—if you are anywheres where it won't do for you to scratch, why you will itch all over in upwards of a thousand places. Pretty soon Jim says:

"Say—who is you? Whar is you? Dog my cats ef I didn' heart sumf'n. Well, I knows what I's gwyne to do. I's gwyne to set down here and listen till I hears it agin."

So he set down on the ground betwixt me and Tom. He leaned his back up against a tree, and stretched his legs out till one of them most touched one of mine. My nose begun to itch. I itched till the tears come into my eyes. But I dasn't scratch. Then it begun to itch on the inside. Next I got to itching underneath. I didn't know how I was going to set still. This miserableness went on as much as six or seven minutes; but it seemed a sight longer than that. I was itching in eleven different places now. I reckoned I couldn't stand it more'n a

Source: Mark Twain, *Adventures of Huckleberry Finn* (London: Chatto & Windus, Piccadilly, 1884), pp. 8–11.

minute longer, but I set my teeth hard and got ready to try. Just then Jim begun to breathe heavy; next he begun to snore—and then I was pretty soon comfortable again.

Tom he made a sign to me—kind of a little noise with his mouth—and we went creeping away on our hands and knees. When we was ten foot off, Tom whispered to me and wanted to tie Jim to the tree for fun; but I said no; he might wake and make a disturbance, and then they'd find out I warn't in. Then Tom said he hadn't got candles enough, and he would slip in the kitchen and get some more. I didn't want him to try. I said Jim might wake up and come. But Tom wanted to resk it; so we slid in there and got three candles, and Tom laid five cents on the table for pay. Then we got out, and I was in a sweat to get away; but nothing would do Tom but he must crawl to where Jim was, on his hands and knees, and play something on him. I waited, and it seemed a good while, everything was so still and lonesome.

As soon as Tom was back, we cut along the path, around the garden fence, and by-and-by fetched up on the steep top of the hill the other side of the house. Tom said he slipped Jim's hat off of his head and hung it on a limb right over him, and Jim stirred a little but he didn't wake. Afterwards Jim said the witches bewitched him and put him in a trance, and rode him all over the State, and then set him under the trees again and hung his hat on a limb to show who done it. And next time Jim told it he said they rode him down to New Orleans; and after that, every time he told it he spread it more and more, till by-and-by he said they rode him all over the world, and tired him most to death, and his back was all over saddle-boils. Jim was monstrous proud about it, and he was more looked up to than any nigger in that country. Strange niggers would stand with their mouths open and look him all over, same as if he was a wonder. Niggers is always talking about witches in the dark by the kitchen fire; but whenever one was talking and letting on to know all about such things, Jim would happen in and say, "Hm!" What you know 'bout witches?" and that nigger was corked up and had to take a back seat. Jim always kept that five-center piece around his neck with a string, and said it was a charm the devil give to him with his own hands and told him he could cure anybody with it and fetch witches whenever he wanted to, just by saying something to it; but he never told what it was he said to it. Niggers would come from all around there and give Jim anything they had, just for a sight of that five-center piece; but they wouldn't touch it, because the devil had had his hands on it. Jim was most ruined, for a servant, because he got so stuck up on account of having seen the devil and been rode by witches.

Source: "Jim," illustration by E. W. Kemble for first edition of Mark Twain's *Adventures of Huckleberry Finn,* Chatto & Windus, Piccadilly, London, 1884, p. 11. Reprinted with the permission of The Poetry/Rare Books Collection, University Libraries, State University of New York at Buffalo.

KEMBLE ON ILLUSTRATING HUCKLEBERRY FINN

Now began the important job of getting a model. The story called for a variety of characters, old and young, male and female. In the neighborhood I came across a youngster, Cort Morris by name, who tallied with my idea of Huck. He was a bit tall for the ideal boy, but I could jam him down a few pegs in my drawing and use him for the other characters.

From the beginning I never depended upon models but preferred to pick my types out of the ether, training my mind to visualize them. So I engaged my youthful model, and I remember that from the very start he became immensely popular among his feminine schoolmates as all of his income went for sweet-meats which were duly distributed on his homeward journeys from the seat of learning.

I had a large room in the top of our house which I used as a studio. Here I collected my props for the work. I spent the forenoon completing the drawing, using "Huck" as soon as he was released from school. He was always grinning, and one side of his cheek was usually well padded with a "sour ball" or a huge wad of molasses taffy. Throwing his wool cap and muslin-covered schoolbooks on a lounge, he would ask what was wanted at this session. I would designate the character. "We will do the old woman who spots Huck as he is trying to pass for a girl." Donning an old sunbonnet and slipping awkwardly into a faded skirt, Cort would squat on a low splint-bottomed chair and become the most woebegone female imaginable. Forthwith he would relieve his extended cheek of its burden of taffy with a mighty gulp. I would make a simple outline sketch on yellow toned paper and then take a rest, during which Cort would pop a "cocoanut strip" into his grinning mouth.

For the King, Cort wore an old frock coat and padded his waist line with towels until he assumed the proper rotundity. Then he would mimic the sordid old reprobate and twist his boyish face into the most outlandish expressions. If I could have drawn the grimaces as they were I would have had a convulsing collection of comics, but these would not have jibed with the text, and I was forced to forego them.

I used my young model for every character in the story—man, woman and child. Jim the Negro seemed to please him the most. He would jam his little black wool cap over his head, shoot out his lips and mumble coon talk all the while he was posing. Grown to manhood, "Huck" is now a sturdy citizen of Philadelphia, connected with an established business house.

This Negro Jim, drawn from a white schoolboy, with face unblackened, started something in my artistic career. Several advance chapters of "Huckleberry Finn" were published in the *Century Magazine,* then under the able editorship of Richard Watson Gilder and a select staff of assistants. My picture caught the fancy of Mr. Gilder and W. Lewis Frazer, the art director. I was asked to call and exhibit my wares. I went to *Life* and borrowed a few originals, but not one picture contained a Negro type.

Source: Edward Windsor Kemble, "Illustrating Huck Finn," *The Colophon,* Part I, (February 1930), unpaginated.

"We want to see some of your Negro drawings," Mr. Frazier said.

"I have none," I replied. "I've never made any until this one in Huck Finn."

The art editor looked dubious. "I have several stories I would like to have you illustrate, but they are all of the South."

"Let me try," I urged, "and if they do not suit the text you need not use or pay for them."

I made the drawings. Mr. Frazer nodded his head as he looked at them.

"I guess they'll go. We'll strike off some proofs and send them to the authors and see what they say."

The proofs were sent and soon came back with the stamp of approval. One author went so far as to declare: "At last you have an artist who knows the South." I had, up to that time, never been further south than Sandy Hook. My coons caught the public fancy. *The Century* then engaged me to work exclusively for their magazine. This continued for several years, and all the stories from those charming writers of the South, Thomas Nelson Page, James Lane Allen, Harry Stilwell Edwards, Richard Malcom Johnson and George W. Cable, were placed in my hands for picture work. I was established as a delineator of the South, the Negro being my specialty, and, as I have mentioned, I had never been South at all. I didn't go for two years more. Then I told Mr. Gilder that it was high time for me to go and see what the real article looked like. He agreed with me. After visiting several plantations and noting the local color, a thing I had missed but had not attempted to carry out to any extent in my pictures, I found that my types were, in most cases, the counterparts of those surrounding me. I had seen the Negro of the city but he was a different bird from the plantation product, both in carriage and dress. It all seems so strange to me now, that a single subject, a Negro, drawn from a pose given me by a lanky white schoolboy, should have started me on a career that has lasted for forty-five years, especially as I had no more desire to specialize in that subject than I had in the Chinaman or the Malay pirate.

D is for Didimus
what blew down a gun;
now he and his sister_

_ain't havin' much fun.

Source: "D is for Didimus," cartoon sequence by E. W. Kemble, *A Coon Alphabet*, Robert Howard Russell, Publisher, New York, 1898. Grosvenor Rare Book Room, Buffalo and Erie County Public Library.

R is fo' Rastus
who poked in de trees
a huntin' fer honey —

— but he found mostly bees.

Source: "R is fo' Rastus," cartoon sequence by E. W. Kemble, *A Coon Alphabet,* Robert Howard Russell, Publisher, New York, 1898. Grosvenor Rare Book Room, Buffalo and Erie County Public Library.

The Deadly Effects of Discrimination:
Devin S. Standard

The previous selections in this chapter have mainly been concerned with the way ideas reflecting racial prejudice have been insinuated into the constructed identities of Indians and African Americans in past centuries. In the latter case, we have seen how burlesque humor was a key ingredient in reducing the ordinary complications of human identity to a mocking and inept simplicity. It was as if there had been broad-based popular collaboration (as indeed there had been) to strip the African American of any serious capacity to compete with the rest of humanity. Yet much actual public and private behavior, in the form of overt expressions of discrimination, indeed contradicted the blithe comic dismissals to reveal instead a deeply felt sense of fear and menace. At the same time that blackface minstrelsy, racial cartoons, and coon songs flourished in the last decade of the nineteenth century, not only were African Americans being ruthlessly deprived of economic opportunity but an inordinate number of them were literally being killed with impunity, most frequently by lynch mobs. In the 1890s and into the early years of the twentieth century, scores—mostly men—were hanged, burned, shot, and mutilated: 112 in 1891, 160 in 1892, 117 in 1893, in the neighborhood of 100 or more in each year of that decade alone. What collective angst, after all, did the breezy racial humor conceal, what perception of menace did it so casually disguise, what roiling discomfort did it mask just beneath its surface? Finally, can we claim, in the latter part of this century, to have achieved a more civilized resolution of these tensions and conflicts? Perhaps to some degree, but not entirely.

Writing in 1989, Devin Standard suddenly feels the cumulative pressures of the threatening and prejudicial character constructed for the African-American male. He is, in a psychological instant, rudely shaken from his complacent sense of being a relatively well-adjusted and accepted member of society. In "A Young Black Man Asks: Will I Be Next?," this 24-year-old New Yorker is shocked into perceiving himself, because he is an African-American male, as a conspicuous target for violent racial eradication. A week earlier, a racially motivated confrontation and killing had taken place that compelled Standard to speak out, to express his sense of the perversity of the situation as well as his "feeling of impending doom." Yusef Hawkins, a 16-year-old African American, had been shot and killed by four white teenagers in the Bensonhurst section of Brooklyn. Provoked by an inextricable mixture of racial and sexual prejudices not uncommonly imposed on black males, they thought the young man was dating a white girl in the neighborhood. Actually, he had innocently come to Bensonhurst to look at a used car he had seen advertised in a newspaper. Standard also refers to a similar event in 1986 when Michael Griffith, a young man, was killed by a car in the Howard Beach section of Queens while trying to flee a gang of white youths attacking him. Taken together, this all feels to Standard like a conspiracy of wanton discrimination. Part of his amazement is

Source: The New York Times, September 2, 1989, 23.

that he has understood his own identity not to be racial, but rather ethnic or national. President of his own import-export firm, he has seen himself as a successful and typical "American," in the past able to ignore what he thought to be trivial racial slights. Now, bearing the full psychological brunt of racial events around him, of the racial identity invented for him by others, he feels his very life threatened.

Another young African-American man has fallen victim to the bullets of prejudice and hatred. Yusuf Hawkins, 16 years old, minding his own business, was shot to death on a New York City sidewalk last week by a gang of white kids.

I am writing this in the middle of the night, unable to sleep. I wonder if I am to be next.

It is incredible. This is 1989. I am 24 years old, a graduate of an elite prep school, an elite college, have started a business of my own and am about to commence graduate studies overseas.

Yet I cannot walk throughout the city in which I was born without fearing for my safety—just because I am an African-American.

It is ironic that my being black could be my death warrant, for until this latest killing I denied to myself the fact that I was a member of a minority group. group.

All of my friends are white, my accent and my vocabulary are white, my education is white, my girlfriend is white and my aspirations of success are the same as those of any American. I listen to country music, I ski and I volunteer for the Republicans.

I write to editors of newspapers supporting the National Rifle Association because I own a rifle and enjoy shooting sports. All this being said, I am intrigued by the fact that apparently there are gangs of white people just waiting to kill me.

What have I done? What have we African-Americans done that makes so many white people hate, fear and disdain us so much that they want to deprive us of our lives, liberty and pursuit of happiness?

Have we offended somebody by aspiring to share in the American dream? None of my white friends has ever told me this. Will somebody please explain this to me?

I thought the Federal Bureau of Investigation, the police and the justice system were supposed to benefit all Americans, but lately it seems as if they are awfully close to the thugs in Howard Beach and Bensonhurst.

In case after case, these officials have been harassing their fellow officers and agents merely because they were minority citizens. In case after case, black men fall victim to mortal wounds while in their custody. There is always an investigation, but frequently nothing happens. Charges are dropped and it is back to business as usual.

I used to ignore the menacing glances of police officers, the contemptuous glares of average white citizens, being followed by security guards whenever I enter a store and my inability to flag down a taxi in Manhattan.

But I cannot help wondering now what brought about this miserable state of affairs. Why is this happening to me in my own beloved country? Do white people secretly aspire to intern us all in jails or concentration camps—to permanently do away with us?

I really believe that I am fulfilling my part of the social contract that is necessary for people to live together in a civilized fashion. I certainly am shouldering my share of the responsibilities that accompany the privileges of American citizenship. Moreover, I and all other Americans, have something positive and meaningful to contribute to this country.

Therefore, I must state that I will not appease those of you who wish me dead. African-Americans will not be led quietly to their deaths, interned, or just disappear. Those murderers among you better realize that, because I am an American, I will defend myself.

I am not advocating violence. I will, however, without hesitation, defend my life, liberty and dignity by whatever legal means I have, including force if necessary.

It is really perverse that someone as educated and as adjusted as I am would feel compelled to make a statement such as this. But you know as well as I do what has happened in this world through silence and appeasement. Sadly, I can no longer blindly believe that the justice system, the media and the common decency of others can protect innocent people in this country.

This latest killing of an innocent, unarmed young black man gives me the feeling of impending doom. I hope that I am overreacting, but unfortunately for me, as well as all other Americans, I doubt it.

SUGGESTIONS FOR FURTHER READING

Robert F. Berkhofer Jr. *The White Man's Indian: Images of the American Indian from Columbus to the Present.* New York: Alfred A. Knopf, 1978.

Ralph Blumenthal, "Black Youth Is Slain in Brooklyn by Whites in Attack Held Racial." *The New York Times* August 25, 1989), pp. B1–B2.

Joseph Boskin, *Sambo: The Rise & Demise of an American Jester.* New York: Oxford University Press, 1986.

Andrew Hacker, *Two Nations: Black and White, Separate, Hostile, and Unequal.* New York: Charles Scribner's Sons, 1992.

Werner Sollors, ed., *The Invention of Ethnicity.* New York: Oxford University Press, 1989.

Marlon Riggs, *Ethnic Notions* (video documentary, 56 minutes). San Francisco: Resolution, Inc./California Newsreel, 1987.

Robert C. Toll, *Blacking Up: The Minstrel Show in Nineteenth-Century America.* New York: Oxford University Press, 1974.

Cornel West, *Race Matters.* Boston: Beacon Press, 1993.

Part III

Communities in Historical Perspective

5

Communities in an Expanding Nation— The Nineteenth Century

Between 1800 and 1900 the United States grew from a string of sparsely populated agricultural settlements on the Atlantic seaboard to an industrial giant that spanned a continent. Folklore has portrayed this as the century of the "rugged individual"—the lone frontiersman, the self-made industrialist, the independent pioneer family. More accurately, however, it was the century of the community. Faced with slavery and Emancipation, westward expansion, immigration, industrialization, and urbanization, individuals and families engaged in a wide range of collective activities in order to survive and, if possible, to direct the changes in their lives.

When the nineteenth century began, Native-American peoples already had a long and varied history of collective life. The tribes that lived on the Great Plains, for example, typically hunted, fought, celebrated, and worshipped as close-knit, cooperative units. Although white military power and the destruction of the buffalo undermined many aspects of their culture, their communal traditions survived. Indeed, a major theme of Indian-white relations throughout the century was Native Americans' resistance to the efforts of Anglo-American missionaries and government agents to convert them to the individualistic life-style of the independent white farmer.

Long traditions of communal life were disrupted when Africans were enslaved and taken to America. By the early nineteenth century, however, enslaved and free African Americans were creating new forms of community to meet new needs. On large plantations in the South, "quarter" communities mitigated the physical and psychological horrors of slavery by sharing food and other resources, helping runaways, caring for unprotected children, organizing religious services, preserving African traditions, and developing leaders and moral standards in opposition to those of the slave holders. In the North, communities of emancipated and escaped African Americans established schools, churches, newspapers, mutual assistance societies, literary societies, and abolitionist societies—an expression of a growing African-American culture as well as a response to racism and white exclusion.

"We are all a little wild here with numberless projects of social reform. Not a reading man but has a draft of a new community in his waistcoat pocket," wrote Ralph Waldo Emerson in 1840—with only slight exaggeration. Hundreds of "intentional" communities, voluntary associations for the pursuit of reformist religious or social agendas, dotted the American landscape throughout the nineteenth century. Religious communities such as the Shakers, the Rappites, and the Oneida Society owed their existence to the rise of evangelical, millenial religion in the antebellum years. Secular communities such as Nashoba, New Harmony, and Brook Farm were influenced by European social reformers, especially Robert Owen and Charles Fourier, as well as by transcendentalist philosophy and Jacksonian democratic idealism. Religious or secular, intentional communities addressed the troubling problems of gender and class relations in the new industrial order. Solutions to the former ranged from celibacy to free love; solutions to the latter focused on cooperative, or socialistic, economic life.

Between 1815 and 1860 about five million immigrants came to the United States, a number equal to the entire population of the nation in 1790. This number doubled between 1860 and 1890 and tripled between 1890 and 1914. Immigrants from similar geographic, linguistic, and religious backgrounds gathered together to socialize and help one another, creating distinctive, conspicuous, and, to many of the native born, threatening ethnic enclaves throughout rural and urban America. Vibrant communities developed within many of these enclaves, as immigrants established local, and in some cases national, networks of churches and synagogues, lodges, insurance companies, nationalist societies, women's clubs, schools, theaters, labor unions, and other institutions that both reinforced ethnic identity and facilitated Americanization.

People of color, immigrants, and social reformers were not the only Americans who created communities in the nineteenth century. "Mainstream" Americans also participated in a variety of informal and formal groupings, local, regional, and national, that formed around geographic, religious, professional, ideological, or other commonalities. Probably the most widespread, and least noticed, communities were those that formed around social class. While social status had long been recognized as an important force differentiating one individual from another, and before the Civil War slavery had created a lower caste, most colonial and early-nineteenth-century Americans prided themselves on avoiding the rigid social stratification common in Europe. However, by the mid-nineteenth century commercial and industrial development had created in every town and city an upper class that passed its wealth along to its children and a lower class that lived from day to day as wage laborers. Common interests, common experiences, and common neighborhoods drew many nineteenth-century Americans together along these social class lines. The wealthy mingled with their peers in "society," business, church, and private schools. The poor formed informal networks of sociability and mutual assistance in the working-class neighborhood, the dance hall, the tenement, and the tavern. As large factories began to replace small handicraft shops, the work place and the fledgling labor union became sources and sites of working-class community.

Communities also formed around gender. Most nineteenth-century Americans considered women different by nature (not nurture) from men, and as men left the household for other work places, everyday activities were increasingly segregated by sex. As a result, gender became a basis for community, both independently and as a category within racial, religious, and other groupings. Female relatives and friends formed support groups that helped one another through childbirth, illness, and marital crises. Women of different classes, races, and ethnic and religious backgrounds organized to pursue a range of agendas, many, but not all, of which were seen as appropriate to the narrow but expanding female "sphere."

Larger than families but more intimate than most other social units, nineteenth-century communities performed important functions. Some of these functions were negative, as when communities reinforced their own identities by attacking other groups or maintained solidarity by ostracizing dissenters. More often, the contributions of communities were positive. Communities offered companionship and support to the many people in transition from overseas to the United States, from slavery to freedom, from East to West, from countryside to city. Communities created and preserved values, including some not widely shared, and provided opportunities for leadership and recognition to individuals whose talents would otherwise have gone unnoticed. Finally, at a time when government assumed little or no responsibility for the welfare of the individual, communities ameliorated the human costs of territorial expansion and economic growth.

Community as Survival: Solidarity and Celebration in the Slave Quarters

In the early nineteenth century the cotton gin and other technological improvements increased the demand for cotton. The result was an increase in large plantations and, consequently, an increase in the size of slave quarters, so that they became large enough to function as communities. This account of community life in the quarter is from a slave narrative first printed in 1836. The author, Charles Ball, is described on the title page as "a Black Man Who Lived Forty Years in Maryland, South Carolina, and Georgia as a Slave," and "twice escaped from the cotton country."

When the passage begins, Ball, recaptured after years of freedom in the North, is a new field hand on a plantation in South Carolina and has been arbitrarily assigned to the cabin of a woman named Dinah. Almost immediately he becomes, in effect, a member of Dinah's family, sharing its meager

Source: Charles Ball, *Slavery in the United States: A Narrative of the Life and Adventures of Charles Ball, A Black Man, Who Lived Forty Years in Maryland, South Carolina, and Georgia as a Slave* (New York: J.S. Taylor, 1837), pp. 192–95, 200–203.

resources and contributing to its support. The narrative illustrates the strong cooperative bonds within the community, which functioned as an extended family for unrelated adults as well as for children whose parents had died or been sold. A weekend of communal celebration after the cotton harvest revives Ball's spirits, enabling him and the entire community to reaffirm their humanity and solidarity in the face of slavery. While this celebration was sponsored by the master, quarter communities often held feasts, religious services, and other communal events secretly, in defiance of their masters and at great risk to themselves.

. . .when I returned to the quarter in the evening, Dinah (the name of the woman who was at the head of our family) produced at supper, a black jug, containing molasses, and gave me some of the molasses for my supper.

I felt grateful to Dinah for this act of kindness, as I well knew that her children regarded molasses as the greatest of human luxuries, and that she was depriving them of their highest enjoyment to afford me the means of making a gourd full of molasses and water. I therefore proposed to her and her husband, whose name was Nero, that whilst I should remain a member of the family, I would contribute as much towards its support as Nero himself; or, at least, that I would bring all my earnings into the family stock, provided I might be treated as one of its members, and be allowed a portion of the proceeds of their patch or garden. This offer was very readily accepted, and from this time we constituted one community, as long as I remained among the field hands on this plantation. After supper was over, we had to grind our corn; but as we had to wait for our turn at the mill, we did not get through this indispensable operation before one o'clock in the morning. We did not sit up all night to wait for our turn at the mill, but as our several turns were assigned to us by lot, the person who had the first turn, when done with the mill, gave notice to the one entitled to the second, and so on. By this means nobody lost more than half an hour's sleep, and in the morning every one's grinding was done.

• • • • •

We were supplied with an abundance of bread, for a peck of corn is as much as a man can consume in a week, if he has other vegetables with it; but we were obliged to provide ourselves with the other articles, necessary for our subsistence. Nero had corn in his patch, which was now hard enough to be fit for boiling, and my friend Lydia had beans in her garden. We exchanged corn for beans, and had a good supply of both; but these delicacies we were obliged to reserve for supper. We took our breakfast in the field, from the cart, which seldom afforded us any thing better than bread, and some raw vegetables from the garden. Nothing of moment occurred amongst us, in this first week of my residence here. On Wednesday evening, called settlement-night, two men and a woman were whipped; but circumstances of this kind were so common, that I shall, in future, not mention them, unless something extraordinary attended them.

I could make wooden bowls and ladles, and went to work with a man who was clearing some new land about two miles off—on the second Sunday of my sojourn here, and applied the money I earned in purchasing the tools necessary to enable me to carry on my trade. I occupied all my leisure hours, for several months after this, in making wooden trays, and such other wooden vessels as were most in demand. These I traded off, in part, to a storekeeper, who lived about five miles from the plantation; and for some of my work I obtained money. Before Christmas, I had sold more than thirty dollars worth of my manufactures; but the merchant with whom I traded, charged such high prices for his goods, that I was poorly compensated for my Sunday toils, and nightly labours; nevertheless, by these means, I was able to keep our family supplied with molasses, and some other luxuries, and at the approach of winter, I purchased three coarse blankets, to which Nero added as many, and we had all these made up into blanket-coats for Dinah, ourselves, and the children.

About ten days after my arrival, we had a great feast at the quarter. One night, after we had returned from the field, the overseer sent for me by his little son, and when I came to his house, he asked me if I understood the trade of a butcher—I told him I was not a butcher by trade, but that I had often assisted my master and others, to kill hogs and cattle, and that I could dress a hog, or a bullock, as well as most people. He then told me he was going to have a beef killed in the morning at the great house, and I must do it—. . .

I doubt if there was in the world a happier assemblage than ours, on this Saturday evening. We had finished one of the grand divisions of the labours of a cotton plantation, and were supplied with a dinner, which to the most of my fellow-slaves, appeared to be a great luxury, and most liberal donation on the part of our master, whom they regarded with sentiments of gratitude, for this manifestation of his bounty.

In addition to present gratification, they looked forward to the enjoyments of the next day, when they were to spend a whole Sunday in rest and banqueting; for it was known that the two fore-quarters of the bullock, were to be dressed for Sunday's dinner; and I had told them that each of these quarters weighed at least one hundred pounds.

Our quarter knew but little quiet this night; singing—playing on the banjoe, and dancing, occupied nearly the whole community, until the break of day. Those who were too old to take any part in our active pleasures, beat time with their hands, or recited stories of former times. Most of these stories referred to affairs that had been transacted in Africa, and were sufficiently fraught with demons, miracles, and murders, to fix the attention of many hearers.

None of our people went out to work for wages, . . . Sunday. Some few, devoted a part of the morning to such work as they deemed necessary, in or about their patches, and some went to the woods, or the swamps, to collect sticks for brooms, and splits, or to gather flats for mats; but far the greater number remained at the quarter, occupied in some small work, or quietly awaiting the hour of dinner, which we had been informed, by one of the house-servants, would be at one o'clock. . . .

One o'clock at length arrived, but not before it had been long desired; and we proceeded with our bowls a second time, to the great kitchen. I acted, as I had done yesterday, the part of commissary for our family; . . . In addition to at least two gallons of soup, about a pound of beef, and a small piece of bacon, I obtained nearly two pounds of pudding, made of corn meal, mixed with lard, and boiled in large bags. This pudding, with the molasses that we had at home, formed a very palatable second course, to our bread, soup, and vegetables.

On Sunday afternoon, we had a meeting, at which many of our party attended. A man named Jacob, who had come from Virginia, sang and prayed; but a great many of the people went out about the plantation, in search of fruits; for there were many peach and some fig trees, standing along the fences, on various parts of the estate. With us, this was a day of uninterrupted happiness.

A man cannot well be miserable, when he sees every one about him immersed in pleasure; and though our fare of to-day, was not of a quality to yield me much gratification, yet such was the impulse given to my feelings; by the universal hilarity and contentment, which prevailed amongst my fellows, that I forgot for the time, all the subjects of grief that were stored in my memory, all the acts of wrong that had been perpetrated against me, and entered with the most sincere and earnest sentiments, in the participation of the felicity of our community.

"Yes, the love of god is best . . . ," The Oneida Community

In this passage a relatively open-minded traveler, Charles Nordhoff, describes his visit to the Oneida community in the early 1870s. One of the most famous and controversial "intentional" communities, Oneida was founded by Dartmouth-educated lawyer and Congregationalist minister John Humphrey Noyes. Believing that the kingdom of God was about to be manifest on earth, Noyes gathered a group of followers, first in Putney, Vermont, in 1840, then in Oneida, New York, in 1848, to create the earthly forerunner of this kingdom. The resulting community was organized as one family, sharing property, sex partners, and child rearing and supporting itself through farming and manufacturing. The community practiced a system of birth control called male continence and a system of discipline called mutual criticism, both invented by Noyes, and conducted perhaps the first practical experiment in human eugenics.

Held together by the charismatic leadership of Noyes and the religious commitment and practical skills of his followers, Oneida prospered longer than most intentional communities. For decades it presented a collectivist alternative to the individualistic, capitalistic, male-dominated American socioeconomic system. Eventually, however, disaffection of the second generation, weakening leadership, and internal factionalism combined with con-

Source: Charles Nordhoff, *The Communistic Societies of the United States: From Personal Visit and Observation, Including Detailed Accounts of the Economists, Zoarites, Shakers, the Amana, Oneida, Bethel, Aurora, Icarian, and Other Existing Societies, Their Religious Creeds, Social Practices, Numbers, and Industries, and Present Condition* (New York: Harper & Brothers, 1875), pp. 268–90.

stant disapproval by the outside world to undermine Oneida's uniqueness. In 1879 the community abandoned "complex" marriage. In 1880 its collectively owned property and businesses were transformed into a joint stock company.

RELIGIOUS BELIEF

They call themselves "Perfectionists."

They hold to the Bible as the "text-book of the Spirit of truth", to "Jesus Christ as the eternal Son of God"; to "the apostles and Primitive Church as the exponents of the everlasting Gospel.". . .

Community of goods and of persons they hold to have been taught and commanded by Jesus: "Jesus Christ offers to save men from all evil—from sin and death itself; but he always states it as a necessary condition of their accepting his help that they shall forsake all other; and particularly that they shall get rid of their private property.". . .

The community system, which they thus hold to have been divinely commanded, they extend beyond property—to persons; and thus they justify their extraordinary social system, in which there is no marriage; or, as they put it, "complex marriage takes the place of simple."

"Complex marriage" means, in their practice: that, within the limits of the community membership, any man and woman may and do freely cohabit, having first gained each other's consent, not by private conversation or courtship, but through the intervention of some third person or persons; that they strongly discourage, as an evidence of sinful selfishness, what they call "exclusive and idolatrous attachment" of two persons for each other, . . . and that the propagation of children is controlled by the society, which pretends to conduct this matter on scientific principles. . . .

DAILY LIFE AND BUSINESS ADMINISTRATION

Their system of administration is perfect and thorough. Their bookkeeping—in which women are engaged as well as men, a young woman being the chief—is so systematized that they are able to know the profit or loss upon every branch of industry they pursue, as well as the cost of each part of their living.

They have twenty-one standing committees: on finance: amusements; patent-rights; location of tenant houses; administration; rents; baths, walks, roads, and lawns; fire; heating; sanitary; education; clothing; real estate and tenant houses; water-works and their supplies; painting; forest; water and steam power; photographs; hair-cutting; arcade; and Joppa—the last being an isolated spot on Oneida Lake, to which they go to bathe, fish, shoot, and otherwise ruralize.

Besides these, they divide the duties of administration among forty-eight departments . . . .

At first view these many committees and departments may appear cumbrous; but in practice they work well. . . .

Every Sunday morning a meeting is held of what is called a "Business Board." This consists of the heads of all the departments, and of whoever, of the whole community, chooses to attend. At this meeting the business of the past week is discussed; and a secretary notes down briefly any action deemed advisable. At the Sunday-evening meeting the secretary's report is read to all, and thereupon discussed; and whatever receives general or unanimous approval is carried out.

Once a year, in the spring, there is a special meeting of the Business Board, at which the work of the year is laid out in some detail. . . .

The appointment of so many committees makes some one responsible for each department, and when any thing is needed, or any fault is to be found, the requisition can be directed to a particular person. Women, equally with men, serve on the committees. . . .

There is no bell or other signal for proceeding to work; but each one is expected to attend faithfully to that which is given him or her to do; and here, as in other communities, no difficulty is found about idlers. Those who have disagreeable tasks are more frequently changed than others. Thus the women who superintend in the kitchen usually serve but a month, but sometimes two months at a time.

Children are left to the care of their mothers until they are weaned; then they are put into a general nursery under the care of special nurses or care-takers, who are both men and women. There are two of these nurseries, one for the smaller children, the other for those above three or four years of age, and able somewhat to help themselves. These eat at the same time with the older people, and are seated at tables by themselves in the general dining-room. The children I saw were plump, and looked sound; but they seemed to me a little subdued and desolate, as though they missed the exclusive love and care of a father and mother.

The men dress as people in the world do, but plainly, each one following his own fancy. The women wear a dress consisting of a bodice, loose trousers, and a short skirt falling to just above the knee. Their hair is cut just below the ears, and I noticed that the younger women usually gave it a curl. The dress is no doubt extremely convenient: it admits of walking in mud or snow, and allows freedom of exercise; and it is entirely modest. But it was to my unaccustomed eyes totally and fatally lacking in grace and beauty. . . .

For the children they have a sufficiently good school, in which the Bible takes a prominent part as a text-book. The young people are encouraged to continue their studies, and they have two or three classes in history, one in grammar, and several in French, Latin, geology, etc. . . .

It is their habit to change their young people from one employment to another, and thus make each master of several trades. The young women are not excluded from this variety; and they have now several girls learning the machinists' trade, ...

SUNDAY AT THE ONEIDA COMMUNITY, WITH SOME ACCOUNT OF"CRITICISM."

I was permitted to spend several days at the Oneida Community, among which was a Sunday. . . .

The people are kind, polite to each other and to strangers, cheerful, and industrious. There is no confusion, and for so large a number very little noise.

I was shown the house, the kitchen and heating arrangements, the barns with their fine stock, the various manufacturing operations; and in the evening was taken to their daily gathering, at which instrumental music, singing, and conversation engage them for an hour, after which they disperse to the private parlors to amuse themselves with dominos or dancing or to the library to read or write letters. Cards are prohibited. The questions I asked were freely answered. . . .

The institution of Criticism, a description of which I have reserved for this place, is a most important and ingenious device, which Noyes and his followers rightly regard as the corner-stone of their practical community life. It is in fact their main instrument of government; and it is useful as a means of eliminating uncongenial elements, and also to train those who remain into harmony with the general system and order.

I am told that it was first used by Mr. Noyes while he was a divinity student at Andover, where certain members of his class were accustomed to meet together to criticise each other. The person to suffer criticism sits in silence, while the rest of the company, each in turn, tell him his faults, with, I judge, an astonishing and often exasperating plainness of speech. . . .

On Sunday evening, about half-past six o'clock, there was a gathering in the large hall to hear some pieces of music from the orchestra. After half an hour's intermission, the people again assembled, this time for a longer session. A considerable number of round tables were scattered about the large hall; on these were lamps; and around them sat most of the women, old and young, with sewing or knitting, with which they busied themselves during the meeting. Others sat on benches and chairs, irregularly ranged about.

After the singing of a hymn, a man rose and read the report of the business meeting held that morning, the appointment of some committees, and so on; and this was then put to vote and accepted, having elicited no discussion, and very little interest apparently. Next a man, who sat near Mr. Noyes in the middle of the room, read some extracts from newspapers, which had been marked and sent in to him by different members for that purpose. Some of these were mere drolleries, and raised laughter. Others concerned practical matters.

To this reading, which was brief, followed a discussion of the power of healing disease by prayer. It was asserted to be "necessary to regard Christ as powerful to-day over diseases of the body as well as of the spirit." . . .

Next a hymn was sung relating to community life, which I copy here as a curiosity:

"Let us sing, brothers, sing,
  In the Eden of heart-love—
Where the fruits of life spring,

And no death e'er can part love;
Where the pure currents flow
   From all gushing hearts together,
And the wedding of the Lamb
   Is the feast of joy forever.
         Let us sing, brothers, sing.

This was presently followed by another song peculiar to the Oneida people. A man sang, looking at a woman near him:

"I love you, O my sister,
But the love of God is better;
Yes, the love of God is better—
O the love of God is best."

To this she replied:

"I love you, O my brother,
But the love of God is better;
Yes, the love of God is better—
O the love of God is best."

Then came the chorus, in which a number of voices joined:

"Yes, the love of God is better,
O the love of God is better;
Hallelujah, Hallelujah—
Yes, the love of God is best."

Soon after the meeting broke up; but there was more singing, later, in the private parlors, which I did not attend. Thus ended Sunday at the Oneida Community; and with this picture of their daily life I may conclude my account of these people.

Education, Americanization, and Community: The Ethnic Press

The large immigrant communities of the nineteenth century came mainly from western Europe and China in the antebellum decades and, after 1880, from eastern and southern Europe, Japan, Mexico, and the West Indies. At first newcomers socialized and exchanged information in saloons, candy stores, boardinghouses, and tenement kitchens. However, most groups soon created formal religious, social, political, and other institutions to fulfill a wide range of communal needs. One of the most important of these institutions was the ethnic press. In this reading, historian Maxine Seller describes the origins of the ethnic press and its diversity, reflecting the diversity among and within immigrant communities. She also describes the

Source: Maxine Schwartz Seller, *To Seek America: A History of Ethnic Life in the United States,* rev. enlarged ed. (Englewood, N.J.: Jerome S. Ozer, Publisher, 1988), pp. 169–76.

dual roles of the ethnic press: it supported the collective life of immigrant communities while it helped educate and Americanize individual immigrants.

Newspapers in Native-American and African-American communities also performed organizational and educational functions in the nineteenth century, as did the English-language newspapers of religious denominations, farmers, workers, suffragists, and other organized groups. By the 1990s, many of the newspapers Seller described had disappeared or were published in English for the Americanized descendants of their original readers. However, a vibrant and growing foreign language press continued to serve new immigrant communities from Asia, Latin America, and the Caribbean.

In little Italy, little Poland, little Syria, the Irish shantytown, the Jewish ghetto, Chinatown, and the Japanese colony—the ethnic press was visible everywhere. Educated immigrants debated its editorials. The semiliterate spelled out headlines and advertisements. The illiterate listened while a friend or relative read. In the sweatshops immigrants pooled their pennies to pay one of their number to read aloud while they worked. By 1920 over a thousand foreign language periodicals and newspapers were being published in the United States with their circulation running into the millions. In urban centers such as New York, Chicago, and Detroit, large ethnic communities supported dozens of newspapers while no group—the Letts, the Estonians, the Wends, the Spanish Catalans—was too small to have at least one.

Foreign language publications were as varied as the communities that produced them. There were dailies, weeklies, monthlies—and papers that came out whenever their editors could assemble the material and the money to print an issue. The smallest had a few dozen subscribers; the largest had circulations of over a hundred thousand. The four leading Yiddish newspapers in New York City alone sold over a third of a million copies every day. Many ethnic publications were local, serving a particular town or village or even a particular neighborhood or parish. Others were national and even international. In *Al Hoda,* for example, Arab-Americans advertised to locate missing relatives in Cuba, Brazil, and Mexico.

Most foreign language papers began as "shoestring" operations, often the work of unemployed immigrant intellectuals. Frequently the original owner was bought out by a businessman, who put the paper on a sound financial basis. The *Desteaptate Romane,* a leading Rumanian newspaper, is a good example. It was begun by an educated but sickly Rumanian immigrant who faced deportation because he had no prospects for employment. On the advice of a helpful immigration official, he collected a few dollars from each of his friends and set up the *Desteaptate Romane.* He was reputed to write well, but could not manage the paper financially. Eventually he was bought out by the owner of a steamship ticket agency.

A successful Japanese born journalist, Shakuma Washizu, left a colorful account of the early days of the Japanese-American press. Washizu's background before immigration was typical of that of many ethnic journalists—"middle class family, published a newspaper or two, ran for a political office or two, went into business, but was never successful. . . ." His first job in the United States was with a newspaper where "the editorial sanctum was at the same time kitchen, dining room, printing shop, parlor, and bedroom, all in one. The editor . . . unshaved face . . . shabby dress . . . gave me the impression of a tramp."

Washizu tried working first for one small paper then another. Finally he issued his own comic magazine called *Agahazushi (Open the Jaws)*. "The magazine continued up to twelve numbers, but the total income . . . was not more than fifteen dollars. I did not eat more than once a day for several months." Eventually he became the manager of a larger paper with brighter prospects. "We got together a number of those press men at a building which became gradually a resort for the homeless and poverty stricken fellows. As I was manager of the paper, everybody called me a great king. I was a sad king indeed—I had to do all the cooking." This venture, too, almost ended in disaster. An unfortunate caricature resulted in a lawsuit. "As we could not hire a lawyer to defend the case, we lost it." Washizu and a colleague went to jail for nine months, not an unmitigated disaster. "During that time both of us really lived, as we had plenty to eat. . . ."

Despite this inauspicious beginning, Washizu's paper, later called the *Japanese-American News*, became the largest and most influential Japanese daily in the United States. Most ethnic newspapers were not so fortunate. Nine out of ten did not survive their first year of publication. The successful ones, however, the *Jewish Daily Forward*, the Italian *Il Progresso Italo-Americano*, the Spanish *La Prensa*, the German *Staats-Zeitung*, and similar papers lived on decade after decade exerting an enormous influence in their respective communities.

Ethnic newspapers reflected a variety of ethnic interests. Many were the organs of mutual aid societies, churches, or lodges. Others were commercial ventures. There were literary papers, humorous papers, and papers for farmers, musicians, socialists, anarchists, trade unionists, religious factions, and freethinkers. Special journals were published for young people and for women. The nationally circulated Bohemian *Zenske Listy* of Chicago was a feminist journal, printed and edited by women and devoted not to "beauty lessons" and "household hints" but to efforts toward women's suffrage and "the uplifting of the attitude of working women."

The contents of ethnic newspapers varied widely, but certain things were characteristic of most. The front page was usually devoted to news of the mother country, so that the press, like other ethnic institutions, served as a link between the Old World and the New. Here the immigrant could find out what the harvest had been like at home, what was happening in the old church, and what political or economic reforms were in the offing. Nineteenth century Irish-American papers, for example (English in language, but ethnic in content), included news of the Great Famine, of the various reform factions in Ireland, and of the arrival of immigrant ships to the United States.

News of the United States was also reported, often summarized and translated from the American press. The better papers taught their readers about American life through skillful coverage and interpretation of national and local news. The socialist press, important among Jews, Finns, and Bohemians, organized the news within a radical ideological framework. Previously uneducated laboring people were stimulated to read and think by a radical press interested in the problems of "workers" and "bosses"—their problems. According to Robert E. Parks' study of the immigrant press, "socialism gave the common man a point of view . . . from which he could think about actual life. It [the socialist ethnic press] made the sweatshop an intellectual problem."

Even after they were able to read the American press, immigrants and their children turned to the ethnic press for news of their own communities. In local ethnic papers they could learn the news of the neighborhood available nowhere else—who had been married, who had died, who had had a baby, who had been baptized, confirmed, or become a *bar mitzvah,* who had been honored with the chairmanship of the church committee, the presidency of the lodge. Here they could follow the progress of the organized community—the success of the latest fundraising drive, the building of the new ethnic school, the arrival of the new minister from overseas, the creation of a new national agency or political lobby. And here they could read about, and rejoice in, the success of their own people, in business, politics, education, or whatever, both within the ethnic community and in the larger world outside.

The editorial columns of the ethnic press aired the controversies of the day. Anarchists, socialists, nationalists, members of religious factions, and secularists debated ideology and tactics, the editors often talking more to one another than to their subscribers. Most readers were more interested in practical subjects that affected everyday life. They welcomed features on child rearing, cooking, health care, how to obtain American citizenship, and how to vote.

Catering to these interests, feature writers were effective agents of Americanization and of education in general. Julian Chupka of the leading Ukrainian paper *Svoboda,* was typical of many such feature writers. He published articles entitled "Pictures of America," "the Constitution of the United States of North America," and "Something about the Laws and Courts of the United States, Especially in Pennsylvania." Abraham Cahan, Abner Tannenbaum, and other Jewish journalists introduced the Yiddish reading public to Darwinism and other scientific ideas, and to the science fiction of Jules Verne. A Lithuanian radical paper introduced its public to the philosophy of Nietzsche with a translation of *Thus Spake Zarathustra.*

The most widely read features were poetry, fiction, and the letters to the editor. Much of the poetry and fiction was sent in by readers with more sentimentality than literary talent. Pulp novels ground out by "hack" writers were published in installments, to keep their following eagerly awaiting the next edition. Not all of the literature published in the ethnic press was the product of amateurs or hacks, however. The foreign language press introduced its readers to the works of many talented professional writers from within the community and outside. . . .

Editors served as priests, psychiatrists, social workers, and friends to readers who had nowhere else to turn. Many papers had "advice" columns, but none was as famous as the "Bintel Brief," (Bundle of Letters") of the *Jewish Daily Forward.* Through the "Bintel Brief," poverty stricken people found jobs, husbands were united with their wives, and parents located children from whom they had been separated many years. Everyone found sensible advice for problems ranging from the most trivial to the most overwhelming:

> My father does not want me to use face powder. Is it a sin?
>   The editor assures a young girl that it is not.

> Since I do not want my conscience to bother me, I ask you to decide whether a married woman has the right to go to school two evenings a week. My husband thinks I have no right to do this.
>   The editor states unequivocally that the wife "absolutely has the right to go to school two evenings a week."

> A long, gloomy year, three hundred and sixty-five days, have gone by since I left my home and I am alone on the lonely road of life. . . . My heart is heavy for my parents whom I left behind. I want to run back. . . .
>   The editor tells this young man that all immigrants suffer similar loneliness and advises him to remain where he is, work hard, and bring his parents to America. . . .

Glancing through the advertisements in an ethnic newspaper is like peering into the tenement windows of the community. The papers of the newer communities—Poles, Italians, Greeks, Armenians—advertised boarding houses, cheap restaurants, and local dry good stores. The papers of longer established communities, Germans, for example, contained the advertisement of ethnic professionals and of "downtown" as well as local merchants.

As food preferences are among the most long-lived ethnic characteristics, all papers carried ads for groceries and delicatessens. Gold watches, the status symbols of the successful immigrant, were also widely advertised, as were electric belts, trusses, and other items dealing with health care. Often professionals of one ethnic group developed specialties which they advertised in other ethnic presses. Thus Chinese physicians advertised syphilis cures in the Greek press of San Francisco, and a Jewish lawyer, Fannie Horovitz, offered her services on "civil and criminal cases" in *Il Progresso Italo-Americano*. . . .

"Wanted—girl or childless widow, 19–27 years old, freethinker, agreeing to a civil marriage, knowing how to read and write in Lithuanian, wanted by a man 29 years old, photographer, using no intoxicants or tobacco," read an advertisement in *Kelevis,* a Lithuanian paper in Boston. Similar ads appeared in many ethnic papers, a symptom of the loneliness of the immigrant cut off from the traditional village matchmaking machinery.

According to the Jewish Communal Register of 1917–1918, "the election of any candidate on the East Side (of New York) is impossible unless the Yiddish press favors him." The impact of the ethnic press on public opinion in all ethnic communities was enormous, a fact which, did not go unnoticed by politicians and other special interest groups. . . .

Ethnic newspapers performed other important functions. Through the ethnic press, communities exchanged ideas and information and were able to take on projects on a scale that would otherwise have been impossible, establishing colleges and universities, seminaries for their ministers, and national charities. The nationalist societies could never have conducted their activities in behalf of the homeland without the ethnic press. The ethnic press also stood as a guardian against unfair treatment of its constituency. One example typical of many was the action taken by *Svoboda* to help 365 Ukrainians tricked into becoming contract laborers in Hawaii. *Svoboda* led a campaign of demonstrations and letter writing to American Congressmen that resulted in the voiding of the harsh contracts and the freeing of the laborers.

People did not read the ethnic press because they wanted to be Americanized or educated or molded into a community. They read the ethnic press because it reflected their interests, their problems, and their feelings. The intimate relationship between loyal readers and their favorite paper is suggested by Ruth Levine, a longtime employee of the Yiddish *Der Tog (The Day)*. According to Levine, readers felt free to come to the editors, day or night, when they needed help with a job, with the police or immigration authorities, or with a medical or personal problem. Readers argued with the columnists, expected to be answered when they wrote, and carried yellowed clippings of their favorite articles in their pockets for years.

Not long ago, an agent for the now defunct Yiddish *Der Tog*, traveling through the Middle West, stopped to call on an old subscriber he had not seen for a long time. The woman who greeted him introduced herself as the subscriber's wife and told the agent that her husband had been dead for a year. "But you never stopped the subscription," said the agent. "I know," she replied simply. "I'm not Jewish but I know how much the paper meant to him. I bring it to his grave."

Solidarity and Diversity in Women's Communities

Like their colonial predecessors, nineteenth-century women relied on intimate family and neighborhood female communities to meet many of their needs for companionship and personal help. Unlike their colonial predecessors, however, they moved beyond these informal communities to create hundreds of formal organizations, local and national. Women used their new organizations to form lasting friendships and to acquire new social, financial, and political skills, as well as to pursue a variety of specifically stated goals. In defining goals, some organizations reached across lines of class and race in the name of gender solidarity; for example, "respectable" middle-class women organized to rescue prostitutes and white women organized to free enslaved black women. In their membership, however, the new organizations were usually homogeneous. Women of different social classes, races, and ethnic and religious groups formed separate organizations to pursue agendas reflecting their distinctive interests and experiences. The readings that follow will illustrate this diversity.

"DAUGHTERS OF FREEMEN STILL"—MILLWORKERS PROCLAIM A STRIKE AT LOWELL, MASSACHUSETTS, 1834

The first reading, a strike manifesto and poem, represents collective action by a white, native-born, working-class women's community, the textile workers of Lowell, Massachusetts, in February of 1834. In the early decades of the century manufacturers recruited "surplus" daughters of New England farm families to work in the newly built textile, shoe, and other factories in nearby towns. To reassure the families of their daughters' physical and moral safety, the manufacturers provided supervised boardinghouses—a policy with unforeseen and, from the employers' perspective, undesirable results. Obliged to eat, sleep, play, and pray as well as work together, the Lowell "girls" (and other female factory workers) formed strong communal bonds that enabled them also to strike together. The strike that inspired this manifesto and poem was called to protest a 15 percent cut in wages. It was unsuccessful; the leaders were fired and the remaining workers were forced to accept lower wages. Note that the manifesto and poem do not refer to the strikers' supposed vulnerability as women. Rather, they stress independence and resistance to tyranny, drawing on republican rhetoric from the still vivid tradition of the American Revolution.

"Daughters of Freemen Still"—Millworkers Proclamation at Lowell Massachusetts, 1834

UNION IS POWER.—Our present object is to have union and exertion, and we remain in possession of our own unquestionable rights. We circulate this paper, wishing to obtain the names of all who imbibe the spirit of our patriotic ancestors, who preferred privation to bondage and parted with all that renders life desirable—and even life itself—to produce independence for their children. The oppressing hand of avarice would enslave us, and to gain their objective they very gravely tell us of the pressure of the times; this we are already sensible of and deplore it. If any are in want of assistance, the ladies will be compassionate and assist them, but we prefer to have the disposing of our charities in our own hands [In this strike, as in others, the strikers set up a fund to help those in need], and as we are free, we would remain in possession of what Kind Providence has bestowed upon us, and remain daughters of freemen still.

All who patronize this effort we wish to have discontinue their labor until terms of reconciliation are made.

Resolved, that we will not go back into the mills to work unless our wages are continued to us as they have been.

Resolved, that none of us will go back unless they receive us all as one.

Resolved, that if any have not money enough to carry them home that they shall be supplied.

> Let Oppression shrug her shoulders
>   And a haughty tyrant frown
>   And little upstart Ignorance
>   In mockery look down
>
> Yet I value not the feeble threats
>   Of Tories in disguise,
> While the flag of Independence
>   O'er our noble nation flies.

Source: The man, Boston, February 22, 1834, and the *Boston Transcript,* February 18, 1834.

"THE SOUND OF OUR OWN VOICES," A WOMEN'S STUDY CLUB

Unlike their working-class sisters, middle-class white women were expected to stay at home, exemplifying the ideals of "true womanhood"—domesticity, purity, piety, and submissiveness. Many used this narrow definition of women's "sphere" to legitimize organizing in the interests of children, religion, and causes (such as temperance) that protected the home. In New England women formed Maternal Associations to read and exchange ideas on the Christian upbringing of their children. Everywhere women formed missionary societies, church auxiliaries, and societies to protect orphans and other "unfortunates." In the post Civil War years, professional women (some of them feminists) started clubs like Sorosis and the New England Women's Club with the less socially acceptable aims of enabling women to "network," to learn about public issues, and to pursue "civic housekeeping" reforms such as protective laws for women workers, child labor laws, and consumer protection laws.

In the selection that follows, a loyal member reminisces in 1892 about her twenty years of membership in one of the most popular white, middle-class women's organizations, the study club. In these clubs, middle-aged married women met weekly to pursue the liberal arts education unavailable to most of them when they were young. The club described here, Friends in Council, began in 1869. It was still active in the 1890s with many of the same members, held together by strong bonds of comradeship and a comfortable clubhouse with a library of over six hundred volumes. Rejecting reform agendas, Friends in Council maintained its exclusive focus on self-education.

Looking over the period of my membership in Friends in Council, a period which dates back to the very early days of the organization, and covers just half the whole number of years in my life, I realize that the society has been in that life one of its great shaping forces. It calls forth my most loyal and grateful feelings, and I am moved to linger awhile among its pleasant reminiscences.

To this day I recall every detail of the interview in which Mrs. Denman, of blessed memory, the founder of the society, called to announce to me my election to membership. The offer of a seat in the Cabinet of the United States would have surprised me less; these ladies, so much older than myself, of whose meetings I had heard, seemed to me like Virgil's women, all "goddess-born." I remember regretting that I should happen to be wearing an apron at such a momentous hour, and I asked timidly what was required of members. Mrs. Denman explained that generally some book was read aloud, that remarks were made or papers written on questions that might come up. I assured her that never, no never, could I speak to such an august company, nor could I write much. She kindly reassured me, and called for me on the following Tuesday to mitigate the trying ordeal of a first appearance.

Source: Anna B. McMahan, speech of February 1892, quoted in J. C. Croly, *The History of the Women's Club Movement in America* (New York: H. G. Allen & Co., c1898), pp. 57–59.

I can only mention a few of the epochs of those early days, such as when I was asked to read a chapter from Cousin's "History of Philosophy," the usual reader being absent; also, when I gained courage, though with quaking limbs and trembling voice, to read aloud something of my own selection. It was about the Middle Ages. In those days we never mentioned anything more modern than mediaeval times. . . . My first original contribution was called "Method of the Study of Mind." I remember that one member praised this very much, saying that "it was so good, that she could scarcely believe that any woman wrote it." The dear old lady may well have indulged her doubts; had she been at all familiar with Maudley's first chapter of the "Physiology of the Mind," she would have discovered similarity too great to be accidental. . . .

In the fall of the same year [1873], the society then being four and a half years old, occurred the most important step that had yet been taken. A programme was outlined on one general subject, continuing through the year, with subdivisions assigned to individuals. . . . The general subject was "The History of Painting"; my special topic, "The Venetian School." Think of it, friends! A person who knew nothing of art principles, who had never seen a painting, nor perhaps even an engraving of any work of the Venetian school, with such a theme!

Those who had been abroad and knew something about the subject at first-hand, were very good not to laugh in my face. But at least I was industrious. Never before had I spent so much labor in the preparation of anything, nor, I presume, shall I ever do so again. Everything that I heard or saw seemed somehow to bear a relation to Venetian art, and into my paper it all went.

Neither was fine writing nor flight of rhetoric wanting, for the spell of Ruskin was upon me. The reading of this paper took nearly two hours. Few subjects in heaven or earth were left untouched, but almost any title beside Venetian art would have been equally fitting. Still, even such an omnivorous compilation was a decided gain over the Maudley cribbing. . . .

This phase of our history lasted about ten years. Ancient philosophy, ancient history, and high-sounding names, these were in turn our topics. One read and the others listened with more or less attention, for in those days fancy work [sewing and embroidering] was often in our hands, but seldom did anyone speak.

. . . .Yet I am not deriding those old days of second-hand work. They were a necessary step in the evolution of our club life; they gave us the habit of expressing ourselves on paper; they taught us not to fear the sound of our own voices; they made us acquainted with each other's mind and thoughts, since even a compilation gives an opportunity for the expression of individuality. . . .

With the year 1883 we entered upon a new epoch . . . the period of original thinking. It is too much to claim of Friends in Council that all of the work done now is of the truly studentlike or creative order; but it is not too much to say that a great deal of it is really admirable and worthy of the larger audience which some of its papers have gained through subsequent publication in journals and magazines. . . .

And now the little moral of all this tale is, that we ought to be somewhat exacting of this society, but not too exacting. For one, I am so grateful for its influence upon my life that I do not care to quarrel with it. When I hear the criticism that we are not public spirited enough, or philanthropic enough, or social enough, it hurts me—hurts as if some friend were maligned. Not any *one* thing can satisfy *all* interests of life, but if earnestness of purpose, high ideals, and steadfast devotion are worth anything, Friends in Council may be congratulated upon having found and possessed them.

". . .TO ELEVATE OUR RACE": REPORT OF THE PHILLIS WHEATLEY CLUB

Like their white counterparts, educated, middle-class African-American women in the northern cities established religious, literary, and abolition societies in the antebellum years. Poorer women created self-help societies, pooling their pennies for insurance against economic crisis. Toward the close of the century, larger, nonsectarian service organizations were formed. Typical of these was the Phillis Wheatley Club of New Orleans, founded in 1894 and described in this 1898 report by its president, S. F. Williams.

Although African-American women's clubs provided similar opportunities for friendship and self-improvement, they differed from middle-class white clubs in important ways. First, despite middle-class leadership, black clubs had large numbers of working-class members, reflecting the class structure of an oppressed community. Second, given racism and the resulting poverty of their communities, black women's clubs did not have the luxury of choosing to focus exclusively on self-education, as Friends in Council did. Instead, they focused on providing their communities with essential services such as health care, day nurseries, kindergartens, adult education, and housing and job training for young women migrating North. Finally, as "race" women, they focused on issues affecting men as well as women. They defended the reputation of African-American women against stereotypes of immorality and launched the first campaigns against the lynching of African-American men.

African-American women offered to join, as women, with white club women. However, they were almost always excluded from membership in white clubs, and their clubs were excluded from the white General Federation of Women's Clubs, founded in 1890. A national network for African-American club women, the National Association of Colored Women, was founded in 1896 in Washington, D.C.

The Phillis Wheatley Club of N.O. was the outcome of the realization among our women that something must be done to elevate our race and that we as women should exercise some executive ability. A few earnest women under the guidance of Mrs. S. F. Williams organized the club October 9, 1894. As it is in all things the beginning of the club was small. The club was divided into several committees viz: Temperance, Social Purity and Anti-Tobacco, Philanthropy and

Source: Report of the Phillis Wheatley Club, January 10, 1898, to the National Association of Colored Women, Washington, D.C.

Prison Work, Night Schools, Literature, Law and History, Law Schools, Fireside Schools and Suffrage Committees. . . .

In the Nurse Training Dept. eight nurses have been registered under the tuition [?] of Drs. Martinet and Newman. One of these nurses, Mrs. M. E. Williams, on the completion of her course successfully passed the examination as midwife before the State Medical Board of Louisiana and is now practicing her profession. Many of these nurses were in constant demand during the last visitation of Yellow Fever. . . . Since the organization much good has been done by these committees. Sewing [?] and Night Schools were established. The prison work has progressed finely. The committee makes weekly visits to the prison distributing reading matter among the inmates and encouraging the attendance of religious services. . . . Shoes and clothing have been distributed among the poor. Some needy ones have been sent to various Homes. Two needy members of the club have been assisted.

The one great object towards which the members have bent their efforts was the establishment of a Sanitorium and Training School for Nurses. We realized the necessity of *trained* nurses, since all professions are now calling for trained hands. Many of our old nurses were deprived of work because they did not hold certificates from a Training School. We needed the Sanitorium in connection with our Medical School to give the students that practice which is such a necessary adjunct to theory. Our colored doctors are not allowed to practice in our city hospitals, not even in the colored wards. Colored patients are not received in their pay wards and we saw that the establishment of such an institution would cover a multitude of needs.

After much hard work under our able Pres. the hope was realized and on Oct. 31, 1898 the doors of the Sanitorium were thrown open to the public. . . . We have a free clinic daily for the poor. . . . We have expended as running expenses for the eight months the sum of six hundred and twenty dollars. The money for the establishment of the institution was raised through the donations of generous friends and of the public. Our budget committee succeeded in obtaining from the city an appropriation of $240 annually. . . . Our membership has reached 97. We have very small dues of 5 cents monthly and have brought in all good moral women so that our work is purely humanitarian and in no way a social affair. We work for the masses and urge individual advancement. We have a Board of Managers composed of the officers and ten members of the club to act as an advisory board in the management of the Sanitorium. We have great hopes for the future of our work and sincerely trust that we may be successful.

Cordially,

Phillis Wheatley Club
S. F. Williams, president

SUGGESTIONS FOR FURTHER READING

Brian Joe Lobley Berry, *America's Utopian Experiments: Communal Havens from Long-wave Crises*. Hanover, N.H.: University Press of New England, 1992.

John W. Blassingame, *The Slave Community: Plantation Life in the Ante Bellum South.* Rev. enlarged ed. New York: Oxford University Press, 1979.

John Bodnar, *The Transplanted: A History of Immigrants in Urban America.* Bloomington: University of Indiana Press, 1985.

Jay P. Dolan, *The Immigrant Church: New York's Irish and German Catholics, 1815–1865.* Baltimore: Johns Hopkins University Press, 1975.

Carol Smith Rosenberg, "The Female World of Love and Ritual: Relations Between Women in Nineteenth Century America." *Signs: Journal of Women in Culture and Society,* Autumn 1975.

Dorothy Sterling, ed., *We Are Your Sisters: Black Women in the Nineteenth Century.* New York: W. W. Norton & Company, 1984.

Barbara Mayer Wertheimer, *We Were There: The Story of Working Women in America,* New York: Pantheon Books, 1977.

6

Continuity and Change: Communities in the Twentieth Century

In the twentieth century as in the nineteenth, community life coalesced around racial, ethnic, gender, religious, and social class groupings. There were significant changes, however, in the composition of these communities and in their relationship to the larger American society of which they were a part. Some changes originated internally, while others reflected changes in the larger American life—urbanization and suburbanization, more active government, two world wars and the Cold War, the cultural revolution of the 1960s, new patterns of immigration, and the transition from an industrial to a postindustrial economy.

During the twentieth century familiar racial and linguistic communities such as African Americans and Spanish-speaking Americans expanded and became more culturally diverse. By the closing decades of the century "black" America included Haitians, Dominicans, Cubans, Nigerians, and Ethiopians, as well as African Americans. The Spanish-speaking population, almost completely Mexican American a century earlier, now included Puerto Ricans, Cubans, Guatemalans, Colombians, Dominicans, and others. Most nineteenth-century intentional communities did not survive into the twentieth century, but new ones were established. Some, like their predecessors, were based on the religious teachings of charismatic leaders. Others, especially in the 1960s, were secular experiments motivated by ecological, antiauthoritarian, or other "countercultural" social concerns. Religious congregations continued to be major foci of community life, but there were changes here as well. By the 1990s, "mainline" Protestant denominations such as the Episcopalians and Presbyterians were losing ground to rapidly growing fundamentalist denominations, Moslems outnumbered Jews, and new communities of Buddhists, Hindus, Jains, and Bahai enlarged the concept of religious pluralism.

Much of the new racial and religious diversity in the late twentieth century stemmed from changing patterns of immigration. Restrictive and racist "national origin" quotas passed by Congress in 1924 had sharply limited the formerly heavy immigration from southern and eastern Europe. When these restrictions were lifted in 1965, the push and pull of political and economic factors resulted in a decline of all European immigration and a rise in immigration from Asia and Latin America, including Cold War refugee populations from Cuba, Hungary, and Southeast Asia and illegal immigrants from Mexico, Central America, and China. The new large Asian and Latino communities changed the cultural tone of major cities, revitalizing old neighborhoods while they integrated and educated new arrivals.

One of the most important changes in community life in the twentieth century was a broadly based increase in "minority" political activism. Individuals and organizations within racial, gender, and working-class groups had pressed for justice for their groups in the nineteenth century. However, larger and often more effective "rights" campaigns were possible in the twentieth century because of the increased numbers and higher educational levels within the groups involved. Perhaps even more important was the twentieth-century activists' access to a new, popular press and, later, to the powerful visual imagery of television.

The opening decades of the century, sometimes called the Progressive Era, saw a nationwide women's movement culminating in the passage of women's suffrage in 1919. It saw the beginning of a century of struggle by African Americans for racial equality, including the founding of the National Association for the Advancement of Colored People and Marcus Garvey's popular movement for Black Pride and pan-African nationalism. It also saw the rise of an ideologically diverse and vigorous labor movement, including trade unionism, socialism, and syndicalism.

A second wave of activism began with the black Civil Rights Movement of the 1950s and 1960s, in which African-American leaders like Dr. Martin Luther King and Rosa Parks rallied blacks (and white allies) to end segregation of schools and other public facilities, to win voting and other civil rights commonly denied in southern states, and to demand equality and respect throughout American society. The movement spread to the Native-American, Latino, and Asian communities, and, through the "new ethnicity" movement, to European immigrant communities as well. Mid-century racial and ethnic activists denounced demeaning stereotypes and demanded equal job and educational opportunities. They explored the history of their groups, urged group pride, and raised complex questions about integration versus separatism, group rights versus individual rights, and the role of government in the pursuit, or imposition, of social change. Similar themes were pursued by second-wave feminism and newly organized groups such as gays and lesbians, the elderly, and the disabled. Activism stimulated the growth of community at two levels. Locally, individuals who worked together to integrate a lunch counter or create a shelter for abused women formed strong bonds among themselves. Nationally, campaigns for group rights stimulated individuals to identify emotionally and organizationally with the larger racial, ethnic, gender, or other grouping of which they were a part. Although the resulting changes were modest and overdue, by the 1990s some white men reacted by seeing themselves as a beleaguered, disadvantaged group.

Protestant riots against Catholics in Philadelphia in 1844 and Irish riots against African Americans in New York in 1863 were two of many nineteenth-century examples of intergroup violence involving destruction of life and property. Comparable intergroup conflict flared in the twentieth century, including race riots in inner-city neighborhoods; bombings, shootings, and barricades at abortion clinics; and less violent but equally bitter battles in the schools, courts, and legislatures. Like their nineteenth-century counterparts, these conflicts reflected not only cultural difference but also competition for control of neighborhoods and access to education, jobs, political power, and government largesse. Moreover, they were exacerbated by increased unemployment and declining living standards in the "deindustrializing" economy of the late twentieth century and by government's increasing inability, or unwillingness, to help ordinary people.

As the twentieth century drew to a close the familiar forms of nineteenth-century community life still existed, but the issues surrounding them were more complex. As racial and ethnic populations shifted, neighborhoods changed, causing crises for individuals and institutions of older groups left behind. Mixed marriages increased dramatically, creating multicultural families and blurring accustomed racial, ethnic, and religious boundaries. As organized communities of women and "minorities" continued to press their claims for group recognition and equality, critics warned of the "disuniting" of America. New immigrant communities worried about rapid loss of culture and language among American-born children, while leaders of old communities worried that the shrinking cultural content of their institutions would soon be limited to nostalgia and food. Some Americans abandoned traditional racial, ethnic, or religious communities altogether, substituting newly created "mini-communities" of friends and colleagues or one or more of an exploding number of hobby, self-help, or prayer and Bible study associations. However, many others continued to seek companionship, support, and identity in traditional communities, struggling to keep them intact and recognizable.

The Labor Movement in the Progressive Era: Congressional Hearings on the Lawrence Textile Strike of 1912

One of the most prominent, and to some Americans one of the most frightening, social movements of the early twentieth century was the labor movement. Working-class neighborhoods had a long tradition of cooperation, of families and friends helping one another through "hard times" with food, shelter, and job referrals. In the early twentieth century, this tradition became institutionalized and politicized through the growth of national labor organizations. The most important was the American Federation of Labor (AFL), which organized mainly white, male, skilled workers. The more radical Industrial Workers of the World (IWW) reached out to organize skilled and unskilled workers of all races, women as well as men.

In fighting for better wages and working conditions, unions provided a focal point for the development of working-class community. Strikes were their most conspicuous activity and, as this passage illustrates, strikes strengthened the sense of working-class community among their participants. Unions also strengthened working-class community by providing a place for working people to meet (sometimes across ethnic lines), sponsoring educational and cultural activities, and providing economic assistance in time of crisis. Despite some successes, unions enrolled only about 10 percent of American workers by 1930. Their growth was checked by internal disputes and, from the outside, by corporate and government hostility and the strength of the American capitalistic, individualistic ethos.

In 1912 the mill workers of Lawrence, Massachusetts, assisted by the IWW, conducted a strike against the American Woolen Manufacturers. While cutting the work week from fifty-six to fifty-four hours to conform to a new state law, the company also cut wages and demanded a speed-up in productivity. In this passage Mr. Lipson, a worker, describes to a congressional investigator the conditions that led to the strike and the organization across ethnic lines that created a united workers' community. He does not describe the major role played by women workers in initiating and supporting the strike, the mass picketing and singing, the violence of the police (which resulted in three deaths and many injuries among the workers), or the skillful newspaper publicity that won outside sympathy and financial support. The strike was successful. The workers won wage increases (the largest increases to go to the lowest paid), a fifty-four-hour week with no pay cut, an improvement in the oppressive premium system described by Mr. Lipson, and amnesty for all the strikers.

MR. BERGER: Why did you go on a strike?

MR. LIPSON: I went out on strike because I was unable to make a living for my family.

Source: U.S. House Committee on Rules, Hearings on H. Res. 409 and 433. *The Strike at Lawrence, Mass.*, Document No. 671, 62d Cong., 2d Sess. (Washington, D.C.: Government Printing Office, 1912), pp. 32–36.

Mr. Berger: How much wages were you receiving?

Mr. Lipson: My average wage, or the average wage of my trade, is from $9 to $10 a week.

Mr. Berger: What kind of work do you do?

Mr. Lipson: I am a weaver.

Mr. Berger: You have been a skilled workman for years and your wages average from $9 to $10 per week?

Mr. Lipson: Yes sir; that was the average.

Mr. Berger: How many children do you have?

Mr. Lipson: I have four children and a wife.

Mr. Berger: You support a wife and four children from a weekly wage averaging from $9 to $10 per week and you are a skilled workman. Do you have steady work?

Mr. Lipson: Usually the work was steady, but there was times when I used to make from $3 to $4 and $5 per week. We have had to live on $3 per week. We lived on bread and water. . . .

Mr. Berger: How much were you reduced by reason of the recent cut in the wages?

Mr. Lipson: From 50 to 65 to 75 cents per week.

Mr. Berger: How much does a loaf of bread cost in Lawrence?

Mr. Lipson: Twelve cents; that is what I pay.

Mr. Berger: The reduction in your wages, according to this, took away five loaves of bread from you every week?

Mr. Lipson: Yes, sir. . . .

Mr. Berger: Do you do piecework?

Mr. Lipson: Yes, sir.

Mr. Berger: What can you tell us about the speeding-up system in the Lawrence mills?

Mr. Lipson: The speeding-up system is according to the premium. . . . When a section makes up a certain amount of cloth, they get a certain premium. Therefore they have us to speed up the machinery. If a man can not come up to it he gets fired out. Sometimes one is sick, and sometimes our stomach is empty, because our pay does not always last to the end of the month. When we come to that, we wish it was Saturday, because we usually get our pay on Saturday, but we stay in the mills just the same. They stay there, sick at the loom.

Mr. Berger: The general tendency, then, is to push the skilled workers harder, so as to compel the rest also to work so much more?

Mr. Lipson: Yes, sir;

Mr. Berger: You are a member of the strike committee, are you not?"

Mr. Lipson: Yes, sir.

Mr. Berger: Tell us the immediate cause of the strike.

Mr. Lipson: The workers in the American Woolen Co.'s mills had meetings and discussed the question of what can we do to make a living. It was unbearable. In one of our meetings we decided to see the agent of the mill, and one committee went up to see the agent of the mill, and he told them to go back to their machines: he did not want to give them any answer at all. At another one of the mills they were absolutely turned down, and in the Washington mill they were told to go to Boston and see the president of the American Woolen Co., Mr. Wood. When they told us to do that, we sent a special delivery letter to Mr. Wood, telling him about how it is in Lawrence. We expected to get an answer, because it was a special-delivery letter, and we are waiting for that answer still. Well, they were trying to make up two hours, and they tried to speed up the machinery in order to make us do 56 hours work in 54 hours time, and try to cut off the pay at the same time. The question was whether we could make a living. . . . we thought we would have to starve.

MR. BERGER: Do you mean to convey by your statement that you were required to do 56 hours work in 54 hours time, because a law was recently passed in Massachusetts cutting down the hours of labor to 54 per week?

MR. LIPSON: Yes, sir. . . .

MR. BERGER: And then suffer a cut in wages besides?

MR. LIPSON: Yes, sir.

MR. BERGER: How many nationalities are there represented among the workers at Lawrence?

MR. LIPSON: Sixteen nationalities.

MR. BERGER: Mention some of them.

MR. LIPSON: There are Germans, Polish, English, Italians, Armenians, Turks, Syrians, Greeks, Belgians, some from France, Jewish, Lithuanians—there are 16 in all.

MR. BERGER: Are there any Bulgarians?

MR. LIPSON: That is so, and Austrians. I can not name them all now; I am not familiar with geography.

MR. BERGER: Are there any Portuguese?

MR. LIPSON: Yes, sir; Portuguese and Armenians. . . .

MR. BERGER: How many nationalities are represented on the strike committee?

MR. LIPSON: Every nationality is represented by four delegates, and also on the subcommittee of that committee by about three or four.

MR. BERGER: How many of the workers of Lawrence are women and children? How many are men?

MR. LIPSON: I can not tell you about how many, but I can tell you that the majority of them are women and children, and as we are speeding up, these children are doing more work. If they can not do the work, they are fired out.

MR. BERGER: Do you mean that the children are discharged?

MR. LIPSON: Yes, sir; and the women who are used in the same place are pushed out sometimes and the children take their places.

MR. BERGER: Do they have any accidents in the factory?

MR. LIPSON: Yes, sir.

MR. BERGER: Give a few instances of accidents.

MR. LIPSON: There is a girl over there, Camella Teoli, and everyone present can see her. She is an Italian girl, but also speaks English. She started to work in the spinning department, on a machine that is a long one, with three or four different sides. The machine was speeded up and was running with such speed that her hair was caught and her scalp was cut by the machine. Her scalp was torn down, as you see. She was there working for the American Woolen Co.

two years ago, and she is still under the treatment of a physician and at work at the same time, because the family consists of seven and she is the oldest. She is 16 years old; her father works in the mill and gets $7 per week. Of course, her parents have no money to have a trial with the company. . . .

MR. BERGER: She would not stand much chance in a lawsuit against the American Woolen Co. The American Woolen Co. is a powerful concern.

MR. LIPSON: Yes, sir; that is true.

MR. BERGER: What are the demands of the strikers now?

MR. LIPSON: The demands are 15 per cent increase in wages, based on 54 hours work per week, and double pay for overtime. The reason I wish to call your attention to the demand for 15 per cent increase is this: These people work sometimes only two or three days in a week. Her [the injured girl's] father works only three days in a week, and has $2.88 per week for the family, and they absolutely live on bread and water. If you would look at the other children, you would see that they look like skeletons. . . .

MR. BERGER: What reception did the strikers get from the mill owners?

MR. LIPSON: I told you before.

MR. BERGER: I want to know whether you got any other answer. You said Mr. Wood did not answer your letter, and that the foreman simply told the committee to go back to your machines.

MR. LIPSON: Yes, sir. They said if we did not like it to get out.

MR. BERGER: Well, you failed to tell us that before, and it is important.

MR. LIPSON: We are so used to it that I did not mention it. To you these things are new, but to us it is an old story. . . .

Community Activism After the Black Civil Rights Revolution

NATIONAL ORGANIZATION FOR WOMEN: AN INVITATION TO JOIN

The mid-twentieth-century black Civil Rights Movement galvanized the national conscience when a quarter of a million people, black and white, assembled in Washington in 1962 to hear Dr. Martin Luther King's now famous "I Have a Dream" speech. The documents that follow deal with group rights movements after this watershed gathering. Their authors draw on the language and goals of the Civil Rights Movement—as formulated by Dr. King and, later, by more militant leaders—and apply them to related but different issues of equality for women, Mexican Americans, and the disabled.

The National Organization for Women (NOW) was founded in 1966

Source: National Organization for Women, Washington, D.C. 20090-6824.

in Washington, D.C., by twenty-eight women who deplored the lack of state and federal action to correct the economic, legal, educational, and other inequalities faced by women as a group. They decided to form a new organization to do for women what the National Association for the Advancement of Colored People had done for African Americans. Their statement of purpose follows, as does their 1967 platform. As the women's movement grew in the late 1960s, some feminists criticized NOW for being too individualist and middle class in its methods and priorities. More radical groups focused on "consciousness raising" among women, emphasized male oppression and female separatism, or called for the abolition of all sex roles and social hierarchies rather than equal opportunities for women to compete in male society. However, in the 1970s and 1980s NOW reached out to focus more explicitly and strongly on issues of importance to lesbians, working-class women, and women from racial minority groups. With 260,000 members in all fifty states by the mid-1980s, NOW was the leading feminist organization in the nation. Its network of national, state, and local branches served as important centers, though by no means the only centers, for the formation of feminist communities throughout the nation.

N.O.W. is a new national organization and has been formed "To take action to bring women into full participation in the mainstream of American society NOW, exercising all the privileges and responsibilities thereof in truly equal partnership with men."

We, 300 men and women who met in Washington October 29 and 30th to constitute ourselves as the National Organization for Women, believe that the time has come for a new movement toward true equality for all women in America, and toward a fully equal partnership of the sexes, as part of the worldwide revolution of human rights now taking place within and beyond our national borders. . . .

We organize to initiate or support action, nationally, or in any part of this nation, by individuals or organizations, to break through the silken curtain of prejudice and discrimination against women in government, industry, the professions, the churches, the political parties, the judiciary, the labor unions, in education, science, medicine, law, religion and every other field of importance in American society. . . .

There is no civil rights movement to speak for women, as there has been for Negroes and other victims of discrimination. The National Organization for Women must therefore begin to speak. . . .

As an organization of individuals, not delegates or representatives, N.O.W. will be able to act promptly. As a private, voluntary, self-selected group it will establish its own procedures and not be limited in its targets for action or methods of operation by official protocol.

Membership is open to any individual who is committed to our purpose. Initial dues of $5.00 are payable to the Secretary-Treasurer.

At its first national conference, in November 1967, NOW members agreed upon their objectives.

WE DEMAND:

I. That the U.S. Congress immediately pass the Equal Rights Amendment to the Constitution . . . and that such then be immediately ratified by the several States.

II. That equal employment opportunity be guaranteed to all women, as well as men. . . .

III. That women be protected by law to ensure their rights to return to their jobs within a reasonable time after childbirth without loss of seniority or other accrued benefits, and be paid maternity leave as a form of social security and/or employee benefit.

IV. Immediate revision of tax laws to permit the deduction of home and child-care expenses for working parents.

V. That child-care facilities be established by law on the same basis as parks, libraries, and public schools, adequate to the needs of children from the pre-school years through adolescence, as a community resource to be used by all citizens from all income levels.

VI. That the right of women to be educated to their full potential equally with men be secured by Federal and State legislation. . . .

VII. The right of women in poverty to secure job training, housing, and family allowances on equal terms with men, but without prejudice to a parent's right to remain at home to care for his or her children; revision of welfare legislation and poverty programs which deny women dignity, privacy, and self-respect.

VIII. The right of women to control their own reproductive lives by removing from the penal codes laws limiting access to contraceptive information and devices, and by repealing penal laws governing abortion.

A CHICANA FEMINIST MANIFESTO

Despite the new focus on gender identity and community in the mid and late twentieth century, women did not always agree on priorities, or even principles. Conservative women's organizations like the Eagle Forum and Concerned Women for America opposed abortion rights, the Equal Rights Amendment, and other feminist agendas and promoted gender solidarity around women's traditional roles as mothers and homemakers. Among feminists there were divisions based on class, race, and ethnicitiy as well as on ideology.

Women of color faced special problems because they were concerned about racism as much as, or more than, sexism. Often these women were alienated from white feminists by racial discrimination, past and present. At the same time, they faced sexism within their homes and communities. To cope with their dual concerns, women of color formed racial caucuses in women's organizations and women's caucuses in racial organizations. The document that follows was written by a women's caucus in El Partido de la Raza Unida (the Party of the United People) in 1972. It expresses their

Source: Manifesto of Women's Caucas, meeting of El Partido de la Raza Unida, 1972.

demand as Chicanas (working-class Mexican-American women) for recognition and equal treatment within their ethnic liberation movement. It also expresses their demand for dignified and culturally appropriate treatment in the larger American community.

We, as *Chicanas,* are a vital part of the *Chicano* community. (We are workers, unemployed women, welfare recipients, housewives, students.) Therefore, we demand that we be heard and that the following resolutions be accepted.

Be it resolved that we, as *Chicanas,* will promote *la hermanidad* [sisterhood] concept in organizing *Chicanas.* As *hermanas,* we have a responsibility to help each other in problems that are common to all of us. . . .

Be it also resolved, that we as *Raza* must not condone, accept, or transfer the oppression of *La Chicana.*

That all *La Raza* literature should include *Chicana* written articles, poems, and other writings to relate the *Chicana* perspective in the *Chicano* movement.

That *Chicanas* be represented in all levels of *La Raza Unida* party and be run as candidates in all general, primary, and local elections.

Jobs
Whereas the *Chicana* on the job is subject to unbearable inhumane conditions, be it resolved that:

Chicanas receive equal pay for equal work; working conditions, particularly in the garment-factory sweatshops, be improved; *Chicanas* join unions and hold leadership positions within these unions; *Chicanas* be given the opportunity for promotions and be given free training to improve skills; there be maternity leaves with pay.

Prostitution
Whereas prostitution is used by a corrupt few to reap profits for themselves with no human consideration for the needs of *mujeres,* and *whereas* prostitutes are victims of an exploitative economic system and are not criminal, and *whereas* legalized prostitution is used as a means of employing poor women who are on welfare, be it resolved that:

(1) those who reap profits from prostitution be given heavy prison sentences and be made to pay large fines;

(2) that *mujeres* who are forced to prostitution not be condemned to serve prison sentences;

(3) that prostitution not be legalized.

Abortions
Whereas we, as *Chicanas,* have been subjected to illegal, dehumanizing, and unsafe abortions, let it be resolved that we endorse legalized medical abortions in order to protect the human right of self-determination. . . .

Community-Controlled Clinics
We resolve that more *Chicano* clinics (self-supporting) be implemented to service the *Chicano* community. . . .

Child-Care Centers

In order that women may leave their children in the hands of someone they trust and know will understand the cultural ways of their children, be it resolved that *Raza* child-care programs be established in *nuestros barrios*, [our neighborhoods]. . . .

BLACK PRIDE AND DISABILITY PRIDE: "MALCOLM TEACHES US, TOO"

Like the women's movement, the disability rights movement was influenced by the Civil Rights Movement. Disheartened by white resistance to change and dismayed by the assassination of Dr. Martin Luther King, some black leaders abandoned King's goal of racial integration to espouse a more radical, separatist ideology. Malcolm X, a leader in the Black Muslim Movement, urged blacks to take pride in their African origin and to seek liberation in the autonomous development of their own communities. In this reading, Marta Russel, a disability rights activist who has just seen a popular film version of Malcolm X's life, urges the struggling disability rights community to apply this black leader's ideology to their situation.

Disability rights activists faced, and continue to face, great difficulties in building a sense of community and a social movement, as their constituency is geographically scattered and divided by class, race, gender, age, and degree and type of disability. Nevertheless, through organizations such as the Berkeley-based Disability Legal and Educational Defense Fund and the more militant ADAPT and publications such as *Disability Rag*, an activist community emerged that theorized, lobbied, and demonstrated in the 1970s and 1980s. Their immediate goals were access to transportation and other public facilities, control of their own medical and attendant care, and equal employment and educational opportunity. The passages of a basic civil rights law, the Americans with Disabilities Act, in 1991 was a major victory for this emerging community.

Spike Lee's film shows us a Malcolm X who is a true cultural revolutionary thinker, one who saw the importance of speaking about what it meant to be black living in a white-supremacist society. And there are parallels to be drawn between the disability rights movement and the movement Malcolm X called for. There are questions to be asked about being disabled in a physicalist society similar to those Malcolm asked about being black in white society.

Malcolm's most important message was to love blackness, to love black culture. Malcolm insisted that loving blackness was itself an act of resistance in a white-dominated society. By exposing the internalized racial self-hatred that deeply penetrated the psyches of U.S.-colonized black peoples, Malcolm taught that blacks could decolonize their minds by coming to blackness to be spiritually renewed, transformed. He believed that only then could blacks unite to gain the equality they rightfully deserved.

Source: Marta Russell, "Malcolm Teaches Us, Too," *The Disability Rag*, March/April, 1993, pp. 23–24.

It is equally important for disabled persons to recognize what it means to live as a disabled person in a physicalist society—that is, one which places its value on physical agility. When our bodies do not work like able-bodied persons' bodies, we're disvalued. Our oppression by able-bodied persons is rife with the message: there is something wrong, something "defective," with us—because we have a disability.

We must identify with ourselves and others like us. Like Malcolm sought for his race, disabled persons must build a culture which will unify us and enable us to gain our human rights.

As we see in Lee's film, the white man's dictionary itself became a revealer of truth for Malcolm. With help, Malcolm discovers that the word "black" is coupled with evil, degeneracy, death and the order of darkness, while "white" is linked to goodness and purity of an angelic order.

When disabled people go through the same exercise, what do we learn? That "able-bodied" is defined as fit and strong. That "able" is defined as "having great ability," "competent." "Disability" is defined as something that disables or disqualifies a person. . . . To "disable" is to "deprive of some ability," to "make unfit or useless." . . .

You bet able-bodied people wrote this dictionary! Our "disability" label has not been taken yet as politically or personally empowering for disabled persons newly embarking on the trail to self discovery.

Many of us insist labels are unimportant. Wrong! Exploitation and oppression are given power through language. In our hierarchical society, it is the social implications of words that do us the greatest damage. Malcolm X knew this. By evolving his self-image, and by changing the words used to describe himself and his race, Malcolm knew he could make the old words disappear, too. Who calls an African American a negro anymore? We inherit language. Our children will inherit language we use today. . . .

If we identify as disabled people, then others should be called "non-disabled." It gives them less power over us. Nondisabled people should not participate in our identification process. The recent coinages of "people with differing abilities" and "physically challenged" are far worse than "disabled." Our socioeconomic and political history teaches us that what we really are is *disvalued* persons.

When a sympathetic white girl asked Malcolm X what she could do for black people, he answered, "nothing." Part of our oppression as disabled people is in believing we need nondisabled people to do things for us. We may need them to be our attendants; we do not need to give our personal or socioeconomic power over to them. We need services, we don't need to be "taken care of."

Before his spiritual transformation, Malcolm inflicted pain on himself to straighten his "nappy" hair to the more desirable look of white peoples. What do we do to ourselves to look nondisabled? We go through painful expensive surgeries to correct our "defects." We submit to the wiles of the medical profession who promise to "cure" our disabilities. Some of us will endure great pain to be able to stand up and walk rather than use a wheelchair, so as to have straight bodies that look more desirable than a cripple's body. Like Malcolm, disabled people must learn to celebrate our own bodies and respect who we are.

Like Malcolm who, before his conversion preferred the company of white women, many of us feel it's a status symbol to have a nondisabled partner. We see it as a mark of success. Like Malcolm the Black Muslim who came to terms with his race and married an African American woman, we need to question our motives for forming relationships with nondisabled persons.

Malcolm's characterization of his people into "house Negroes" and "field Negroes" has parallels for us, too. The "house Negro" lived in the master's house, cooked, cleaned and did the masters every wish, often to his own degradation. When the "field Negroes," living among themselves, planned an escape," the "house Negroes" rarely went along. They became known as Uncle Toms. In the disability community we have our Uncle Toms, too—we call them Uncle Tiny Tims. They're thankful for whatever crumbs they're given by nondisabled people; they fear the stigma of associating with the rest of us. Uncle Tiny Tims are addicted to the charity—the enslavement—mode of thinking. They're ashamed of being disabled and will not identify with our movement. You won't hear Uncle Tiny Tims refer to themselves as "disabled."

When we wonder where the mass of disabled people are, we must recognize that many still hold to the Uncle Tiny Tim slave mentality.

Though Malcolm X largely considered Martin Luther King, Jr. an Uncle Tom, I think he'd agree with King's contention that freedom is never voluntarily given by the oppressor but must be demanded by the oppressed. And that leads to the real question: Where are the real leaders in our community? By leaders, I mean those capable of empowering others to celebrate who they are—disabled persons—rather than running from it; to embrace who they are, not disown it; to associate en masse with one another, indeed, to prefer it to nondisabled peoples' company—in short, to love disability.

When we can love disability, then we will have a real movement, not a token one. Thank you, Malcolm X.

Communities in Conflict in South Central Los Angeles, 1991

ALICE CHOI ON KOREAN–BLACK TENSIONS

Intergroup conflict in the late twentieth century arose from many causes, including ignorance, prejudice, scapegoating (blaming minorities for personal or social problems whose causes lie elsewhere), cultural misunderstandings, and real conflicts of interest. Many individuals identified with, or were identified by others with, specific communities, and many political leaders, rightly or wrongly, associated particular problems with particular

Source: Alice H. Choi, "A Closer Look at the Conflict Between the African American and the Korean American Communities in South Central Los Angeles," *Asian American Pacific Islands Law Journal,* UCLA School of Law, I:1 (1991), 69–78.

groups. It is not surprising, therefore, that competition for jobs, education, health, and other services, as well as for status and power—all in limited supply in postindustrial America—produced conflict between communities. With real wages declining and poverty increasing, conflict was often most intense among groups at or near the bottom of the social ladder. Conflict was also intense between working-class minorities and "middlemen" minorities, such as Jews or, in this reading, Koreans, who provided professional and commercial services in inner-city minority neighborhoods.

In this reading, Alice Choi, then a law student at the University of California, analyzed the many complex factors causing conflict between African Americans and Koreans in Los Angeles. The conflict was highlighted by the fatal shooting of an African-American teenager, Latasha Harlins, by an elderly female Korean shopkeeper, Soon Ja Din, in 1991. Other intergroup conflicts with different participants but similar causes and similarly tragic results occurred in many major cities.

I. Introduction

On March 16, 1991, Latasha Harlins, a fifteen year old African American female, entered the Empire Liquor Market in South Central Los Angeles. In the store, the proprietor, Soon Ja Du, a fifty-one year old Korean American female, was working behind the cash register. Harlins walked to the back of the store, picked up a bottle of orange juice and placed it in her knapsack. She then went to the counter, holding some cash in her hand. Du believed that Harlins was shoplifting because she had placed the orange juice in her knapsack before approaching the cash register. Du accused Harlins of shoplifting and reached for the orange juice in Harlins' knapsack. She then grabbed Harlins by her shirt. Harlins reacted by punching Du's face several times, forcing Du to the floor. Harlins then took the orange juice out of her knapsack and placed it on the counter. As Harlins turned toward the exit away from Du, Du got up from the floor, threw a stool over the counter, reached under a cash register, and took out a gun. Du fired and fatally wounded Harlins. Du was arrested the following morning and was charged with murder.

The fatal shooting of Latasha Harlins by Soon Ja Du was a flash point between the African American and the Korean American communities in Los Angeles. The incident sparked protests and boycotts, and it continues to be a source of conflict. Both communities have been hurt and angered by the incident. The African American community grieves for the death of Latasha, who symbolized hope for the future and the tragedies of the present. To the Korean American community, Soon Ja Du symbolized the struggling small business owner who has become the easy target of animosity and fury. Neither community has yet to accept that the incident may have been caused by the greater problems in the economic and political failure of our social institutions.

This article explores several factors contributing to the conflict between the African and Korean Americans using the Du/Harlins incident as the point of departure.

II. Sources of Conflict

The Du/Harlins incident was a culmination of diverse factors that added up to an explosive situation. The prominent factors of agitation included: (a) racism; (b) tension among ethnic minorities; (c) economic strife in the African American community juxtaposed against the apparent success of Korean Americans doing business in the community; and, (d) exploitation of all of the above by the media.

A. Racism

Racism is defined as a belief that race is the primary determinant of an individual's capabilities and worth, and that racial differences account for an inherent superiority or inferiority of a particular group. Racist attitudes have been (and continue to be) prevalent in the United States, . . . bigotry . . . is a defense mechanism in a society where prejudice is embraced and encouraged. Consequently, minority groups adopt some of the racist beliefs held by the majority about other minority groups.

B. Tension Among Ethnic Minorities

Racial tension among minority groups is pervasive in Los Angeles; it can be seen on street corners, in businesses, in schools and at political roundtables. In 1991, the Los Angeles County Human Relations Commission reported that the number of racial hate crimes has increased from a handful to nearly 300 a year. The victims are as likely to be Cambodian or Central American as they are to be African American, and those committing the hate crimes are as likely to be African American or Latino as they are to be white.

Examples of the human toll taken by inter-racial conflict that goes unchecked have been plentiful. For example, ethnic conflict arose between Latin and African Americans when three African Americans were charged with setting an apartment on fire, killing five Latin American family members in the Jordan Downs Housing Project. This tragedy was a product of our failure to address the tensions that existed. Ethnic conflict was also played out in the redistricting lobby efforts. The *Los Angeles Times* reported that "[i]n the city of Los Angeles, the fear is that Latinos and blacks could goad each other into a bitter redistricting battle in the heart of South-Central Los Angeles, where traditional black political dominance is being tested by a new Latino majority." Tension was also seen between Asian and Latin Americans in redistricting plans:

Among immigrant groups, tensions appear to arise from cultural or regional differences. Focusing on Latino immigrants, journalist Hector Tobar stated,

> [t]he prejudices and stereotypes swirling through South Los Angeles' immigrant community may have their roots in a single cultural fact: The Latinos come from regions like the highlands of Guatemala and the deserts of northern Mexico, places with only minuscule black populations. Often, their only prior knowledge of black America comes from the movies and television programs that Hollywood exports to Latin America.

Likewise, Koreans come from a monolingual and mono-cultural country where exposure to African American people and their history is nearly nonexistent.

On the other hand, resentment toward immigrant groups has been voiced by the African American community based on the belief that immigrants take away jobs and increase the competition for scarce economic resources. The newcomers are perceived to be troublemakers who disturb the peace of the familiar neighborhoods. Korean Americans are perceived as being rude and ruthless merchants.

One factor that has contributed to this image is the language barrier. . . . Many immigrants do not speak English well.

. . .While it may be true that certain individuals may be discourteous or unfriendly toward their customers, it is also true that cultural differences account for part of this negative image. In the Korean culture, strangers are kept at a distance—even in business. Generally, Korean women are taught to keep to themselves to preserve their reputation of chastity. Korean men are indoctrinated to appear solemn as a sign of maturity and manhood. Many first generation Korean Americans still retain the old customs and thus have difficulty modifying their behavior despite being in the U.S. Korean tradition also embodies the Confucian teachings of age hierarchy in which a person is expected to treat an elder with courtesy and reverence. This value of age hierarchy often conflicts with the American value of individual equality, and may have played a part in intensifying the conflict between Du and Harlins. It is possible that Du, being the older woman, expected the same courtesy from Harlins, a teenager, and Harlins, as a customer, expected the same courtesy from Du, a merchant. Resentment may have intensified when neither had her expectation met.

Furthermore, various misconceptions and misunderstandings among the minority groups are exaggerated when people mistake innocent gestures as insults. This happens when the groups who experience oppression get defensive at the slightest hint of insensitivity from others. Itabari Njeri, a journalist stated,

> [Most interethnic conflicts] have a psychological aspect—rigidity of thinking, low self-esteem, compensatory behavior. . . . [T]hese are especially significant in disputes between historically subordinate groups. In the case of Koreans, they carry not only the historical memory of subjugation under the Japanese, but the day-to-day reality of anti-Asian prejudice in the United States and the isolation caused by language and cultural differences. African-Americans carry not only the historical memory of slavery but status as America's most stigmatized minority. In many respects, . . . Korean-Americans and African-Americans [seem] to be very similar. Accustomed to being targets of abuse, members of both groups are quick to defend themselves if anyone seems ready to violate their humanity.

In sum, the pervasive racist atmosphere in America coupled with cultural and language barriers create a dangerous background for conflicts between Korean and African Americans.

C. Economic Strife of African Americans and Economic Success of Korean Americans

In exploring the Du/Harlins incident, it is necessary to go beyond the language or cultural difference between the Korean and African Americans in

South Central Los Angeles. The relationship between African and Korean Americans in South Central Los Angeles is defined by the economic dynamics of the two groups. South Central Los Angeles is economically depressed and isolated. In a column entitled Urban Perspective in the *Los Angeles Sentinel*, Los Angeles County Human Relations deputy, Larry Aubry stated,

> [t]he broader context within which Latasha's death occurred should be kept upper-most in everyone's mind. South Central Los Angeles is an economic graveyard, ravaged by time and neglect; government services are inadequate, public education is a failure, and housing and employment are worse than in 1965, at the time of the Watts riots; drastic demographic changes compound and aggravate the area's problems . . . .

"South Los Angeles' economy was devastated in the late 1970s and early 1980s as major industrial employers such as General Motors, Goodyear, Firestone and Bethlehem Steel shut aging factories. . . . Bankers and insurers . . . dealt the area another crushing blow by redlining the area and investing elsewhere." Consequently, the residents of South Central Los Angeles suffer from a glaring lack of employment opportunities and capital for economic development.

Furthermore, the absence of big retail stores leaves the residents of South Central Los Angeles with small family-run businesses where high overhead costs get passed on to consumers in the form of higher prices for goods. "Many in the community believe that the dependence on liquor stores and other small shops has contributed to ethnic tensions because such businesses—many owned by Korean Americans—cannot match big-store prices or provide many jobs for residents."

By virtue of their involvement in small retail stores, Korean Americans seem to fit [Edna Bonacich's] definition of the middleman minority and consequently are susceptible to the pitfalls inherent in that status.

For example, the middleman minority tends to be made up of recent immi-grants with separate and distinct cultures. They tend to concentrate in trade or in small scale entrepreneurships—usually family-owned and operated. It is com-mon to enlist help from family members to cut down on overhead and labor costs. In addition, the businesses are often marginal and considered undesir-able. . . .

Also, the middleman minority is regarded as clannish and resistant to assim-ilation; but at the same time, they are considered pushy for wanting to enter a social order in which they are unwelcome. On the whole, the middleman minor-ity image is filled with contradictions.

Finally, the middleman minority serves as a buffer between the elites and subordinate groups in times of trouble. Because the elite has removed itself from daily interaction with the subordinated group, the outrage of the subordinated group is re-directed to the middleman minority who is within reach. Conse-quently, the real source of oppression is often overlooked and the middleman minority becomes a scapegoat.

Korean Americans fit the description of the classic middleman minority. . . . By virtue of their position, the Korean American entrepreneurs in South Central Los Angeles are prime targets of scapegoating by the African American community.

D. Media Sensationalism

The media plays a significant role in perpetuating racist stereotypes and racist attitudes. By constantly highlighting the conflicts, the media feeds the anger of the people. Larry Aubry stated,

> [t]he problem is the media, which regularly skews and sensationalizes stories about Blacks and Koreans who are easy targets and apparently make "good copy." . . . By highlighting the violence between African Americans and Koreans as the media often does, with no reference to other areas of conflict and crime in South Central, it distorts reality and does a disservice to communities. Selective reporting clearly exacerbates Black-Korean problems, while at the same time diverting attention from other, more serious problems that beset the African American community.

The media can also fuel the anger of certain community groups by inaccurate reporting.

III. Conclusion

The Korean-African American tension is complicated and not likely to be resolved overnight. We can all learn from the Du/Harlins incident and attempt to understand the forces that gave rise to the tragedy. A failing economy, crumbling social and political conditions and unchecked racism and bigotry lead communities to destruction. Korean Americans and African Americans are not the source of the problems; they are victims of the larger failures of our institutions and public policies. Much of the problem lies in the dynamics of poverty and racism. The question is how to go beyond these problems. . . . Education in general is an important first step in bridging the gap between the two communities. Moreover, building coalitions is imperative. Koreans and other Asians share a common experience with racial minorities. In the common struggle for minority rights, they will need to continue to form coalitions with African Americans and Latinos. Koreans have benefited greatly from the fruits of the civil rights struggle led by American Blacks during the 1950s and 1960s. It is time for them to contribute to the broader movement by giving back their talent, skills, experiences and resources to the efforts to end discrimination.

" . . . IT'S A MISUNDERSTANDING OF ONE ANOTHER": UNIVERSITY OF CALIFORNIA STUDENTS DISCUSS THE LOS ANGELES RIOT

> Despite warnings by Alice Choi and others, there was little constructive response to the intergroup conflict that smoldered in Los Angeles in the months following the shooting of Latasha Harlins. Then, on April 29, 1992, East Los Angeles erupted into a violent riot that destroyed a billion dollars in property and left fifty-eight people dead. The riot began after a mostly white jury acquitted white police officers for the beating of Rodney

Source: Kariann Yokota, "Understanding Each Other: African and Asian Students at UCLA," *Pacific Ties: UCLA's Asian Pacific Newsmagazine,* 16:5 (April 1993), 34–35.

King, an African American. Although Mexican Americans and whites also participated, the media portrayed the riot as a rampage by angry African Americans against businesses owned by Korean immigrant families.

In the reading that follows, Kariann Yokota, a student at the University of California at Los Angeles, interviews African-American and Asian-American students soon after the riot. Yokota's article demonstrates that the college campus was not immune to the intergroup tensions in Los Angeles and, indeed, in the nation. Her article also demonstrates, however, that rather than assigning blame, students of African-American and Korean backgrounds were trying to understand each other. At a time when conservative critics were attacking multicultural curricula as divisive, these students praised African-American and Asian-American history courses for building bridges, helping them appreciate each other's backgrounds, problems, and experiences.

UCLA students were preparing for midterms when the L.A. uprisings shook the city's deteriorating infrastructure. In light of the uprising, many students from the African-American and Asian-American communities have been forced to confront issues of ethnic identity, perceptions of other groups, and the influence of university education on these ideas. The students expressed differing opinions, but these differences are tempered by an open-minded attitude towards each other and a shared concern for the future.

"I could have easily put the blame (for the uprising) on African-Americans, like a lot of Koreans have," said student activist Alyssa Kang. "But I choose not to because I understand that there are bigger issues involved. I felt a lot of pain and sympathy for what the African-Americans are going through."

"I just think it's a misunderstanding of one another," said Kevin Goines, a second-year African-American student majoring in history. "Africans look at Koreans as coming fresh into the country, barely speaking English . . . and all of a sudden they have something. And here you have a people who have been enslaved for over 500 years and we are still at the bottom with nothing. I think that is the real problem which no one wants to deal with."

Students voiced their concern about minorities such as African- and Korean-Americans blaming each other for their discontent rather than addressing the economic and social inequities of American society and also in the university setting.

"I don't think Korean people have been the direct cause of the condition of black people," stated Paul Moon, a 22-year-old Korean-American, majoring in political science. "Historically, this country exploited and neglected black people and other minority groups and it continues to do so. I think that's the direct cause of the uprising. Koreans are still fighting the oppression also."

Goines, a reporter for the African-American newsmagazine *Nommo*, believes that different communities need to connect on a human level to bridge gaps. "Right now, the minority classes don't see each other as people . . . it's like we're completely different. I think if we just have an understanding of one another, we'd see that we're not."

Both African- and Asian-American students overwhelmingly agree that an awareness of other ethnic groups' culture and history is crucial for improving race relations. But, before this is accomplished, they agree that people must bridge the existing gap between the groups.

Despite the fact that UCLA's 1992–93 catalog boasts the distinction of having the "most ethnically mixed . . . [student body of] any university in the country, both in terms of total students and percentage of enrollment, students such as Greg Warren, see the current situation on campus as being far from utopian.

"Every ethnic group is completely segregated in Los Angeles, so why would anybody think things would be different here on campus?" questioned Warren, an African-American senior in communication studies. . . .

Some students were discouraged by the lack of integration and what they perceived as problems with UCLA in terms of racial equality.

"When I got here I was disappointed," confessed Tracy Greathouse, a recent African-American graduate. "I realized that UCLA has got its racist problems. They may have all the money in the world, but in terms of equity, it's really bad here. I couldn't believe that this school was just as messed up as everything else in the city. People just don't notice it unless they are going here. Then, everything starts to unravel."

Although students noted inequality and institutional racism on campus, they also conceded that the things they learned in various classes at UCLA served to increase their understanding of themselves and others. Both Asian- and African-Americans believed that as students at UCLA, they became more open-minded about people of other races.

Students felt that they benefited from classes which examined history from their ethnic perspective. For many students this was a new experience. "When you get here, it's like wow, they have African history classes," said Tammy Thompson, an English major.

"Half of the (African-American) people that I know who come to UCLA as pre-meds end up in history because you get so caught up in learning about . . . something that was never taught before," said Thompson, who aspires to become a journalist upon graduating. "There's a spirit here of revolution. Learning about African-American history, you learn who are the major instigators of change. You understand their struggles and ideals and you want to implement those."

Many African- and Asian-American students found that after studying their own history, they were inspired to learn about other cultures. Goines was fascinated when he started reading about Latino history and realized, "how similar" the two groups' historical experiences were. "Reading those works just opened up different things for me. I began to see things in a different light," he said.

"I've become more educated about other minority communities and I found themes of commonality," said Kang. "I realized we are not in the struggle by ourselves. When I see African-Americans, I wish I could go up to them and say, "Look, even though there's been all of these false images and stereotypes on TV and even though there's been this so-called conflict, we really need to talk about this and educate ourselves about each other."

For Teresa Magno, a Pilipina history/Asian-American studies student, the "turning point" in developing her "ethnic identity" came when she joined Sam-ahang Pilipino club during her freshman year. Magno traced the expansion of her ethnic awareness which gradually exposed her to people of different eth-nicities. Her first two years as a UCLA student was spent "knowing about my own culture" through activities with the Samahang club. The next year she "branched outward" and worked with various Asian groups as editor-in-chief of *Pacific Ties*. This year Magno is working with African-American and Chi-cano/Latino students through her job with Academic Advancement Program (AAP).

Many of the Asian-American individuals indicated that their experience as students at UCLA and the classes that they have taken have liberalized their political views. . . .

Tom Park, a Korean-American major, experienced a profound change in his political views. He commented that taking various social science classes has opened his eyes to different perspectives, subsequently making him more sensi-tive to the oppression that the African-American community has faced in Amer-ica. "I'm getting a wider, fairer point of view," said Park.

Park stated that his high school education at a private school in Orange County had an extremely Eurocentric emphasis, which in turn influenced his political and social views. "In high school I was a complete Twinkie (yellow on the outside white on the inside). But as a student here I had to take general education classes with professors that were more liberal than me," he said. "They really put me in touch with the struggles that the blacks went through during the Civil Rights era and how much we as minorities owe to them."

"I know people in my community who didn't go to college. I'm different from them because of the education I got," continued Park. "If you are just stuck in your Korean community, stereotypes of other races are just perpetuated."

Students felt that the pervasiveness and persistence of racial stereotypes was an integral element that hindered the mutual understanding between African-Americans and Asian-Americans on campus before and after the uprising.

"One of the problems is we have negative images of different people," said Goines. "Basically, it's stereotypes. Also, it's like when you have a problem in class, it's like, those damn Asians are pushing up the curve. The truth is, they work harder . . . the ones I have come into contact with value education more; they come from a different background."

"The same stigma applies to Africans," explained Goines. "Some people say we're naturally good in sports, but we work at that too. I walk into the Wooden Center and it's like, I want that big black guy on my team. . . . why? Its very insulting."

Greathouse considers the prevailing stereotype of the "model minority" Asian-American student that many African-Americans hold as detrimental to her community. "Asians don't have any more brain power than anyone else. That is so whack, I don't think they are any smarter, they just work harder. If you took their color away and follow them around and find out why they are getting good grades . . . , then you would say, 'Hey, I can do that.' But as soon as you given the color back, you go from what is their mode of operandi to thinking the Asians' success is because of their color," she said.

"Like Public Enemy said, 'Don't believe the hype,'" warned Greathouse. "If you hear something and you wonder if it is true, go educate yourself. Go to the source. Go to an Asian-American and ask them."

This demystification of other racial groups is the beginning of understanding people in their full humanity. "I think that if you don't take that chance and break down that barrier to find out what the other person is into, what they're about, you can never know them," said Goines.

"Granted, I don't think I could ever pretend to be black and maybe will never fully understand their issues or what they are going through," admitted Nozaki. "But what it all boils down to is respect."

Amid the devastation of last year's uprising, African-American and Asian-American UCLA students were able to pick up the pieces and start again. "I saw some positive things come out of this too," said Kang. "A lot of things changed because of it. People are forming multiethnic coalitions and starting to work with other communities, which I don't think people thought of before the uprising."

One year after the Los Angeles uprising, African-American and Asian-American UCLA students are still struggling with the complexity of race relations between their communities. Although the students recognize that inequality and injustice persist, their ability to engage in dialogue gives them hope for the future.

"If we aren't willing to discuss these issues, they will never be addressed," said Warren. "It is only through discussion that you can educate others and attempt to find solutions."

Kariann Yokota is a first-year graduate student in Asian American Studies. She is also a staff writer at the Japanese-American daily The Rafu Shimpo.

"Sharing the Journey: The Small Group Movement

As old community institutions adapted to change or disappeared, some of the people who had used them (or their children and grandchildren) developed new, more flexible forms of social connection to meet the needs of new, more flexible lifestyles. In this selection from a book of the same title, sociologist Robert Wuthnow describes what was in the 1980s and early 1990s the most popular and rapidly growing solution to the problem of companionship and emotional support for a mobile society, the small group movement.

Wuthnow notes that while small groups included everything from Great Books clubs to Alcoholics Anonymous, the most numerous were prayer and Bible study groups. He notes, too, that while small groups appeared to be a new departure in American life, they were, in fact, heirs to a nineteenth-century tradition of voluntary associations. (Although he does not point this out, they can also be considered the successors of con-

Source: Robert Wuthnow, *Sharing the Journey: Support Groups and America's New Quest for Community* (New York: The Free Press), 1994.

sciousness-raising groups, encounter groups, and other small groups of the 1960s and 1970s.) Recognizing the support and satisfaction many people get from their participation in small groups, Wuthnow warns that these groups do not provide the depth, longevity of attachment, or spirituality offered by traditional cultural or religious communities. Indeed, he suggests that people who substitute small groups for traditional community life may be, in fact, redefining community, not only for themselves but for other Americans as well.

In the driveway across the street, a vintage silver Porsche sits on blocks as its owner tinkers with the engine. Next door, a man with thinning gray hair applies paint to the trim around his living room window. But at 23 Springdale something quite different is happening. About two dozen people are kneeling in prayer, heads bowed, elbows resting on folding chairs in front of them. After praying, they will sing, then pray again, then discuss the Bible. They are young and old, men and women, black and white. A teenage girl remarks after the meeting that she comes every week because the people are so warm and friendly. "They're not geeks; they just make me feel at home."

At the largest gothic structure in town, several people slip hastily through the darkness and enter a small door toward the rear of the building. Inside is a large circle of folding chairs. On the wall a felt banner reads "Alleluia Alleluia" (the two As are in red). Before long all the chairs are filled and an attractive woman in her late thirties calls the group to order. "Hi, my name is Joan, and I'm an alcoholic." "Hi, Joan," the group responds. After a few announcements, Betty, a young woman just out of college, tells her story. Alcohol nearly killed her. Then, close to death in a halfway house, she found God. "I thought God hated me. But now I know there is a higher power I can talk to and know."

These are but two examples of a phenomenon that has spread like wildfire in recent years. These cases are so ordinary that it is easy to miss their significance. Most of us probably are vaguely aware of small groups that meet in our neighborhoods or at local churches and synagogues. We may have a coworker who attends Alcoholics Anonymous or a neighbor who participates in a Bible study group. We may have scanned lists of support groups in the local newspaper and noted that anything from underweight children to oversexed spouses can be a reason to meet. Members of our family may have participated in youth groups, couples groups, prayer groups, book discussion clubs, or Sunday school classes at one time or another. Perhaps we attend one ourselves. But we may not have guessed that these groups now play a major role in our society.

At present, four out of every ten Americans belong to a small group that meets regularly and provides caring and support for its members. These are not simply informal gatherings of neighbors and friends, but organized groups: Sunday school classes, Bible study groups, Alcoholics Anonymous and other twelve-step groups, youth groups and singles groups, book discussion clubs, sports and hobby groups, and political or civic groups. Those who have joined these groups testify that their lives have been deeply enriched by the experience. They have found friends, received warm emotional support, and grown in their spirituality. They have learned how to forgive others and become more accepting of themselves. Some have overcome life-threatening addictions. Many say their identity has been changed as a result of extended involvement in their group. In fact, the majority have been attending their groups over an extended period of time, often for as long as five years, and nearly all attend faithfully, usually at least once a week. . . .

Providing people with a stronger sense of community has been a key aim of the small-group movement from its inception. There is a widespread assumption that community is sputtering to an undignified halt, leaving many people stranded and alone. Families are breaking down. Neighbors have become churlish or indifferent. The solution is thus to start intentional groups of like-minded individuals who can regain a sense of community. Small groups are doing a better job than many of their critics would like to think. The communities they create are seldom frail. People feel cared for. They help one another. They share their intimate problems. They identify with their groups and participate regularly over extended periods of time. . . .

But in another sense small groups may not be fostering community as effectively as many of their proponents would like. Some small groups merely provide occasions for individuals to focus on themselves in the presence of others. The social contract binding members together asserts only the weakest of obligations. Come if you have time. Talk if you feel like it. Respect everyone's opinion. Never criticize. Leave quietly if you become dissatisfied. Families would never survive by following these operating norms. Close-knit communities in the past did not, either. But small groups, as we know them, are a phenomenon of the late twentieth century. There are good reasons for the way they are structured. They reflect the fluidity of our lives by allowing us to bond easily but to break our attachments with equivalent ease. If we fail to understand these reasons, we can easily view small groups as something other than what they are. We can imagine that they really substitute for families, neighborhoods, and broader community attachments that may demand lifelong commitments, when, in fact, they do not.

The common view is that small groups are successful because they fill needs otherwise unmet in contemporary society; these needs include emotional support, friendship, and ways to develop spiritually. By filling such needs, the small-group movement is seen to be stemming the tide. I do not deny that many individuals who participate in small groups feel that their groups are meeting such needs. The data show that group members do feel this way. But the mistake is to infer then that small groups are fundamentally at odds with larger societal trends and are working mainly to counter them. It makes more sense, in my view, to see that small groups are helping people adapt to these trends. . . . Voluntary associations have long been a favored way of meeting needs in the United States rather than depending on government programs or trying to create traditions that were not strong here in the first place. Small groups carry on the voluntaristic emphasis. They also adapt it to meet new challenges, such as helping individuals cope with addictions, helping them find spirituality when large religious organizations fail to do so, or rebuilding their personal identities after families and other primary groups have become inadequate to the task. Many small groups help to maintain the social equilibrium. They extend trends that are already under way, but do not set forth visions of a better world that would radically transform the way things are. And in extending these trends, small groups may also contribute to some of the problems inherent in such developments. Rather than putting the brakes on marital dissolution, for example, they may make it easier for spouses to separate and remarry, or they may even make it possible for employers to put greater pressures on working women because there will be support groups to pick up the pieces.

If small groups are the glue holding together American society (as some argue), they are then a social solvent as well. They provide a way out of the traditional attachments that formerly may have bound people tightly to their communities. Former Mennonites who have grown weary of church customs and moved to urban areas can leave the fold more comfortably, not having to become pure secularists or isolated individualists, by joining a prayer fellowship in their neighborhood. Adult children who have fled the dysfunctional families of their youth can get along without kin networks by spending time each week attending a twelve-step group. The solvent helps people slip away from previous forms of social organization. At the same time, it facilitates the enormous adjustments required. Group members are, indeed, making a journey, quite literally into the unknown. It helps to share the journey.

"Today's Strength from Yesterday's Traditions": Northern Arapaho Indian Women

Robert Wuthnow suggests that many small-group participants have chosen to leave the racial, religious, or other traditional communities in which they had formerly been rooted. Virginia Sutter writes about people who made a different choice, who struggled in the face of social change to maintain ancestral racial, religious, and gender ties. A Northern Arapaho Indian from the Wind River reservation in Wyoming, Sutter spent several summers gathering material for a book on Arapaho women, a project initiated by her daughter's questions. In reporting her conversations with women who attended tribal celebrations, Sutter describes the tension in the lives of Native Americans who try to combine traditional culture and community ties with often incompatible modern jobs and lifestyles. Similar tensions exist in the lives of Orthodox Jews, the Amish, and to a greater or lesser extent any group that tries to preserve a distinctive tradition against the inroads of mainstream American culture. Some individuals compromise (as did most of Sutter's subjects), others assimilate, and still others create schools, museums, and other institutions to preserve their heritage, sometimes seeking government grants or, at the very least, exemption from laws that violate their traditions. (Jehovah's Witnesses, for example, are exempt from compulsory flag salutes in the public schools.) Recognizing the inevitability of some change, Sutter nevertheless agrees with the women she interviews on the positive value of tradition and community in helping people cope with modern life.

Source: Virginia Sutter, "Today's Strength from Yesterday's Traditions—the Continuity of the American Indian Woman," *Frontiers*, VI:3 (1982), 53–57.

Sometimes in traveling from state to state, taking part in both social and religious ceremonies, I would see the same women and their families. It was the women of these families that held my interest; I wanted to hear from them why they spent their vacations, weekends, and any other free time traveling to be with other Indians at celebrations. Some even quit their jobs when summer came. Jobs were available later, but for now they felt the pull of tribal tradition from hundreds of years back. . . .

Some Indians are continually working at the assimilation of two cultures. "Norms" are "culture bound" and Indians are often faced with conflicting norms. When summer comes, their tribal culture says, "Let's get together, let's be a family again, let's renew our faith in our religion and in our people." But the other culture says, "Keep your job, do your religion on Sundays, stay in your working pattern, there is no extra time for family, friends, or visiting. If you do not keep your nose to the grindstone the year around, there will be no raises, no promotions, no move up to the next level of social status, and no security."

But what about the security of the soul and peace of mind that come from being among your loved ones and those who care for you, not for your social status? You either go with your heart and years of tribal tradition or you change to another culture full time—or you compromise. You grab what you can in your two-week vacation time and long weekends. You work eight hours on the job to maintain today's lifestyle, but whenever possible, you hold on to the Indian way. Your heart and soul know that only you are the one to dictate.

I have spoken to many women in the old Indian way—learning by listening—and the consensus was unanimous. Contemporary Indian women return to their tribes for social activities and religious ceremonies to retain their tradition and culture, maintain their equilibrium and gain strength for the coming year.

One of the first Indian women to take part in my discussions for the book was a breed. She was sixty-one years of age. She and her husband were raising a six-year-old grandchild. This woman has not lived on a reservation for many years, but had originally been raised there until her marriage. Her father and two of her sons had taken part in the Sun Dance.* During a certain period in her life—when her children were small and the family business just starting out—she did not attend the celebrations regularly. However, as the stress of raising a family and keeping up the business increased, she began going back more often. She goes for many reasons, but mostly for the release of business tension. There she can be with her family and friends, rest, relax, dance, visit, and go home with a brighter outlook on life to carry her through the year. The Sun Dance trips were significant, not only because of her sons' participation, but also because her Indian beliefs regarding religion are still strong.

It was during her tribal Sun Dance that I spoke with this woman. She told me that even though she knew and sang the Indian songs as she was growing up, she had not sung for over twenty years. That night, long after midnight, as the

---

*The Sun Dance is considered by many tribes as the most significant ceremony of Indian religious life. The rituals involved are too complex to explain with brevity, and any discussion of religious ceremonies is never to be taken lightly.

Sun Dancers were dancing, behind the drummers with the women singers stood this woman, her voice joining the others, high and clear. The stars shone the same as they had twenty years ago; the songs were the same. This Indian woman had truly come home.

Another woman, who talked to me about contemporary Indian women, was in her middle twenties. The family included herself, her husband, and their three-month-old baby. She was a blood married to a blood of a different tribe. Amazingly enough, this woman attended some type of Indian celebration, mostly powwows, on an average of three weekends a month. Her husband had recently started contesting in the traditional dances, not always for money, but often in "fun contests."

This young woman knew without hesitation why she attended. She said that there is a special feeling when you hear the drums; you know who you are—an Indian. You are among friends and family—the workday world drops away. You feel good, secure in a familiar atmosphere, one that has held Indians together for time eternal. The night of our discussion we were at a powwow in the South. The night was warm, and the summer moon shone bright and beautiful. In the background the drums beat strong and vibrant while muted tones of animated conversation flowed back and forth. I watched this young mother visiting, laughing with first one woman, then another, showing off her baby with pride. . . .

A third woman, in her late forties, married out of her tribe and has lived in the South with her husband's tribe for over twenty years. She has four boys, two married with families of their own and two at home. In winter, when jobs are scarce, they sometimes all live at home.

She attended at least two Indian social events a month during the winter and many more in the summer. Religious ceremonies were the most planned for and always attended. Even if the ceremony is only a few miles away from their modern home, the family prefers to camp, cooking outside under a shade, and sleeping in tents. They like being close to friends and relatives as the campers arrange tent after tent in a circle around the ceremonial grounds, just as it used to be. . . .

She felt no need to explain her feelings on religious ceremonies. We had cooked side by side for the Sun Dances of both our tribes, and our respect and need for Indian religion was understood. We, along with other Indian women, have known and lived the uncertainties of change, but we are still immersed in enough traditional emotions that for us religious ceremonies are the Indian way, and, as the old ones say, "that's the way it is."

The fourth and youngest Indian woman I questioned was a college student, age twenty. She explained that she was greatly interested in meeting eligible young men, and she felt that in college activities Indian men sometimes "put on an act" to impress the girls. At Indian ceremonies she could meet their families and friends. There she could learn more about them before getting emotionally involved. Also at celebrations, especially powwows, she had a chance to see young men from many different tribes.

There is a "courting walk" around the circle of spectators who are watching the dancing, and while strolling around the outside of the group, boys and girls have a chance to meet. . . . They are taking part in a ritual that also goes back many years, as her grandmother laughingly told us. . . .

Near the end of the summer, late one evening I sat watching two older Indian women, leaning close together. . . . I could not help but smile to myself, remembering my conversation with one of them. She was in her early seventies, with a sharp mind and a great sense of humor. Some of her grandmother's stories about the white man who copied the Indian, even told in places with Indian words, were among the funniest I had ever heard.

She and her husband live alone in a modern house in town, with occasional visits from grandchildren. In the Indian way, some of her grandchildren have made their home with her at various times. They would attend school and do all the things youngsters do, but at the same time they would gain traditional knowledge from their grandmother as in yesteryear.

This woman remembers camping for many Indian events in quiet places among the rolling hills that are now in the center of urban areas. She still attends the ceremonies for the same reasons she did then, to be close to her people, to visit, to hear the drumming and singing.

She is there, with other grandmothers, to help and encourage young girls to prepare for their traditional dance contests. She will dance in a "Special" with pride when a relative or friend achieves the distinction of being one of the best in some field of endeavor. By attending and participating, she is one of the many thousands of Indians who are keeping a culture alive.

During the time we talked, she told me of her grandparents, the Southern Arapaho, Sitting Bull, and his wife Dropping Lip. Sitting Bull, because of his tribal status, was allowed to have four wives, all sisters. When the white superintendent protested his multiple marriage, Sitting Bull kept only the youngest sister, Dropping Lip, as his wife. He took her to Oklahoma from the Wind River Reservation. She made the trip riding a horse, and her baby girl rode in a horsedrawn travois. Two other horses carried the family belongings over the prairie, where there were no roads or trails; dried meat provided the food for the trip. She herself lives in a lifestyle quite changed from the time her mother traveled on that travois from north to south, to marry and bear a child who still attends the ceremonies each year, as she hopes her grandchildren will have the privilege of doing in the generations to come.

I spoke to many Indian women. . . . One thing is quite certain: these women attend the religious ceremonies because it is necessary for them to have a renewal of faith to survive in what is still an alien lifestyle. They need the security and reassurance that comes from knowing that generations of their people have been able, and still are able, to pledge themselves to a greater Spirit who cares for them and looks after them—"the way it has always been"—to take part in the rituals, changed only by time, as the mountains and streams are changed by the natural elements of time. This is why they travel many miles to join their tribe. They still believe a family worships together and Indian people are their family. . . .

There was an exceptional feeling as I listened to the soft melodious voices of the Indian women speaking of the things they remembered. Their eyes were expressive with emotion as they occasionally lapsed into their native tongue, recalling the good times and those of hardship.

With quiet respect, as we talked, I cannot help feeling that perhaps the good spirits of those grandmothers past may linger with us. And when the Sun Dance drum begins and the Indian people gather, stretching their camps out over the prairie, the women of the tribe will be there, and Manito (Man-Above) willing, so will I.

SUGGESTIONS FOR FURTHER READING

David Brody, *In Labor's Cause: Main Themes on the History of the American Worker.* New York: Oxford University Press, 1993.

Stewart Burns, *Social Movement of the 1960s: Searching for Democracy.* Boston: Twayne Publishers, 1990.

Amitai Etzioni, ed., *New Communitarian Thinking: Persons, Virtues, Institutions, and Communities.* Charlottesville: University Press of Virginia, 1995.

Sara Evans, *Personal Politics: The Roots of Women's Liberation in the Civil Rights Movement and the New Left.* New York: Knopf, 1979.

Frances FitzGerald, *Cities on a Hill: A Journey Through Contemporary American Cultures.* New York: Simon and Schuster, 1986.

Henry Hampton and Steve Fayer, *Voices of Freedom: An Oral History of the Civil Rights Movement from the 1950s through the 1980s.* New York: Bantam Books, 1990.

Donald L. Horowitz, *Ethnic Groups in Conflict.* Berkeley and Los Angeles: University of California Press, 1985.

Neil Miller, *Out of the Past: Gay and Lesbian History from 1869 to the Present.* New York: Vintage Books, 1995.

Part IV

Permission to Enter and the Right to Belong

7

Opening and Closing the Door: The Debate over Immigration

It is safe to say that the great majority of Americans have at least one immigrant among their ancestors. Certainly all descendants of indigenous people living here when the Europeans first arrived are descendants of immigrants since their remote ancestors ventured from Asia in prehistoric times. The only Americans not descending from immigrants are those whose every foreign ancestor who lived in America was brought here forcefully as a slave and never mated with an immigrant or a descendant of an immigrant. But many African Americans, descendants of slaves, are also partly descendants of immigrants.

Most Americans can identify their foreign ancestry and are generally aware that immigration has shaped American history in a significant way. But immigration is not a thing of the past. Foreigners in large numbers continue to enter the United States, legally or illegally, and history repeats itself with respect to the reasons for immigration and the attitudes of Americans toward newcomers. Foreigners have been settling in the United States since the nation was founded, chiefly for the purpose of improving their lot. Economic opportunities here (real or perceived), coupled with hard times in their country of origin, have propelled many people to seek a new life in America. But immigrants have also come for noneconomic reasons. Many fleeing oppression of whatever nature— political, religious, or cultural—have been attracted to the promise of living in what they perceive as a democracy of orderly laws and extraordinary personal liberties.

In turn, throughout American history and up to the present time, Americans, including descendants of immigrants, have either welcomed immigrants or regarded them as unwelcome, for economic as well as noneconomic reasons. Ever since the country was founded, the American credo has included the ideal that the United States serves as a refuge for the oppressed from other lands. But when this ideal has come into conflict with economic interests, it is usually economic considerations that have won out, leading to legislation aimed at keeping foreigners out. At the same time, some noneconomic justification has been provided for the exclusion.

The conflict between the desire to welcome the oppressed and the perceived need to exclude them on economic grounds manifested itself sharply toward the end of the nineteenth century. At that time the United States was in the midst of a great industrial expansion and in need of cheap unskilled labor in great quantities. This need coincided with population expansion and poor economic conditions in other countries. At the same time there was considerable improvement in methods of transportation. The conjunction of all these factors brought to the United States an unprecedented number of economic immigrants, mostly from Europe but also from Asia. The year 1886 saw the dedication of the Statue of Liberty as an icon of welcomeness at the entrance to the Port of New York. "Give me your tired, your poor/your huddled masses yearning to breathe free . . ." says the sonnet by Emma Lazarus inscribed on the base of the statue. But just four years before, Congress had passed the first Chinese Exclusion Act, outlawing Chinese immigration. Originally, the Chinese had come in large numbers when labor was needed to build the railroads. Once the job was finished, cheap Chinese labor was available to compete with a growing American labor force. The drive to protect native workers brought about Chinese exclusion, but a powerful noneconomic justification was offered: the Chinese were an inferior race undeserving of American citizenship. Moreover, they posited a threat to the genetic purity of the white race—they were "the yellow peril."

Considerations of racial inferiority and genetic purity regarding immigrants have not been limited to nonwhites. Early this century Francis Walker, president of the prestigious Massachusetts Institute of Technology, characterized incoming Italians, Greeks, Poles, and Russians—ancestors of many present-day Americans—as "beaten men from beaten races, representing the worst failures in the struggle for existence." Racial inferiority was cited as the justification for severely restricting immigration from southern and eastern Europe as part of immigration laws passed in the 1920s. These restrictions had tragic consequences for a particular ethnic group in eastern Europe. Thousands of Jews who sought refuge in the United States at the outset of the Nazi era were unable to enter because of quotas that discriminated particularly against countries in eastern Europe. Many of the people refused entry very probably perished in the Holocaust.

A persistent antiimmigrant strain in American history has always been counterbalanced by an equally persistent proimmigrant strain. The debate over immigration continues to this day. On one side are those who believe that immigrants have been a positive force in American history and will continue to be so. In this view new immigrants are not different from immigrants of the past and will successfully assimilate and be productive citizens. Therefore immigration should be encouraged. The opposite view is that new immigrants constitute not only an economic threat but also a social and cultural one. (Presently it is not popular to speak openly about a racial threat.) Those with an antiimmigrant view believe that foreigners are bound to engage in antisocial behavior and alien cultural practices since they have values different from our own. In this view new immigrants are unlike the immigrants of the past, who are held up as exemplary.

The selections in this chapter reflect the debate between these two views on immigration at different points in our history.

A Friend of Immigrants: At the Height of Nativism a Doctor Publishes a Lecture in Favor of Immigration, 1845

Thomas L. Nichols (1815–1901) was a medical doctor as well as a social historian and journalist. In 1845 he published in New York a spirited defense of immigration under the title *Lecture on Immigration and Right of Naturalization,* from which the following selection is excerpted.

Nichols endeavors to provide an antidote to the views of what was then called Native Americanism—a political movement that would lead to the formation of the Native American Party, which held its initial convention the same year that Nichols' lecture appeared. Nativists, as they called themselves, had as their cause the defense of the native born against the ever increasing number of foreigners coming into the country, an invasion which they looked upon as a political, economic, and cultural threat.

To nativists, only natives had a natural title to the inalienable rights of life, liberty, and the pursuit of happiness. If these rights were extended to foreigners, it was merely as a favor, not a privilege to which they were entitled. Nichols thinks otherwise and argues that such rights are not tied to particular nationalities.

Nativists saw European nations as ridding themselves through emigration of the burden of their poor, their idle, and their feebleminded. Nichols considers immigrants to be the very best of their respective lands and stresses the contributions that productive and patriotically minded foreigners have made to American life.

Nativists regarded immigrants as subversive elements holding views antithetical to democracy. Nichols sees them as wanting to live in political freedom and as indisposed to tearing down the institutions that guarantee such freedom.

And nativists thought that the racial purity of America was threatened by the influx of great numbers of inferior stock. To them the native Anglo-American majority belonged to a superior Anglo-Saxon race. In contrast, Nichols holds a nonracist view of immigrants and is not alarmed by their number.

The questions connected with emigration from Europe to America are interesting to both the old world and the new—are of importance to the present and

Source: Edith Abbott, ed., *Historical Aspects of the Immigration Problem* (New York: Arno Press, 1969), pp. 749–55.

future generations. They have more consequence than a charter or a state election; they involve the destinies of millions; they are connected with the progress of civilization, the rights of man, and providence of God!

I have examined this subject the more carefully, and speak upon it the more earnestly, because I have been to some extent, in former years, a partaker of the prejudices I have since learned to pity. A native of New England and a descendant of the puritans, I early imbibed, and to some extent promulgated, opinions of which reflection and experience have made me ashamed. . . .

But while I would speak of the motives of men with charity, I claim the right to combat their opinions with earnestness. Believing that the principles and practices of Native Americanism are wrong in themselves, and are doing wrong to those who are the objects of their persecution, justice and humanity require that their fallacy should be exposed, and their iniquity condemned. It may be unfortunate that the cause of the oppressed and persecuted, in opinion if not in action, has not fallen into other hands; yet, let me trust that the truth, even in mine, will prove mighty, prevailing from its own inherent power!

The right of man to emigrate from one country to another, is one which belongs to him by his own constitution and by every principle of justice. It is one which no law can alter, and no authority destroy. "Life, liberty, and the pursuit of happiness" are set down, in our Declaration of Independence, as among the self-evident, unalienable rights of man. If I have a right to live, I have also a right to what will support existence—food, clothing, and shelter. If then the country in which I reside, from a superabundant population, or any other cause, does not afford me these, my right to go from it to some other is self-evident and unquestionable. The *right to live,* then, supposes the right of emigration. . . .

I proceed, therefore, to show that the emigration of foreigners to this country is not only defensible on grounds of abstract justice—what we have no possible right to prevent, but that it has been in various ways highly beneficial to this country.

Emigration first peopled this hemisphere with civilized men. The first settlers of this continent had the same right to come here that belongs to the emigrant of yesterday—no better and no other. They came to improve their condition, to escape from oppression, to enjoy freedom—for the same, or similar, reasons as now prevail. And so far as they violated no private rights, so long as they obtained their lands by fair purchase, or took possession of those which were unclaimed and uncultivated, the highly respectable natives whom the first settlers found here had no right to make any objections. The peopling of this continent with civilized men, the cultivation of the earth, the various processes of productive labor, for the happiness of man, all tend to "the greatest good of the greatest number," and carry out the evident design of Nature or Providence in the formation of the earth and its inhabitants.

Emigration from various countries in Europe to America, producing a mixture of races, has had, and is still having, the most important influence upon the destinies of the human race. It is a principle, laid down by every physiologist, and proved by abundant observation, that man, like other animals, is improved and brought to its highest perfection by an intermingling of the blood and qualities of various races. That nations and families deteriorate from an opposite course has been observed in all ages. The great physiological reason why Americans are superior to other nations in freedom, intelligence, and enterprise, is because that they are the offspring of the greatest intermingling of races. The mingled blood of England has given her predominance over several nations of Europe in these very qualities, and a newer infusion, with favorable circumstances of climate, position, and institutions, has rendered Americans still superior. The Yankees of New England would never have shown those qualities for which they have been distinguished in war and peace throughout the world had there not been mingled with the puritan English, the calculating Scotch, the warm hearted Irish, the gay and chivalric French, the steady persevering Dutch, and the transcendental Germans, for all these nations contributed to make up the New England character, before the Revolution, and ever since to influence that of the whole American people.

It is not too much to assert that in the order of Providence this vast and fertile continent was reserved for this great destiny; to be the scene of this mingling of the finest European races, and consequently of the highest condition of human intelligence, freedom, and happiness; for I look upon this mixture of the blood and qualities of various nations, and its continual infusion, as absolutely requisite to the perfection of humanity. . . . Continual emigration, and a constant mixing of the blood of different races, is highly conducive to physical and mental superiority.

This country has been continually benefited by the immense amount of capital brought hither by emigrants. There are very few who arrive upon our shores without some little store of wealth, the hoard of years of industry. Small as these means may be in each case, they amount to millions in the aggregate, and every dollar is so much added to the wealth of the country, to be reckoned at compound interest from the time of its arrival, nor are these sums like our European loans, which we must pay back, both principal and interest. Within a few years, especially, and more or less at all periods, men of great wealth have been among the emigrants driven from Europe, by religious oppression or political revolutions. Vast sums have also fallen to emigrants and their descendants by inheritance, for every few days we read in the papers of some poor foreigner, or descendant of foreigners, as are we all, becoming the heir of a princely fortune, which in most cases, is added to the wealth of his adopted country. Besides this, capital naturally follows labor, and it flows upon this country in a constant current, by the laws of trade.

But it is not money alone that adds to the wealth of a country but every day's productive labor is to be added to its accumulating capital. Every house built, every canal dug, every railroad graded, has added so much to the actual wealth of society; and who have built more houses, dug more canals, or graded more railroads, than the hardy Irishmen? I hardly know how our great national works could have been carried on without them then; while every pair of sturdy arms has added to our national wealth, every hungry mouth has been a home market for our agriculture, and every broad shoulder has been clothed with our manufactures.

From the very nature of the case, America gets from Europe the most valuable of her population. Generally, those who come here are the very ones whom a sensible man would select. Those who are attached to monarchical and aristocratic institutions stay at home where they can enjoy them. Those who lack energy and enterprise can never make up their minds to leave their native land. It is the strong minded, the brave hearted, the free and self-respecting, the enterprising and the intelligent, who break away from all the ties of country and of home, and brave the dangers of the ocean, in search of liberty and independence, for themselves and for their children, on a distant continent; and it is from this, among other causes, that the great mass of the people of this country are distinguished for the very qualities we should look for in emigrants. The same spirit which sent our fathers across the ocean impels us over the Alleghenies, to the valley of the Mississippi, and thence over the Rocky mountains into Oregon.

For what are we not indebted to foreign emigration, since we are all Europeans or their descendants? We cannot travel on one of our steamboats without remembering that Robert Fulton was the son of an Irishman. We cannot walk by St. Paul's churchyard without seeing the monuments which admiration and gratitude have erected to Emmet, and Montgomery. Who of the thousands who every summer pass up and down our great thoroughfare, the North River, fails to catch at least a passing glimpse of the column erected to the memory of Thaddeus Kosciusko? I cannot forget that only last night a portion of our citizens celebrated with joyous festivities the birthday of the son of Irish emigrants, I mean the Hero of New Orleans!

Who speaks contemptuously of Alexander Hamilton as a foreigner, because he was born in one of the West India Islands? Who at this day will question the worth or patriotism of Albert Gallatin, because he first opened his eyes among the Alps of Switzerland—though, in fact, this was brought up and urged against him, when he was appointed special minister to Russia by James Madison. What New Yorker applies the epithet of "degraded foreigner" to the German immigrant, John Jacob Astor, a man who has spread his canvas on every sea, drawn to his adopted land the wealth of every clime, and given us, it may be, our best claim to vast territories!

Who would have banished the Frenchman, Stephen Girard, who, after accumulating vast wealth from foreign commerce, endowed with it magnificent institutions for education in his adopted land? So might I go on for hours, citing individual examples of benefits derived by this country from foreign immigration. . . .

I have enumerated some of the advantages which such emigration has given to America. Let us now very carefully inquire, whether there is danger of any injury arising from these causes, at all proportionable to the palpable good.

"Our Country is in danger," is the cry of Nativism. During my brief existence I have seen this country on the very verge of ruin a considerable number of times. It is always in the most imminent peril every four years; but, hitherto, the efforts of one party or the other have proved sufficient to rescue it, just in the latest gasp of its expiring agonies, and we have breathed more freely, when we have been assured that "the country's safe." Let us look steadily in the face of this new danger.

Are foreigners coming here to overturn our government? Those who came before the Revolution appear to have been generally favorable to Republican institutions. Those who have come here since have left friends, home, country, all that man naturally holds dearest, that they might live under a free government—they and their children. Is there common sense in the supposition that men would voluntarily set about destroying the very liberties they came so far to enjoy?

"But they lack intelligence," it is said. Are the immigrants of today less intelligent than those of fifty or a hundred years ago? Has Europe and the human race stood still all this time? . . . The facts of men preferring this country to any other, of their desire to live under its institutions, of their migration hither, indicate to my mind anything but a lack of proper intelligence and enterprise. It has been charged against foreigners, by a portion of the whig press, that they generally vote with the democratic party. Allowing this to be so, I think that those who reflect upon the policy of the two parties, from the time of John Adams down to that of Mayor Harper, will scarcely bring this up as the proof of a lack of intelligence!

The truth is, a foreigner who emigrates to this country comes here saying, "Where Liberty dwells, there is my country." He sees our free institutions in the strong light of contrast. The sun seems brighter, because he has come out of darkness. What we know by hearsay only of the superiority of our institutions, he knows by actual observation and experience. Hence it is that America has had no truer patriots—freedom no more enthusiastic admirers—the cause of liberty no more heroic defenders, than have been found among our adopted citizens. . . .

But if naturalized citizens of foreign birth had the disposition, they have not the power, to endanger our liberties, on account of their comparatively small and decreasing numbers. There appears to be a most extraordinary misapprehension upon this subject. To read one of our "Native" papers one might suppose that our country was becoming overrun by foreigners, and that there was real danger of their having a majority of votes. . . .

There is a point beyond which immigration cannot be carried. It must be limited by the capacity of the vessels employed in bringing passengers, while our entire population goes on increasing in geometrical progression, so that in one century from now, we shall have a population of one hundred and sixty millions, but a few hundred thousands of whom at the utmost can be citizens of foreign birth. Thus it may be seen that foreign immigration is of very little account, beyond a certain period, in the population of a country, and at all times is an insignificant item. . . .

In the infancy of this country the firstborn native found himself among a whole colony of foreigners. Now, the foreigner finds himself surrounded by as great a disproportion of natives, and the native babe and newly landed foreigner have about the same amount, of either power or disposition, to endanger the country in which they have arrived; one, because he chose to come—the other because he could not help it.

I said the power or the disposition, for I have yet to learn that foreigners, whether German or Irish, English or French, are at all disposed to do an injury to the asylum which wisdom has prepared and valor won for the oppressed of all nations and religions. I appeal to the observation of every man in this community, whether the Germans and the Irish here, and throughout the country, are not as orderly, as industrious, as quiet, and in the habit of performing as well the common duties of citizens as the great mass of natives among us.

The worst thing that can be brought against any portion of our foreign population is that in many cases they are poor, and when they sink under labor and privation, they have no resources but the almshouse. Alas! shall the rich, for whom they have labored, the owners of the houses they have helped to build, refuse to treat them as kindly as they would their horses when incapable of further toil? Can they grudge them shelter from the storm, and a place where they may die in peace?

Raising Alarm: An Antiimmigration Politician Speaks at the Convention to Revise the Constitution of Kentucky, 1849

Following are excerpts from a speech that Kentucky politician Garrett Davis (1801–1872) delivered at a session of the 1849 Kentucky Constitutional Convention in which he called for restricting immigration and immigrants' right to vote. The convention had been called to revise the state's constitution at a time when the criteria for admitting or rejecting immigrants and for granting or denying naturalization were at issue. At that time states were still considered to have the power to set their own immigration regulations. Davis' position was that the rules for naturalizing citizens were too lax. In this he reflected the general view of antiimmigrant politicians in the 1840s.

For understanding Davis' remarks, it is important to take into account that he delivered his speech at a time when Ireland and Germany had largely replaced Great Britain as the main source of immigration. There were also many immigrants from Slavic countries.

At the time of its constitutional convention, Kentucky was a slave state. It nonetheless never joined the rebellion that was to erupt twelve years later, bringing about the U.S. Civil War—a conflict that Davis anticipates in his speech. That Kentucky never seceded from the Union was due to the presence there of strong antislavery forces. But Davis—who at different times served as a senator and congressman from Kentucky—was proslavery and was furthermore a racist who believed in the superiority of what he called the "noble Anglo-American race." As his words make clear, it was precisely his views on slavery and race that inspired his opposition to European immigration.

When arguing in favor of excluding foreigners from the political process, Davis invokes Thomas Jefferson's concerns that giving immigrants the

Source: Edith Abbott, ed., *Historical Aspects of the Immigration Problem* (New York: Arno Press, 1969), pp. 767–74.

vote will lead dangerously to having to share the legislative power with them because they will be great in number. The people that both Jefferson and Davis had in mind were non-English Europeans. For Jefferson it was the Germans. For Davis it was the latter plus the Irish and those from Slavic countries such as Russians and Poles, which he called the Slavonics. For him all these were not national groups but "races" ranking below the Anglo-American.

Why am I opposed to the encouragement of foreign immigration into our country, and disposed to apply any proper checks to it? Why do I propose to suspend to the foreigner, for twenty-one years after he shall have signified formally his intention to become a citizen of the United States, the right of suffrage, the birthright of no man but one native-born? It is because the mighty tides of immigration, each succeeding one increasing in volume, bring to us not only different languages, opinions, customs, and principles, but hostile races, religions, and interests, and the traditionary prejudices of generations with a large amount of the turbulence, disorganizing theories, pauperism, and demoralization of Europe in her redundant population thrown upon us. This multiform and dangerous evil exists and will continue, for "the cry is, Still they come!". . .

The most of those European immigrants, having been born and having lived in the ignorance and degradation of despotisms, without mental or moral culture, with but a vague consciousness of human rights, and no knowledge whatever of the principles of popular constitutional government, their interference in the political administration of our affairs, even when honestly intended, would be about as successful as that of the Indian in the arts and business of civilized private life; and when misdirected, as it would generally be, by bad and designing men, could be productive only of mischief, and from their numbers, of mighty mischief. The system inevitably and in the end will fatally depreciate, degrade, and demoralize the power which governs and rules our destinies.

I freely acknowledge that among such masses of immigrants there are men of noble intellect, of high cultivation, and of great moral worth; men every way adequate to the difficult task of free, popular, and constitutional government. But the number is lamentably small. There can be no contradistinction between them and the incompetent and vicious; and their admission would give no proper compensation, no adequate security against the latter if they, too, were allowed to share political sovereignty. The country could be governed just as wisely and as well by the native-born citizens alone, by which this baleful infusion would be wholly excluded. . . .

This view of the subject is powerfully corroborated by a glance at the state of things in Europe. The aggregate population of that continent in 1807 was 183,000,000. Some years since it was reported to be 260,000,000 and now it is reasonably but little short of 283,000,000; showing an increase within a period of about forty years of 100,000,000. The area of Europe is but little more than that of the United States, and from its higher northern positions and greater proportion of sterile lands, has a less natural capability of sustaining population.

All her western, southern, and middle states labor under one of the heaviest afflictions of nations—they have a redundant population. The German states have upward of 70,000,000, and Ireland 8,000,000; all Germany being not larger than three of our largest states, and Ireland being about the size of Kentucky. Daniel O'Connell, in 1843 reported 2,385,000 of the Irish people in a state of destitution. The annual increase of population in Germany and Ireland is in the aggregate near 2,000,000; and in all Europe it is near 7,000,000. Large masses of these people, in many countries, not only want the comforts of life, but its subsistence, its necessaries, and are literally starving. England, many of the German powers, Switzerland, and other governments, have put into operation extensive and well-arranged systems of emigrating and transporting to America their excess of population, and particularly the refuse, the pauper, the demoralized, and the criminal. Very many who come are stout and industrious, and go to labor steadily and thriftily. They send their friends in the old country true and glowing accounts of ours, and with it the means which they have garnered here to bring, too, those friends. Thus, immigration itself increases its means, and constantly adds to its swelling tides. Suppose some mighty convulsion of nature should loosen Europe, the smaller country, from her ocean-deep foundations, and drift her to our coast, would we be ready to take her teeming myriads to our fraternal embrace and give them equally our political sovereignty? If we did, in a few fleeting years where would be the noble Anglo-American race, where their priceless heritage of liberty, where their free constitution, where the best and brightest hopes of man? All would have perished! It is true all Europe is not coming to the United States, but much, too much of it, is; and a dangerous disproportion of the most ignorant and worst of it, without bringing us any territory for them; enough, if they go on increasing and to increase, and are to share with us our power, to bring about such a deplorable result. The question is, Shall they come and take possession of our country and our government, and rule us, or will we, who have the right, rule them and ourselves? I go openly, manfully, and perseveringly for the latter rule, and if it cannot be successfully asserted in all the United States, I am for taking measures to maintain it in Kentucky, and while we can. Now is the time—prevention is easier than cure.

The governments of Europe know better than we do that they have a great excess of population. They feel more intensely its great and manifold evils, and for years they have been devising and applying correctives, which have all been mainly resolved into one—to drain off into America their surplus, and especially their destitute, demoralized, and vicious population. By doing so, they not only make more room and comfort for their residue, but they think—and with some truth—that they provide for their own security, and do something to avert explosions which might hurl kings from their thrones. . . .

We have a country of vast extent, with a great variety of climate, soil, production, industry, and pursuit. Competing interests and sectional questions are a natural and fruitful source of jealousies, discords, and factions. We have about four millions of slaves, and the slaveholding and free states are nearly equally divided in number, but the population of the latter greatly preponderating, and every portion of it deeply imbued with inflexible hostility to slavery as an institution. Even now conflict of opinion and passion of the two great sections of the Union upon the subject of slavery is threatening to rend this Union, and change confederated states and one people into hostile and warring powers. Cession has recently given to us considerable numbers of the Spanish race, and a greatly increasing immigration is constantly pouring in upon us the hordes of Europe, with their hereditary national animosities, their discordant races, languages, and religious faiths, their ignorance and their pauperism, mixed up with a large amount of idleness, moral degradation, and crime; and all this "heterogeneous, discordant, distracted mass," to use Mr. Jefferson's language, "sharing with us the legislation" and the entire political sovereignty. . . .

Washington and Jefferson and their associates, though among the wisest and most far-seeing of mankind, could not but descry in the future many formidable difficulties and dangers, and thus be premonished to provide against them in fashioning our institutions. If they had foreseen the vast, the appalling increase of immigration upon us at the present, there can be no reasonable doubt that laws to naturalize the foreigners and to give up to them the country, its liberties, its destiny, would not have been authorized by the constitution. The danger, though great, is not wholly without remedy. We can do something if we do it quickly. The German and Slavonic races are combining in the state of New York to elect candidates of their own blood to Congress. This is the beginning of the conflict of races on a large scale, and it must, in the nature of things, continue and increase. It must be universal and severe in all the field of labor, between the native and the stranger, and from the myriads of foreign laborers coming to us, if it does not become a contest for bread and subsistence, wages will at least be brought down so low as to hold our native laborers and their families in hopeless poverty. They cannot adopt the habits of life and live upon the stinted meager supplies to which the foreigner will restrict himself, and which is bounteous plenty to what he has been accustomed in the old country. Already these results are taking place in many of the mechanic arts. Duty, patriotism, and wisdom all require us to protect the labor, and to keep up to a fair scale the wages of our native-born people as far as by laws and measures of public policy it can be done. The foreigner, too, is the natural foe of the slavery of our state. He is opposed to it by all his past associations, and when he comes to our state he sees 200,000 laborers of a totally different race to himself excluding him measurably from employment and wages. He hears a measure agitated to send these 200,000 competitors away. Their exodus will make room for him, his kindred and race, and create such a demand for labor, as he will reason it, to give him high wages. He goes naturally for the measure, and becomes an emancipationist. While the slave is with us, the foreigner will not crowd us, which will postpone to a long day the affliction of nations, an excess of population; the slaves away, the great tide of immigration will set in upon us, and precipitate upon our happy land this, the chief misery of most of the countries of Europe. Look at the myriads who are perpetually pouring into the northwestern states from the German hives—making large and exclusive settlements for themselves, which in a few years will number their thousands and tens of thousands, living in isolation; speaking a strange language, having alien manners, habits, opinions, and religious faiths, and a total ignorance of our political institutions; all handed down with German phlegm and inflexibility to their children through generations. In less than fifty years, northern Illinois, parts of Ohio, and Michigan, Wisconsin, Iowa, and Minnesota will be literally possessed by them; they will number millions and millions, and they will be essentially a distinct people, a nation within a nation, a new Germany. We can't keep these people wholly out, and ought not if we could; but we are getting more than our share of them. I wish they would turn their direction to South America, quite as good a portion of the world as our share of the hemisphere. They could there aid in bringing up the slothful and degenerate Spanish race; here their deplorable office is to pull us down. Our proud boast is that the Anglo-Saxon race is the first among all the world of man, and that we are a shoot from this noble stock; but how long will we be as things are progressing? In a few years, as a distinctive race, the Anglo-Americans will be as much lost to the world and its future history as the lost tribes of Israel. . . .

No well-informed and observant man can look abroad over this widespread and blessed country without feeling deep anxiety for the future. Some elements of discord and disunion are even now in fearful action. Spread out to such a vast extent, filling up almost in geometrical progression with communities and colonies from many lands, various as Europe in personal and national characteristics, in opinions, in manners and customs, in tongues and religious faiths, in the traditions of the past, and the objects and the hopes of the future, the United States can, no more than Europe, become one homogeneous mass—one peaceful, united, harmonizing, all self-adhering people. When the country shall begin to teem with people, these jarring elements being brought into proximity, their repellant and explosive properties will begin to act with greater intensity; and then, if not before, will come the war of geographical sections, the war of races, and the most relentless of all wars, of hostile religions. This mournful catastrophe will have been greatly hastened by our immense expansion and our proclamation to all mankind to become a part of us.

Proimmigration Reform: The President of the United States Argues for the Elimination of National Origin Quotas, 1963

John Fitzgerald Kennedy (1917–1963) worked actively in favor of immigrants and refugees while he served in the U.S. Congress, first as a congressman and later as a senator from Massachusetts. He was also a talented writer. His book *Profiles in Courage* won the prestigious Pulitzer Prize in 1956.

In 1958, Kennedy, a great-grandson of Irish immigrants, published *A Nation of Immigrants,* a book in which he highlighted the contributions made by immigrants to American life and criticized existing immigration legislation, which he regarded as racist and unfair.

Source: John Fitzgerald Kennedy, *A Nation of Immigrants* (New York: HarperCollins Publishers, 1964), pp. 69–83.

The book was relatively simple and straightforward and was intended to create an awareness in the general public not only of the central role of immigration in American life but also of the need for legislative reform.

Kennedy was elected President in 1960 and he made immigration reform an important part of his legislative program. Late in July 1963, he sent to the U.S. Congress a set of proposals to liberalize immigration laws. He decided then that it was time to revise *A Nation of Immigrants* so that it would serve as "a weapon of enlightenment in the coming legislative battle"—as his brother Robert F. Kennedy tells us in his introduction to the 1964 edition. The President was working on the book at the time of his assassination, in November 1963, and it appeared posthumously.

The following selection draws from the last two chapters of the book. Kennedy provides a clear historical background for his proposals, many of which were enacted into law in 1965, during the presidency of his successor, Lyndon B. Johnson.

From the start, immigration policy has been a prominent subject of discussion in America. This is as it must be in a democracy, where every issue should be freely considered and debated.

Immigration, or rather the British policy of clamping down on immigration, was one of the factors behind the colonial desire for independence. Restrictive immigration policies constituted one of the charges against King George III expressed in the Declaration of Independence. And in the Constitutional Convention James Madison noted, "That part of America which has encouraged them [the immigrants] has advanced most rapidly in population, agriculture and the arts." So, too, Washington in his Thanksgiving Day Proclamation of 1795 asked all Americans "humbly and fervently to beseech the kind Author of these blessings. . .to render this country more and more a safe and propitious asylum for the unfortunate of other countries."

Yet there was the basic ambiguity which older Americans have often shown toward newcomers. In 1797 a member of Congress argued that, while a liberal immigration policy was fine when the country was new and unsettled, now that America had reached its maturity and was fully populated, immigration should stop, an argument which has been repeated at regular intervals throughout American history. . . .

By the turn of the century the opinion was becoming widespread that the numbers of new immigrants should be limited. Those who were opposed to all immigration and all "foreigners" were now joined by those who believed sincerely, and with some basis in fact, that America's capacity to absorb immigration was limited. This movement toward restricting immigration represented a social and economic reaction, not only to the tremendous increase in immigration after 1880, but also to the shift in its main sources, to Southern, Eastern and Southeastern Europe.

Anti-immigration sentiment was heightened by World War I, and the disillusionment and strong wave of isolationism that marked its aftermath. It was in this climate, in 1921, that Congress passed and the President signed the first major law in our country's history severely limiting new immigration by establishing an emergency quota system. An era in American history had ended; we were committed to a radically new policy toward the peopling of the nation.

The Act of 1921 was an early version of the so-called "national origins" system. Its provisions limited immigration of numbers of each nationality to a certain percentage of the number of foreign-born individuals of that nationality resident in the United States according to the 1910 census. Nationality meant country of birth. The total number of immigrants permitted to enter under this system each year was 357,000.

In 1924 the Act was revised, creating a temporary arrangement for the years 1924 to 1928, under which the national quotas for 1924 were equal to 2 percent of the number of foreign-born persons of a given nationality living in the United States in 1890, or about 164,000 people. The permanent system, which went into force in 1929, includes essentially all the elements of immigration policy that are in our law today. The immigration statutes now establish a system of annual quotas to govern immigration from each country. Under this system 156,987 quota immigrants are permitted to enter the United States each year. The quotas from each country are based upon the national origins of the population of the United States in 1920.

The use of the year 1920 is arbitrary. It rests upon the fact that this system was introduced in 1924 and the last prior census was in 1920. The use of a national origins system is without basis in either logic or reason. It neither satisfies a national need nor accomplishes an international purpose. In an age of interdependence among nations such a system is an anachronism, for it discriminates among applicants for admission into the United States on the basis of accident of birth.

Because of the composition of our population in 1920, the system is heavily weighted in favor of immigration from Northern Europe and severely limits immigration from Southern and Eastern Europe and from other parts of the world.

To cite some examples: Great Britain has an annual quota of 65,361 immigration visas and used 28,291 of them. Germany has a quota of 25,814 and used 26,533 (of this number, about one third are wives of servicemen who could enter on a nonquota basis). Ireland's quota is 17,756 and only 6,054 Irish availed themselves of it. On the other hand, Poland is permitted 6,488 and there is a backlog of 61,293 Poles wishing to enter the United States. Italy is permitted 5,666 and has a backlog of 132,435. Greece's quota is 308; her backlog is 96,538. Thus a Greek citizen desiring to emigrate to this country has little chance of coming here. And an American citizen with a Greek father or mother must wait at least eighteen months to bring his parents here to join him. A citizen whose married son or daughter, or brother or sister, is Italian cannot obtain a quota number for them for two years or more. Meanwhile, many thousands of quota numbers are wasted because they are not wanted or needed by nationals of the countries to which they are assigned.

In short, a qualified person born in England or Ireland who wants to emigrate to the United States can do so at any time. A person born in Italy, Hungary, Poland or the Baltic States may have to wait many years before his turn is reached. This system is based upon the assumption that there is some reason for keeping the origins of our population in exactly the same proportions as they existed in 1920. Such an idea is at complete variance with the American traditions and principles that the qualification of an immigrant do not depend upon his country of birth, and violates the spirit expressed in the Declaration of Independence that "all men are created equal."

One writer has listed six motives behind the Act of 1924. They were: (1) postwar isolationism; (2) the doctrine of the alleged superiority of Anglo-Saxon and Teutonic "races"; (3) the fear that "pauper labor" would lower wage levels; (4) the belief that people of certain nations were less law-abiding than others; (5) the fear of foreign ideologies and subversion; (6) the fear that entrance of too many people with different customs and habits would undermine our national and social unity and order. All of these arguments can be found in Congressional debates on the subject and may be heard today in discussions over a new national policy toward immigration. Thus far, they have prevailed. The policy of 1924 was continued in all its essentials by the Immigration and Nationality Act of 1952. . . .

The Immigration and Nationality Act of 1952 undertook to codify all our national laws on immigration. This was a proper and long overdue task. But it was not just housekeeping chore. In the course of the deliberation over the Act, many basic decisions about our immigration policy were made. The total racial bar against the naturalization of Japanese, Koreans and other East Asians was removed, and a minimum annual quota of one hundred was provided for each of these countries. Provision was also made to make it easier to reunite husbands and wives. Most important of all was the decision to do nothing about the national origins system.

The famous words of Emma Lazarus on the pedestal of the Statue of Liberty read: "Give me your tired, your poor, your huddled masses yearning to breathe free." Until 1921 this was an accurate picture of our society. Under present law it would be appropriate to add: "as long as they come from Northern Europe, are not too tired or too poor or slightly ill, never stole a loaf of bread, never joined any questionable organization, and can document their activities for the past two years."

Furthermore, the national origins quota system has strong overtones of an indefensible racial preference. It is strongly weighted toward so-called Anglo-Saxons, a phrase which one writer calls "a term of art" encompassing almost anyone from Northern and Western Europe. Sinclair Lewis described his hero, Martin Arrowsmith, this way: "a typical pure-bred-Anglo-Saxon American—which means that he was a union of German, French, Scotch-Irish, perhaps a little Spanish, conceivably of the strains lumped together as 'Jewish,' and a great deal of English, which is itself a combination of primitive Britain, Celt, Phoenician, Roman, German, Dane and Swede."

Yet, however much our present policy may be deplored, it still remains our national policy. As President Truman said when he vetoed the Immigration and Nationality Act (only to have that veto overridden): "The idea behind this discriminatory policy was, to put it boldly, that Americans with English or Irish names were better people and better citizens than Americans with Italian or Greek or Polish names. . . . Such a concept is utterly unworthy of our traditions and our ideals.". . .

There is, of course, a legitimate argument for some limitation upon immigration. We no longer need settlers for virgin lands, and our economy is expanding more slowly than in the nineteenth and early twentieth centuries. . . .

The clash of opinion arises not over the number of immigrants to be admitted, but over the test for admission—the national origins quota system. Instead of using the discriminatory test of where the immigrant was born, the reform proposals would base admission on the immigrant's possession of skills our country needs and on the humanitarian ground of reuniting families. Such legislation does not seek to make over the face of America. Immigrants would still be given tests for health, intelligence, morality and security. . . .

Religious and civic organizations, ethnic associations and newspaper editorials, citizens from every walk of life and groups of every description have expressed their support for a more rational and less prejudiced immigration law. Congressional leaders of both parties have urged the adoption of new legislation that would eliminate the most objectionable features of the McCarran-Walter Act and the nationalities quota system. . . .

The Presidential message to Congress of July 23, 1963, recommended that the national origins system be replaced by a formula governing immigration to the United States which takes into account: (1) the skills of the immigrant and their relationships to our needs; (2) the family relationship between immigrants and persons already here so that the reuniting of families is encouraged; and (3) the priority of registration. Present law grants a preference to immigrants with special skills, education or training. It also grants a preference to various relatives of the United States' citizens and lawfully resident aliens. But it does so only within a national origins quota. It should be modified so that those with the greatest ability to add to the national welfare, no matter where they are born, are granted the highest priority. The next priority should go to those who seek to be reunited with their relatives. For applicants with equal claims, the earliest registrant should be the first admitted. . . .

These changes will not solve all the problems of immigration. But they will insure that progress will continue to be made toward our ideals and toward the realization of humanitarian objectives.

We must avoid what the Irish poet John Boyle O'Reilly once called

Organized charity, scrimped and iced,
In the name of a cautious, statistical Christ.

Immigration policy should be generous; it should be fair; it should be flexible. With such a policy we can turn to the world, and to our own past, with clear hands and a clear conscience. Such a policy would be but a reaffirmation of old principles. It would be an expression of our agreement with George Washington that "The bosom of America is open to receive not only the opulent and respectable stranger, but the oppressed and persecuted of all nations and religions; whom we shall welcome to a participation of all our rights and privileges, if by decency and propriety of conduct they appear to merit the enjoyment."

Doubts on Assimilation: A Conservative Demographer Does not Think that Third World Immigrants Will Adapt to U.S. Culture, 1990

In a 1990 article in *Conservative Review,* Robert N. Hopkins, a demographer, presents a pessimistic view of immigrants from Asia, Africa, and Latin America as potential members of the U.S. society. The following selection is excerpted from his article.

Hopkins argues that the dominant political forces in the United States have a view of assimilation that is different from the one that prevailed in the era of the great immigration waves from Europe. For Hopkins there is no longer an official insistence that immigrants assimilate to American culture: the notion of America as a melting pot has been replaced, according to Hopkins, by cultural pluralism, including linguistic pluralism. He traces this change in official philosophy to the immigration reforms in the 1960s that eliminated the old national origins quotas. Hopkins points out that regulations now favor immigrants from Asian, African, and Latin American nations in the Third World, which are also the source of illegal immigration.

The Third World is generally considered to be composed of the technologically less advanced nations outside North America and Europe. Indeed, since the passage of the 1965 Immigration and Naturalization Act, the great majority of immigrants have come from Latin America and Asia, which combined have accounted for 80 percent of legal arrivals. In contrast, in the period 1931–1960, 60 percent of legal immigrants came from northern and western Europe and North America.

Hopkins' argument is that since there is now no official pressure to assimilate, the new immigrants will tend to retain their many distinct cultures.

Though Hopkins does not propose in his article that Third World immigration be restricted or ended, he presents as an obstacle to assimilation a factor that antiimmigrationists fixed upon in the past to support excluding southern and eastern Europeans—that the new immigrants are coming from countries with strong antidemocratic traditions.

The problem of assimilating immigrant peoples into the United States culture and society has had a varied history, depending largely on who the immigrant peoples were and what the dominant culture of America was at that time.

When the majority population of the United States was still British by origin, the ideal of "Anglo-conformity" was the standard. This demanded, in the words of Milton M. Gordon, in his book *Assimilation in American Life: The Role of Race, Religion and National Origins,* the "renunciation of the immigrant's ancestral culture in favor of the behavior and value of the Anglo-Saxon core group."

Although early America had almost as many settlers of German, Dutch and

Source: Robert Hopkins, "Can the United States Assimilate the Wave of New Immigrants?" *Conservative Review,* April 1990.

French descent as of Anglo-Saxon origin, the concurrent values and ethnic similarities shared by all West, Northwest and North European immigrants ensured that collaboration and harmony was attained with little if any friction. Indeed, there was a generally widespread acceptance of the English language and of the Anglo-Saxon character of the common law legal system and Constitution of the United States.

This attitude prevailed until the closing decade of the nineteenth century, when the immigration of numbers of immigrants from southern, central and eastern European countries stimulated people to begin to think consciously about a process of assimilation which they called the "melting pot." Because the immigrants were almost all of European origin, America did partially become a melting pot, but with the essential persistence of the "Old American" culture as the basis of "Americanism."

With this change of philosophy it has become popular to assume that the future of American society involves the preservation of distinctive immigrant cultures within a broadly overriding concept of American citizenship, and with only a steadily increasing integration of the immigrants into the American economic and political scene. The possibility that the immigrants might go so far as wishing to retain their own language was, at first, seldom considered as a serious question of any significance.

While America had acquired a small immigrant community of Asians, imported mainly as laborers in the nineteenth century, these were regarded with a tolerant nature as a rather amusing and quaint anachronism. The large black community, which had been a part of the fabric of America since colonial days, and the surviving American Indian element, were both likewise generally accepted as subgroups essentially subordinate to the truly "American" population of European provenance. In short, America was still a nation, albeit one with several relatively small, accepted, but definitely subordinate minorities.

The way in which America thinks it can absorb new immigrant minorities while still remaining a nation is important, since prevailing beliefs about assimilation may be more significant in determining public policy concerning immigration than the reality of assimilation. In daily life, moreover, relations between the "Old Americans" and the new Third World immigrants may be significantly affected by the ideal of assimilation which they do or do not hold in common; an ideal which may be perceived as inspiring, or threatening, depending upon the status of the individuals involved. Finally, the extent to which the "Old Americans" and the immigrants are able to identify with the nation—their implicit answer to the question whether they think of themselves and of others as being a part of "our nation"—is significantly influenced by the concept of assimilation and of national identity that they hold.

Assuming that elites do exist in a nation, and that these elites may or may not share the same views as the larger majority population, it becomes necessary also to ask whether the elite which dominates the political scene holds the same view on the question of how to absorb large immigrant minorities into the "American" culture, or indeed, whether such minorities should be absorbed at all. It is worth mentioning here that demands for "English only" in education have been attacked as "racist." This is nonsense, since a real racist would obviously prefer other stocks to remain separated by linguistic barriers, rather than risk the possibility of their children interbreeding with the original European stock.

During the 1920's the concept of Anglo-Saxon culture as constituting the root of American culture and of European stock as constituting the root base of the American ethnic type was still sufficiently strong among both the elite and the majority of the population of "Old Americans," to ensure a common desire to restrict immigration largely to people of European origin.

But the Anglo-Saxon cultural tradition and white America ideal has in recent decades found neither sufficient spokesmen in the governing elite and media nor sufficient grass roots support to constitute an effective mass movement. What feelings many of them had on this matter have been more recently weakened by the phenomenon of "neo-conservative" propagandists who continually portray every issue solely in economic terms, as though no other human goals or values existed. Although it could be argued that the elements of the "national" concept were still implicit in the Walter-McCarran Immigration Act of 1952, which reaffirmed the principle of quotas based on country of origin, the spirit of this ideal had died by the time John F. Kennedy, in 1963, came to publish his book, *A Nation of Immigrants*. This treatise expressed quite contrary views which were to become official policy with the Immigration Act of 1965 and all subsequent immigrant legislation—which effectively reversed the former policy of discrimination in favor of European immigrants to discrimination in favor of Third World immigrants. The official target now seems to be the reshaping of the American population into a miniature replica of the entire world.

Simply, the Kennedy viewpoint argued that America was traditionally a nation of immigrants, and that the "Old Americans" who had founded America, fought for its independence, given it its language, constitution and legal system, was no more "American" than any other immigrant group. The concept of the melting pot, with a subsidiary concession to the cultural pluralism view, has subsequently prevailed.

But the belief in the melting pot theory has come to be questioned as a result of the arrival of increasing numbers of non-European immigrants. Instead, the theory of America as a land of "cultural pluralism" has caught the official imagination—the idea of America as a multi-cultural and multi-racial microcosm of the entire world.

Since the legislation presently governing immigration gives preference not to the Northwest European countries that established the United States, but to the surplus populations of the overcrowded and teeming Third World—which are also entering the country in large numbers illegally, only to be given the legal right to remain and become American citizens after they have effected illegal entry successfully (not a difficult thing to do) and have managed to evade the law for a further period of time, again successfully. It is quite clear that it is no longer realistic to assume that this vast and growing number of immigrants, who also prove to be more prolific in child-bearing than the native white American population, are likely to comply with the cultural ideal of conformity to "Old American" ideals and institutions.

This has become particularly obvious in areas which have been heavily settled by Hispanics, where even the Spanish language has taken root, and political pressures by the immigrants have ensured that they receive permission to operate radio and T.V. stations dedicated to their own language and culture. Interestingly, this has sometimes caused tension amongst resident minorities, particularly the black minority, when a decision had to be made whether a new T.V. station should be allocated to the black minority or to the Hispanic minority.

Indeed, recent legislation has affirmed the right of illegal immigrants who have been permitted to stay in the U.S. under the amnesty provision to benefit from Affirmative Action programs, which is thus unfair to the American blacks and American Indians who were originally targeted to benefit from such programs in light of past disadvantages.

Surprisingly, one aspect of the "Old American" conformity concept does linger on as a phantom "residue," much like the whiff of scent which remains in a long-emptied bottle. Although realistically it seems apparent that this is currently a politically unrealizable ideal, the notion that the new immigrants will be absorbed into the historic Anglo-Saxon culture is allowed to survive as a perennial source of solace whenever anyone dares to suggest that future immigration might challenge the national premise of *e pluribus unum*.

This notion assures those who believe in it that, even if the "Old American" core group continues to dwindle in numbers and power to the point of becoming marginal, the political heritage of the Founding Fathers will survive. According to the most optimistic exponents of this belief, the republic will endure even if the descendants of its founders go into extinction, because it is based on an imperishable tradition going back to William Blackstone, John Locke, Magna Carta and Anglo-Saxon common law. Some even argue that these values will be better defended by Third World immigrants than by the "Old American" members of the nation which created that heritage.

This last "residue" of belief in the ability of the "Old American" institutions to survive simply because of their innate superiority would be simply an innocuous illusion were there not indications that official public policy is in fact moving in a direction directly contrary to those traditions. Today the government deliberately gives no recognition to race or ethnicity, except to advance the interests of minority ethnic and racial groups, which are thereby encouraged to maintain their own identity and to avoid being absorbed into the "Old American" tradition so readily accepted by most earlier immigrants of European origin.

But the reality is that there is no evidence that the European tradition can or will be transmitted to immigrants of African, Asian and Hispanic origin, or to any other of the millions of Third World immigrants who are now entering the country at an increasing rate.

Indeed, the social comforts of being among 'people of one's own kind,' and the political advantages of ethnic unity and ability to form pressure groups become significant forces now that the philosophy of cultural pluralism has gained broad acceptance in ruling circles.

As evidence that the new ethnic pluralism is becoming official public policy, author Gordon cites "recently introduced measures such as government-mandated affirmative action procedures in employment, education, and stipulated public programs, and court-ordered busing of school children across neighborhood district lines to effect racial integration. . . . As is widely known, the federal government has experienced difficulties implementing such measures with its present population. It is certainly not unreasonable, therefore, to expect that the present problems will only be exacerbated with the incorporation—one cannot call it assimilation—of masses of Third World immigrants."

There are optimists who still believe that the melting pot process will lead to the assimilation of today's immigrants into the "Old American" way of life—with all that means in respect of liberty, justice, democracy, and cultural tradition. They hope for an end result that will congeal in favor of the survival of the traditionally prized political and legal heritage of freedom and rational democracy.

Forecasting, it is to be admitted, is a hazardous enterprise, but major anomalies can be expected as the United States becomes the host country to truly massive numbers of Third World immigrants.

Asia, for example, has an enduring heritage of not simply feudalism, but of that Oriental Despotism, masterfully analyzed in Karl Wittfogel's thus named book, which has shown a capacity to overwhelm liberalizing Western tendencies. Japan, supposedly a parliamentary democracy, has given evidence—not limited to the widely-publicized statements of Prime Minister Nakasone—of being one of the most ethnocentric nations in the world. China remains a one-party state. The parliamentary democracy of India may not survive internecine warfare among the subcontinent's linguistic and religious power blocs. The future of democracy in the Philippines is very uncertain. The massacres in Cambodia are indistinguishable in enormity from the depredations of Tamerlane.

Latin America, with few exceptions, reveals a history of rotating authoritarian rule with failing democratic government, in which *el caudillo* follows *el golpe de estado,* and vice versa, in a succession without end. Mexico experienced a long period of what in effect has been corrupt one-party rule. The one notable exception to this pattern, Costa Rica, is virtually a European country, and possibly may not endure much longer. Democracy is, if anything, in even more disarray in Africa. The one African nation with any history of democratic forms, Liberia, fell to a military dictatorship several years ago which is now threatened by another military insurrection.

After even a cursory survey of the Third World, anyone can see that only a foolish ethnocentrism can account for the fond belief of many Americans that their political heritage—imperfectly received in the past by immigrants from nations having cultures closely related to that of the nation's founders—will in the future transform and overwhelm all that is alien. Such a universal constant cannot anywhere be found in the records of political history.

On Being an American in a Pluralistic Society: A Hispanic View, 1986

The National Council of La Raza, a Hispanic organization, lobbies in congress on behalf of Americans of Hispanic descent. In one of their publications, *Beyond Ellis Island: Hispanics—Immigrants and Americans,* from which the following selection is taken, they address certain beliefs about Hispanic immigration that are held in segments of the general population but have no foundation in reality. One is that Hispanics are different from older immigrants in their attitudes toward American culture and English: many people think that Hispanics are resisting assimilation, and one manifestation of this is their refusal to learn English.

La Raza makes the argument that immigrants do not think they have to shed their ethnic heritage entirely to become American and this attitude is not new but was held by the ethnic groups of the old immigration. According to La Raza, Americans of different ethnic origins share a certain set of beliefs, and it is having these beliefs that makes an individual an American.

La Raza points out that one important difference between Hispanic immigrants and the immigrants of the past is that U.S. Hispanics often travel to their countries of origin because they are close to the United States and travel to them is easy—as is the case for example of Mexico and Puerto Rico. This would seem to facilitate their continuing to speak Spanish. In addition, new immigrants from Hispanic countries often settle in Hispanic communities that already exist.

Yet, La Raza points out, Hispanics learn English at the same rate as the old immigrants did. It is a generational process that takes as long now as it did then. Moreover, an obstacle to Hispanic adults learning English is not any negative attitude they harbor toward the language but rather the lack of opportunities to study it—they do want to learn it.

Another belief that La Raza aims at correcting is that Hispanics are separatists and therefore not loyal to the United States. La Raza points to the high degree of patriotism that Hispanics have displayed in times of war as proof of their integration into American society.

Americans have always been ambivalent about immigration, cherishing their immigrant heritage while at the same time fearing new immigration. According to sociologist Charles Keely of the Population Council:

> On the one hand, the country has historically been a place of refuge, a place of new beginnings, accepting and even recruiting new settlers to build the nation and its economy. On the other hand, the theme of protectionism has found recurrent expression in the capacity of the culture and economy to absorb newcomers, in the desire to limit labor market competition and assure minimal health standards, and even in nativism and racist theories. The history of immigration policy is a dialectic of these two themes of acceptance and protection.

Source: National Council of La Raza, *Beyond Ellis Island: Hispanics—Immigrants and Americans* (Washington, D.C.: National Council of La Raza, 1990).

These two themes have dominated immigration policy debates from the birth of the nation. With rare exceptions, however, major changes in immigration policy have resulted when protectionism is in the ascendancy. Public opinion polls dating back to the late 1800s confirm that the protectionist or restrictionist view has almost always commanded a majority of popular opinion. . . .

Much of the protectionism in American attitudes toward immigration is based on fear of "different" ethnic and nationality groups—people the public believes may not become "real Americans." While a part of this fear and mistrust stems from active racism and nativism, much of it is rooted in ignorance and a lack of historical perspective. The descendants of most of the feared immigrants of the nineteenth century have become the respected mainstream Americans of today. More than a century ago, Germans were a culturally distinct, and therefore a threatening, immigrant group; today more than one-fifth of all Americans claim some German ancestry.

The process of acculturation was probably never as rapid as it appears to us in retrospect; it has usually taken several generations. However, today's mass media increase immigrant visibility and therefore may create unwarranted concerns. A century ago, the arrival of immigrants from east Europe was evident primarily in the cities where they settled. Today, the evening news makes Americans in every part of our nation aware of new Indochinese immigrants in California or Cubans in Florida. The short-term visibility of new immigrants with their distinctive language and culture can make native Americans uneasy, but over the long term, the effects of acculturation and time make these immigrants and their children and grandchildren less identifiable and more familiar. We do not notice them because they have become a part of American society.

The experience of history and the evidence of recent research both indicate that today's immigrants, like their predecessors, will become tomorrow's accepted Americans.

Immigrants become a part of American society by a process of acculturation. Typically, they do not totally assimilate; they do not lose their culture entirely and become part of a homogeneous existing culture in their new country. In fact, there is no homogeneous American culture. The melting pot was always part myth; if it existed, it would probably be incredibly boring, compared to the vibrancy and variety of American society. When differing cultures come into long-term contact, changes occur in both; the dominant culture changes least, but the acculturation process requires some adaptation by everyone. What results is a changing, developing society that adopts the strengths of its varied ethnic components.

Each major immigrant group over the past two centuries has contributed to, and enriched, American culture. The value of immigration was recognized even earlier, by the framers of our democracy. As James Madison noted during the Constitutional Convention: "That part of America which has encouraged them [immigrants] the most has advanced most rapidly in population, agriculture, and the arts."

Our pluralistic society has been identified in recent years as a salad bowl or a stew; it was more eloquently described by Horace Kallen and John Dewey as an orchestra, in which the different instruments play in harmony. From music to food to crafts, the United States is a patchwork of unique ethnic components which complement each other. Kallen and Dewey also note that the hyphen sometimes used in ethnic American designations—Mexican-American, Italian-American—connects; it need not separate.

Alexis de Tocqueville considered Americans unique in their ability to set aside their individualism when necessary for the greater good; for example, when a neighbor's barn burned down, the neighbors helped to build another. He considered Americans more able to tolerate and accept differences and less xenophobic than other peoples, attributing this to their recognition that because they were all members of different ethnic groups they themselves could be targets; he viewed this recognition as "self-interest rightly understood."

The motto of the United States, *E pluribus unum* ("from many, one"), reflects the American confidence that diversity can strengthen unity. In spite of tremendous ethnic and racial variation—or perhaps because of it—Americans are an identifiable people not because of how they look, but because of the political values they share. To "become American" is not to lose all ethnic heritage, but adopt and share certain basic beliefs. Lawrence Fuchs, former executive director of the Select Commission on Immigration and Refugee Policy, made this point:

> The genius of the American system has been that loyalty to the United States is compatible with other ties of affection—regional, local, religious, and ethnic. The ties which bind Americans are the ideals of individual freedom and equality of opportunity, regardless of ethnicity or other social characteristics.

These beliefs have been adopted and treasured by immigrants and their children for more than 200 years, regardless of their native language or place of birth.

Most Americans accept these concepts of acculturation and recognize that ours has always been a nation of immigrants. Our veneration for the Statue of Liberty reflects pride in our pluralism and our immigrant heritage. Yet many Americans also fear that today's immigrants will be different from those who have come before them, that they will not become a part of American culture.

One stated cause for concern is the relatively small number of nationality groups which currently make up most of the recent immigrant population. Recent immigrants and refugees are predominantly Hispanic (Mexican, Cuban, and Salvadoran) and Asian (Filipino, Chinese, Vietnamese, Cambodian, and Laotian). Yet historically, immigration during any single year or decade has always been dominated by just a few nationality groups. Starting in 1821, and for the next four decades, at least 35% of new immigrants to the United States were Irish. From the 1830s through the 1880s, Germans constituted at least 25% of all immigrants. Mexicans today constitute about 13 to 14% of legal immigrants and perhaps 50% of undocumented entrants; even if the largest estimates are used, Mexicans probably constitute less than 25% of total immigrants today. The actual proportion of immigrants is far lower if we exclude the large number of Mexican entrants who do not plan to stay in the United States permanently.

Another cause for fear has been the seemingly large number of immigrants in recent years. In fact, there are proportionately fewer foreign-born people in the United States now than during almost any earlier period in our history. Between 1860 and 1920, for example, the foreign-born never dropped below 13% of the total population. In 1980, the figure was 6.2%. In a 1908 survey of 37 U.S. cities, a U.S. Senate immigration commission found that 60 nationalities were represented in the school population and that 58% of all students had fathers born outside the United States. Even if Latin American immigration, legal and illegal, were to double for the next 60 years, Hispanics would still constitute only 18% of the population at the end of that time (they now constitute at least 7.2%). Notes Fuchs: "Only those who lack confidence in the acculturation power of American society could give a second thought to the idea that the number of foreign entries in recent years by itself constitutes a threat to American unity."

Concerns about acculturation frequently show themselves in public worries about whether new immigrants will learn English. Too often, this translates into a fear of bilingualism. In fact, having Americans who can speak two or more languages is not a threat; even poorly educated people in many countries speak at least two languages, as do educated persons in nearly all European countries. The legitimate concern is not whether people speak their native language, but whether they learn English. Historically, immigrants have tended to learn some English but speak their native language better, and their children have typically been bilingual. Their grandchildren, however, have almost always been English-dominant, and the native language has largely disappeared by the fourth generation. A study of the French-speaking community in the United States indicates that language shifts may be occurring even more rapidly—that children of immigrants generally are English-dominant and use French only occasionally. The research also indicates that this language shift occurs more quickly in the United States than in other countries. Many experts concerned with world economic interdependence believe that such loss of language represents a serious waste of national resources, but it has been—and remains—the norm.

Available information indicates that Hispanics follow the same acculturation process as other immigrants. Several studies have concluded that by the third generation, the vast majority of Hispanic-Americans are English-dominant. Surveys in San Antonio and Los Angeles found that 89% of Mexican-American citizens were bilingual or spoke only English; for those 18 to 25 years of age the figure was 94%. A study by the Rand Corporation found that 90% of the Mexican-American children of immigrants in California were proficient in English, and more than half of their children were monolingual English speakers. The study concluded that "the transition to English begins almost immediately and proceeds very rapidly."

This fact, however, is not always obvious, because there is significant new immigration; in communities with large Hispanic populations, new arrivals whose primary language is Spanish are much in evidence. As with earlier immigrant groups, the children and grandchildren of immigrants, speaking English, are far less visible. In addition, there is considerable movement between the United States and Puerto Rico and Latin America, which tends to encourage language maintenance. Puerto Ricans, who move freely between the island and the mainland, are educated in Spanish on the island and in English on the mainland, and many Mexican-Americans retain family ties south of the border because of the proximity of their homeland. For earlier immigrants, especially before the advent of air travel and international long-distance telephone systems, continued contact with their native country was far less likely.

Recent immigrants also face real obstacles in their quest to learn English. Only a minority of limited-English-proficient children receive special language services in school. Adult literacy programs have been severely reduced because of federal budget cuts, and almost no existing programs are geared to limited-English-proficient adults. There are far too few English as a second language programs for adult immigrants, and the result is that hundreds of thousands of new immigrants who want to learn English find it difficult to do so.

An often unspoken but very real public fear is that, rather than acculturating, Hispanic immigrants, especially Mexicans, will pursue a goal of separatism, perhaps seeking to reunite the southwestern states with Mexico. Parallels with Quebec are often drawn, but most expert observers believe that the two situations are totally dissimilar. In fact, no national Hispanic organization or leader supports such separatism, and Hispanic groups are unanimous in their advocacy of additional opportunities to learn English. People of Mexican origin do not constitute anything approaching a majority of the population in any state except New Mexico (36%), and they are increasingly dispersed. Nor do Mexican-Americans face anything approaching the religious, linguistic, political, or historical differences which separate English-speaking from French-speaking Canadians. Throughout the United States, Hispanic leaders seek increased opportunities for Hispanics to join the economic mainstream. . . .

Bilingual ballots are also sometimes attacked as preventing acculturation. In fact, available evidence indicates that one of the best ways of "Americanizing" immigrants is by helping them to participate in the political process. Bilingual ballots and assistance not only help native-born Americans who had limited educational opportunities but also encourage new citizens who are not fully English-proficient to become involved. One of the requirements of naturalization is some capacity in English, but for many older immigrants, extra help is needed at the ballot box. Such participation helps show new Americans that representative democracy is a reality, not just an ideal, in the United States.

Sometimes, other Americans express concern that Hispanics don't seem to become part of the mainstream quickly enough. This typically occurs not as a result of Hispanic preferences but because of a legacy of discrimination. Hispanics face special obstacles to acculturation, primarily because most are recognizable minorities who may encounter discrimination in housing, education, employment, and other areas of life. They must overcome the effects of limited opportunities which have kept both native-born and immigrant Hispanics concentrated in certain neighborhoods and denied them full political and economic access. Making Hispanics part of the mainstream requires eliminating discrimination and encouraging full Hispanic participation in American society.

Given such opportunities, "the behavior of the children and grandchildren of Hispanic-ethnic immigrants. . .tends to veer sharply toward middle-class norms," according to studies reported by the Select Commission on Immigration and Refugee Policy.

Perhaps the best proof of loyalty and Americanism on the part of Hispanics can be found in the stated beliefs and actions of Hispanic-Americans. All available attitude surveys show an exceptionally high level of patriotism among Hispanic-Americans, and this is reflected in their behavior. Puerto Ricans have consistently been overrepresented as members of our Armed Forces. As Henry Ramos has noted in his history of the American G.I. Forum, a national Hispanic veterans group, Hispanics were overrepresented on military casualty lists in World War II, Korea, and Vietnam. Seventeen Mexican-Americans received the Congressional Medal of Honor for action in World War II and Korea; this represents the highest proportion of Medal winners for any identifiable ethnic group, a distinction that continued in Vietnam. During World War II, not a single Spanish-surnamed soldier was reported to have deserted or was ever charged with cowardice or treason. Like the 442nd Regional Combat Team, made up of Japanese-Americans, the predominantly Mexican-American 36th Combat Divisions of Texas distinguished themselves in World War II; the 36th had the highest casualty rate of any division. . . .

More than 200 years of experience show that this nation can best meet the challenges of the twenty-first century by continuing its tradition as a nation of refuge, providing opportunities to individuals and families willing to risk the physical dangers and psychological stresses of immigration. The lessons of history tell us that the nation as a whole will benefit by keeping the torch lit, as a symbol to the world of America's unique heritage and ideals.

SUGGESTIONS FOR FURTHER READING

Frank D. Bean, et al., *Undocumented Migration to the United States*. Santa Monica, Calif.: Rand Corporation, 1990.

Stanley Feldstein and Lawrence Costello, eds., *The Ordeal of Assimilation*. New York: Anchor Books, 1974.

Oscar Handlin, *The Uprooted: The Epic Story of the Great Migrations that Made the American People*. New York: Grossett and Dunlap, 1951.

Reed Ueda, *Postwar Immigrant America: A Social History*. New York: St. Martin's Press, 1994.

Bernard A. Weisberger, *The American People*. New York: American Heritage, 1971.

8

The State, Citizenship,
and Naturalization

Since the founding of the United States there have been a number of significant ways in which state institutions, through law and the agencies of government, have come to play a role in structuring American pluralism. The laws that have created and maintained public schools are another example. Tuition-free public schools, which constitute the largest and oldest social welfare project undertaken in our history, have introduced generation after generation of young people, of both native and foreign background, to American culture. Immigration laws are an obvious example, too, for they have played a vital role in determining which peoples and individuals are allowed to reside permanently in the United States.

These state activities often have been controversial and at times have caused social conflict. For the most part, they have sought to foster homogeneity and unity, at best balancing these goals against the valued sources of diversity in the population, but at worst, especially in times of crisis as in war, making diversity the victim of a quest for a reliable sameness. This is one way in which the state has played an active role in legitimizing and in stigmatizing various groups throughout our history. State activities have also created sources of opportunity (for example, government employment, elected office, scholarships, and military careers) as well as of obligation (for example, taxes and the military draft) for residents of the United States, and in this connection have set in motion a sometimes divisive competition for public resources. Still, in a democracy, in which groups are encouraged to organize to defend and to advance their rights, such competition actually serves to advance into society's mainstream those people who are allowed to compete, even as it sets them against one another.

Naturalization is one highly significant state activity native-born Americans do not think much about. Naturalization is the conferral to foreign-born residents of such basic citizenship rights that native-born Americans enjoy as the right to live permanently in the United States and to gain access to the various privileges and protections, such as the right to vote and to hold office or to travel abroad with an American passport. If we think about this at all, it is usually in the context not of the prolonged naturalization process or even the general shape of citizen's rights, including voting, but rather of the patriotic ceremony in a federal courtroom that lies at its conclusion. It is here that immigrants take an oath of allegiance to the United States and become citizens.

It was not always as easy as it is today to take naturalization for granted. The process of conferring citizenship had implications, beyond the case of the immigrant, that were of critical significance to the shaping of the American state. For almost a century after the founding of the United States, citizenship and naturalization were highly controversial matters, at the heart of which lay at least two types of conflicts. One was the dispute between the federal government and the individual states over which of them had the power to define the requirements of citizenship for all people. The other was the question of diversity, especially in regard to race but also to some extent gender. Many native-born, white Americans were not pleased with the ease by which foreign-born whites could become citizens and thus voters, but they were even more set against African-American citizenship. In the early nineteenth century more than three million African-American slaves lived in the United States as a class of permanent foreigners in their relationship to the government. They were under the authority of the U.S. government, but in the South and, even to some extent in the North where a small percentage of the pre-Civil War black population were not enslaved, they were almost totally excluded from the protection and obligations of the law.

As a result of the Civil War and Emancipation, the Fourteenth Amendment (1868), which finally formalized a national standard of citizenship, was passed. It said simply that all native-born residents were citizens of both the states they lived in and the United States itself. The amendment did not resolve all outstanding issues of citizenship for native-born Americans. The states retained power to create qualifications, such as the length of time of residence, that worked to define the size of the voting population in state and local elections. In spite of the Fifteenth Amendment, which sought to guarantee political rights to black men, blacks were gradually disfranchised in the late nineteenth and early twentieth centuries by the actions of individual southern states. Native Americans, too, have had a complex status. Though the original Americans, they, too, lived as permanent foreigners because of a combination of racial discrimination and their ambiguous political status. While they were individuals born and living in the United States, they were often as well members of recognized, self-governing peoples residing on their own tribal lands. Only those Native Americans who abandoned tribal affiliations, left reservations, and sought to assimilate into European-American society were able to vote. Other even more basic rights, such as the right to security from attacks upon one's person, were in practice routinely violated or simply did not exist for racial minorities. Under restrictive circumstances, Asians might be allowed to immigrate to America and to work, but they could not become citizens until well into the twentieth century. Women enjoyed the full protection of laws but could not vote in most elections, anywhere in the country, until the passage of the Nineteenth Amendment (1920).

These exceptions notwithstanding, the Fourteenth Amendment did create a basis for systematically addressing the question of citizenship henceforth. On a closely related, parallel track the procedures for naturalization evolved out of the original legislation that addressed the issue in the 1790s and in 1802.

To examine the matter of naturalization and citizenship rights is to gain insight into a number of fundamental and often very divisive issues in the American past. After all, as we see in the selections in this chapter, the question of who we allow to become a citizen and thus to enjoy the full rights and obligations of citizenship exposes our assumptions about democracy and our visions of democratic equality.

Deciding Membership in the American Political Community: The First National Debate on Naturalization and Citizenship, 1790

The Constitution empowered Congress to create a national standard for defining American citizenship and a common national process by which those not born in the country could become citizens. Between 1790 and 1802, Congress debated the matter frequently and passed a variety of laws, finally settling on a formula, which was written into the Naturalization Act of 1802, that has remained largely unchanged for almost two centuries.

The basic outlines of the debate over naturalization emerged in the earliest discussion in the first Congress (1789–1790). On the one hand, there was a desire to encourage immigration in order to build up the country, and an aspiration to provide a place of refuge for people oppressed by authoritarian governments and illiberal social systems in Europe. On the other hand, there was a fear that immigration could lead to excessive and even dangerous foreign influences in American politics and government.

Out of these competing considerations, a naturalization policy began to emerge that bore the marks of compromise between these hopes and fears. Immigrants could settle in the country and obtain property, but they could not become citizens, and hence members of the political community as voters and officeholders, without waiting for five years, during which they would be expected to learn American values and habits. No sooner than three years after coming to the United States, those wishing to become citizens had to take two oaths in a court, one announcing the intention to become an American citizen and the other renouncing loyalties to foreign governments and leaders. (Thus, officially sanctioned dual citizenship was discouraged, a fact that makes the United States different today from many other societies, such as Canada, that allow for dual citizenship.) After five years of residence they were required to provide a court with satisfactory

Source: Annals of Congress, 1st Congress, 2nd Session, 1789–1790, 1109–18.

proof of good moral character and to swear attachment to the Constitution, out of which requirement grew the policy of actually testing the applicant's knowledge of American law and government.

There remained, however, significant gaps in the process for many years. The states controlled their own elections, and state criteria for participation in nonnational elections continued to be employed. In addition, local as well as federal courts were able to administer the process of citizenship, and this provided an opportunity for political machines to manipulate the process to enroll new voters in time for use in hotly contested races.

In this selection, taken from the 1790 Congressional debates on naturalization and citizenship, members of the first House of Representatives articulated their hopes and fears about naturalization. They anticipated many of the problems that would trouble the process of naturalization well into the twentieth century.

The proposed law being debated would have allowed free white immigrants to the United States to become citizens after one year of residence and upon taking an oath affirming the intention to live in and swearing allegiance to the United States. An additional two years residence, however, was necessary under the proposal before the immigrant could hold state or federal office. The debate was enlivened by an amendment offered by Representative Thomas Tucker of South Carolina who wanted to abolish the residency requirement for voting (but not for officeholding). Tucker's thinking was that since there was no residency requirement for the ownership of land, there should not be one for voting either.

The remarks by the various congressmen reprinted here react both to the proposed law and to Tucker's proposed amendment. These remarks were reported simply as summaries, so the sense of the give-and-take of the usual Congressional debate is somewhat absent. The statements are chosen to illustrate the development of typical opinions that influenced the final votes in the House of Representatives. (Some of the participants who had particularly significant insights are quoted more than once.)

Tucker's amendment was defeated. In its final form, the Naturalization Act of 1790 allowed those free white persons who had resided in the United States for two years and for at least one year in the state where they sought admission to citizenship to become citizens, if they could prove "good character" and took an oath to "support the Constitution of the United States."

*Mr. Hartley** said, he had no doubt of the policy of admitting aliens to the rights of citizenship; but he thought some security for their fidelity and allegiance was requisite besides the bare oath; that is, he thought an actual residence of such a length of time as would give a man an opportunity of esteeming the

---

*Those quoted here, from among the participants in the debates of February 3 and 4, 1790, are: Thomas Hartley (Pennsylvania), James Jackson (Georgia), John Lawrence (New York), James Madison (Virginia), John Page (Virginia), Michael Stone (Maryland), and Alexander White (Virginia).

Government from knowing its intrinsic value, was essentially necessary to assure us of a man's becoming a good citizen. The practice of almost every State in the Union countenanced a regulation of this nature; and perhaps it was owing to a wish of this kind, that the States had consented to give this power to the General Government. The terms of citizenship are made too cheap in some parts of the Union; to say, that a man shall be admitted to all the privileges of a citizen, without any residence at all, is what can hardly be expected.

The policy of the old nations of Europe has drawn a line between citizens and aliens: that policy has existed to our knowledge ever since the foundation of the Roman Empire; experience has proved its propriety, or we should have found some nation deviating from a regulation inimical to its welfare. From this is may be inferred, that we ought not to grant this privilege on terms so easy as is moved by the gentleman from South Carolina. If he had gone no further in his motion than to give aliens a right to purchase and hold lands, the objection would not have been so great; but if the words are stricken out that he has moved for, an alien will be entitled to join in the election of your officers at the first moment he puts his foot on shore in America, when it is impossible, from the nature of things, that he can be qualified to exercise such a talent; but if it was presumable that he was qualified by a knowledge of the candidates, yet we have no hold upon his attachment to the Government.

Mr. Page was of opinion, that the policy of European nations and States respecting naturalization, did not apply to the situation of the United States. Bigotry and superstition, or a deep-rooted prejudice against the Government, laws, religion, or manners of neighboring nations had a weight in that policy, which cannot exist here, where a more liberal system ought to prevail. I think, said he, we shall be inconsistent with ourselves, if, after boasting of having opened an asylum for the oppressed of all nations, and establishing a Government which is the admiration of the world, we make the terms of admission to the full enjoyment of that asylum so hard as is now proposed. It is nothing to us, whether Jews or Roman Catholics settle amongst us; whether subjects of Kings, or citizens of free States wish to reside in the United States, they will find it their interest to be good citizens and neither their religious nor political opinions can injure us if we have good laws, well executed.

Mr. White noticed the inconvenience which would result from permitting an alien to all the rights of citizenship, merely upon his coming and taking an oath that he meant to reside in the United States. Foreign merchants and captains of vessels might by this means evade the additional [taxes] laid on foreign vessels; he thought, therefore if the words were struck out, that another clause ought to be added, depriving persons of the privilege of citizenship, who left the country and staid abroad for a given length of time.

Mr. Lawrence said that the reason of admitting foreigners to the rights of citizenship among us in the encouragement of emigration, as we have a large tract of country to people. Now, he submitted to the sense of the committee, whether a term, so long as that prescribed in the bill, would not tend to restrain rather than encourage emigration? It has been said, that we ought not to admit them to vote at our elections. Will they not have to pay taxes from the time they settle amongst us? And is it not a principle that taxation and representation ought to go hand and hand? Shall we then restrain a man from having an agency in the disposal of his own money? It has been also observed, that persons might come and reside amongst us for some time, and then leave the country; he did not doubt that such might be the case, but it was not presumable, that after they had once taken an oath that they meant to reside here, and had become citizens, that they would return as soon as the occasion which required their absence had terminated.

Mr. Madison.—When we are considering the advantages that may result from an easy mode of naturalization, we ought also to consider the cautions necessary to guard against abuses. It is no doubt very desirable that we should hold out as many inducements as possible for the worthy part of mankind to come and settle amongst us, and throw their fortunes into a common lot with ours. But why is this desirable? Not merely to swell the catalogue of people. No, sir, it is to increase the wealth and strength of the community; and those who acquire the rights of citizenship, without adding to the strength or wealth of the community are not the people we are in want of. And what is proposed by the amendment is, that they shall take nothing more than an oath of fidelity, and declare their intention to reside in the United States. Under such terms, it was well observed by my colleague, aliens might acquire the right of citizenship, and return to the country from which they came, and evade the laws intended to encourage the commerce and industry of the real citizens and inhabitants of America, enjoying at the same time all the advantages of citizens and aliens.

I should be exceedingly sorry, sir, that our role of naturalization excluded a single person of good fame that really meant to incorporate himself into our society; on the other hand, I do not wish that any man should acquire the privilege, but such as would be a real addition to the wealth or strength of the United States.

It may be a question of some nicety, how far we can make our law to admit an alien to the right of citizenship, step by step; but there is no doubt we may, and ought to require residence as an essential.

Mr. Hartley said, that the subject had employed his thoughts for some time, and that he had made up his mind in favor of requiring a term of residence. The experience of all nations, and the Constitution of most of the States induced the same opinion. An alien has no right to hold lands in any country, and if they are admitted to do it in this, we are authorized to annex to it such conditions as we think proper. If they are unreasonable, they may defeat the object we have in view, but they have no right to complain; yet, considering the circumstances of this country, he was favorable to easy terms of admission, because, he thought, it might be some inducement to foreigners to come and settle among us. It has been remarked, that we must admit those whom we call citizens to all the rights of citizenship at once. This opinion, he presumed, was not well founded; the practice of this country in no instance warrants it. The Constitutions of the several States admit aliens to the privilege of citizenship, step by step; they generally require a residence for a certain time, before they are admitted to vote at elections; some of them annex to it the condition of payment of taxes and other qualifications; but he believed none of the States render a foreigner capable of being elected to serve in a legislative capacity, without a probation of some years. This kind of exception is also contemplated in the Constitution of the United States. It is there required, that a person shall be so many years an inhabitant before he can be admitted to the trust of legislating for the society. He thought, therefore, that this part of the objection is not well supported.

With respect to the policy of striking out the words altogether from the clause, and requiring no residence before a man is admitted to the rights of election, the objections are obvious. If, at any time, a number of people emigrate into a seaport town, for example, from a neighboring colony into the State of New York, will they not, by taking the oath of allegiance, be able to decide the fate of an election contrary to the wishes and inclinations of the real citizens? And are gentlemen disposed to throw such an undue influence into the hands of a foreigners? Besides, they will acquire a capacity of evading your revenue laws, intended for the encouragement of the citizens. I have mentioned this example, and might enumerate many others, to point out the impropriety of this policy; but presuming them to be within every gentleman's knowledge, I shall not enlarge upon it.

With respect to the propriety of enabling foreigners to acquire and hold lands on a qualified tenure, I have no objection to such a clause.

Mr. Stone.—I would let the term of residence be long enough to accomplish two objects, before I would consent to admit a foreigner to have any thing to do with the politics of this country. First, that he should have an opportunity of knowing the circumstances of our Government, and in consequence thereof, shall have admitted the truth of the principles we hold. Second, that he shall have acquired a taste for this kind of Government. And in order that both these things may take place, in such a full manner as to make him worthy of admission into our society, I think a term of four or seven years ought to be required. A foreigner who comes here is not desirous of interfering immediately with our politics; nor is it proper that he should. His emigration is governed by a different principle; he is desirous of obtaining and holding property. I should have no objection to his doing this, from the first moment he sets his foot on shore in America; but it appears to me, that we ought to be cautious how we admit emigrants to the other privileges of citizenship, and that for a reason not yet mentioned; perhaps it may allude to the next generation more than to this, because the present inhabitants, or most of them have been engaged in a long, hazardous and expensive war. They have been active in rearing up the present Government, and feel, perhaps, a laudable vanity in having effected what the most sanguine hardly dared to contemplate. There is no danger of these people losing what they so greatly esteem; but the admission of a great number of foreigners to all the places of Government, may tincture the system with the dregs of their former habits, and corrupt what we believe the most pure of all human institutions.

Mr. Jackson conceived the present subject to be of high importance to the respectability and character of the American name; the veneration he had for, and the attachment he had to, this country, made him extremely anxious to preserve its good fame from injury. He hoped to see the title of a citizen of America as highly venerated and respected as was that of a citizen of old Rome. I am clearly of opinion, that rather than have the common class of vagrants, paupers, and other outcasts of Europe that we had better be as we are, and trust to the natural increase of our population for inhabitants. If the motion made by the gentleman from South Carolina should obtain, such people will find an easy admission to the rights of citizenship; much too easy for the interests of the people of America. Nay, sir, the terms required by the bill on the table are, in my mind, too easy. I think, before a man is admitted to enjoy the high and inestimable privileges of a citizen of America, that something more than a mere residence amongst us is necessary. I think he ought to pass some time in a state of probation, and at the end of the term, be able to bring testimonials of a proper and decent behavior; no man, who would be a credit to the community, could think such terms difficult or indelicate: if bad men should be dissatisfied on this account, and should decline to emigrate, the regulation will have a beneficial effect; for we had better keep such out of the country than admit them into it. I conceive, sir, that an amendment of this kind would be reasonable and proper; all the difficulty will be to determine how a proper certificate of good behaviour should be obtained; I think it might be done by vesting the power in the grand jury or district courts to determine on the character of the man, as they should find it.

Mr. Jackson had an objection to any persons holding land in the United States without residence, and an intention of becoming a citizen; under such a regulation the whole Western Territory might be purchased up by the inhabitants of England, France, or other foreign nations; the landholders might combine, and send out a large tenantry, and have thereby such an interference in the Government as to overset the principles upon which it is established. It will be totally subversive of the old established doctrine, that allegiance and land go together; a person owing no allegiance to a Sovereign ought not to hold lands under its protection, because he cannot be called upon and obliged to give that support which invasion or insurrection may render necessary. But, with respect to residence and probation, before an alien is entitled to the privilege of voting at elections, I am very clear it is necessary; unless gentlemen mean to render the rank of an American citizen the maygame of the world. Shall stories be told of our citizenship, such as I have read in the *Pennsylvania Magazine* of the citizenship there? If my memory serves me right, the story runs, that at a contested election in Philadelphia, when parties ran very high, and no stone was left unturned, on either side, to carry the election, most of the ships in the harbor were cleared of their crows [sailors], who, ranged under the masters and owners, came before a Magistrate, took the oath of allegiance, and paid half a crown tax to the Collector, as the Constitution required, then went and voted, and decided the contest of the day. On the return of one of the vessels, whose crew had been employed in the affair of the election, they fell in with a shoal of porpoises off Cape Henlopen: "Ha!" said one of them, "what merry company have we got here! I wonder where they are going so cheerfully?" "Going," replied one of his comrades, "why, going to Philadelphia, to be sure, to pay taxes, and vote for Assembly men!" I hope, Mr. Chairman, we have more respect for our situation as citizens, than to expose ourselves to the taunts and jeers of a deriding world, by making that situation too cheap.

Is It Too Easy to Become an American?, 1845

In the nineteenth century, the ease with which one could become an American citizen stood in sharp contrast to the practice of most European nations, in which one could often reside legally for many years without ever becoming a member of the political community. There have always been those who believe that American citizenship is too easily attained, because the time period of five years residence is too brief or because the legally defined process is corrupted and easily violated by those, such as politicians, with an interest in increasing the number of voters. Protests have been the loudest in periods in which Americans have become preoccupied with the increasing volume of immigration and the fear of foreign influences in American life. One such period was the 1840s and 1850s when a massive wave of immigration flooded the country, originating in Germany and Ireland.

Representative Lewis Levin of Philadelphia, a leader of the Native American Party, was typical of these Americans. Members of this party were convinced, among other claims, that the antidemocratic European aristocracy and the hierarchy of the Roman Catholic Church were using Roman Catholic immigrants to subvert the American republic. This subversion was prompted by a fear that the democratic example of the United States would spread to Europe and destroy the privileges enjoyed by the Catholic clergy and the reactionary aristocrats. The answer of Levin and other nativists was not to cut off immigration, for they too accepted the economic value of immigration. Instead they wished to make it much more difficult for persons to become American citizens, by defining as twenty-one years, which was the standard then accepted in American law for the maturation of the individual, the period immigrants had to wait to become enfranchised. In effect, immigrant males, no matter what their age, were being asked to be born and grow up again in the United States in order to enter the political community and vote.

Since our last national conflict with England, the monarchs of Europe have changed their tactics, not abandoned their object. Invulnerable as they have found us to be, to all their belligerent assaults by physical power, they have since resorted to a moral and political warfare, to compel our free institutions to conform to their feudal establishments. The conflict is the same; but the weapons used are new ones—the ballot-box, the naturalization law, and a class alien vote—all of which can achieve greater destruction than their armies or their navies. Am I asked, how is this manifested? I answer, in the moral impression made on the minds of the people who are hourly brought to sympathize with foreign monarchies, and to esteem the royalist, hot from the atmosphere of thrones as equal to—nay, as superior—to the native-born American, nursed in the lap and nourished from the bosom of Democratic institutions! Yes, superior—for that is the term made use of to the native; because, as the [repre-

Source: "Naturalization Law," speech of Hon. Lewis C. Levin of Pennsylvania in the House of Representatives, December 18, 1845, *Congressional Globe,* 29th Congress, 1st Session, 1845, pp. 46–50.

sentative] from Maryland had asserted, "the alien is a citizen from choice;" and choice implies preference of a Republic, which implies superior virtue and patriotism. Now, sir, are aliens citizens by choice? To make aliens "citizens by choice," they must have no motives of a compulsory character to drive them from their native homes to seek a foreign, strange, and remote land. . . . Man must eat first, and think afterwards. Show me a nation on the face of the earth where mankind can obtain so abundantly all the comforts of life, at so little cost of labor as in the United States? Show me any nation of Europe where the mass of population do not suffer for want of subsistence? Here is the grand necessity which drives the swarms of Europe to our shores. Is not this necessity? The worst of all necessities—the physical force of famine. Can such men say they come here from "choice"—from love of freedom, or from love of bread? We may pity their destitution, but Heaven save us from lavishing ridiculous applause upon their patriotism for having chosen this country as their abode. . . .

But grant that some score or two in a thousand have made this country their abode from "choice," and not from dread of famine or lust of gold, what does it prove? Does it furnish any reason why those who are driven among us from necessity should contaminate our ballot-boxes by spurious votes, spoiled under the dictation of foreign agents? There exists no reason why we should bow down to foreign dictators, because a few—a very few—republicans have made "choice" of this country for their abode—because they preferred a free Government to a royal tyranny? No, sir; we have no aliens who are citizens from "choice."

. . . . Other parties, sir, may boast their ten thousand ideas of imbecility and corruption. We boast of but one; and that one, thank God, is honest, wise, benevolent, comprehensive: and last, not least, American. But, even on the supposition that we aimed at but one idea—the extension of the naturalization law to twenty-one years—still that would not subject us to the imputation of one idea; for such a law involves more ideas than some of our opponents appear able to comprehend. . . .

Does not a naturalization law extend to the idea of the ballot-box? Does not that idea generate the idea of the good citizen of the sound republican, of the glorious patriot? . . . And now, sir, when we propose to erect bulwarks in defense of American rights, American institutions, and the American Constitution, a spurious appeal is made in behalf of the banded foreign legion, and we are asked to substitute the liberal spirit of the Declaration of American Independence for the venerated charter of our republican rights. This suggestion has long since been made by the demagogue of Europe to whom I have alluded, and I blush to find it re-echoed on our republican shores. By which document are we bound as citizens of these United States? The Declaration of American Independence is an exposition of the rights of man, which applies to the whole human family. The Constitution is a settled system of Government for the American people only. The cry raised here of natural rights, under an organized Government, is little better than the ravings of insanity. Natural rights are the offspring of revolution, that struggle through anarchy to settled system of law. Nations have a natural right to independence, but individuals under an organized Government can claim no rights not embraced in their legal institutions. Life, liberty, and the pursuit of happiness, are recognized, defined, and limited by the law. All such fallacies produce mischief, Mr. Speaker, and none more than that which supposes naturalization to be a right, a boon, or a favor granted to the alien. No alien has a right to naturalization; neither is it granted as a boon. . . .

Exclusion is the original object of naturalization—not admission to citizenship; for, if that were the object, we should have no naturalization laws; in which case, all foreigners would become American citizens the moment they landed on our shores. To prevent this universal admission to citizenship, we frame naturalization laws, and prescribe forms that operate as a check upon the interference of foreigners in our institutions. At the epoch of the Federal convention, the broad line was drawn between native Americans and foreign emigrants. The Constitution, while it prescribed nativity as the qualification of our American rulers, also vested in Congress the power to pass uniform laws of naturalization as corresponding checks and supports of the precedence given to natives in the first and secondary offices of the Republic. Why, I ask, was this power vested in Congress? Certainly to protect American institutions from foreign influence—to secure Congress from foreign influence—to prevent aliens from filling the offices of the Republic—and to prevent the States from naturalizing aliens to suit the cupidity, ambition, and intrigue of local demagogues. . . . I have avoided touching upon the merits of the main question, which we ask to bring in proper form to the consideration of the House, and which, I repeat, a select committee will alone enable us to accomplish. Will the House permit us to place before the nation such records, drawn from the proper departments, as will show that, unless some remedy be applied to this great and growing evil, THE DAY IS NOT FAR DISTANT WHEN THE AMERICAN-BORN VOTER WILL FIND HIMSELF IN A MINORITY IN HIS OWN LAND! Or will you continue to tell us that because we are not as liberal as we might be to foreign ignorance and foreign crime, you will shut out this appeal, which comes up to you in all its freshness from the hearts of the American people?

View this great subject in any light, and it still flings back upon us the reflected rays of reason, patriotism, and philanthropy. The love of our native land is an innate, holy, and irradicable passion. Distance only strengthens it—time only concentrates the feeling that causes the tear to gush from the eye of the emigrant, as old age peoples by the vivid memory in the active present with the happy past. In what land do you behold the foreigner, who denies this passion of the heart? It is nature's most holy decree, nor is it in human power to repeal the law, which is passed on the mother's breast, and confirmed by the father's voice. The best policy of the wise statesman is to model his laws on the holy ordinances of nature. If the heart of the alien is in his native land—if all his dearest thoughts and fondest affections cluster around the altar of this native gods—let us not distune his enjoyments by placing time burden of new affections on his bosom, through the moral force of an oath of allegiance, and the onerous obligation of political duties that jar against his sympathies, and call on him to renounce feelings that he can never expel from his bosom. Let us secure him the privilege at least of mourning for his native land, by withholding obligations that he cannot discharge either with fidelity, ability, or pleasure. Give him time, sir, to wean himself from his early love. Why should he not, like our own sons, enjoy twenty-one years of infant freedom from political cares, to look around him, grow familiar with the new scene in which he finds himself placed—become acquainted with all the new and intricate relations by which man is made a sovereign by the voice of his fellow-man, and yet still remains all the responsibilities of the citizen, even while he exercises all the power of a monarch. A long list of innumerable duties will engage all his attention during his political noviciate, in addition to those comprised in reforming the errors and prejudices of the nursery, and in creating and forming new opinions, congenial to the vast field which lies spread before him in morals, politics, and life. A due reflection will convince every alien, when his passions are not inflamed by the insidious appeals of selfish demagogues, that his highest position is that of a moral agent in the full enjoyment of all the attributes of civil freedom, preparing the minds and hearts of his children to become faithful, intelligent, and virtuous republicans, born to a right that vindicates itself by the holy ties of omnipotent nature, and which, while God sanctions and consecrates, no man can dispute.

We, as Native Americans, and the people of these United States, as patriots and republicans, have now attained that climax of foreign influence, when to pause in our onward career of reforming the abuse that subjects us to the degradation, is to surrender forever the high dignity of moral independence, and the peculiar exalted, distinctive character of a homogeneous nation.

The Experience of Becoming a Citizen: New York City, 1900

As nativists often charged, the naturalization process was easily corrupted and influenced by politics. Yet both government officials and the immigrants themselves usually took it much more seriously than nativists grasped. This selection suggests both the weakness and the often unanticipated strengths of the American process of becoming a citizen. The reporter is not particularly partial to immigrants, and writes with the condescending tone that native-born Americans frequently adopted when describing foreign newcomers. Moreover, the article proceeds from the premise, which was no doubt mostly correct, that the "rush to be naturalized" usually coincided with the fulfillment of residence requirements for voting in upcoming elections. The article also reveals, however, that the immigrants have prepared themselves fairly well to answer the questions about American history and law they are asked, and that the officials who administer the process did attempt to give it the dignity that nativists charged it lacked. Those uncomfortable with mass democracy probably would not have been completely convinced that the naturalization process worked effectively, for in the end their fears were as much about losing power in their own society to people they could not completely accept as true Americans, as about how American laws were administered.

Source: New York *Evening Post*, August 7, 1900.

This is what is known as the "busy season" in naturalization work at the United States District Court. The busy season is an annual phenomenon. Especially manifest once in every four years, the present anniversary, according to the statements of the government officers at the federal building, shows every indication of being a "recordbreaker."

There is, of course, more or less naturalization business to be done throughout the year, but there seems to be a particular incentive to ambitious foreigners in the latter part of July and the early part of August. A ninety-day citizenship is required of all electors in the state before they are entitled to vote. In the case of the unnaturalized, this means that unless their papers are dated August 8, or earlier, they will not be permitted to participate in the Presidential and state elections this fall. As a matter of fact, unless the applications are signed by the Commissioner today, it will be impossible for the applicants to be sworn in by Judge Thomas tomorrow. To all intents and purposes, today is the latest period for naturalization of aliens who hope to vote this year. The applicants for citizenship have been, for the most part, perfectly well aware of that fact, for the numerous [leaders] and small politicians in both parties who cultivate the foreign vote had taken pains that they should not forget. Long before the Commissioner's court opened for business this morning, the line had begun to form. Those desirous of an early interview began to arrive at the Post Office building before seven o'clock. When Commissioner Alexander, who relieves the judges of the actual work of examining the candidates, made his appearance soon after nine, he found an interested and somewhat excited throng awaiting him. The deputy United States marshals had had their hands full for some time in attempting to arrange the crowd in an orderly array. They had formed them into two lines—one extended from Commissioner Alexander's room into the hall and to the rear of the Post Office building, and the other reached from the room of Commissioner York along the other side of the hall to the rear. When Commissioner York's applicants secured their papers, they were transferred to the tail of the line extending into Commissioner Alexander's rooms. Their eagerness, owing to the fact that no applicants would be received after today, was especially annoying to the deputy marshals. Latecomers resorted to any number of tricks to secure places near the head of the line; they were continually pushing and crowding and constantly disputed with one another for the right of precedence.

Both lines were made up, for the most part, of Russian Jews and Italians, though an occasional Irishman or German insisted upon his right to have an earlier hearing than an ordinary *dago*. At rare intervals still, an Englishman appeared to acknowledge his willingness to forswear his allegiance to the Queen. In one respect, the crowds were deceptive, for each applicant was accompanied by a witness to take the necessary oath as to the former's age, good character, and other qualifications for citizenship. Aside from the witnesses, however, the officers expected to prepare for naturalization today about 250 men, which, added to the 1,363 who have received their papers since July 18, gives a total of 1,613 for the "rush season" of 1900. The record for the same period in 1896 was 1,157.

None of the officers of the court could remember any time when they have had their hands so full in making citizens as they have had for about ten days. In the main, the present rush of foreigners for citizenship papers is attributed to the prosperity of the country. This is especially true, it was said today, in the case of the Italians, whose chief interest in the country previously had seemed to be as a temporary abiding place—a place in which to make a "little pile" and then return to their fatherland. Their anxiety to escape the military conscription and the burdensome military taxes of the Italian government have inclined them to adopt the United States as their permanent home.

Most of the aliens who appeared before Commissioner Alexander today were fairly intelligent and orderly. They attacked his questions upon the Constitution of the United States and upon a few elementary facts in American history not only without trepidation, but with considerable eagerness. Just how far these replies, which were usually correct, displayed an intelligent grasp of the principles of American government, the officers do not say. There could be no doubt that the aliens had learned their lesson well; they had of course, been coached in their answers by their compatriots for some weeks. At any time in the course of recent weeks, visitors to the Italian or Jewish quarter would have found male members of a family who were of voting age poring over slips of paper prepared and distributed by the local leaders. Nearly all the candidates had these same slips with them, upon which their eyes were riveted up to the moment that the Commissioner took them in charge. A translation of these modest treatises upon the American Constitution—for they were all printed in the language with which the candidate is most familiar—would contain such bits of information as these:

Q: Who makes the laws of the United States? A: The Congress at Washington.

Q: Of how many houses is it composed? A: Two; the House of Representatives and the Senate.

Q: How many members of the House? A: According to population.

Q: How many members of the Senate? A: Two from each state.

Q: By whom is the President elected? A: By the electors.

Q: Who is the President now? A: Mr. McKinley.

Q: Who was the first President? A: George Washington.

Q: How many Representatives from New York? A: Thirty-four.

Q: How long do they hold office? A: Two years.

Q: How many Senators? A: Two.

Q: How long do they hold office? A: Six years.

There are several other questions and answers upon the printed slips, but these are the principle ones. That the candidates learn them more or less in parrot fashion is evident when they begin to deluge the Commission with their learning. Few are so ignorant as to make Mr. McKinley the first President of the United States and General Washington the present executive, though this sometimes happens. Even today, an alien, in reply to the question as to the present President, gave the name of "William McCleveland." It is upon the fundamental principles of the Constitution, however, that they more frequently go astray. They are likely to confuse the senators and representatives, to give New York

State thirty-four men in the more dignified chamber and only two congressmen. Neither can they understand why a senator should be elected for a six-year term and a representative for two, and they are likely to say that the former are chosen by the people and the latter by the legislatures. On one question, however, they seldom go astray:

"When was the Declaration of Independence signed?" asks the Commissioner.

"July 4, 1776," comes the proud reply in a loud tone.

"Who's the Governor of New York State?" he asks, quickly, jumping from past to present history.

The sudden transition is confusing; this is as intended. The candidate stammers and shifts from one foot to the other.

"Teodoro Rosevelta!" hisses a man at the end of the line, bursting with his own stock of information and with his desire to help out a fellow countryman in trouble. He is promptly pulled out of his place by the marshal and placed at the end of the procession as a punishment for furnishing surreptitious information.

With the exception of little incidents of this kind the examiners have little trouble, and they expressed today their satisfaction both with the intelligence and the good behavior of the candidates.

Exclusion: Race and Powerlessness, 1857

The relative ease by which immigrant men could attain citizenship stood time in sharp contrast to the politically powerless condition of both women and racial minorities in the nineteenth century and even well into the twentieth century.

As the next reading makes clear, these exclusions were justified in a variety of ways specific to each group. One of the most important cases in the history of the Supreme Court, *Dred Scott v. Sandford* (1857) concerned the effort of Dred Scott, a slave, to win his freedom on the basis of a claim that years of residence in a free state, to which he had been taken by his master, gave him the right to freedom under the terms of the Constitution. Writing for the majority of seven of the nine judges of the Supreme Court, Chief Justice Roger B. Taney (1777–1864), a proslavery Southerner, argued that because there was never any intention on the part of the Founding Fathers to admit African Americans to citizenship, they had no rights under the Constitution. Thus, Dred Scott could not sue for his freedom, or anything else, in a federal court. The decision left African Americans, one of the longest-resident groups in the United States, in a state of virtual rightlessness; and without rights protected by law, they were powerless to use law and government to defend themselves against a racist white majority. Only after the Civil War, with slavery abolished and the nation facing the task of reconstructing the civil status of four million African Americans, was the citizenship of the nations' largest racial minority finally written into the

Source: Dred Scott v. Sandford, 19 Howard 393 (U.S., 1857).

Constitution. Even then, however, these formal constitutional guarantees would be widely violated for the next century.

In this excerpt from Justice Taney's decision, he argues that African Americans were never intended to be citizens by those who founded the United States and that, thus, there existed at the time no mechanism for making them citizens and endowing them with the rights and protections of citizens. Among other arguments he marshals, to make his case, Taney contrasts their status under the Constitution with that of American Indians, the nation's other longest-resident racial minority.

The question is simply this: Can a negro, whose ancestors were imported into this country, and sold as slaves, become a member of the political community formed and brought into existence by the Constitution of the United States, and as such become entitled to all the rights, and privileges, and immunities, guarantied by that instrument to the citizen? One of which rights is the privilege of suing in a court of the United States in the cases specified in the Constitution. . . .

•　•　•　•　•　•

The situation of this population was altogether unlike that of the Indian race. The latter, it is true, formed no part of the colonial communities, and never amalgamated with them in social connections or in government. But although they were uncivilized, they were yet a free and independent people, associated together in nations or tribes, and governed by their own laws. Many of these political communities were situated in territories to which the white race claimed the ultimate right of dominion. But that claim was acknowledged to be subject to the right of the Indians to occupy it as long as they thought proper, and neither the English nor colonial Governments claimed or exercised any dominion over the tribe or nation by whom it was occupied, nor claimed the right to the possession of the territory, until the tribe or nation consented to cede it. These Indian Governments were regarded and treated as foreign Governments, as much so as if an ocean had separated the red man from the white; and their freedom has constantly been acknowledged, from the time of the first emigration to the English colonies to the present day, by the different Governments which succeeded each other. Treaties have been negotiated with them, and their alliance sought for in war; and the people who compose these Indian political communities have always been treated as foreigners not living under our Government. It is true that the course of events has brought the Indian tribes within the limits of the United States under subjection to the white race; and it has been found necessary, for their sake as well as our own, to regard them as in a state of pupilage, and to legislate to a certain extent over them and the territory they occupy. But they may, without doubt, like the subjects of any other foreign Government, be naturalized by the authority of Congress, and become citizens of a State, and of the United States; and if an individual should leave his nation or tribe, and take up his abode among the white population, he would be entitled to all the rights and privileges which would belong to an emigrant from any other foreign people.

We proceed to examine the case as presented by the pleadings.

The words "people of the United States" and "citizens" are synonymous terms, and mean the same thing. They both describe the political body who, according to our republican institutions, form the sovereignty, and who hold the power and conduct the Government through their representatives. They are what we familiarly call the "sovereign people," and every citizen is one of this people, and a constituent member of this sovereignty. The question before us is, whether the class of persons described in the plea in abatement compose a portion of this people, and are constituent members of this sovereignty? We think they are not, and that they are not included, and were not intended to be included, under the word "citizens" in the Constitution, and can therefore claim none of the rights and privileges which that instrument provides for and secures to citizens of the United States. On the contrary, they were at that time considered as a subordinate and inferior class of beings, who had been subjugated by the dominant race, and, whether emancipated or not, yet remained subject to their authority, and had no rights or privileges but such as those who held the power and the Government might choose to grant them. . . .

*   *   *   *   *

It becomes necessary, therefore, to determine who were citizens of the several States when the Constitution was adopted. And in order to do this, we must recur to the Governments and institutions of the thirteen colonies, when they separated from Great Britain and formed new sovereignties, and took their places in the family of independent nations. We must inquire who, at that time, were recognised as the people or citizens of a State, whose rights and liberties had been outraged by the English Government; and who declared their independence, and assumed the powers of Government to defend their rights by force of arms.

In the opinion of the court, the legislation and histories of the times, and the language used in the Declaration of Independence, show, that neither the class of persons who had been imported as slaves, nor their descendants, whether they had become free or not, were then acknowledged as a part of the people, nor intended to be included in the general words used in that memorable instrument.

It is difficult at this day to realize the state of public opinion in relation to that unfortunate race, which prevailed in the civilized and enlightened portions of the world at the time of the Declaration of Independence, and when the Constitution of the United States was framed and adopted. But the public history of every European nation displays it in a manner too plain to be mistaken.

They had for more than a century before been regarded as beings of an inferior order, and altogether unfit to associate with the white race, either in social or political relations; and so far inferior, that they had no rights which the white man was bound to respect; and that the negro might justly and lawfully be reduced to slavery for his benefit. He was bought and sold, and treated as an ordinary article of merchandise and traffic, whenever a profit could be made by it. This opinion was at that time fixed and universal in the civilized portion of the white race. It was regarded as an axiom in morals as well as in politics, which no one thought of disputing, or supposed to be open to dispute; and men in every grade and position in society daily and habitually acted upon it in their private pursuits, as well as in matters of public concern, without doubting for a moment the correctness of this opinion.

And in no nation was the opinion more firmly fixed or more uniformly acted upon than by the English Government and English people. They not only seized them on the coast of Africa, and sold them or held them in slavery for their own use; but they took them as ordinary articles of merchandise to every country where they could make a profit on them, and were far more extensively engaged in this commerce than any other nation in the world.

The opinion thus entertained and acted upon in England was naturally impressed upon the colonies they founded on this side of the Atlantic. And, accordingly, a negro of the African race was regarded by them as an article of property, and held, and bought and sold as such, in every one of the thirteen colonies which united in the Declaration of Independence, and afterwards formed the Constitution of the United States. The slaves were more or less numerous in the different colonies, as slave labor was found more or less profitable. But no one seems to have doubted the correctness of the prevailing opinion of the time. . . .

•　•　•　•　•

We refer to these historical facts for the purpose of showing the fixed opinions concerning that race, upon which the statesmen of that day spoke and acted. It is necessary to do this, in order to determine whether the general terms used in the Constitution of the United States, as to the rights of man and the rights of the people, was intended to include them, or to give to them or their posterity the benefit of any of its provisions.

The language of the Declaration of Independence is equally conclusive:

It begins by declaring that, "when in the course of human events it becomes necessary for one people to dissolve the political bands which have connected them with another, and to assume among the powers of the earth the separate and equal station to which the laws of nature and nature's God entitle them, a decent respect for the opinions of mankind requires that they should declare the causes which impel them to the separation."

It then proceeds to say: "We hold these truths to be self-evident: that all men are created equal; that they are endowed by their Creator with certain unalienable rights; that among them is life, liberty, and the pursuit of happiness; that to secure these rights, Governments are instituted, deriving their just powers from the consent of the governed."

The general words above quoted would seem to embrace the whole human family, and if they were used in a similar instrument at this day would be so understood. But it is too clear for dispute, that the enslaved African race were not intended to be included, and formed no part of the people who framed and adopted this declaration; for if the language, as understood in that day, would embrace them, the conduct of the distinguished men who framed the Declaration of Independence would have been utterly and flagrantly inconsistent with the principles they asserted; and instead of the sympathy of mankind, to which they so confidently appeared, they would have deserved and received universal rebuke and reprobation.

Yet the men who framed this declaration were great men—high in literary acquirements—high in their sense of honor, and incapable of asserting principles inconsistent with those on which they were acting. They perfectly understood the meaning of the language they used, and how it would be understood by others; and they knew that it would not in any part of the civilized world be supposed to embrace the negro race, which, by common consent, had been excluded from civilized Governments and the family of nations, and doomed to slavery. They spoke and acted according to the then established doctrines and principles, and in the ordinary language of the day, and no one misunderstood them. The unhappy black race were separated from the white by indelible marks, and laws long before established, and were never thought of or spoken of except as property, and when the claims of the owner or the profit of the trader were supposed to need protection.

This state of public opinion had undergone no change when the Constitution was adopted, as is equally evident from its provisions and language.

The brief preamble sets forth by whom it was formed, for what purposes, and for whose benefit and protection. It declares that it is formed by the *people* of the United States that is to say, by those who were members of the different political communities in the several States; and its great object is declared to be to secure the blessings of liberty to themselves and their posterity. It speaks in general terms of the *people* of the United States, and of *citizens* of the several States, when it is providing for the exercise of the powers granted or the privileges secured to the citizen. It does not define what description of persons are intended to be included under these terms, or who shall be regarded as a citizen and one of the people. It uses them as terms so well understood, that no further description or definition was necessary.

But there are two clauses in the Constitution which point directly and specifically to the negro race as a separate class of persons, and show clearly that they were not regarded as a portion of the people or citizens of the Government then formed.

One of these classes reserves to each of the thirteen States the right to import slaves until the year 1808, if it thinks proper. And the importation which it thus sanctions was unquestionably of persons of the race of which we are speaking, as the traffic in slaves in the United States had always been confined to them. And by the other provision the States pledge themselves to each other to maintain the right of property of the master, by delivering up to him any slave who may have escaped from his service, and be found within their respective territories. By the first above-mentioned clause, therefore, the right to purchase and hold this property is directly sanctioned and authorized for twenty years by the people who framed the Constitution. And by the second, they pledge themselves to maintain and uphold the right of the master in the manner specified, as long as the Government they then formed should endure. And these two provisions show, conclusively, that neither the description of persons therein referred to, nor their descendants, were embraced in any of the other provisions of the Constitution; for certainly these two clauses were not intended to confer on them or their posterity the blessings of liberty, or any of the personal rights so carefully provided for the citizen.

No one of that race had ever migrated to the United States voluntarily; all of them had been brought here as articles of merchandise. The number that had been emancipated at that time were but few in comparison with those held in slavery; and they were identified in the public mind with the race to which they belonged, and regarded as a part of the slave population rather than the free. It is obvious that they were not even in the minds of the framers of the Constitution when they were conferring special rights and privileges upon the citizens of a State in every other part of the Union. . . .

Taney then proceeded to review the laws of the individual states, both slave holding and non-slave holding, before continuing:

It is impossible, it would seem, to believe that the great men of the slave-holding States, who took so large a share in framing the Constitution of the United States, and exercised so much influence in procuring its adoption, could have been so forgetful or regardless of their own safety and the safety of those who trusted and confided in them.

Besides, this want of foresight and care would have been utterly inconsistent with the caution displayed in providing for the admission of new members into this political family. For, when they gave to the citizens of each State the privileges and immunities of citizens in the several States, they at the same time took from the several States the power of naturalization, and confined that power exclusively to the Federal Government. No State was willing to permit another State to determine who should or should not be admitted as one of its citizens, and entitled to demand equal rights and privileges with their own people, within their own territories. The right of naturalization was therefore, with one accord, surrendered by the States, and confided to the Federal Government. And this power granted to Congress to establish a uniform rule of *naturalization* is, by the well-understood meaning of the word, confined to persons born in a foreign country, under a foreign Government. It is not a power to raise to the rank of a citizen any one born in the United States, who, from birth or parentage, by the laws of the country, belongs to an inferior and subordinate class. And when we find the States guarding themselves from the indiscreet or improper admission by other States of emigrants from other countries, by giving the power exclusively to Congress, we cannot fail to see that they could never have left with the States a much more important power—that is, the power of transforming into citizens a numerous class of persons, who in that character would be much more dangerous to the peace and safety of a large portion of the Union, than the few foreigners one of the States might improperly naturalize. The Constitution upon its adoption obviously took from the States all power by any subsequent legislation to introduce as a citizen into the political family of the United States any one, no matter where he was born, or what might be his character or condition; and it gave to Congress the power to confer this character upon those only who were born outside of the dominions of the United States. And no law of a State, therefore, passed since the Constitution was adopted, can give any right of citizenship outside of its own territory.

Shared Political Values and Language
Inform the Effort to Combat Exclusion:
American Women, 1848

The political history of a number of American groups has been characterized by the effort to attain greater power to effect the course of day-to-day existence and to help decide the direction of the nation. To that end, some have wished greater inclusion in the existing American society, while others have wished to bring about a more or less comprehensive restructuring of society, changing the basic laws and political principles of American life.

In light of the broad and long-term inequalities that have been present in the lives of some Americans, it is interesting and significant to understand the extent to which they have opted not to dream of a completely different America, but rather of a more inclusive America that is true to its own historic ideals. Evidence of this commitment to American political ideals is seen in the extent to which groups protesting exclusion have often framed a statement of protest that is patterned directly on the language, form, and ideals of the Declaration of Independence. The historian Philip S. Foner pointed this out some years ago, at the time of the Bicentennial of the Declaration of Independence, in a collection of just such statements of protest, *We, the Other People: Alternative Declarations of Independence by Labor Groups, Farmers, Women's Rights Advocates, Socialists, and Blacks, 1829–1975*.

Such was the case, for example, with the first organized convention held in the United States to demand political equality for women. About two hundred persons, including thirty-two men, met at Seneca Falls, New York, on July 19, 1848, and approved a series of resolutions on women's rights. The next selection, which was drafted at that meeting by women's rights advocate Elizabeth Cady Stanton, concerns the vote. Stanton closely followed the Declaration of Independence in drafting it. In doing so, she made the point that the assembled delegates wanted America to continue to live up to the ideals that had influenced its revolution. By using the Declaration of Independence as a model, Stanton was also able to point to the gap, in the case of women's rights, between American ideals and American realities. The document is a pointed attack on women's powerlessness and subordination to men, whom alone, it was then widely believed by most people of

Source: "Declaration of Sentiments," Elizabeth Cady Stanton, Susan B. Anthony, and Matilda Joslyn Gage, eds., *History of Woman Suffrage* (New York: Fowler and Wells, 1881), pp. 70–74.

both genders, were endowed by God and nature with the ability to govern. The very existence of this articulate document, modeled on the premier document of American liberty, subverted the argument that men alone were capable of thinking and acting politically.

When, in the course of human events, it becomes necessary for one portion of the family of man to assume among the people of the earth a position different from that which they have hitherto occupied, but one to which the laws of nature and of nature's God entitle them, a decent respect to the opinions of mankind requires that they should declare the causes that impel them to such a course.

We hold these truths to be self-evident: that all men and women are created equal; that they are endowed by their Creator with certain inalienable rights; that among these are life, liberty, and the pursuit of happiness; that to secure these rights governments are instituted, deriving their just powers from the consent of the governed. Whenever any form of government becomes destructive of these ends, it is the right of those who suffer from it to refuse allegiance to it, and to insist upon the institution of a new government, laying its foundation on such principles, and organizing its powers in such form, as to them shall seem most likely to effect their safety and happiness. Prudence, indeed, will dictate that governments long established should not be changed for light and transient causes; and accordingly all experience hath shown that mankind are more disposed to suffer, while evils are sufferable, than to right themselves by abolishing the forms to which they were accustomed. But when a long train of abuses and usurpations, pursuing invariably the same object evinces a design to reduce them under absolute despotism, it is their duty to throw off such government, and to provide new guards for their future security. Such has been the patient sufferance of the women under this government, and such is now the necessity which constrains them to demand the equal station to which they are entitled.

The history of mankind is a history of repeated injuries and usurpations on the part of man toward woman, having in direct object the establishment of an absolute tyranny over her. To prove this, let facts be submitted to a candid world.

He has never permitted her to exercise her inalienable right to the elective franchise.

He has compelled her to submit to laws, in the formation of which she had no voice.

He has withheld from her rights which are given to the most ignorant and degraded men—both natives and foreigners.

Having deprived her of this first right of a citizen, the elective franchise, thereby leaving her without representation in the halls of legislation, he has oppressed her on all sides.

He has made her, if married, in the eye of the law, civilly dead.

He has taken from her all right in property, even to the wages she earns.

He has made her, morally, an irresponsible being, as she can commit many crimes with impunity, provided they be done in the presence of her husband. In the covenant of marriage, she is compelled to promise obedience to her husband, he becoming, to all intents and purposes, her master—the law giving him power to deprive her of her liberty, and to administer chastisement.

He has so framed the laws of divorce, as to what shall be the proper causes, and in case of separation, to whom the guardianship of the children shall be given, as to be wholly regardless of the happiness of women—the law, in all cases, going upon a false supposition of the supremacy of man, and giving all power into his hands.

After depriving her of all rights as a married woman, if single, and the owner of property, he has taxed her to support a government which recognizes her only when her property can be made profitable to it.

He has monopolized nearly all the profitable employments, and from those she is permitted to follow, she receives but a scanty remuneration. He closes against her all the avenues to wealth and distinction which he considers most honorable to himself. As a teacher of theology, medicine, or law, she is not known.

He has denied her the facilities for obtaining a thorough education, all colleges being closed against her.

He allows her in Church, as well as State, but a subordinate position, claiming Apostolic authority for her exclusion from the ministry, and, with some exceptions, from any public participation in the affairs of the Church.

He has created a false public sentiment by giving to the world a different code of morals for men and women, by which moral delinquencies which exclude women from society, are not only tolerated, but deemed of little account in man.

He has usurped the prerogative of Jehovah himself, claiming it as his right to assign for her a sphere of action, when that belongs to her conscience and to her God.

He has endeavored, in every way that he could, to destroy her confidence in her own powers, to lessen her self-respect, and to make her willing to lead a dependent and abject life.

Now, in view of this entire disfranchisement of one-half the people of this country, their social and religious degradation—in view of the unjust laws above mentioned, and because women do feel themselves aggrieved, oppressed, and fraudulently deprived of their most sacred rights, we insist that they have immediate admission to all the rights and privileges which belong to them as citizens of the United States.

In entering upon the great work before us, we anticipate no small amount of misconception, misrepresentation, and ridicule; but we shall use every instrumentality within our power to effect our object. We shall employ agents, circulate tracts, petition the State and National legislatures, and endeavor to enlist the pulpit and the press in our behalf. We hope this Convention will be followed by a series of Conventions embracing every part of the country.

RESOLUTIONS

Whereas, The great precept of nature is conceded to be, that "man shall pursue his own true and substantial happiness." Blackstone in his *Commentaries* remarks, that this law of Nature being coeval with mankind, and dictated by God himself, is of course superior in obligation to any other. It is binding over all the globe, in all countries and at all times; no human laws are of any validity if contrary to this, and such of them as are valid, derive all their force, and all their validity, and all their authority, mediately and immediately, from this original; therefore,

Resolved, That such laws as conflict, in any way, with the true and substantial happiness of woman, are contrary to the great precept of nature and of no validity, for this is "superior in obligation to any other."

Resolved, That all laws which prevent woman from occupying such a station in society as her conscience shall dictate, or which place her in a position inferior to that of man, are contrary to the great precept of nature, and therefore of no force or authority.

Resolved, That woman is man's equal—was intended to be so by the Creator, and the highest good of the race demands that she should be recognized as such.

Resolved, That the women of this country ought to be enlightened in regard to the laws under which they live, that they may no longer publish their degradation by declaring themselves satisfied with their present position, nor their ignorance, by asserting that they have all the rights they want.

Resolved, That inasmuch as man, while claiming for himself intellectual superiority, does accord to woman moral superiority, it is pre-eminently his duty to encourage her to speak and teach, as she has an opportunity, in all religious assemblies.

Resolved, That the same amount of virtue, delicacy, and refinement of behavior that is required of woman in the social state, should also be required of man, and the same transgressions should be visited with equal severity on both man and woman.

Resolved, That the objection of indelicacy and impropriety, which is so often brought against woman when she addresses a public audience, comes with a very ill-grace from those who encourage, by their attendance, her appearance on the stage, in the concert, or in feats of the circus.

Resolved, That woman has too long rested satisfied in the circumscribed limits which corrupt customs and a perverted application of the Scriptures have marked out for her, and that it is time she should move in the enlarged sphere which her great Creator has assigned her.

Resolved, That it is the duty of the women of this country to secure to themselves their sacred right to the elective franchise.

Resolved, That the equality of human rights results necessarily from the fact of the identity of the race in capabilities and responsibilities.

Resolved, therefore, That, being invested by the Creator with the same capabilities, and the same consciousness of responsibility for their exercise, it is demonstrably the right and duty of woman, equally with man, to promote every righteous cause by every righteous means; and especially in regard to the great subjects of morals and religion, it is self-evidently her right to participate with her brother in teaching them, both in private and in public, by writing and by speaking, by any instrumentalities proper to be used, and in any assemblies proper to be held; and this being a self-evident truth growing out of the divinely implanted principles of human nature, any custom or authority adverse to it, whether modern or wearing the hoary sanction of antiquity, is to be regarded as a self-evident falsehood, and at war with mankind.

Excluding Asians, 1889

Most Asian immigration to the United States has come from China and Japan. It began in the mid-nineteenth century, at the time of the California Gold Rush, when thousands of Chinese laborers joined the flood of immigrants, generally single men, from all over the world and the United States going to find opportunity in California. Immigration from Asia was never large relative to that from Europe, but it was concentrated in the West, especially in California, where it was highly unpopular among the majority white population. Differences of race and culture between Asians and European Americans provide an explanation for this white hostility, as does the economic competition of Asians, who were often willing to work for much lower wages and thus were blamed for threatening the living standards of other workers.

In the 1870s a growing demand for exclusion of Asians, coming from California, led Congress to act. Beginning in 1882 and 1888, a series of laws were passed that barred Chinese from entering the United States and made it impossible for the existing Chinese population to become naturalized. Additional laws and some court decisions would extend this policy to the Japanese, East Asians, and other Asian peoples during the next half century, so that Asians, and particularly Asian men, might be allowed to enter the country and to work but could never hope to become citizens. Asian immigration and naturalization were not placed on the same plane with European immigration until as late as the mid-twentieth century, when Congress passed the McCarran-Walter Act in 1952.

The Chinese population in the United States when these restrictive laws were passed in the 1880s was allowed to stay, but if individuals left the country they could be barred from returning. The Chinese population largely comprised single men or men who had left their families in China, often in the hope that they would someday be able to bring them to the United States. The new laws, which now barred Chinese women from entering the country, imposed great hardship, because they made family reconstitution impossible and made it impossible as well for those single Chinese men who wished to stay in the United States to find Chinese wives.

Under a treaty agreed to by both China and the United States in 1868, both nations had pledged to the mutual protection of those of their citizens resident in the other country. The laws of 1882 and 1888 certainly contradicted this treaty. In a case involving a Chinese laborer who had resided in the United States, gone back to China, and then attempted to reenter the United States, the Supreme Court was asked to decide whether Congress

Source: Chae Chan Ping v. United States, 130 U.S. 581 (1889).

could, in fact, take the step of nullifying the terms of a treaty, in spite of the fact that it was an agreement with another sovereign nation. In a unanimous decision the justices answered emphatically. "Yes." They argued the highly contestable point that treaties carried no greater obligation than other acts of Congress, and that Congress frequently revised its previous actions. Underlying this constitutional point, however, is the subtext of the decision. In a selection from that decision, which was written by Judge Stephen J. Field, we see that, even as it praised the Chinese for their industriousness, the court accepted the racial stereotypes and fears that haunted Californians when they considered Chinese immigration and thus, allowed prejudice to dictate policy and law.

. . . The discovery of gold in California in 1848, as is well known, was followed by a large immigration thither from all parts of the world, attracted not only by the hope of gain from the mines, but from the great prices paid for all kinds of labor. The news of the discovery penetrated China, and laborers came from there in great numbers, a few with their own means, but by far the greater number under contract with employers, for whose benefit they worked. These laborers readily secured employment, and, as domestic servants, and in various kinds of out-door work, proved to be exceedingly useful. For some years little opposition was made to them except when they sought to work in the mines, but, as their numbers increased, they began to engage in various mechanical pursuits and trades, and thus came in competition with our artisans and mechanics, as well as our laborers in the field.

The competition steadily increased as the laborers came in crowds on each steamer that arrived from China, or Hong Kong, an adjacent English port. They were generally industrious and frugal. Not being accompanied by families, except in rare instances, their expenses were small; and they were content with the simplest fare, such as would not suffice for our laborers and artisans. The competition between them and our people was for this reason altogether in their favor, and the consequent irritation, proportionately deep and bitter, was followed, in many cases, by open conflicts, to the great disturbance of the public peace.

The differences of race added greatly to the difficulties of the situation. Notwithstanding the favorable provisions of the new articles of the treaty of 1868, by which all the privileges, immunities, and exemptions were extended to subjects of China in the United States which were accorded to citizens or subjects of the most favored nation, they remained strangers in the land, residing apart by themselves, and adhering to the customs and usages of their own country. It seemed impossible for them to assimilate with our people or to make any change in their habits or modes of living. As they grew in numbers each year the people of the coast saw, or believed they saw, in the facility of immigration, and in the crowded millions of China, where population presses upon the means of subsistence, great danger that at no distant day that portion of our country would be overrun by them unless prompt action was taken to restrict their immigration. The people there accordingly petitioned earnestly for protective legislation.

In December, 1878, the convention which framed the present constitution of California, being in session, took this subject up, and memorialized Congress upon it, setting forth, in substance, that the presence of Chinese laborers had a baneful effect upon the material interests of the State, and upon public morals; that their immigration was in numbers approaching the character of an Oriental invasion, and was a menace to our civilization; that the discontent from this cause was not confined to any political party, or to any class or nationality, but was well-nigh universal; that they retained the habits and customs of their own country, and in fact constituted a Chinese settlement within the State, without any interest in our country or its institutions; and praying Congress to take measures to prevent their further immigration. This memorial was presented to Congress in February, 1879.

So urgent and constant were the prayers for relief against existing and anticipated evils, both from the public authorities of the Pacific Coast and from private individuals, that Congress was impelled to act on the subject. Many persons, however, both in and out of Congress, were of opinion that so long as the treaty remained unmodified, legislation restricting immigration would be a breach of faith with China. A statute was accordingly passed appropriating money to send commissioners to China to act with our minister there in negotiating and concluding by treaty a settlement of such matters of interest between the two governments as might be confided to them.

This court is not a sensor of the morals of other departments of the government; it is not invested with any authority to pass judgment upon the motives of their conduct. When once it is established that Congress possesses the power to pass an act, our province ends with its construction, and its application to cases as they are presented for determination. Congress has the power under the Constitution to declare war, and in two instances where the power has been exercised—in the war of 1812 against Great Britain, and in 1846 against Mexico—the propriety and wisdom and justice of its action were vehemently assailed by some of the ablest and best men in the country, but no one doubted the legality of the proceeding, and any imputation by this or any other court of the United States upon the motives of the members of Congress who in either case voted for the declaration, would have been justly the cause of animadversion. We do not mean to intimate that the moral aspects of legislative acts may not be proper subjects of consideration. Undoubtedly they may be, at proper times and places, before the public, in the halls of Congress, and in all the modes by which the public mind can be influenced. Public opinion thus enlightened, brought to bear upon legislation, will do more than all other causes to prevent abuses; but the province of the courts is to pass upon the validity of laws, not to make them, and when their validity is established, to declare their meaning and apply their provisions. All else lies beyond their domain.

There being nothing in the treaties between China and the United States to impair the validity of the act of Congress of October 1, 1888, was it on any other ground beyond the competency of Congress to pass it? If so, it must be because it was not within the power of Congress to prohibit Chinese laborers who had at the time departed from the United States, or should subsequently depart, from returning to the United States. Those laborers are not citizens of the United States; they are aliens. That the government of the United States, through the action of the legislative department, can exclude aliens from its territory is a proposition which we do not think open to controversy. Jurisdiction over its own territory to that extent is an incident of every independent nation. It is a part of its independence. If it could not exclude aliens it would be to that extent subject to the control of another power.

For local interests the several States of the Union exist, but for national purposes, embracing our relations with foreign nations, we are but one people, one nation, one power.

To preserve its independence, and give security against foreign aggression and encroachment, is the highest duty of every nation, and to attain these ends nearly all other considerations are to be subordinated. It matters not in what form such aggression and encroachment come, whether from the foreign nation acting in its national character or from vast hordes of its people crowding in upon us. The government, possessing the powers which are to be exercised for protection and security, is clothed with authority to determine the occasion on which the powers shall be called forth; and its determination, so far as the subjects affected are concerned, are necessarily conclusive upon all its departments and officers. If, therefore, the government of the United States, through its legislative department, considers the presence of foreigners of a different race in this country, who will not assimilate with us, to be dangerous to its peace and security, their exclusion is not to be stayed because at the time there are no actual hostilities with the nation of which the foreigners are subjects.

SUGGESTIONS FOR FURTHER READING

David H. Bennett, *The Party of Fear: From Nativist Movements to the New Right in American History*. New York: Vintage-Random House, 1990.

Ellen Carol DuBois, *Feminism and Suffrage: The Emergence of An Independent Women's Movement in America, 1848–1869*. Ithaca, NY: Cornell University Press, 1978.

Bill Ong Hing, *Making and Remaking Asian America through Immigration Policy, 1850–1990*. Stanford, Calif.: Stanford University Press, 1993.

John Higham, *Strangers in the Land: Patterns of American Nativism, 1860–1925*. Rev. Ed. New York: Atheneum, 1963.

Kenneth L. Karst, *Belonging to America: Equal Citizenship and the Constitution*. New Haven, Conn.: Yale University Press, 1989.

Part V

Enduring Conflicts

9

The Question of a National Language

Legend has it that in 1795 the U.S. Congress almost made German the official language of the United States, but the proposal lost by one vote. Actually, a group of Virginia Germans proposed that all federal laws be printed in German as well as in English and it was this proposal that lost by one vote. The proposal itself and the closeness of the vote reflected the fact that many German immigrants were choosing consciously to retain their language in America. This situation caused alarm in some natives, including—twenty some years before the republic was founded—one Benjamin Franklin. Germans were only one of several linguistic minority groups living in America when the nation was founded. There were also, for instance, groups from other non-English-speaking European countries, including many refugees from the French Revolution. Though the German proposal was defeated in Congress, the general attitude in the new republic was one of tolerance toward the use of languages other than English in public life. This was motivated in part by the need to secure the loyalty of foreign groups to the fledgling republic and in part by a favorable disposition toward the many foreigners who had fought alongside the revolutionaries in the War of Independence.

At the beginning of the nation, people who thought that English should be the exclusive language of public life were not in the majority. The majority of citizens in the former colonies spoke English as their mother tongue and apparently did not perceive any threat to English from the use of other languages. The existence of a generally favorable attitude toward the public use of other languages explains why the framers of the Constitution saw no need to include in it any declaration that English was the official language of the United States. On the other hand, the climate of tolerance toward European languages did not extend to the languages of the indigenous peoples that the American republic vanquished in its inexorable expansion toward the west. Indian children on reservations were taught in English-only schools. The general policy was to stamp out what authorities considered "barbarous" languages.

At the dawn of the nation, there was some debate about the question of a national language. Anti-British sentiment led some people to propose that the new nation adopt a language different from English—some proposed Hebrew, others Greek. But the main preoccupation was not whether English should or should not be used but rather what kind of English should be used. Noah Webster began his efforts to standardize American English according to educated usage in the United States, not in Britain. And John Adams proposed an American Academy of the language that would improve and refine English. Adams' proposal did not prosper because then—as later in history—most Americans believed that English could take care of itself.

Today, those who think that the use of other languages poses no threat to English will find support for their view in the history of ethnic languages in America. No matter how loyal an immigrant group was to its mother tongue, language loyalty was usually felt only by adults. Children learned English and tended to use it exclusively, passing it along to their own children. After a few generations the ethnic language was totally lost.

One enduring myth is that the switch to English occurred very rapidly among immigrant children of the past, thanks to English-only schools where they acquired the preparation that allowed them later, as adults, to enter the middle class. However, the record indicates that many children of the great European immigration waves of the late nineteenth century and early twentieth century performed poorly in schools because they did not know English well. Many of them eventually dropped out and could take only jobs that did not require a lot of education. As late as 1950, large numbers of whites in the working class were European ethnics.

Today, belief in the efficiency of English-only schools of the distant past is usually accompanied by the belief that contemporary immigrants are not learning English fast enough and in fact have no desire to learn it. History shows that this accusation was leveled against immigrants in the past. It was probably false. Opinion polls conducted among immigrant parents in the 1980s showed that the overwhelming majority of them thought it very important for their children to learn English and wanted to learn English themselves.

The belief that English is secure in the United States and no special legislation is needed to protect it has been dominant in American history. However, there have always been people for whom the persistent use of an ethnic language has meant not only a threat to English but to the nation as well. In this view, if an immigrant group is not shedding its language quickly, it means that the members of that group harbor separatist views: they want to create their own nation within the nation and this will lead to political fragmentation and the destruction of national unity when every immigrant group chooses to do the same. To people who think that way, English is the most important common bond that has held the nation together throughout its history. In the face of the threat posed by other languages, English-only advocates have proposed legislation mandating that no language other than English should be used in public life.

An early success for English-only forces came in 1920 when a state constitutional amendment made English the official language of the State of Nebraska and specified that all official dealings as well as all education had to be in English. This was the product of anti-German sentiment remaining in the state after World War I.

In 1923 Montana Representative Washington J. McCormick introduced a bill in Congress that would make *American*, not English, the official language of the United States. McCormick was inspired by anti-British rather than anti-ethnic sentiments, but it was the first attempt to establish an official language at the federal level. McCormick's proposal did not prosper. However, it inspired the passing of a state law making American the official language of Illinois. In 1969, the Illinois legislature passed a law changing "American" to English, making Illinois only the second state after Nebraska to have an official language.

Official-English efforts came very much to the fore in the 1980s as a response to what English-only advocates regarded as a dangerous rise in the public use of foreign languages, especially Spanish. To English-only advocates, two particularly alarming manifestations of this rise were Congress mandating voting ballots and voting information in languages other than English and the funding by the federal government of bilingual education programs (serving primarily Hispanics).

Non-English voting ballots and related material were mandated by the Voting Rights Act as amended in 1975, and were intended to incorporate non-English speakers into the political process. To English-only advocates, such ballots discouraged the learning of English and encouraged manipulation of voters by ethnic bosses. Proponents of bilingual ballots countered that the record showed an increase in voter participation in the areas in which they were used, and naturalized immigrants still wanted to learn English and were trying to do so.

As to bilingual education, English-only advocates characterized it as an ineffective method of educating non-English-speaking children and a source of separatist feelings. To English-only advocates, teaching non-English-speaking children in their native language prevented their learning English; in addition, such programs, in promoting the culture of the child, prevented assimilation into the American mainstream.

Modern public bilingual education began in metropolitan Miami, Florida, in 1963, with the establishment of an experimental program serving the children of Cuban exiles. The program proved successful in teaching the children English while maintaining the use of their native Spanish, as their parents desired. In the mid-sixties the feasibility of bilingual education attracted the attention of Chicano activists who wanted to put an end to the educational failures of Mexican children in English-only schools in the Southwest. Chicano pressure eventually brought about the passing by Congress of the 1968 Bilingual Education Act, which provided funding for demonstration programs nationwide. These programs served only a small percentage of children of no or limited English-speaking ability.

The law was revised in 1978 to specify that programs were to be transitional only: as soon as children learned English, they would be transferred to regular programs. No funds would be provided to maintain the native language of the child. In the late seventies transitional bilingual education was the method that the federal government insisted upon. A 1984 revision allowed the establishment of programs that would maintain the native language. However, in the typical bilingual program of the late twentieth century, children were "exited" early and placed in regular English-only programs. Some programs were bilingual only in name: all instruction was actually in English, but special English language instruction was provided. In addition, bilingual education programs continued to serve only a relatively small portion of the population in need of help.

Despite all these facts, opponents of bilingual education depicted bilingual education as actually promoting the educational failure of students by teaching them in their native tongue instead of in English. Defenders of bilingual education countered that instruction in English was by law an obligatory component of any federally funded program. Furthermore, they pointed out that quality maintenance programs, such as the one established for Cubans in the early sixties, proved to be successful. In fact, they argued, when those programs were compared with transitional programs, it was found that the longer the children were taught in Spanish the better they learned English and the better they performed in courses taught in English. They also pointed out that transitional bilingual programs exited the children too soon. Children might be good in communicating orally in English (they had learned "playground" English) but their English was not sufficiently developed for them to do well in courses taught in English (they still lacked "academic" English). These considerations did not reach the general public, where they would have been at odds with the view—commonsensical to many—that young children have no trouble picking up a new language.

The characterization of bilingual education as an expensive, inefficient method found an echo in many white ethnics who resented the expense on the grounds that their ancestors learned English without the help of any special program. But people opposed to bilingual education on those grounds did not tend to contemplate the fact that many young immigrant children of the past had been academically unsuccessful.

At the beginning of the eighties, English-only organizations were formed to combat the federal government's efforts on behalf of non-English speaking groups in electoral matters and in education. Perhaps the most successful of these organizations was U.S. English, founded in 1983 by S. I. Hayakawa and John Tanton.

California Republican Hayakawa, a naturalized Canadian immigrant of Japanese descent and a noted linguist, served in the U.S. Senate from 1977 to 1983. Tanton, a physician from Michigan, headed also an organization that advocated restrictions to immigration. He resigned from U.S. English in 1988 after a memorandum of his was made public in which he expressed strong racist and nativist views regarding Mexican immigrants.

U.S. English lobbied Congress for repealing laws mandating multilingual ballots and voting materials and for limiting government funding for bilingual education to short-term transitional programs only. It also lobbied for a constitutional amendment declaring English the official language of the United States. The first English Language Amendment had been introduced by then Senator Hayakawa in 1981.

In the mid-nineties, efforts to bring about a constitutional language amendment had not yet met with success. The controversy over bilingual education was dormant and the government was still funding programs, though at a lower level. In addition, bilingual ballots continued in use. But U.S. English was successful, especially in the eighties, in bringing about English-only legislation at the state and local levels. Between 1980 and 1990 fifteen states adopted English as their official language. Joining Nebraska and Illinois were Alabama, Arizona, Arkansas, California, Colorado, Florida, Georgia, Indiana, Kentucky, Mississippi, North Carolina, North Dakota, South Carolina, Tennessee, and Virginia. Perhaps the most restrictive law—incorporated into the state constitution—was that of Arizona, whose Article 28 required every state official to use English exclusively in official business. A bilingual state insurance claims administrator challenged the law in court because she feared that her using Spanish with Hispanic clients would violate her oath to uphold the state constitution. In 1990 Article 28 was ruled unconstitutional by a federal judge, who found it in violation of the First Amendment of the U.S. Constitution protecting free speech. The ruling did not immediately affect official English laws in other states, but introduced the possibility of challenging such laws in court.

They Should Speak English: Benjamin Franklin Complains About the Germans in Pennsylvania, 1753

On May 9, 1753, twenty-three years before the founding of the United States, Benjamin Franklin wrote a letter to Peter Collinson, a British member of Parliament, complaining about the Germans in Pennsylvania. Franklin seems to be particularly riled about the Germans' linguistic behavior: they are using their native language in their business activities and even in the courts of justice, where they are allowed to do so—to Franklin's chagrin.

Franklin's accusations and warnings are early manifestations of a theme that has recurred throughout American history and has involved languages and nationalities other than German: "There are too many of them and they keep on using their language" is the recurring refrain. It was said for example of Italians and Yiddish-speaking Jews in the late nineteenth and early twentieth century and of Hispanics and Asian groups in the late twentieth century.

Source: The Papers of Benjamin Franklin, ed. Leonard W. Labaree (New Haven, Conn.: Yale University Press. 1961), Vol. 4, p. 234.

Those [Germans] who come hither are generally the most ignorant Stupid Sort of their own Nation, and as Ignorance is often attended with Credulity when Knavery would mislead it, and with Suspicion when Honesty would set it right; and as few of the English understand the German Language, and so cannot address them either from the Press or Pulpit, 'tis almost impossible to remove any prejudices they once entertain. Their own Clergy have very little influence over the people; who seem to take an uncommon pleasure in abusing and discharging the Minister on every trivial occasion. Not being used to Liberty, they know not how to make a modest use of it. . . .

I remember when they modestly declined intermeddling in our Elections, but now they come in droves, and carry all before them, except in one or two Counties; Few of their children in the Country learn English; they import many Books from Germany; and of the six printing houses in the Province, two are entirely German, two half German half English, and but two entirely English; They have one German News-paper and one half-German. Advertisements, intended to be general are now printed in Dutch [German] and English; the Signs in our Streets have inscriptions in both languages, and in some places only German: They begin of late to make all their Bonds and other legal Writings in their own Language, which (though I think it ought not to be) are allowed good in our Courts, where the German Business so increases that there is continued need of Interpreters; and I suppose in a few years they will also be necessary in the Assembly, to tell one half of our Legislators what the other half say; In short, unless the stream of their importation could be turned from this to other Colonies, as you very judiciously propose, they will soon so out number us, that all the advantages we have will not, in My Opinion, be able to preserve our language, and even our government will become precarious.

Attempting to Establish English as the Official Language: Three Proposed Amendments to the Constitution of the United States, 1981, 1983, 1989

Between 1981 and 1990 sixteen English Language amendments were introduced in the U.S. Congress. We reproduce three of them in the following selection.

English Language amendments have generally been of two types. One type—of which the 1983 version is an example—mainly declares that English is the official language of the nation and leaves to Congress and the courts to determine what the consequences of this declaration should be. The other type—of which the 1981 and 1989 versions are examples—*mandates* the use of English at all levels of government but makes exceptions for certain areas such as public safety, court interpretation, and education—

Source: S.J. Res. 72 (1981), S.J. Res. 167 (1983), H.J. Res. 81 (1989), U.S. Congress.

the latter especially with regard to the teaching of English to foreigners and of foreign languages to those who know English. Notice that the 1989 version, in providing more exceptions, is less restrictive than the 1981 version, which allows exceptions only in the area of bilingual education.

Notice also that the 1981 version was introduced by Senator S. I. Hayakawa, who two years later would launch U.S. English, which, as you will recall, has lobbied Congress for an English Language amendment. Hayakawa's view that bilingual education should be exclusively transitional is reflected in Section 5 of the amendment sponsored by him.

For English to become the official language, a constitutional language amendment would have to be approved by two-thirds of each house of Congress and ratified by three-quarters of state legislatures. The Senate held hearings on official English in 1984, and the House in 1988. But the decade ended without any English Language amendment coming to a vote in Congress. Not even in a Congressional committee was a vote taken on such an amendment. This reflected perhaps the sentiment of a majority of Americans that an English Language amendment was not needed because the dominant status of English was secure.

S.J. RES. 72 (1981)

Sponsored by Senator S. I. Hayakawa (R-Calif.)

Section 1. The English language shall be the official language of the United States.

Section 2. Neither the United States nor any State shall make or enforce any law which requires the use of any language other than English.

Section 3. This article shall apply to laws, ordinances, regulations, orders, programs, and policies.

Section 4. No order or decree shall be issued by any court of the United States or of any State requiring that any proceedings, or matters to which this article applies, be in any language other than English.

Section 5. This article shall not prohibit educational instruction in a language other than English as required as a transitional method of making students who use a language other than English proficient in English.

Section 6. The Congress and the States shall have power to enforce this article by appropriate legislation.

S.J. RES. 167 (1983)

Sponsored by Senators Walter Huddleston (D-Ky.) and Steve Symms (R-Idaho)

Section 1. The English language shall be the official language of the United States.

Section 2. The Congress shall have the power to enforce this article by appropriate legislation.

H.J. RES. 81 (1989)

Sponsored by Representative Norman Shumway (R-Calif.)

Section 1. The English language shall be the official language of the United States.

Section 2. Neither the United States nor any State shall require, by law, ordinance, regulation, order, decree, program, or policy, the use in the United States of any language other than English.

Section 3. This article shall not prohibit any law, ordinance, regulation, order, decree, program, or policy—

(1) to provide educational instruction in a language other than English for the purpose of making students who use a language other than English proficient in English,

(2) to teach a foreign language to students who are already proficient in English,

(3) to protect public health and safety, or

(4) to allow translators for litigants, defendants, or witnesses in court cases.

Section 4. The Congress and the States may enforce this article by appropriate legislation.

Language and Equality in Education: The Supreme Court *Lau* Decision, 1974

In the wake of the Civil Rights Movement that led to the passing of the Civil Rights Act of 1964, Chicano (Mexican-American) organizations in the Southwest—seeking to put an end to the failure of Chicano children in English-only schools—agitated for the establishment of bilingual education programs. Pressure from Chicanos led eventually to the passing of the Bilingual Education Act of 1968. This legislation set up demonstration programs in areas with populations of children who spoke little or no English. But the programs served a small percentage of these children nationwide and school districts were under no legal obligation to use such programs.

In 1970, a class-action suit, on behalf of Kinney Lau and 1,789 other Chinese children enrolled in public schools in San Francisco, California, was brought against the San Francisco Unified School District. The suit argued that the plaintiffs—the children—were not being provided with an equal education because all instruction and materials were in English, a language these children did not understand. Furthermore, it argued that English-only education for non-English-speaking children was unconstitutional because it violated the Fourteenth Amendment, which guarantees to all citizens the equal protection of the laws. It also argued that such education was illegal under Title VI of the Civil Rights Act, which rules that "no person in the

Source: 414 U.S. 563 (1974).

United States shall . . . be subjected to discrimination under any program receiving Federal financial assistance" and the San Francisco School District was receiving funds from the federal government.

The case, known as *Lau v. Nichols,* was decided by the Supreme Court in 1974. Overturning an earlier decision by a lower court, the Court ruled unanimously in favor of the Chinese students. However, the Court avoided the constitutional argument and ruled only on the basis of the Civil Rights Act. The Court ruled that English-only programs violated the civil rights of non-English-speaking students on the ground of national origin and it determined that some educational remedy must be provided for these students. However, it left it up to local school boards to determine what the specific remedy should be.

The *Lau* decision later served as the basis for litigation against school boards that were not providing language services to students of limited English-speaking ability.

This class suit brought by non-English-speaking Chinese students against officials responsible for the operation of the San Francisco Unified School District seeks relief against the unequal educational opportunities which are alleged to violate, *inter alia,* the Fourteenth Amendment. No specific remedy is urged upon us. Teaching English to the students of Chinese ancestry who do not speak the language is one choice. Giving instructions to this group in Chinese is another. There may be others. Petitioners ask only that the Board of Education be directed to apply its expertise to the problem and rectify the situation. . . .

The Court of Appeals reasoned that "every student brings to the starting line of his educational career different advantages and disadvantages caused in part by social, economic and cultural background, created and continued completely apart from any contribution by the school system." Yet in our view the case may not be so easily decided. This is a public school system of California and §71 of the California Education Code states that "English shall be the basic language of instruction in all schools." That section permits a school district to determine "when and under what circumstances instruction may be given bilingually." That section also states as "the policy of the state" to insure "the mastery of English by all pupils in the schools." And bilingual instruction is authorized "to the extent that it does not interfere with the systematic, sequential, and regular instruction of all pupils in the English language."

Moreover, §8573 of the Education Code provides that no pupil shall receive a diploma of graduation from grade 12 who has not met the standards of proficiency in "English," as well as other prescribed subjects. Moreover, by §12101 of the Education Code (Supp. 1973) children between the ages of six and 16 years are (with exceptions not material here) "subject to compulsory full-time education."

Under these state-imposed standards there is no equality of treatment merely by providing students with the same facilities, textbooks, teachers, and curriculum; for students who do not understand English are effectively foreclosed from any meaningful education. Basic English skills are at the very core of what these public schools teach. Imposition of a requirement that, before a child can effectively participate in the educational program, he must already have acquired those basic skills is to make a mockery of public education. We know that those who do not understand English are certain to find their classroom experiences wholly incomprehensible and in no way meaningful.

We do not reach the Equal Protection Clause argument which has been advanced but rely solely on §601 of the Civil Rights Act of 1964 to reverse the Court of Appeals. That section bans discrimination based "on the ground of race, color, or national origin," in "any program or activity receiving federal financial assistance." The school district involved in this litigation receives large amounts of federal financial assistance. The Department of Health, Education, and Welfare (H.E.W.), which has authority to promulgate regulations prohibiting discrimination in federally assisted school systems, in 1968 issued one guideline that "[s]chool systems are responsible for assuring that students of a particular race, color, or national origin are not denied the opportunity to obtain the education generally obtained by other students in the system." In 1970 H.E.W. made the guidelines more specific, requiring school districts that were federally funded "to rectify the language deficiency in order to open" the instruction to students who had "linguistic deficiencies." . . .

It seems obvious that the Chinese-speaking minority receive fewer benefits than the English-speaking majority from respondents' school system, which denies them a meaningful opportunity to participate in the educational program—all earmarks of the discrimination banned by the Regulations. In 1970 H.E.W. issued clarifying guidelines which include the following:

> Where inability to speak and understand the English language excludes national origin-minority group children from effective participation in the educational program offered by a school district, the district must take affirmative steps to rectify the language deficiency in order to open its instructional program to these students.
>
> Any ability grouping or tracking system employed by the school system to deal with the special language skill needs of national origin-minority group children must be designed to meet such language skill needs as soon as possible and must not operate as an educational deadend or permanent track.

Respondent school district contractually agreed to "comply with Title VI of the Civil Rights Act of 1964 . . . and all requirements imposed by or pursuant to the Regulation" of H.E.W. which are "issued pursuant to that title . . ." and also immediately to "take any measures necessary to effectuate this agreement." The Federal Government has power to fix the terms on which its money allotments to the States shall be disbursed. Whatever the limits of that power, they have not been reached here. Senator Humphrey, during the floor debates on the Civil Rights Act of 1964, said:

> Simple justice requires that public funds, to which all taxpayers of all races contribute, not be spent in any fashion which encourages, entrenches, subsidizes, or results in racial discrimination

We accordingly reverse the judgment of the Court of Appeals and remand the case for the fashioning of appropriate relief. . . .

Justice Harry Blackmun, who concurred in the decision, added the following caveat, joined by Chief Justice Warren Burger:

Against the possibility that the Court's judgment may be interpreted too broadly, I stress the fact that the children with whom we are concerned here number about 1,800. This is a very substantial group that is being deprived of any meaningful schooling because the children cannot understand the language of the classroom. We may only guess as to why they have no exposure to English in their preschool years. Earlier generations of American ethnic groups have overcome the language barrier by earnest parental endeavor or by the hard fact of being pushed out of the family or community nest and into the realities of broader experience.

I merely wish to make plain that when, in another case, we are confronted with a very few youngsters, or with just a single child who speaks only German or Polish or Spanish or any language other than English, I would not regard today's decision . . . as conclusive upon the issue whether the statute and the guidelines require the funded school district to provide special instruction. For me, numbers are at the heart of this case and my concurrence is to be understood accordingly.

Speaking for English as the Official Language: A U.S. Senator Explains Why He Is Sponsoring an English Language Amendment to the Constitution, 1983

Kentucky Democrat Walter Huddleston represented his state in the U.S. Senate from 1973 to 1985. In 1983 he cosponsored (with Idaho Republican Steve Symms) an amendment to the Constitution of the United States. We have seen the text of the amendment (S.J. Res. 167) in the first selection of this chapter.

As is obvious, Section 1 of the Huddleston–Symms amendment declares the official language to be English without specifying what consequences this may have. Section 2 leaves to Congress the task of spelling out the consequences while at the same time suggesting that use of English will be required.

On September 21, 1983, Huddleston stood before the Senate and explained why this amendment was needed. The following selection is excerpted from his remarks.

Huddleston's argument may perhaps be synthesized as follows. For the United States to be a strong, united nation where everyone shares the same political ideals and beliefs in democracy, everyone should speak the same language. That language should be English. However, there are now factors discouraging non-English-speaking foreigners living in the United States

Source: Congressional Record, 98th Congress, 1st session, September 21, 1983, pp. S12640–43.

from learning English. One factor is their own attitude: the new immigrants are resisting learning English, so unlike the immigrants of the past. Other factors are actions of the federal government itself. The government discourages the use of English by requiring that voting ballots be printed in languages other than English, by printing informational material in those languages, by requiring interpreters in court proceedings and federal social programs, and by allowing bilingual education to have a bicultural component. The latter sends to foreign parents and children the wrong message, that it is all right to retain their native language.

Huddleston does not tell exactly how his amendment will put an end to the public use of languages other than English. But it is logical to assume that he thinks the amendment will allow for laws that will prohibit the official use of other languages. This in turn will discourage foreigners from keeping their native tongues and will encourage them to learn English.

The remarks I am about to make will be readily understood by my distinguished colleagues in the Congress. They will be understood by my constituents in Kentucky. They will be understood by the journalists in the press gallery, and by most of their readers across the country. No simultaneous interpreters will be needed for those in this chamber, and no translators will be needed for most of those who will be reading these words in the *Congressional Record*. In order to guarantee that this current state of affairs endures, as it has for over two hundred years, I am introducing today a constitutional amendment (S.J. Res. 167) to make English the official language of the United States (*see* p. 241).

The amendment addresses something so basic, so very fundamental to our sense of identity as Americans, that some who are in full agreement with the objectives of this amendment, will nevertheless question the necessity for it. So widely held is the assumption that English is already our national language that the notion of stating this in our national charter may seem like restating the obvious. However, I can assure my colleagues that this is not the case and that the need for a constitutional amendment grows stronger every day.

Almost alone among the world's very large and populous nations, the United States enjoys the blessings of one primary language, spoken and understood by most of its citizens. The previously unquestioned acceptance of this language by immigrants from every linguistic and cultural background has enabled us to come together as one people. It has allowed us to discuss our differences, to argue about our problems, and to compromise on solutions. It has allowed us to develop a stable and cohesive society that is the envy of many fractured ones, without imposing any strict standards of homogeneity, or even bothering to designate the language, which is ours by custom, as the nation's official one.

As a nation of immigrants, our great strength has been drawn from our ability to assimilate vast numbers of people from many different cultures and ethnic groups into a nation of people that can work together with cooperation and understanding. This process was often referred to as the melting pot and in the past it has been seen as an almost magical concept that helped to make the United States the greatest nation on earth. But for the last fifteen years, we have experienced a growing resistance to the acceptance of our historic language, an antagonistic questioning of the melting pot philosophy that has traditionally helped speed newcomers into the American mainstream.

Initially, the demands to make things easier for the newcomers seemed modest enough; and a generous people, appreciative of cultural diversity, was willing to make some allowances. For example, the English language requirements for naturalization were removed for elderly immigrants living here for twenty years who were still unable to meet them; and the use of a child's home language was encouraged, in a well-intentioned attempt to soften the pain of adjustment from the home to the English-speaking society that the school represents.

However, the demands have sharply escalated, and so has the tone in which they are presented. Bilingual education has gradually lost its role as a transitional way of teaching English, and now mandates a bicultural component. This mandate has been primarily shaped by the federal government. The unfortunate result is that thousands of immigrant and nonimmigrant children are languishing in near-permanent bilingual-bicultural programs, kept in a state of prolonged confusion, suspended between two worlds, and not understanding what is expected of them. They and their parents are given false hopes that their cultural traditions can be fully maintained in this country, and that the mastery of English is not so important, after all.

This misdirected public policy of bilingualism has been created primarily by the federal government, at the insistence of special interest groups, and it continues today because elected officials do not want to run the risk of taking a position that could, in some way, offend these groups. Over the last few years the federal government has spent approximately $1 billion on the bilingual education program. What we have bought with this money is a program that strives to keep separate cultural identities rather than a program that strives to teach English. It is a program which ignores the basic fact that in order to learn another language the student must talk, read, and use that language on a regular basis. Even though the bilingual education program has received failing marks by many reputable educators, it still survives because it is a political issue rather than an educational issue. What this means is that we will continue to finance an expensive bilingual program that does more to preserve cultural identities that it does to teach children to speak English.

In the area of voting rights, we have also formulated a national policy that encourages voting citizens not to learn to speak English. The Voting Rights Act, which was reauthorized in 1982, requires bilingual ballots if more than 5 percent of the citizens of voting age in a jurisdiction are of specified language minority groups and the illiteracy rate is higher than the national rate. As a result, bilingual ballots are required by federal law to be provided in thirty states—even if there is no demand for them. The wisdom of this policy is clearly lacking when you consider that the vast bulk of political debate, whether it is in the printed press or the electronic media, is conducted in English. By failing to provide a positive incentive for voting citizens to learn English, we are actually denying them full participation in the political process. Instead, we are making them dependent upon a few interpreters or go-betweens for information as to how they should vote. Although this process helps to preserve minority voting blocs, it seriously undercuts the democratic concept that every voting individual should be as fully informed as possible about the issues and the candidates.

There are other less prominent provisions of federal law which now require the use of foreign languages; for example, the use of interpreters in federal civil and criminal proceedings for parties whose primary language is other than English; and the use of foreign language personnel in connection with federally funded migrant health centers and alcohol-abuse treatment programs. Although I can understand that this kind of assistance is helpful, the fact that it must be legislated strongly indicates that we are failing miserably in our efforts to teach immigrants and many of our native born how to speak, read, and write English.

These federal laws are only the tip of the iceberg. I recently sent a request to all of the state governors and the major federal agencies asking for information regarding non-English forms and publications that their offices produce which are intended for use in this country. Although my staff is still in the process of reviewing the data, and I have not yet received responses to all of my letters, we know that hundreds of different, non-English forms and publications are now being printed and distributed on a wide scale throughout the United States. These publications cover a broad spectrum and range from White House press releases in Spanish to National Labor Relations Board notices in thirty-two languages. The non-English materials which I have received are in a stack that is about three feet high, and we are adding to it almost daily. I am told that if copies of all bilingual educational materials were sent, we could fill a large room. While distribution of these materials may be seen as providing just another government service, it can also be seen as reducing the incentive to learn English. It demonstrates a growing nationwide problem.

At the nongovernmental level there is a great deal of emphasis being placed on the use of non-English languages. In some major metropolitan areas, English is the second language; minorities who speak only English are being told that they must learn a foreign language to be eligible for a job; in many stores non-English languages are the only ones used to conduct business. It is not uncommon to find areas in this country where individuals can live all of their lives having all their social, commercial, and intellectual needs met without the use of English.

If this situation were static and merely a reflection of the large-scale legal and illegal immigration the United States has been experiencing over the last few years—in 1980 more immigrants entered the United States than at any time other than the peak years at the turn of the century—there would not be cause for concern. However, what we are seeing is a decrease in the use of English and a widely accepted attitude that it is not necessary to learn English. The United States is presently at a crucial juncture. We can either continue down the same path we have walked for the last two hundred years, using the melting pot philosophy to forge a strong and united nation, or we can take the new path that leads in the direction of another Tower of Babel.

National unity does not require that each person think and act like everyone else. However, it does require that there be some common threads that run throughout our society and hold us together. One of these threads is our common belief and support of a democratic form of government, and the right of every person to fully participate in it. Unfortunately, this right of full participation means very little if each individual does not possess the means of exercising it. This participation requires the ability to obtain information and to communicate our beliefs and concerns to others. Undoubtedly, this process is greatly hindered without the existence of a commonly accepted and used language.

In essence, what a policy of bilingualism-biculturalism does is to segregate minorities from the mainstream of our politics, economy, and society because we are not making it possible for them to freely enter into that mainstream. We are pushing them aside into their own communities, and we are denying them the tools with which to break out. I have always been against segregation of any kind, and by not assuring that every person in this country can speak and understand English, we are still practicing segregation. It was wrong when we segregated blacks because of their color, and it is just as wrong when we create a system which segregates any group of people by language.

As Americans we are a unique people, and one of the things that makes us uniquely American is our common language—English. My proposed constitutional amendment would assure that anyone in this country can fully take part in the American dream and that future generations also will have this privilege.

Against Official English: A U.S. Representative Explains Why There Should not Be an English Language Constitutional Amendment, 1988

During a 1988 Congressional hearing on several proposed English Language amendments, then U.S. Representative Stephen Solarz, a New York Democrat, testified against adopting any such amendment. The following selection presents an excerpt from his testimony.

Solarz considers that the threat to English from use of other languages by foreigners in the United States has been exaggerated. He cites statistics to support his point.

Solarz sees danger in a language amendment that could serve as the ground to eliminate certain language services that translate into social services.

He also argues that having an official language would retard, rather than facilitate, assimilation of foreigners into American society.

Solarz does not accept the idea of America as a melting pot based on language uniformity. In his view, what unites a culturally diverse America is the fact that people share the same set of democratic ideals.

At the time Solarz testified, the Soviet Union still existed, holding sway over ethnic minorities. Solarz compares the stifling quality of the Soviet

Source: English Language Constitutional Amendments: Hearing on H.J. Res. 13, H.J. Res. 33, H.J. Res. 60, and H.J. Res. 83, 100th Congress, second session, May 11, 1988, pp. 67–70.

system with an America in which he can serve some of his New York constituents, refugees from Soviet oppression who do not know English, by sending them printed information in Russian. He seems to imply that this would not be possible if only English were allowed in governmental communications.

On the face of it, the establishment of English as our official language seems to be an innocuous endeavor—free of controversy and devoid of any real dangers. However, like the metaphorical patch of quicksand, once you step into the issues surrounding this proposal, the severe problems that accompany this initiative become readily apparent.

We are not in danger of becoming another Quebec, or the national equivalent of the Tower of Babel, as some of my colleagues have suggested. Census data reveal there are fewer non-English-speaking citizens in the United States today than there were in 1900. A 1985 Rand Corporation survey of Mexican Americans, a community often cited during discussions of these amendments, reported that 95 percent of those individuals who were born in the United States are English-proficient. There is nobody more cognizant of the disability of non-English proficiency than the individual who is struggling to make it in this country without being able to speak English. I see no reason, therefore, to enact legislation that would only punish a huge segment of a society for a disability that they themselves are earnestly trying to correct.

I believe that the proposals that have been offered here this morning are unnecessary and unwise. They are unnecessary because it is clear that English is unquestionably our primary language, and I see no evidence that its position, as such, is in danger. They are unwise for two reasons. First, there is the potential that an English Language Amendment could pose significant threats to the civil and constitutional rights of citizens with little or no English proficiency. Second, the proposals represent a concession to nativist instincts and are incompatible with the cultural diversity and ethnic pluralism that constitute fundamental strengths of our nation.

If this amendment were adopted, it is entirely conceivable, if not certain, that the courts of our country could subsequently rule unconstitutional a whole series of legislative measures designed to provide linguistic assistance and relief to those limited number of Americans who are not able to read or converse fluently in English. It is my understanding that the sponsors of these amendments would like to see fewer government programs in languages other than English. I respectfully disagree. On the federal level, several critical statutes could be threatened, including the bilingual ballot provisions of the Voting Rights Act, the Court Interpreters Act, and statutes mandating language services at federally funded migrant-health and substance-abuse centers. Other routine federal services could also be seriously jeopardized, among them the Surgeon General's enlightened policy of sending out his groundbreaking AIDS information mailing in Spanish. The Internal Revenue Service currently uses forms and materials in other languages, as does the Department of Commerce in conducting the census.

The possible consequences of the proposed constitutional amendments are disturbing and, in my view, are not worth risking. There is too real a danger that court rulings and legislation in the wake of such an amendment could undermine the civil rights of millions of Americans. But even if an English Language Amendment were purely symbolic, I would oppose it. Such an amendment would have the perverse effect of making huge segments of our society feel unwanted and *not wanted*, strangers and not citizens. In my view, this amendment would have the very opposite effect than that intended by its authors, by serving to hinder the assimilation of non-English-speaking Americans into the mainstream of our society.

The time-worn cliché dictates that America is a "melting pot." This is no longer an apt description. We are instead a tapestry of many races, creeds, religions, and ethnic backgrounds—each independent, but all interwoven with one another. Like no other country in the world, this diversity creates not a clash of cultures, but a nation in which each culture leaves its own imprint and enriches us all.

I am proud to say that during a walk through my district, one would hear my constituents speaking over a dozen languages, including Yiddish, Russian, Hebrew, Greek, Arabic, Farsi, Polish, Hungarian, German, Spanish, Italian, Haitian Creole, Korean, and Chinese. The glue that bonds these diverse communities together is not commonality of language, but a commitment to the democratic ideals on which our country was founded. Among these principles are freedom of speech, equality of opportunity, and tolerance for minorities.

Proponents of the English Language Amendment have often claimed that the use of other languages in any official capacity dilutes American unity and prevents ethnic groups from participating in the mainstream of our country's economic and political pursuits. I believe that just the opposite is true. During the Second World War, at a time when the very survival of our nation was at stake, when our capacity to defeat the fascist foe depended on our ability to muster all of the resources at our command, the Office of War Information sent out publications in seventeen different languages—Baltic, Chinese, Czechoslovakian, Filipino, Finnish, French, German, Greek, Hungarian, Italian, Japanese, Polish, Portuguese, Scandinavian, Spanish, Serbo-Croatian, and Yiddish. Did anybody say then, at the height of the Second World War with the *Wehrmacht* on the loose, the Japanese Imperial Army rampaging through Asia and the Pacific, that we didn't want the contributions of these Americans in a war effort that would bring us to victory? Of course not. But if there had been an English Language Amendment to the Constitution at that time, we might not have been able to reach out to those people.

Let me give you a more contemporary example. I happen to have in my district in Brooklyn probably the largest number of Russian immigrants in America. Most of them have moved into a neighborhood called Brighton Beach, which they have renamed Odessa-by-the-Sea. Some of them already have become citizens. They are trying to learn English, all of them without exception, but many, particularly the older folks, still can't speak it or read it that well, so they have to rely on Russian. I recently sent out a Congressional newsletter to these people printed in the Cyrillic script because a newsletter in English would not have been understandable to them. In this newsletter I spoke about problems facing those Russian Jews who were still not able to get out of the Soviet Union, and I asked them to let me know of examples of people living in the Soviet Union who had been denied permission to emigrate. Dozens of Soviet Jewish families responded to this newsletter. In their letters to me—most of them also written in Russian—I learned of many *refusenik* cases of which I was previously unaware. I was then able to contact Soviet officials in an effort to expedite their emigration requests.

I believe that this newsletter is a perfect example of why the English Language Amendment—however well-intentioned—is not in the best interests of our nation. I think it passing strange that many of my colleagues in Congress who have joined me in condemning the Soviet Union for stifling expressions of ethnic diversity would support an initiative that could have a similar effect here in the United States. My Russian-speaking constituents have finally arrived in a country that respects pluralism and human rights. They are actively trying to learn English. They are as patriotic as any ethnic group in our nation and are actively involved in our political process. To prevent these individuals—and any other immigrant group—from being able to use their native language a part of any governmental activity would make it harder, not easier, for them to enter the American mainstream. The Congress would commit a grave error if it amended the Constitution in a way that would circumvent the very purposes for which that document was written.

They Are not Learning English: The Secretary of Education Attacks Bilingual Education, 1985

William J. Bennett was U.S. Secretary of Education when he delivered a speech in New York City on September 26, 1985, declaring that bilingual education was a failure. The text of the speech is taken from a collection of Bennett's writings published in 1988.

Bennett's arguments against bilingual education may be summarized as follows: after many years of special educational efforts on behalf of Hispanic children, many of them continue to perform in school below the national average and eventually drop out. Since bilingual education has been the method preferred by the federal government to teach these children, bilingual education has not worked. Therefore, other programs should be tried.

Bennett is of the opinion that we should not go back to the days of "sink-or-swim," meaning the time when public schools made no concession to the native language of immigrant children: instruction was all in English and you either swam—learned English—or you sank—failed, dropped out.

Of possible methods that should be tried instead of bilingual education, Bennett mentions, but does not define, only two: ESL and structured immersion. ESL stands for English as a Second Language. It consists of teaching English the way a foreign language is taught—that is to say, the

Source: William J. Bennett, *Our Children and Our Country: Improving America's Schools and Affirming the Common Culture* (New York: Simon & Schuster, 1988).

focus of instruction is on the language itself. For example, the objective of an ESL lesson may be to teach when to use and when not to use the verb *to do*. In contrast, structured immersion means subject matter—for example, health, geography, history, math—entirely in English, but the language is *simplified* so that the child who is not proficient in English can follow.

Bennett does not mention that ESL has normally been an essential component of bilingual education programs in which school subjects are taught in the non-English language, since English instruction is mandated in all federally funded programs.

Bennett seems to think that using more English is the key to success. To him bilingual education has failed precisely because the children have been taught in their native language instead of English. However, he does not advocate getting rid of all instruction in the native language: some may be needed to help the child keep up with subject matter while becoming fluent in English.

The ultimate goal is for everyone to have English as their common language. For Bennett, any special program is transitional toward that goal.

Our origins are diverse. Yet we live together as fellow citizens, in harmony. In America, and perhaps especially in New York, we can say, *E pluribus unum;* out of many we have become one. We cherish our particularities, and we respect our differences. Each of us is justly proud of his own ethnic heritage. But we share this pride, in common, as Americans, as American citizens. To be a citizen is to share in something common—common principles, common memories, and a common language in which to discuss our common affairs. Our common language is, of course, English. And our common task is to ensure that our non-English-speaking children learn this common language.

We entrust this task, in part, to our schools. We expect them, in this as in other respects, to prepare our youth to participate fully in the opportunities and challenges of American society. That is why we become so concerned when we discover that our schools are, in various ways, falling short of what we expect of them. We expect much of them—to impart basic skills, to help form character, to teach citizenship. And we expect our schools to help teach all of our students English, the common language that will enable them to participate fully in our political, economic, and social life.

Teaching non-English-speaking children English is not a new task for this nation. It has been performed, with fair success, in communities across this nation since its beginning. But only in the mid-1960s did the federal government accept responsibility for assisting in this task. The timing was no accident. For America was then engaged in a peaceful revolution—our civil rights revolution—in which the federal government stepped in to make good on the great American promise of equal opportunity for all. And this promise extends with full force to those of our children who speak no English, or little English.

Many of these children are the sons and daughters of immigrants and refugees, who have left behind their homes, and all that was familiar to them, to come to this land of freedom and opportunity. Many of these children grow up in circumstances that are not easy, their parents struggling day to day for the sake of a brighter future for their children. Other Americans have always, in their churches and communities, done their part to help give such children a chance to achieve that brighter future. It was reasonable and proper, twenty years ago, for the federal government to step in to play a role as well.

How has our government done by these children? The answer, I am afraid, is not very well. But not from a lack of trying. We began with the best of intentions. We began with two legislative landmarks, the Civil Rights Act of 1964 and the Elementary and Secondary Education Act of 1965. But in both cases, after sound beginnings, federal policies went astray. In a now-familiar pattern of events, over the next two decades our policies gradually became confused as to purpose, and overbearing as to means. As a result, too many children have failed to become fluent in English, and have therefore failed to enjoy the opportunities they deserve. Now is the time to get our policies back on track; now is the time to deliver on the promise of equal opportunity so solemnly pledged twenty years ago.

Despite the *Lau v. Nichols* decision's endorsement of flexibility of approach,the federal government moved in another direction. In 1975 the Department of Health, Education, and Welfare (H.E.W.) began to require that educational programs for non-English-speaking students be conducted in large part *in the student's native language,* as virtually the only approved method of remedying discrimination. These regulations were never formally published, for public notice and comment. Indeed, when H.E.W. was sued and forced to publish them in August 1980, they aroused a storm of opposition, and they were withdrawn in February 1981. By that time, however, they had served as the basis of some five hundred "compliance agreements" negotiated with school districts across the nation. Because of their intrusiveness and heavy-handedness, these regulations came close to giving bilingual education a bad name. More important, by the time they were withdrawn in 1981, the evidence was becoming increasingly clear that this educational method imposed from Washington was doing very little to help students learn English.

Why did the government turn down this path? Partly because of a foolish conviction that only Washington meant well and knew best. Local school districts, it was thought, could not be trusted to devise the best means, given their own circumstances, to teach their students English. But our government made this fateful turn for another reason as well. And that was that we had lost sight of the goal of learning *English* as the key to equal educational opportunity. Indeed, H.E.W. increasingly emphasized bilingual education as a way of enhancing students' knowledge of their native language and culture. Bilingual education was no longer seen so much as a means to ensure that students learned English, or as a transitional method until students learned English. Rather, it became an emblem of cultural pride, a means of producing a positive self-image in the student.

Let us be clear: Pride in one's heritage is natural and commendable. We in the United States cherish our diversity, and local schools should be free—and more, should be encouraged—to foster the study of the languages and heritages of their students in the courses they offer. But the responsibility of the federal government must be to help ensure that local schools succeed in teaching non-

English-speaking students English, so that every American enjoys access to the opportunities of American society.

The Bilingual Education Act was most recently reauthorized last year. Congress had before it yet more evidence that the mandated method of instruction in the native language was no more effective than alternative methods of special instruction using English, and in some cases the mandated method was demonstrably less so. Indeed, the English-language skills of students in bilingual education programs seemed to be no better than the skills of those who simply remained in regular classrooms where English was spoken, without *any* special help. In addition, Hispanic children, the largest subgroup of the eligible population, have continued to perform educationally far below the national average. The recent news of gains by Hispanic students in Scholastic Aptitude Test scores is welcome indeed, and is a testimony to the impressive efforts of many Hispanic parents and children. Yet we cannot take these scores as a sign that all is well. The scores of Hispanics remain unacceptably below the national average and, more important, these scores only reflect the achievement of *half* of all Hispanic children. For almost half of all Hispanic high school students in the United States drop out *before* graduation, and of these dropouts, 40 percent never reach the tenth grade. This figure is as tragically high now as it was twenty years ago.

In response to these facts, and in response to immigrants from various parts of Asia and elsewhere, for many of whom it is practically impossible for schools to provide native-language instruction, Congress last year recognized the need for programs using alternative instructional methods. These methods include English as a second language (E.S.L.) and "structured immersion," and provide special instruction *in English* to students of limited English proficiency. Congress did allow, in its 1984 reauthorization, for such alternative programs, but it limited funding for those programs to 4 percent of the total appropriation, leaving local school districts still very much constrained. And Congress unfortunately further backed away from a clear statement of the goal of learning English, by authorizing for the first time funding for programs designed simply to maintain student competence in the native language.

This, then, is where we stand: After seventeen years of federal involvement and after $1.7 billion of federal funding, we have no evidence that the children whom we sought to help—that the children who deserve our help—have benefited. And we have the testimony of an original sponsor of the Bilingual Education Act, Congressman James Scheuer of New York, that the Act's "original purposes were perverted and politicized"; that instead of helping students learn English, "the English has been sort of thinned out and stretched out and in many cases banished into the mists and all of the courses tended to be taught in Spanish. That was not the original intent of the program."

What, then, are we to do? Give up on the promise of equal educational opportunity for those of our children who are not proficient in English? Our sense of what we owe our fellow Americans will not permit this. Continue down the same failed path on which we have been traveling? This is an equally bankrupt course. We ought to do more for our fellow citizens than throw good money after bad, and we ought to offer more than increasingly hollow protestations of concern and gestures of solidarity.

We intend to make good on the promise of real equal educational opportunity for all Americans. We shall therefore explore with Congress the possibility of removing the 4 percent cap on alternative instructional methods, as well as other legislative changes. We shall move, through regulatory and administrative changes, to allow greater flexibility for local school districts. And we shall take care, in the course of ensuring that the civil rights of minority-national-origin students are respected, that we do not impose a particular method of instruction. These reforms will allow local school districts to choose the sort of program, or to design the combination of programs, best suited to their particular needs. School districts serving recent immigrants who speak seventy different languages may after all need different sorts of programs from school districts whose students speak only two languages.

These reforms will allow local school districts the flexibility to adapt to local circumstances. They will also allow them to take advantage of research results which are now coming in. Let me be clear: We do not intend to prescribe one method or another. Many school districts will undoubtedly continue to pursue programs with some instruction in the native language. In some circumstances, these can be very useful in helping students keep up with their classwork until they become fluent in English. We do not intend to prescribe one method or another. But the goal of any method should be clear—fluency in English. As President Reagan has said: "Bilingual programs should serve as a bridge to full participation in the American mainstream. They should never segregate non-English-speaking students in a way that will make it harder, not easier, for them to succeed in life."

Our movement away from exclusive reliance on one method, and our endorsement of local flexibility should not be mistaken for a return to the old days of sink-or-swim. Many children in earlier generations learned English in such circumstances, but some did not, and at times the cost was high. We intend to enforce the requirement that school districts provide equal opportunity for students deficient in English by providing programs that address their needs. And we intend to continue funding programs that address the needs of school children who need to learn English. But we believe that local flexibility will serve the needs of these students far more effectively than intrusive federal regulation.

Paradoxically, we have over the last two decades become less clear about the goal—English-language literacy—at the same time as we have become more intrusive as to the method. But there ought to be no confusion or embarrassment over our goal. The rise in ethnic consciousness, the resurgence of cultural pride in recent decades, is a healthy thing. The traditions we bring with us, that our forefathers brought with them to this land, are too worthwhile to be discarded. But a sense of cultural pride cannot come at the price of proficiency in English, our common language.

As fellow citizens, we need a common language. In the United States that language is English. Our common history is written in English. Our common forefathers speak to us, through the ages, in English. This is not contradicted by the fact that it is an enduring glory of this nation to have welcomed with open arms immigrants from other lands, speaking other languages; nor by the fact that it is a feature of our free society that these languages can continue to find a place here, in the United States. But beneath the wonderful mosaic of cultures here, beyond the remarkable variety of languages, we are one people.

We are one people not by virtue of a common blood, or race, or origin. We are one people, above all, because we hold these truths to be self-evident: that all men are created equal, that they are endowed by their Creator with certain unalienable rights, and that therefore just government is by consent of the governed. And government by consent means government by discussion, by debate, by discourse, by argument. Such a common enterprise requires a common language. We should not be bashful about proclaiming fluency in this language as our educational goal. And we should not be timid in reforming our policies so as to secure it. For with this goal comes the reward of full participation in this remarkable nation of ours—"not merely a nation but a teeming nation of nations," Walt Whitman said—but still, at the end of the day, beneath all the differences of politics and color and creed, one nation, one people.

In Defense of Bilingual Education: A Response to Secretary Bennett's Attack, 1985

James Lyons was counsel to the National Association for Bilingual Education (NABE), a professional organization of bilingual educators, when he responded to Secretary William Bennett's attack on bilingual education (see previous selection) in the following piece, published in the NABE newsletter.

Lyons considers that Bennett has misrepresented the role of bilingual education in the educational failure of Hispanics, since most Hispanics have not been served by these programs.

According to Lyons, focusing on the teaching of English implies not learning the content areas—mathematics, history, and so on. He means that since these areas will be taught in English and children are only in the process of learning it, they will be automatically denied mastery of them. Lyon's unstated conclusion is that children, while learning English, should be taught school subjects in the language they know best—their native language.

Lyons points out that ESL, one of the methods mentioned by Bennett as a possible substitute for bilingual education, is a required component in all bilingual education programs.

Lyons observes that the legislation funding bilingual education programs is not as inflexible as represented by Bennett, since most programs do not receive any funding. In addition, the Department of Education under Bennett has refused to fund English language programs aimed at parents in which the native language will not be used at all.

Source: James J. Lyons, "Education Secretary Bennett on Bilingual Education: Mixed up or Malicious?", *NABE News* 9, 1 (Fall 1985), 1, 14.

Secretary of Education William J. Bennett launched the Reagan administration's "initiative" on bilingual education September 26. In a media-hyped speech to the Association for a Better New York, Bennett attacked the new Bilingual Education Act, passed by an overwhelming bipartisan majority in Congress in the fall of 1984, following three years of study, hearings, and debate. At the same time, Bennett branded as "a failure" two decades of federal policies to help educate language-minority students. Lost upon many listeners of the Secretary's lengthy address was a more fundamental message: Equality of educational opportunity no longer means what it used to. Language-minority students—native-born Americans, immigrants, and refugees—must be satisfied with only a partial education.

Veteran Washington observers were shocked by the vehemence of the Secretary's attack. Both prior to and immediately following the Secretary's confirmation last February, Bennett repeatedly declined to give his views on how the federal government should help communities across the land to educate more than 4 million language-minority students who don't know English well enough to learn successfully in monolingual English classrooms. Exhibiting uncharacteristic reticence and thoughtfulness, Mr. Bennett promised that he would undertake a thorough examination of this complex and compelling issue. In his New York address, however, lawyer-philosopher Bennett, who recently has taken to teaching high school American history under the doting eye of network television, recounted the development of federal bilingual education policy. In so doing, Bennett not only rewrote the history of bilingual education, but he redefined the meaning of equal educational opportunity.

According to Bennett, "the responsibility of the federal government must be to help ensure that local schools succeed in teaching non-English-speaking students English, so that every American enjoys access to the opportunities of American society." Certainly, none of the members of Congress who developed and voted for the new Bilingual Education Act last year would question the importance of effectively teaching English to language-minority students. And the Hispanic leaders and advocates of bilingual education whom Education Department officials charge are out of touch with their constituents have *never* discounted the importance of teaching English to language-minority students.

However, no one with an ounce of sense would say that a child who has mastered English, but who has not learned mathematics, history, geography, civics, and the other subjects taught in school was educated or prepared for life in this society. Why Secretary Bennett, who generally champions a rigorous comprehensive education, has so narrowly set out the purpose and goal of schooling for language-minority students is anyone's guess. It may be that Bennett finally knuckled under to U.S. English, a well-financed private lobby group which opposes use of non-English languages in public education (or, for that matter, for any public purpose). What is clear is that Bennett's narrow and unworkable definition of what constitutes equal educational opportunity is central to his confused attack on federal law and policy. Secretary Bennett cited the tragic and dangerously high dropout rates of Hispanic students as proof that these laws and policies were wrong. Nowhere in his seventeen-page speech did Bennett acknowledge the fact that most Hispanic students—indeed, most students eligible for federal bilingual education services—have never attended bilingual education classes.

And so, Secretary Bennett has declared that English as a second language (E.S.L.) and undefined "immersion" programs are viable alternatives to bilingual education. Yes, E.S.L. is a sound method of teaching English to non-English-language-background students, especially when carried out by bilingual school personnel. And that is exactly why the new Bilingual Education Act now requires that *every* federally funded program of bilingual education provide intensive "structured English language instruction." The trouble, however, is that E.S.L. and so-called "immersion" programs often fail to teach anything but English.

Prior to enactment of the 1968 Bilingual Education Act, language-minority students who didn't know English were universally ignored. Either they were segregated in inferior schools, or instruction was tailored to the needs of students from English language backgrounds. A majority of the parents of limited-English-proficient students today are themselves the casualties of this earlier educational neglect. Thanks to federal policy—the Bilingual Education Act and other compensatory education programs, the 1974 U.S. Supreme Court decision in *Lau v. Nichols,* and technical assistance to help school districts achieve civil rights compliance—the situation has improved. Because of federal encouragement and financial support, E.S.L. and native-language instructional methods have been developed, teachers have been trained, classroom materials have been prepared and published, evaluation instruments have been written and refined—the list goes on and on. Now, many more teachers can comprehend a student's question or even the simple plea, "I don't understand" when it is delivered in the only language the child knows.

Federal education and civil rights policies have increased the number of school personnel who can communicate with non-English-speaking students and parents. It has, if you will, opened the schoolhouse door. Moreover, the new Bilingual Education Act requires that parents receive information about the placement and progress of students in programs funded under the Act, and gives parents the right to decline placement of their children in these programs. Most important, federal bilingual education policy has made it possible for parents who don't know English to become active partners in their children's education. The principle of parent choice—championed so ardently by Secretary Bennett —is at the heart of bilingual education law and policy.

In support of his pared-down concept of equal educational opportunity, Secretary Bennett decried the "lack of flexibility" in current law. At the same time, the Secretary conveniently ignored a number of facts. He ignored the fact that more than three hundred school districts applied for supposedly "inflexible" Transitional Bilingual Education program grants this year, but that the Department of Education was able to fund just over one hundred applications. He ignored the fact that forty-eight school districts and community organizations asked for seed money to start Family English Literacy programs, but the department awarded grants to only four. And he did not tell his audience that the Reagan administration has already asked Congress to eliminate all funding for these programs next year. Unlike the other programs authorized under the

Bilingual Education Act, Family English Literacy has a single objective: to teach English to parents. The law does not require *any* use of the parent's native language in these simple, straightforward English instruction programs.

Since taking office, William Bennett has traveled widely and talked loosely. Some of what he says makes sense: "Parents are the first and most influential teachers of their children; they should spend more time with their children, reading to them and teaching them to read." But Mr. Bennett's message on bilingual education, coupled with facts the Secretary knew but never disclosed, does not make sense. At best he is mixed up; at worst he is malicious.

SUGGESTIONS FOR FURTHER READING

Dennis E. Baron, *The English-Only Question: An Official Language for Americans.* New Haven, Conn.: Yale University Press, 1990.

James E. Crawford, ed., *Language Loyalties: A Source Book on the Official Language Controversy.* Chicago: University of Chicago Press, 1992.

Joshua Fishman, et al., eds., *Language Loyalty in the United States.* New York: Arno Press, 1978.

Kenji Hakuta, *Mirror of Language: The Debate on Bilingualism.* New York: Basic Books, 1986.

Calvin J. Veltman, *Language Shift in the United States.* Berlin: Mouton Publishers, 1983.

10

Church, State, and Society

Religious differences have a particularly disruptive potential in a pluralistic society. Disagreements over matters of faith and divinely revealed truth are not easily subject to the ordinary give-and-take of social compromise. It seems practical, of course, to suggest that a society create guidelines in matters of faith by drawing a line between public and private life. We might find ways to protect religion in private life from public interference, while protecting our common public life from the possibility of disruption based on our inability to resolve disputes over deeply felt matters of faith.

That is what the men who wrote the American Constitution and, soon thereafter in 1791, the first ten amendments (the Bill of Rights), appear to have done. Section 3 of Article 6 of the Constitution stated firmly that "no religious test shall ever be required as a qualification to any office or public trust under the United States," thus establishing equal access to national political power among the various religious denominations that then populated the new country. The First Amendment to the Constitution stated just as firmly that, "Congress shall make no law respecting an establishment of religion, or prohibiting the free exercise thereof." The Amendment's first clause ("the Establishment Clause") seemed to imply the principle that no one religious faith would receive public support to attain dominance over others. The second clause (the "Free Exercise Clause") implied that all faiths would be free to strive to maintain themselves, to organize their worship, and to pursue their own religious truths free of public interference. In manners of religion, it would seem, the intention was that the government of the United States was officially to be neutral, and hence secular. Government could not interfere with religion, and religion could not interfere with government.

But the boundaries drawn by the founding generation did not prove sufficiently precise to ensure that the United States would be free of conflict over the place of religion in American public life. In fact, in spite of these constitutional guarantees, there has never been a universally agreed upon understanding of exactly what that place was intended to be. The founding generation's intentions did not prove to be transparently clear when analyzed systematically or in the context of particular, deeply felt issues. The very general language used in the First Amendment is too lacking in specific instructions to provide practical guidelines for dealing with all of the realms of public life that can be penetrated by religious feeling and concern in a population that is inclined, as Americans are, to religiosity. Americans may not be much more formally religious, in the sense of attendance at places of worship, than others. Still, more of them, whatever their formal religious affiliation and personal religious identity, profess to believe in God than in most other large, developed societies.

These contradictory currents of public policy and popular feeling have been there throughout our history. The Founding Fathers may not have intended the U.S. government to recognize religion, but the first president's inaugural address explicitly asked God to bless the new country, a prelude to such inconsistencies for a secular state as having "In God We Trust" on its money and allowing clergy to open sessions of Congress with prayers and employing them in the armed forces to serve as spiritual advisors. Moreover, the founding generation had little concept of the United States as officially a "Christian nation." But a number of Protestant clergy and laity in the early nineteenth century began to insist that it should be. The idea has been argued continuously by a vocal minority since then, though what exactly it implies for public policy has never been clear. There is no denying, however, that from the beginning of American history the majority of Americans have been Protestant Christians, who showed an active preference for their own Christianity over both other forms of Christianity, especially Catholicism, and non-Christian religions.

It is not surprising, therefore, that the standards established for the government of the United States were not the same ones that prevailed in the individual states where these statesmen themselves lived. There seemed too many different standards, rooted in deep and often intolerant feeling, to try to adopt a uniform rule. It may be a surprise to learn that at the time the Bill of Rights was adopted, at least two states, Connecticut and Massachusetts, had established (in other words state-subsidized) religious denominations. For more than a century after the writing of the Constitution and the Bill of Rights, furthermore, non-Christians and non-Protestants were subject to varieties of civil and political discriminations, such as not being able to vote or allowed to hold elective office, in a few states. It is no wonder that those framing the First Amendment simply restricted *Congress* from certain actions in regard to religion. Gradually, however, just as in other realms of law, a national standard did come to prevail.

Thus, the boundaries between church and state, and indeed the very idea of the United States as an officially secular country that respects all private faiths but is unwilling to place any one of them over the others, have been matters of contention throughout our history. The controversies over the relations of church and state have always been present in American history, though they have grown or declined in intensity at different times in response to cultural, political, and social changes. The late twentieth century provides an example of the growth of concern over church and state relations. After years of seemingly little public concern, the 1980s and 1990s witnessed the rise of increasing conflict over the place of religion in public life. Contemporary Christian political movements particularly have attempted to shift the boundaries of church-state relations to make religion more a feature of public life. Issues such as school prayer are now in the forefront of political debate.

In this chapter we are going to survey some statements for and against the notion that religion in general, and Christianity in particular, should attain a privileged status in American life, and to examine some of the efforts of the Supreme Court, with the general principle laid out in the First Amendment and past court decisions as its guide, to sort out the question of what the limits of religion in public life should be. Why look at the issue from the standpoint of the opinions of judges and of court decisions? The ambiguity of the First Amendment has created a long and continuous tradition of debate about church-state relations. The issue has ultimately been decided by the Supreme Court, which is the final authority in matters of constitutional law. In following this judicial history, we become aware that contemporary conflicts over church-state relations reiterate tensions that have been present in American life almost from the start of the nation's history, and have been taken so seriously that they required a decision at the highest levels of American government. In this way, we can learn about the conflicts and compromises that have shaped American pluralism as we know it today, and decide for ourselves whether and to what extent to allow the past to continue to guide us. It is important, however, to understand that these same issues have also touched individual people deeply. The chapter concludes, therefore, with a short story that examines the place of religion in public life from the perspective of a Jewish boy who has come to terms with pressures in a public school to conform to majority, Christian ways at Christmas time.

Separating Church and State: What Did the Founders Have in Mind?, 1784

In attempting to interpret the very general formulations of the Constitution and the Bill of Rights on the subject of religion, it is logical that we try to understand what those who wrote these documents thought at the time they wrote them. Centuries later, it is not always practical to be bound by the ideas forged in the distant past. But such ideas may help instruct us about how to interpret and act upon our own experiences.

Useful to any effort to interpret these documents is an analysis of the ideas of James Madison (1751–1836), one of the most influential of the political philosophers among the Founders and one of the most effective

Source: Charles F. James, *Documentary History of the Struggle for Religious Liberty in Virginia* (Lynchberg, Va.: J. P. Bell Company, 1900), pp. 256–62.

practical politicians, too. Madison was deeply involved in thinking about church-state issues. While serving in the first elected House of Representatives in 1789–1790, he was a member of the committee that drafted the First Amendment. It is doubtful that he drafted the specific language of the First Amendment, which in its final form did not go quite so far as Madison had wished it to. (He wanted the amendment explicitly to bar the states from infringing upon the rights of individuals in religious matters.) But Madison was one of the most articulate spokesmen on the subject, known in particular for his clearly "separationist" (i.e., for separation of church and state) views.

We may know these views better by looking into an incident several years previous to the drafting of the First Amendment. In 1784, while he was serving in the Virginia legislature, Madison was involved in a struggle over a proposal to use state tax revenues to subsidize the salaries of Christian clergymen. On the basis of his principled opposition to state involvement in religion, Madison led the forces that successfully opposed this plan. Out of this struggle came the *Memorial and Remonstrance* that is the first selection of this chapter. The extent of Madison's authorship of this document, which was submitted to influence the legislature in the way a petition would be, is not completely clear, but there is no doubt of the influence of his ideas on the document, which speaks clearly to the rights of individual conscience in matters of religion and calls for the separation of church and state.

This document bears the mark of the political principles and religious concerns of the Christian separationism that characterized many prominent American statesmen of Madison's generation. Madison and most of his generation of political leaders were not enemies of religion, but committed Christians of one sort or another. Looking at European history, they had come to believe that whenever religion and government became too closely intertwined, persecution, war, discrimination, and prejudice resulted. Both government and religion had been corrupted by their close, mutual relations in Europe, and religious minorities were continually victimized. Religious liberty for individuals and separation of church and state seemed to Madison and others to be necessary if the new nation they were forming was to be free of the tyranny they associated with Europe.

TO THE HONORABLE GENERAL ASSEMBLY OF THE COMMONWEALTH OF VIRGINIA A MEMORIAL AND REMONSTRANCE (1784)

We the subscribers, citizens of the said Commonwealth, having taken into serious consideration, a Bill printed by order of the last Session of General Assembly, entitled "A Bill establishing a provision for Teachers of the Christian Religion," and conceiving that the same if finally armed with the sanctions of a law, will be a dangerous abuse of power, are bound as faithful members of a free State to remonstrate against it, and to declare the reasons by which we are determined. We remonstrate against the said Bill,

1. Because we hold it for a fundamental and undeniable truth, "that Religion or the duty which we owe to our Creator and the manner of discharging it, can be directed only by reason and conviction, not by force or violence." The Religion then of every man must be left to the conviction and conscience of every man; and it is the right of every man to exercise it as these may dictate. This right is in its nature an unalienable right. It is unalienable, because the opinions of men, depending only on the evidence contemplated by their own minds cannot follow the dictates of other men: It is unalienable also, because what is here a right towards men, is a duty towards the Creator. It is the duty of every man to render to the Creator such homage and such only as he believes to be acceptable to him. This duty is precedent, both in order of time and in degree of obligation, to the claims of Civil Society. . . .

2. Because if Religion be exempt from the authority of the Society at large, still less can it be subject to that of the Legislative Body. The latter are but the creatures and viceregents of the former. Their jurisdiction is both derivative and limited: it is limited with regard to the co-ordinate departments, more necessarily is it limited with regard to the constituents. The preservation of a free Government requires not merely, that the metes and bounds which separate each department of power be invariably maintained; but more especially that neither of them be suffered to overleap the great Barrier which defends the rights of the people. . . .

3. Because it is proper to take alarm at the first experiment on our liberties. We hold this prudent jealousy to be the first duty of Citizens, and one of the noblest characteristics of the late Revolution. The free men of America did not wait till usurped power had strengthened itself by exercise, and entangled the question in precedents. They saw all the consequences in the principle, and they avoided the consequences by denying the principle. We revere this lesson too much soon to forget it. Who does not see that the same authority which can establish Christianity, in exclusion of all other Religions, may establish with the same ease any particular sect of Christians, in exclusion of all other Sects? [;] that the same authority which can force a citizen to contribute three pence only of his property for the support of any one establishment, may force him to conform to any other establishment in all cases whatsoever?

4. Because the Bill violates that equality which ought to be the basis of every law, and which is more indispensible, in proportion as the validity or expediency of any law is more liable to be impeached. If "all men are by nature equally free and independent," all men are to be considered as entering into Society on equal conditions; as relinquishing no more, and therefore retaining no less, one than another, of their natural rights. Above all are they to be considered as retaining an "*equal* title to the free exercise of Religion according to the dictates of Conscience." Whilst we assert for ourselves a freedom to embrace, to profess and to observe the Religion which we believe to be of divine origin, we cannot deny an equal freedom to those whose minds have not yet yielded to the evidence which has convinced us. . . .

5. Because the Bill implies either that the Civil Magistrate is a competent Judge of Religious Truth; or that he may employ Religion as an engine of Civil policy. The first is an arrogant pretension falsified by the contradictory opinions

of all Rulers in all ages, and throughout the world: the second an unhallowed perversion of the means of salvation.

6. Because the establishment proposed by the Bill is not requisite for the support of the Christian Religion. To say that it is, is a contradiction to the Christian Religion itself, for every page of it disavows a dependence on the powers of this world: it is a contradiction to fact; for it is known that this Religion both existed and flourished, not only without the support of human laws, but in spite of every opposition from them, and not only during the period of miraculous aid, but long after it had been left to its own evidence and the ordinary care of Providence. . . .

7. Because experience witnesseth that ecclesiastical establishments, instead of maintaining the purity and efficacy of Religion, have had a contrary operation. During almost fifteen centuries has the legal establishment of Christianity been on trial. What have been its fruits? More or less in all places, pride and indolence in the Clergy, ignorance and servility in the laity, in both, superstition, bigotry and persecution.

8. Because the establishment in question is not necessary for the support of Civil Government. . . . A just Government instituted to secure & perpetuate it needs them not. Such a Government will be best supported by protecting every Citizen in the enjoyment of his Religion with the same equal hand which protects his person and his property; by neither invading the equal rights of any Sect, nor suffering any Sect to invade those of another.

9. Because the proposed establishment is a departure from that generous policy, which, offering an Asylum to the persecuted and oppressed of every Nation and Religion, promised a lustre to our country, and an accession to the number of its citizens. What a melancholy mark is the Bill of sudden degeneracy? Instead of holding forth an Asylum to the persecuted, it is itself a signal of persecution. It degrades from the equal rank of Citizens all those whose opinions in Religion do not bend to those of the Legislative authority. . . .

10. Because it will have a like tendency to banish our Citizens. The allurements presented by other situations are every day thinning their number. To superadd a fresh motive to emigration by revoking the liberty which they now enjoy, would be the same species of folly which has dishonoured and depopulated flourishing kingdoms.

11. Because it will destroy that moderation and harmony which the forbearance of our laws to intermeddle with Religion has produced among its several sects. Torrents of blood have been spilt in the old world, by vain attempts of the secular arm, to extinguish Religious discord, by proscribing all difference in Religious opinion. . . . Instead of Levelling as far as possible, every obstacle to the victorious progress of Truth, the Bill with an ignoble and unchristian timidity would circumscribe it with a wall of defence against the encroachments of error.

12. Because the policy of the Bill is adverse to the diffusion of the light of Christianity. The first wish of those who enjoy this precious gift ought to be that it may be imparted to the whole race of mankind. . . .

13. Because attempts to enforce by legal sanctions, acts obnoxious to so great a proportion of Citizens, tend to enervate the laws in general, and to slacken the bands of Society. . . .

14. Because a measure of such singular magnitude and delicacy ought not to be imposed, without the clearest evidence that it is called for by a majority of citizens, and no satisfactory method is yet proposed by which the voice of the majority in this case may be determined, or its influence secured. . . .

15. Because finally, "the equal right of every citizen to the free exercise of his Religion according to the dictates of conscience" is held by the same tenure with all our other rights. If we recur to its origin, it is equally the gift of nature; if we weigh its importance, it cannot be less dear to us; if we consult the "Declaration of those rights which pertain to the good people of Virginia, as the basis and foundation of Government," it is enumerated with equal solemnity, or rather studied emphasis. Either then, we must say, that the Will of the Legislature is the only measure of their authority; and that in the plentitude of this authority, they may sweep away all our fundamental rights; or, that they are bound to leave this particular right untouched and sacred: Either we must say, that they may control the freedom of the press, may abolish the Trial by Jury, may swallow up the Executive and Judiciary Powers of the State; nay that they may despoil us of our very right of suffrage, and erect themselves into an independent and hereditary Assembly or, we must say, that they have no authority to enact into law the Bill under consideration. We the Subscribers say, that the General Assembly of this Commonwealth have no such authority: And that no effort may be omitted on our part against so dangerous a usurpation, we oppose to it, this remonstrance; earnestly praying, as we are in duty bound, that the Supreme Lawgiver of the Universe, by illuminating those to whom it is addressed, may on the one hand, turn their Councils from every act which would affront his holy prerogative, or violate the trust committed to them: and on the other, guide them into every measure which may be worthy of his blessing, may redound to their own praise, and may establish more firmly the liberties, the prosperity and the happiness of the Commonwealth.

A "Wall of Separation": Thomas Jefferson's View, 1802

The separationist position of Thomas Jefferson (1743–1826) was probably even stronger than Madison's. While recognizing the validity of the philosophical and emotional claims of religion upon the individual, Jefferson had a deep distrust of the institutions of organized religion, such as the clergy and ecclesiastical hierarchies. Early in his first presidential administration, Jefferson took the opportunity presented by a declaration of principles on the subject of separation of church and state by a Baptist organization to formulate a strong, terse statement of his views on separation. (American Baptists have been one of the most strongly separationist of any American religious denomination.) The "wall of separation" was Jefferson's powerful

Source: Thomas Jefferson to Nehemiah Dodge, Ephriam Robbins, and Stephen S. Nelson, A Committee of the Baptist Association, in the State of Connecticut, in Andrew A. Lipscomb and Albert Ellery Bergh, eds., *The Writings of Thomas Jefferson* (Washington, D.C.: Thomas Jefferson Memorial Association, 1905), vol. 16, pp. 281–82.

metaphor for expressing his own position. First employed years before by the colonial religious dissenter, Roger Williams (1603–1683), it is nonetheless most associated with Jefferson. It has long been an emotional rallying point for American separationists.

Believing with you that religion is a matter which lies solely between man and his God, that he owes account to none other for his faith or his worship, that the legislative powers of government reach actions only, and not opinions, I contemplate with sovereign reverence that act of the whole American people which declared that their legislature should "make no law respecting an establishment of religion, or prohibiting the free exercise thereof," thus building a wall of separation between Church and State. Adhering to this expression of the supreme will of the nation in behalf of the rights of conscience, I shall see with sincere satisfaction the progress of those sentiments which tend to restore to man all his natural rights, convinced he has no natural right in opposition to his social duties.

Is The United States a "Christian Nation?": Justice David Brewer's View, 1892

One of the most widely quoted antiseparationist pronouncements was made in 1892 by Supreme Court Justice David Brewer (1837–1910) in rendering a decision in the case of *Holy Trinity Church v. United States*.

The case did not involve the usual issues, such as public funding of religious schools, that prompt church-state debates. It centered around a federal law that barred the importation of contract labor. New York City's Holy Trinity Church was prosecuted under the law because it had hired a foreign minister who was not a resident of the United States. Writing for the majority of the court, Justice Brewer stated that the law under which the church was charged was intended to apply only to low-wage foreign workers, whose employment would bring down American wage scales and living standards. But Justice Brewer went further in rendering his decision. He was indignant over the idea that Christianity should be put in the degrading position of having to defend itself against petty legal persecution. As he says at the end of this selection, which is excerpted from his 1892 decision, the United States is not a secular but rather a "Christian nation." He marshalled evidence that to his mind proved the point.

To this day, Christian antiseparationists frequently quote Brewer to back the claim that the wall of separation is wrong and at odds with American traditions. Yet it is unclear whether Brewer meant that the laws should reflect Christian moral principles and create special protections for Christianity, or simply that most Americans were Christians and that Christianity has played an important role in our history and culture. In later judicial decisions and published essays, Brewer seems to lean toward the latter view, which is not necessarily at odds with separationist arguments. But the ques-

Source: Church of The Holy Trinity v. United States, 143 U.S. 471 (1892).

tion of what Brewer thought is still debated. Under any circumstance, whatever Brewer's actual beliefs, the Supreme Court has never given the "Christian nation" concept official and binding status in its jurisprudence.

. . .Beyond all these matters no purpose of action against religion can be imputed to any legislation, state or national, because this is a religious people. This is historically true. From the discovery of this continent to the present hour, there is a single voice making this affirmation. The commission to Christopher Columbus, prior to his sail westward, is from "Ferdinand and Isabella, by the grace of God, King and Queen of Castile," etc., and recites that "it is hoped that by God's assistance some of the continents and islands in the ocean will be discovered," etc. The first colonial grant, that made to Sir Walter Raleigh in 1584, was from "Elizabeth, by the Grace of God, of England, Fraunce and Ireland, queene, defender of the faith," etc.; and the grant authorizing him to enact statutes for the government of the proposed colony provided that "they be not against the true Christian faith nowe professed in the Church of England." The first charter of Virginia, granted by King James I in 1606, after reciting the application of certain parties for a charter, commenced the grant in these words: "We, greatly commending, and graciously accepting of, their Desires for the Furtherance of so noble a Work, which may, by the Providence of Almighty God, hereafter tend to the Glory of his Divine Majesty, in propagating of Christian Religion to such People, as yet live in Darkness and miserable Ignorance of the true Knowledge and Worship of God, and may in time bring the Infidels and Savages, living in those parts, to human Civility, and to a settled and quiet Government; DO, by these our Letters-Patents, graciously accept of, and agree to, their humble and well-intended Desires."

Language of similar import may be found in the subsequent charters of that colony, from the same king, in 1609 and 1611; and the same is true of the various charters granted to the other colonies. In language more or less emphatic is the establishment of the Christian religion declared to be one of the purposes of the grant. The celebrated compact made by the Pilgrims in the Mayflower, 1620, recites: "Having undertaken for the Glory of God, and Advancement of the Christian Faith, and the Honour of our King and Country, a Voyage to plant the first Colony in the northern Parts of Virginia; Do by these Presents, solemnly and mutually, in the Presence of God and one another, covenant and combine ourselves together into a civil Body Politick, for our better Ordering and Preservation, and Furtherance of the Ends aforesaid."

. . . In the charter of privileges granted by William Penn to the province of Pennsylvania, in 1701, it is recited: "Because no People can be truly happy, though under the greatest Enjoyment of Civil Liberties, if abridged of the Freedom of their Consciences, as to their Religious Profession and Worship; And Almighty God being the only Lord of Conscience, Father of Lights and Spirits; and the Author as well as Object of all divine Knowledge, Faith and Worship, who only doth enlighten the Minds, and persuade and convince the Understandings of People, I do hereby grant and declare," etc.

Coming nearer to the present time, the Declaration of Independence recognizes the presence of the Divine in human affairs in these words: "We hold these truths to be self-evident, that all men are created equal, that they are endowed by their Creator with certain unalienable Rights, that among these are Life, Liberty, and the pursuit of Happiness."

. . .If we examine the constitutions of the various States we find in them a constant recognition of religious obligations. Every constitution of every one of the forty-four States contains language which either directly or by clear implication recognizes a profound reverence for religion and an assumption that its influence in all human affairs is essential to the well being of the community. This recognition may be in the preamble, such as is found in the constitution of Illinois, 1870: "We, the people of the State of Illinois, grateful to Almighty God for the civil, political and religious liberty which He hath so long permitted us to enjoy, and looking to Him for a blessing upon our endeavors to secure and transmit the same unimpaired to succeeding generations," etc.

It may be only in the familiar requisition that all officers shall take an oath closing with the declaration "so help me God." It may be in clauses like that of the constitution of Indiana, 1816, Article XI, section 4: "The manner of administering an oath or affirmation shall be such as is most consistent with the conscience of the deponent, and shall be esteemed the most solemn appeal to God." Or in provisions such as are found in Articles 36 and 37 of the Declaration of Rights of the Constitution of Maryland, 1867: "That as it is the duty of every man to worship God in such manner as he thinks most acceptable to Him, all persons are equally entitled to protection in their religious liberty; wherefore, no person ought, by any law, to be molested in his person or estate on account of his religious persuasion or profession, or for his religious practice, unless, under the color of religion, he shall disturb the good order, peace or safety of the State, or shall infringe the laws of morality, or injure others in their natural, civil or religious rights; nor ought any person to be compelled to frequent or maintain or contribute, unless on contract, to maintain any place of worship, or any ministry; nor shall any person, otherwise competent, be deemed incompetent as a witness, or juror, on account of his religious belief: *Provided*, He believes in the existence of God, and that, under His dispensation, such person will be held morally accountable for his acts, and be rewarded or punished therefor, either in this world or the world to come. That no religious test ought ever to be required as a qualification for any office of profit or trust in this State other than a declaration of belief in the existence of God; nor shall the legislature prescribe any other oath of office than the oath prescribed by this constitution." Or like that in Articles 2 and 3, of Part 1st, of the Constitution of Massachusetts, 1780: "It is the right as well as the duty of all men in society publicly and at stated seasons, to worship the Supreme Being, the great Creator and Preserver of the universe. . . . As the happiness of a people and the good order and preservation of civil government essentially depend upon piety, religion and morality, and as these cannot be generally diffused through a community but by the institution of the public worship of God and of public instructions in piety, religion and morality: Therefore, to promote their happiness and to secure the good order and preservation of their government, the people of this commonwealth have a right to invest their legislature with power to authorize and require, and the legislature shall, from time to time, authorize and require, the several towns, parishes, precincts and other bodies-politic or religious societies to make suitable provision, at their own expense, for the institution of the public worship of God and for the support and maintenance of public Protestant teachers of piety, religion and morality in all cases where such provision shall not be made voluntarily." Or as in sections 5 and 14 of Article 7, of the constitution of Mississippi, 1832: "No person who denies the being of a God, or a future state of rewards and punishments, shall hold any office in the civil department of this State. . . . Religion, morality and knowledge being necessary to good government, the preservation of liberty, and the happiness of mankind, schools and the means of education, shall forever be encouraged in this State." Or by Article 22 of the constitution of Delaware, 1776, which required all officers, besides an oath of allegiance, to make and subscribe the following declaration: "I, . . . , do profess faith in God the Father, and in Jesus Christ His only Son, and in the Holy Ghost, one God, blessed for evermore; and I do acknowledge the Holy Scriptures of the Old and New Testament to be given by divine inspiration."

Even the Constitution of the United States, which is supposed to have little touch upon the private life of the individual, contains in the First Amendment a declaration common to the constitutions of all the States, as follows: "Congress shall make no law respecting an establishment of religion, or prohibiting the free exercise thereof," etc. And also provides in Article 1, section 7, (a provision common to many constitutions,) that the Executive shall have ten days (Sundays excepted) within which to determine whether he will approve or veto a bill.

There is no dissonance in these declarations. There is a universal language pervading them all, having one meaning; they affirm and reaffirm that this is a religious nation. These are not individual sayings, declarations of private persons: they are organic utterances; they speak the voice of the entire people. While because of a general recognition of this truth the question has seldom been presented to the courts, yet we find that in *Updegraph v. The Commonwealth,* 11 S. & R. 394, 400, it was decided that, "Christianity, general Christianity, is, and always has been, a part of the common law of Pennsylvania; . . . not Christianity with an established church, and tithes, and spiritual courts; but Christianity with liberty of conscience to all men." And in *The People v. Ruggles,* 8 Johns. 290, 294, 295, Chancellor Kent, the great commentator on American law, speaking as Chief Justice of the Supreme Court of New York, said: "The people of this State, in common with the people of this country, profess the general doctrines of Christianity, as the rule of their faith and practice; and to scandalize the author of these doctrines is not only, in a religious point of view, extremely impious, but, even in respect to the obligations due to society, is a gross violation of decency and good order. . . . The free, equal and undisturbed enjoyment of religious opinion, whatever it may be, and free and decent discussions on any religious subject, is granted and secured; but to revile, with malicious and blasphemous contempt, the religion professed by almost the whole community, is an abuse of that right. Nor are we bound, by any expressions in the Constitution as some have strangely supposed, either not to punish at all, or to punish indiscriminately, the like attacks upon the religion of *Mahomet* or of the Grand *Lama;* and for this plain reason, that the case assumes that we are a Christian people, and in the morality of the country is deeply ingrafted upon Christianity, and not upon the doctrines or worship of those impostors."

. . . . If we pass beyond these matters to a view of American life as expressed by its laws, its business, its customs and its society, we find everywhere a clear recognition of the same truth. Among other matters note the following: The form of oath universally prevailing, concluding with an appeal to the Almighty; the custom of opening sessions of all deliberative bodies and most conventions with prayer; the prefatory words of all wills, "In the name of God, amen;" the laws respecting the observance of the Sabbath, with the general cessation of all secular business, and the closing of courts, legislatures, and other similar public assemblies on that day; the churches and church organizations which abound in every city, town and hamlet; the multitude of charitable organizations existing everywhere under Christian auspices; the gigantic missionary associations, with general support, and aiming to establish Christian missions in every quarter of the globe. These, and many other matters which might be noticed, add a volume of unofficial declarations to the mass of organic utterances that this is a Christian nation. In the face of all these, shall it be believed that a Congress of the United States intended to make it a misdemeanor for a church of this country to contract for the services of a Christian minister residing in another nation?

Defining Boundaries for Church and State: School Prayer, 1962

The Constitution's refusal to spell out the precise boundaries of church-state relationships has necessitated a long history of struggles in the courts between separationists and antiseparationists. The former wish to see the courts build up and maintain Jefferson's "wall," while the latter, to varying degrees, wish to see American public life open itself to religious influences. The former believe that religion is essentially a private matter. The latter see religion as a prerequisite, if not *the* prerequisite, for morality in the life of the individual and the life of society.

Because of the crucial role public schools play in forming the next generation of workers and leaders, they have been a central location for the struggle over religion in American life. The case of *Engel v. Vitale,* which was decided by the Supreme Court in 1962, is an illustration. The case was prompted by New York State education officials, who wrote an official state prayer and required that it be recited at the start of each school day in public schools throughout the state. Though the prayer did not endorse the views of any particular religion, and though students who wished to remain silent or leave the room during the recitation of the prayer were allowed to do so, the Supreme Court ruled unanimously that New York State's prayer policy was an unconstitutional violation of the First Amendment. This selection spells out the court's reasoning in what proved to be a landmark and controversial decision.

Source: Engel et al. v. Vitale et al., 370 U.S. 421 (1962).

. . . There can be no doubt that New York's state prayer* program officially establishes the religious beliefs embodied in the Regents' prayer. The respondents' argument to the contrary, which is largely based upon the contention that the Regents' prayer is "non-denominational" and the fact that the program, as modified and approved by state courts, does not require all pupils to recite the prayer but permits those who wish to do so to remain silent or be excused from the room, ignores the essential nature of the program's constitutional defects. Neither the fact that the prayer may be denominationally neutral nor the fact that its observance on the part of the students is voluntary can serve to free it from the limitations of the Establishment Clause, as it might from the Free Exercise Clause, of the First Amendment, both of which are operative against the States by virtue of the Fourteenth Amendment. Although these two clauses may in certain instances overlap, they forbid two quite different kinds of governmental encroachment upon religious freedom. The Establishment Clause, unlike the Free Exercise Clause, does not depend upon any showing of direct governmental compulsion and is violated by the enactment of laws which establish an official religion whether those laws operate directly to coerce nonobserving individuals or not. This is not to say, of course, that laws officially prescribing a particular form of religious worship do not involve coercion of such individuals. When the power, prestige and financial support of government is placed behind a particular religious belief, the indirect coercive pressure upon religious minorities to conform to the prevailing officially approved religion is plain. But the purposes underlying the Establishment Clause go much further than that. Its first and most immediate purpose rested on the belief that a union of government and religion tends to destroy government and to degrade religion. The history of governmentally established religion, both in England and in this country, showed that whenever government had allied itself with one particular form of religion, the inevitable result had been that it had incurred the hatred, disrespect and even contempt of those who held contrary beliefs. That same history showed that many people had lost their respect for any religion that had relied upon the support of government to spread its faith. The Establishment Clause thus stands as an expression of principle on the part of the Founders of our Constitution that religion is too personal, too sacred, too holy, to permit its "unhallowed perversion" by a civil magistrate. Another purpose of the Establishment Clause rested upon an awareness of the historical fact that governmentally established religions and religious persecutions go hand in hand. The Founders knew that only a few years after the Book of Common Prayer became the only accepted form of religious services in the established Church of England, an Act of Uniformity was passed to compel all Englishmen to attend those services and to make it a criminal offense to conduct or attend religious gatherings of any kind—a law which was consistently flouted by dissenting religious groups in England and which contributed to widespread persecutions of people like John Bunyan who persisted in holding "unlawful [religious]

---

*The prayer read, "Almighty God, we acknowledge our dependence upon Thee, and we beg Thy blessings upon us, our parents, our teachers, and our Country."

meetings . . . to the great disturbance and distraction of the good subjects of this kingdom. . . ." And they knew that similar persecutions had received the sanction of law in several of the colonies in this country soon after the establishment of official religions in those colonies. It was in large part to get completely away from this sort of systematic religious persecution that the Founders brought into being our Nation, our Constitution, and our Bill of Rights with its prohibition against any governmental establishment of religion. The New York laws officially prescribing the Regents' prayer are inconsistent both with the purposes of the Establishment Clause and with the Establishment Clause itself.

It has been argued that to apply the Constitution in such a way as to prohibit state laws respecting an establishment of religious services in public schools is to indicate a hostility toward religion or toward prayer. Nothing, of course, could be more wrong. The history of man is inseparable from the history of religion. And perhaps it is not too much to say that since the beginning of that history many people have devoutly believed that "More things are wrought by prayer than this world dreams of." It was doubtless largely due to men who believed this that there grew up a sentiment that caused men to leave the cross-currents of officially established state religions and religious persecution in Europe and come to this country filled with the hope that they could find a place in which they could pray when they pleased to the God of their faith in the language they chose. And there were men of this same faith in the power of prayer who led the fight for adoption of our Constitution and also for our Bill of Rights with the very guarantees of religious freedom that forbid the sort of governmental activity which New York has attempted here. These men knew that the First Amendment, which tried to put an end to governmental control of religion and of prayer, was not written to destroy either. They knew rather that it was written to quiet well-justified fears which nearly all of them felt arising out of an awareness that governments of the past had shackled men's tongues to make them speak only the religious thoughts that government wanted them to speak and to pray only to the God that government wanted them to pray to. It is neither sacrilegious nor antireligious to say that each separate government in this country should stay out of the business of writing or sanctioning official prayers and leave that purely religious function to the people themselves and to those the people choose to look to for religious guidance.

It is true that New York's establishment of its Regents' prayer as an officially approved religious doctrine of that State does not amount to a total establishment of one particular religious sect to the exclusion of all others—that, indeed, the governmental endorsement of that prayer seems relatively insignificant when compared to the governmental encroachments upon religion which were commonplace 200 years ago. To those who may subscribe to the view that because the Regents' official prayer is so brief and general there can be no danger to religious freedom in its governmental establishment, however, it may be appropriate to say in the words of James Madison, the author of the First Amendment:

> "[I]t is proper to take alarm at the first experiment on our liberties. . . . Who does not see that the same authority which can establish Christianity, in exclusion of all

other Religions, may establish with the same ease any particular sect of Christians, in exclusion of all other Sects? That the same authority which can force a citizen to contribute three pence only of his property for the support of any one establishment, may force him to conform to any other establishment in all cases whatsoever?"

Defining Boundaries for Church and State: Federal Aid to Church-affiliated Private Schools, 1971

Should public monies, raised by taxation, be used to support nonpublic schools maintained by religious denominations? This issue has been at the center of an intense controversy for decades. In the 1971 case, *Lemon v. Kurtzman,* the Supreme Court attempted to define under what circumstances tax monies may be used to support such schools. The case resulted from a 1968 Pennsylvania law that allowed the state's Superintendent of Public Instruction to assist nonpublic, largely Roman Catholic, schools. The superintendent was authorized to "purchase" certain "secular educational services" (teachers' salaries, textbooks, and instructional materials) from such schools. In effect, the state rented educational services from these schools in order to help them improve the quality of the education they offered. Aid was barred to courses containing "any subject matter expressing religious teaching or the morals or forms of worship of any sect." Nonetheless, in a unanimous decision, the Court ruled Pennsylvania's law, and a similar Rhode Island law, were unconstitutional.

In doing so, the Court significantly reinforced its "excessive entanglement" doctrine, which said, in effect, that though such state programs might seek to differentiate between secular and religious elements in education in the subsidies they offered, the administration of such programs created a relationship between church and state that could not be legally sustained under the First Amendment. The doctrine remains an important principle in cases involving the boundaries of church and state. While some public subsidies to religiously affiliated schools have been ruled constitutional, the Supreme Court's ruling in this and other cases has set definite boundaries around the scope and scale of such assistance. In consequence, those concerned with the maintenance of sectarian education have pursued avenues other than direct government subsidies in seeking ways to support such schools. Advocacy of the voucher system, by which, in one formulation, parents can direct the taxes they presently pay to support public education to pay tuition at private schools, is in large part motivated by the search for ways to finance education that is rooted in religious tradition.

In the absence of precisely stated constitutional prohibitions, we must draw lines with reference to the three main evils against which the Establishment Clause was intended to afford protection: "sponsorship, financial support, and

Source: Lemon et al. v. Kurtzman, Superintendent of Public Instruction of Pennsylvania, et al., 403 U.S. 602 (1971).

active involvement of the sovereign in religious activity." *Walz v. Tax Commission*, 397 U.S. 664, 668 (1970).

Every analysis in this area must begin with consideration of the cumulative criteria developed by the Court over many years. Three such tests may be gleaned from our cases. First, the statute must have a secular legislative purpose; second, its principal or primary effect must be one that neither advances nor inhibits religion, *Board of Education v. Allen*, 392 U.S. 236, 243 (1968); finally, the statute must not foster "an excessive government entanglement with religion." *Walz, supra*, at 674.

Inquiry into the legislative purposes of the Pennsylvania and Rhode Island statutes affords no basis for a conclusion that the legislative intent was to advance religion. On the contrary, the statutes themselves clearly state that they are intended to enhance the quality of the secular education in all schools covered by the compulsory attendance laws. There is no reason to believe the legislatures meant anything else. A State always has a legitimate concern for maintaining minimum standards in all schools it allows to operate. As in *Allen*, we find nothing here that undermines the stated legislative intent; it must therefore be accorded appropriate deference.

In *Allen* the Court acknowledged that secular and religious teachings were not necessarily so intertwined that secular textbooks furnished to students by the State were in fact instrumental in the teaching of religion. . . . The legislatures of Rhode Island and Pennsylvania have concluded that secular and religious education are identifiable and separable. In the abstract we have no quarrel with this conclusion.

The two legislatures, however, have also recognized that church-related elementary and secondary schools have a significant religious mission and that a substantial portion of their activities is religiously oriented. They have therefore sought to create statutory restrictions designed to guarantee the separation between secular and religious educational functions and to ensure that State financial aid supports only the former. All these provisions are precautions taken in candid recognition that these programs approached, even if they did not intrude upon, the forbidden areas under the Religion Clauses. We need not decide whether these legislative precautions restrict the principal or primary effect of the programs to the point where they do not offend the Religion Clauses, for we conclude that the cumulative impact of the entire relationship arising under the statutes in each State involves excessive entanglement between government and religion.

Our prior holdings do not call for total separation between church and state; total separation is not possible in an absolute sense. Some relationship between government and religious organizations is inevitable. . . . Fire inspections, building and zoning regulations, and state requirements under compulsory school-attendance laws are examples of necessary and permissible contacts. . . .

Judicial caveats against entanglement must recognize that the line of separation, far from being a "wall," is a blurred, indistinct, and variable barrier depending on all the circumstances of a particular relationship. . . .

In order to determine whether the government entanglement with religion is excessive, we must examine the character and purposes of the institutions that are benefited, the nature of the aid that the State provides, and the resulting relationship between the government and the religious authority. . . .

PENNSYLVANIA PROGRAM

The Pennsylvania statute . . . provides state aid to church-related schools for teachers' salaries. The complaint describes an educational system that is very similar to the one existing in Rhode Island. According to the allegations, the church-related elementary and secondary schools are controlled by religious organizations, have the purpose of propagating and promoting a particular religious faith, and conduct their operations to fulfill that purpose. Since this complaint was dismissed for failure to state a claim for relief, we must accept these allegations as true for purposes of our review.

As we noted earlier, the very restrictions and surveillance necessary to ensure that teachers play a strictly nonideological role give rise to entanglements between church and state. The Pennsylvania statute, like that of Rhode Island, fosters this kind of relationship. Reimbursement is not only limited to courses offered in the public schools and materials approved by state officials, but the statute excludes "any subject matter expressing religious teaching, or the morals or forms of worship of any sect." In addition, schools seeking reimbursement must maintain accounting procedures that require the State to establish the cost of the secular as distinguished from the religious instruction.

The Pennsylvania statute, moreover, has the further defect of providing state financial aid directly to the church-related school. . . . The history of government grants of a continuing cash subsidy indicates that such programs have almost always been accompanied by varying measures of control and surveillance. The government cash grants before us now provide no basis for predicting that comprehensive measures of surveillance and controls will not follow. In particular the government's post-adult power to inspect and evaluate a church-related school's financial records and to determine which expenditures are religious and which are secular creates an intimate and continuing relationship between church and state.

A broader base of entanglement of yet a different character is presented by the divisive political potential of these state programs. In a community where such a large number of pupils are served by church-related schools, it can be assumed that state assistance will entail considerable political activity. Partisans of parochial schools, understandably concerned with rising costs and sincerely dedicated to both the religious and secular educational missions of their schools, will inevitably champion this cause and promote political action to achieve their goals. Those who oppose state aid, whether for constitutional, religious, or fiscal reasons, will inevitably respond and employ all of the usual political campaign techniques to prevail. Candidates will be forced to declare and voters to choose. It would be unrealistic to ignore the fact that many people confronted with issues of this kind will find their votes aligned with their faith.

Ordinarily political debate and division, however vigorous or even partisan, are normal and healthy manifestations of our democratic system of government, but political division along religious lines was one of the principal evils against which the First Amendment was intended to protect. . . . To have States or communities divide on the issues presented by state aid to parochial schools would tend to confuse and obscure other issues of great urgency. We have an expanding array of vexing issues, local and national, domestic and international, to debate and divide on. It conflicts with our whole history and tradition to permit questions of the Religion Clauses to assume such importance in our legislatures and in our elections that they could divert attention from the myriad issues and problems that confront every level of government. The highways of church and state relationships are not likely to be one-way streets, and the Constitution's authors sought to protect religious worship from the pervasive power of government. The history of many countries attests to the hazards of religion's intruding into the political arena or of political power intruding into the legitimate and free exercise of religious belief. . . .

The potential for political divisiveness related to religious belief and practice is aggravated in these two statutory programs by the need for continuing annual appropriations and the likelihood of larger and larger demands as costs and populations grow. The Rhode Island District Court found that the parochial school system's "monumental and deepening financial crisis" would "inescapably" require larger annual appropriations subsidizing greater percentages of the salaries of lay teachers. Although no facts have been developed in this respect in the Pennsylvania case, it appears that such pressures for expanding aid have already required the state legislature to include a portion of the state revenues from cigarette taxes in the program.

In *Walz* it was argued that a tax exemption for places of religious worship would prove to be the first step in an inevitable progression leading to the establishment of state churches and state religion. That claim could not stand up against more than 200 years of virtually universal practice imbedded in our colonial experience and continuing into the present.

The progression argument, however, is more persuasive here. We have no long history of state aid to church-related educational institutions comparable to 200 years of tax exemption for churches. Indeed, the state programs before us today represent something of an innovation. We have already noted that modern governmental programs have self-perpetuating and self-expanding propensities. These internal pressures are only enhanced when the schemes involve institutions whose legitimate needs are growing and whose interests have substantial political support. Nor can we fail to see that in constitutional adjudication some steps, which when taken were thought to approach "the verge," have become the platform for yet further steps. A certain momentum develops in constitutional theory and it can be a "downhill thrust" easily set in motion but difficult to retard or stop. Development by momentum is not invariably bad; indeed, it is the way the common law has grown, but it is a force to be recognized and reckoned with. The dangers are increased by the difficulty of perceiving in advance exactly where the "verge" of the precipice lies. As well as constituting an independent evil against which the Religion Clauses were intended to protect, involvement or entanglement between government and religion serves as a warning signal. . . .

An Outsider's View of Christmas: "The Other Cheek," by Jay Kaplan, 1958

It is difficult to imagine a more agreeable occasion than Christmas, with its message of peace, hope, and good will, its celebration among family and friends, its decorations and constant media attention, and its exchange of gifts. In the warm glow of these familiar and widely shared aspects of the holiday season, Christmas takes on the proportions of a wintertime national festival that is less a religious than a civic event. It is in the context of these emotions and perceptions that the majority on the Supreme Court, in *Lynch v. Donnelly* (1984), could come to the conclusion that a creche display, erected in a public park and paid for with public money, was essentially a secular phenomenon. The purpose of the display, said the Court's majority, was simply to brighten the mood of holiday shoppers and make the city's central business district more attractive. It was not really religious in nature, and thus constituted no threat to the doctrine of separation of church and state.

Yet, as the majority acknowledged in *Lynch v. Donnelly,* Christmas is also, inescapably, the commemoration of the events central to the origins of Christianity, the religious faith of the large majority of Americans, past and present. No matter how universal its message, in this guise Christmas speaks specifically to the faith and culture of Christians. In doing so, the appearance of Christmas creates a complex problem for non-Christians to negotiate. On the one hand, they might wish to participate in the social and civic aspects of the holiday, but on the other, they cannot accept its religious meanings and still be true to their identities and beliefs. It has often been children who have been most exposed to the pressures of these negotiations, because of both their pluralistic networks of neighborhood friends and because of the difficulties of keeping such a beloved and congenial celebration out of their public school classrooms.

This selection is the story of one Jewish boy's negotiation of the pressures—from his parents, teacher, and peer group and his own conscience—he faces in dealing with Christmas. Like other children, he is reluctant to stand out, to be different, yet the situation forces this on him. The fierceness of his reaction to his teacher's insistence that he take part in the class's celebratory activities and his abiding hatred for her may seem extreme to those who have not been in the boy's place. But the dilemma he faces is no less real, even if we are convinced we would not react to it in exactly the same way. Some have urged that avoidance in our public life of the emotional burden such dilemmas impose, especially on children, is the very reason we must strive to build Jefferson's "wall" everywhere government has the legitimate power to do so. Others, however, argue that there is no practical way to shield religious minorities from occasionally feeling different and that to go to great lengths to do so may ultimately end up depriving the majority of its own liberty and happiness. It is a dilemma

Source: Jay Kaplan, "The Other Cheek," *Commentary* 26 (September 1958), 238–42.

basic to the determination of the fairness of the cultural arrangements of a pluralistic society.

Over twenty years have passed since all of this happened, and probably I do not really remember it accurately, yet I cannot be very far wrong. The details are too clear in my memory. . . .

It was early December. I was nine and a half. We lived in the University Heights section of the west Bronx; our block was the eighteen hundred block of Loring Place. My school was . . . Public School No. 26. . . .

What things are like there today when December rolls around I do not know. But in my day, the coming of December raised certain problems for me. Although the school was at least a third Jewish, December was purely the month of Christmas. None of the teachers I had ever made mention of Chanukkah, or even asked about the mysteries of the odd candelabras they may have glimpsed in some shop window.

There was, of course, no attempt to inflict any sort of worship on the class. But since it was a holiday—and a kind of a national holiday—surely some celebration was in order. Cards were made for the poor in orphanages; sometimes there was a play—not of the manger variety, but illustrative of the Christmas spirit; caroling was treated as a pleasant diversion, not only in assembly periods but in occasional classroom sessions.

When I was only six, my father had spoken quite seriously to me. "Soon," he said, "it will be Christmastime. Christmas is not our holiday. They may do things in school to celebrate Christmas—but you will not do any of it. You will sit quietly and do nothing . . . or do homework . . . or do whatever else the teacher may tell you. But if the name Jesus or Xmas or a tree like this is in anything—" (and as illustrations for both words and pictures, he had a stack of clippings which he had used over the years with my older brother) "—this is not for you. If your teacher asks, you tell her politely this is not your holiday. Say your father said so."

From near the door, my mother burst in "Tell him about Mary," she said. "Tell him! Anything with Virgins is also not for him!"

I was not embarrassed that first year; but in the next two, my self-consciousness grew; I was the only one in my class who did nothing at all. The other Jewish children either participated unself-consciously, or used one technique or another to avoid real participation. In the fourth grade, at age nine and a half, I decided to speak to my father.

"Papa," I said, "This week . . . in school . . . they'll begin with some of that Christmas business—"

My father spoke through his newspaper. "Well, it can't be helped. A good country. But in some things—thoughtless."

A few seconds passed. "Papa," I said, "I been thinking. Instead of doing nothing at all—"

Now my father put aside his newspaper. "Yes. Go on."

"I could do what a lot of the other kids do. Not draw the cards as good as I can really do it. Or be sloppy with my printing. Or just move my mouth when I sing."

"No," my father said. "You do nothing."

"But Papa," I said, "I'm the only one."

"In this country, it's all right to be the only one." His voice stayed even and soft, but very definite, very full. "If no one else wants to be just what they are— you can be it anyhow. You're not hurting anyone. This isn't your holiday. You don't believe in it. So you don't do anything."

It was another week before Christmas came to P.S. 26. In that week I tried several times to raise the issue again with my father; but each time I subsided after only a few words. Somehow, I couldn't muster any enthusiasm for arguing with him. To be absolutely honest, the Christmas season never seemed to have any appeal for me. Perhaps it was that all the sidewalk Santas in the Bronx looked so bedraggled and unjolly, standing beside their iron kettles and clanging their bells. Or possibly it was that the bare figure of Christ on the Cross (as I saw it in a churchyard some blocks away) always struck me as forbidding and a little eerie. The manger scene, in some obscure way, reminded me of my relatives coming to call and passing me by to go make a fuss over my baby sister.

So I had no heart for a struggle with my father. Or was it something deeper?

Whatever it was, I sat in school those days, not exactly calm but not fright-ened or apprehensive. Finally, the announcement was made: joyous Noël was upon us; we would share our joy with those less fortunate than ourselves, and make cards for the poor children who had no parents and no real home. Draw-ing paper was given out; a variety of cutouts was offered to use as tracing figures—a Christmas tree, a fat Santa, a huge stocking.

On the board our teacher—call her Mrs. Allen—printed two messages. Merry Xmas. Season's Greetings. These we were to print by ourselves.

Mrs. Allen was a stout, bulky woman who looked clearly older than my mother (my yardstick of age in those days). That would have put her near forty. Perhaps she was beyond it, although (at least as I remember) her hair was all brown and her skin was not wrinkled. She had a voice which was gravelly, even though it was nearly always pitched at a very soft level. She used to walk about the room as we children worked. Perhaps, that was prescribed in the Teacher's Guide of the day, but she really seemed to enjoy it. She used to move a few steps and pause, and survey—then nod or look perplexed—then move and pause again. For the child under scrutiny, it was possible to feel her nod or her frown even without looking up.

That December afternoon, sitting with my blank drawing paper before me, I felt Mrs. Allen frown. I was holding my pencil, and staring at my desk top, and I felt her there, and somehow I managed to sit absolutely quiet.

"You're not working, Jerome," she said. Oh, so softly . . . "Don't you feel well?"

"I'm all right," I said.

"If you don't get started soon, you won't have time to make a good card."

"I'm not making a card," I said.

"Not making a card?" Mrs. Allen said. "Why not?"

"This isn't my holiday," I said. "I don't believe in it."

Mrs. Allen moved closer. "Some little orphan is going to be very sad—if he's the one not to have a card."

"This isn't my holiday," I said.

"Look," Mrs. Allen said. "You can print Season's Greetings. There's nothing wrong in printing Season's Greetings."

Probably it was not just chance: the colorless, odorless, non-sectarian message. Mrs. Allen was a planner—or again, was it the code for all such activities? Still, there were the cutouts; and to my nine-and-a-half-year-old mind, all was not quite as it should be. So my back stayed up, and I spoke the magic defensive words. "My father said no," I muttered. "My father said nothing."

There was a silence of a few seconds. Then Mrs. Allen said: "Very well, Jerome. You may read your history book while we continue to draw."

This was not punishment: it was not intended as punishment. I am bound, in all honesty, to say here and now that Mrs. Allen had never singled me out for punishment or reward, up to that time. Nor did I think to myself, as she passed along the aisle, that I had made an enemy. I had no reason to think that. Her discipline was strong; her homework assignments were longer than the other fourth-grade teachers; but we had never found her to be vindictive.

The next day or two—perhaps three—all was serene in the classroom. Christmas was unmentioned. Mrs. Allen seemed hardly aware of my existence. I got no dark forbidding glances, and my name was called only in its due time.

Then, one afternoon, we had a music period, and midway in our singing Mrs. Allen, paused and spoke of the next song we would sing. It was, according to her soft explanation, a song much beloved "all over the world." A song translated into many different languages. A song of peace and hope. A song of all people who ever hoped for a better world. And yet, she continued, all of us knew it. It began with the word Silent . . . Now what was it?

The answer came in many voices. Then she led the class into the song. The temptation to move my lips was strong. In our music work, it was her gaze—not her feet—that traveled painstakingly to each of us; and this gaze I felt—once, then again, then again. My lips all but twitched. The temptation to mouth the words grew stronger. And yet, something held me back. It was somehow Mrs. Allen herself. She seemed to look at me too often. I felt almost a kind of demand.

Elsewhere in the class, there were others only moving their lips. Surely she knew. Surely she recognized it. I could see it myself—out of the corner of an eye. Why was I the one singled out? It was unfair.

The carol ended. Another was introduced. Again we were led into song and again I was silent. More minutes of discomfort, indecision, resentment. More glances. I glanced determinedly at the floor; my throat was dry and choked. Still another carol followed. I heard Mrs. Allen come to my side of the room, but she stayed up in front of the class, serving with dignity in her role of conductor or choirmaster.

Finally, the singing over, the rest of the day settled into the old ordinary pattern. Occasionally, as I worked, I would feel some vague indefinable discomfort—and glancing up, I would find Mrs. Allen at another part of the room, but with her eyes on me. Perhaps I was oversensitive. Had anything really happened after all? Mrs. Allen had not even spoken disapprovingly to me.

A few more days passed. All was not serene. I could not shake the feeling—

the sense—that there was something between Mrs. Allen and myself. I did not speak of this at home: somehow, it seemed to be a thing that belonged to me alone. What could I have said, anyway? What was there to say?

It was on a Monday that everything exploded. The time was perhaps one-thirty; most of our cultural, semi-recreational activities were placed in the afternoons. What we had just finished doing, I do not remember; but suddenly, out from a drawer came her large book of music. She was seated at the moment, but she soon rose and stood before us, leaving the book on the desk.

"Boys and girls," she said, "before we begin our singing, I'd like to tell you something about music. Most of us don't appreciate just what music really is. It isn't only words and a tune. It's a special kind of language. It's one way that people who don't speak the same language can still feel like friends. That's why music is often called the universal language. When people come to a different country, and they don't understand anything at all in the country, they can still understand the music. If it's happy, they can feel that. If it's sad, they can feel that, too. And sometimes—to show how friendly they feel toward the people who are singing—they hum along . . . or sing along. And it doesn't matter if the words don't come out just right. It's the friendliness that counts. Even if they're told by someone what the words mean, and they don't really believe or feel what these people feel, they can still sing. It's a mark of how friendly they feel.

"Singing together is a way of saying: I like you. I feel friendly to you. And the world needs that. The world always needs more friendliness."

Once or twice, while she was speaking, she'd looked over at me. And I'd looked aside. Now, after a few more comments and introduction, she carried the class into the lesson. The opening selection was announced as "O come All Ye Faithful . . ."

The voices rose. Silent and somehow fearful, I heard the words loud in my ears:

O come, all ye faith-ful, joy-ful and tri-um-phant,
O come ye, O come ye to Beth-le-hem;
Come and be-hold Him, born the King of angels.
O come, let us a-dore Him
O come, let us a-dore Him
O come, let us a-dore Him
Christ, the Lord . . . Amen.

The carol ended. There was a long silence. Then abruptly it came: soft yet frightening. "Jerome . . ."

Guiltily, I raised my glance. Mrs. Allen's face was serious but showed no anger. When she spoke—after a moment or so—her voice was somewhat thick. "Will you please come up here, Jerome?"

I moved up the aisle. The hot glare of my classmates' attention was all around me. At the head of the aisle—still a few feet from Mrs. Allen I paused. Somehow my eyes remained focused on her face.

"Jerome," Mrs. Allen said, coming closer, "I noticed you haven't been singing. Last week . . . and now today."

"Sometimes I sing—" I said, irrelevantly.

"I understand," Mrs. Allen said. "When you don't sing, it's for a reason."

"It's—" I began falteringly.

"It's just that Christmas isn't your holiday," Mrs. Allen said. "Well, that's true. Christmas isn't everyone's holiday. But the feeling of friendliness—that's something you have, I know. Even if some of your classmates celebrate different things than you celebrate, you still want to say to them—I LIKE YOU, I HOPE YOU HAVE A GOOD TIME ON YOUR HOLIDAY. Isn't that so?"

"Yes," I said.

"Well, we can say that by singing with people."

"No," I said, "I can't. These songs—"

"It's the words," Mrs. Allen said. "I understand. You can't say certain words. It doesn't seem right . . . for you to say them . . ." Now she paused. "Well—I know how we can fix that. We all want to be friendly and we all want to have a good time and sing together—so I have a song we can all sing. I'm sure you learned it when you were in the lower grades. It's a beautiful little song the English Children sing. It's called "Deck the Halls . . ." Now she turned to the class. "Is there anyone who can sing it all the way through—just to refresh our memories?"

One of the girls raised her hand. Mrs. Allen nodded her recognition. The words came tinkling out.

Deck the halls with boughs of holly,
    fa la la la la . . . la la la la . . .
'Tis the season to be jolly,
    fa la la la la . . . la la la la . . .
Don we now our gay apparel,
    fa la la la la . . . la la la la . . .
Troll the ancient Yule-tide carol . . .

"There," Mrs. Allen exclaimed, "not a word in it that everyone can't sing. Is there? Just a song about children enjoying themselves. We'll all sing it together now."

I started to turn to go to my seat, but Mrs. Allen said: "No. You help me Jerome. You help me lead the class. That'll be fun."

A gesture of her hand brought absolute silence to the class. Then, with another gesture and her own voice rising clear, it began. "Deck the halls with boughs of holly," etc, etc.

But for me—no words would come. Though the carol had no mention of Christ, the Lord—or Mary—or the infant Jesus—I couldn't sing. By any name, by any words, it was a Christmas song to me. Anger was rising within me; but even stronger than anger at that moment was a feeling that I would not let myself be duped. It was some kind of trick—what kind I could not have explained.

Suddenly I was nudged. "Sing, Jerome," Mrs. Allen said. "Sing."

I shook my head.

"Sing," she said.

Much of the class was still by now, watching what was happening. The other voices were a weak chorus: "See the blazing yule before us, Fa la la la la . . . la la la la . . . Strike the harp and join the chorus . . ."

"Sing!" she said.

Now with anger and hate filling me—I shouted: "No. I won't!" Blindly, I fled for the door—brushing her as I passed.

A few minutes later, one of my classmates found me in my place of hiding—the boys' bathroom. It was one of the other Jewish boys. "The singing is over," he said. "You can come back now."

I shook my head, not even looking at him.

"It's all right, she said she wasn't going to punish you."

I went back with him, and went to my seat without looking at anyone. I did not feel like any kind of hero. I felt curiously marked . . . stamped . . . branded. . . .

I was in my seat when Mrs. Allen came slowly down the aisle and paused near-by. "Jerome," she said, but her voice was strong and clear enough so that it could be heard throughout the class. "It's all over. We'll forget about the whole thing. If you feel you can't sing, then you don't have to sing. And I want you to know . . . even though you hurt me, I forgive you. I've never been shouted at like you shouted at me and I've never been pushed like that, but I forgive you, I forgive you because that's what I was taught to do"—and here she paused—"in my home. Other people may teach different things in their home—but that's what I was taught. It's called 'turning the other cheek.' It means a person should forgive . . . and try to be friends with other people . . . no matter what."

There may've been more. I heard nothing. I sat there hating her, wishing her dead, wanting to die myself or be somewhere far away.

Within a day I had stopped wanting to die. Within a few days I had stopped wanting to be far away. Within a month I had stopped wishing her dead.

I have never stopped hating her.

I have not even tried.

I will not lie about it, either to myself or to anyone else. The hate I feel, though dimmed by the years, still somehow seems right and clean to me. . . .

SUGGESTIONS FOR FURTHER READING

Robert S. Alley, *School Prayer: The Court, the Congress, and the First Amendment.* Buffalo: Prometheus Books, 1994.

Stephen L. Carter, *The Culture of Disbelief: How American Law and Politics Trivialize Religious Devotion.* New York: Basic Books, 1993.

Thomas J. Curry, *The First Freedoms: Church and State in America to the Passage of the First Amendment.* New York: Oxford University Press, 1986.

Robert T. Handy, *A Christian America: Protestant Hopes and Historical Realities.* 2d ed. New York: Oxford University Press, 1984.

Leonard Levy, *The Establishment Clause: Religion and the First Amendment.* 2d ed. Chapel Hill: University of North Carolina Press, 1994.

Wayne R. Swanson, *The Christ Child Goes to Court.* Philadelphia: Temple University Press, 1990.

11

Individual Rights or Group Rights? The Question of Affirmative Action

In 1961, recently elected President John F. Kennedy issued Executive Order 10925, which established the President's Equal Employment Commission and spelled out the obligations of contractors doing business with the government: "The contractor will take *affirmative action* to ensure that applicants are employed, and employees are treated during their employment, without regard to their race, creed, color, or national origin" (emphasis added). Kennedy was trying to accomplish executively what the U.S. Congress was in no mood to bring about legislatively: extend to racial minorities the same civil rights enjoyed by the white majority. At that time, Southerners in the House and Senate were opposed to any civil rights legislation and were ready to talk down any proposal.

In 1963, Kennedy submitted a Civil Rights bill to Congress. Title VII of that bill reproduced the language of Executive Order 10925 with regard to affirmative action. But Southern resistance to civil rights legislation continued and Kennedy's proposal languished on Capitol Hill.

In the aftermath of Kennedy's November 1963 assassination—in a climate of sorrow and guilt—Kennedy's successor, President Lyndon B. Johnson, was able to persuade Congress to pass Kennedy's bill as the Civil Rights Act of 1964. To be sure, the law did not automatically change the backward social and economic situation of African Americans after years of disenfranchisement, as it put an end only to legal discrimination. It was clear to many in the Civil Rights Movement that a remedy was needed to counteract the effect of almost a century of discrimination.

Enter affirmative action. Kennedy had used the term to refer to positive efforts aimed at ensuring that members of a racial minority who were qualified for a job would have the same opportunities to compete for it as other qualified individuals, regardless of race or ethnicity. This was also the general frame of mind in Congress when the Civil Rights Act was finally passed.

But the Johnson administration soon imparted a completely different meaning to the term. In a speech delivered in 1965, at historically black Howard University, in Washington, D.C., President Johnson declared that giving equal rights to blacks by law was not enough. Johnson said: "You do not take a person who, for years, has been hobbled by chains and liberate him, bring him to the starting line of a race and then say, 'You are free to compete with all others' and still justly believe you have been completely fair." Johnson called for "not just legal equity," but for "equality as a result." That is to say, blacks were to receive special considerations. The concept of affirmative action as compensatory action for past discrimination was later extended to cover other nonwhite minorities and women.

In the seventies and eighties, affirmative action continued to have the meaning that it had acquired in the Johnson administration. It referred generally to policies aimed at giving jobs, or awarding contracts, or granting academic admission, to individuals on the basis of their membership in a group defined by race, ethnicity, or sex—on the grounds that such a group had been subjected to discrimination in the past.

Advocates of affirmative action pointed out that affirmative action was not intended to be used forever. A time would come when women and minorities would be represented in the marketplace and in academia in the same proportion that they were in the population. After that was accomplished there would be no further need for affirmative action programs. In the meantime, individual white men would have to lose out.

Since white men constituted a significant portion of the U.S. population, it was no wonder that public opinion polls in the eighties showed affirmative action to be very unpopular. Polls showed that the great majority of white Americans were in favor of equal opportunities for all, regardless of race, sex, or ethnicity, but at the same time opposed preferential treatment based on group membership.

Opponents of affirmative action pointed out that any preferential treatment for women or minorities constituted *reverse discrimination* against innocent white men. In their view, it was as morally wrong to exclude white men from jobs or government contracts or academic programs as it had been to exclude blacks socially and economically before the Civil Rights era. In both cases exclusion was race based.

In attacks on affirmative action, opponents said that preferential programs established *quotas*—or a fixed number of slots in employment, government contracting, or academic admission—that were set aside exclusively for minorities or women. Opponents of affirmative action argued that quotas were both illegal and unconstitutional. They were illegal because the Civil Rights Act of 1964 prohibited discrimination based on race, sex, or national origin. And they were unconstitutional because they denied white men the equal protection of the laws enshrined in the Fourteenth Amendment to the U.S. Constitution.

In contrast, advocates of affirmative action, declaring that programs established *goals* and *timetables* rather than quotas, argued that affirmative action was neither unconstitutional nor illegal. It was not unconstitutional because there was nothing in the constitution that specified that all government action must be color-blind. In fact, argued advocates of affirmative action, to undo the effects of past discrimination it was imperative to take race (or ethnicity or sex) into account. Furthermore, they argued, affirmative action was not illegal because the criterion of group membership was only one of several criteria that could be used in choosing one person over another. To its advocates, affirmative action did not mean hiring an unqualified woman or an unqualified minority over a qualified white male. Rather, it meant that if two individuals were equally qualified, being a woman or being a minority might be a better qualification for a job than being a man when the job was in a category in which women or minorities (or both) were underrepresented. In that case, being a woman or a minority was a better qualification because it was better for society in general if no groups were underrepresented.

But that kind of reasoning contradicted certain fundamental beliefs that have been part of the American ethos throughout the nation's history. One such belief is that individual rights are supreme and always take precedence over group rights. Another is that individuals are to be judged only by their personal qualifications and merits. In the late twentieth century many Americans remained convinced that U.S. society has always been a true *meritocracy,* where success is directly related to individual effort: if you succeed, it will be through your own efforts; if you do not succeed, it will be because you did not try hard enough. However, supporters of affirmative action pointed out that this view disregarded the fact that everyone does not start out with the same social and economic endowment, and this was precisely the position taken by President Johnson in his 1965 speech calling for special measures in favor of blacks.

Because of essentially irreconcilable views on how to undo the effects of past discrimination in a fair and just way, affirmative action became one of the most divisive issues in American society, especially in the 1980s. Bitter debate over it continued in public and in private. Many times the issue reached the courts of law, including the court of last appeal, the U.S. Supreme Court.

Between 1974 and 1995 the Supreme Court heard thirteen affirmative action cases. It favored affirmative action policies in seven of them and disallowed them in the other six cases. Decisions were never unanimous and the vote was 5 to 4 in eight of the thirteen cases. The Court seemed to move back and forth between the poles of an insoluble conflict. At times it allowed taking race into account for the purpose of eliminating inequalities created by past discrimination. At other times it ruled that making such an allowance was itself discriminatory. To illustrate, in the 1978 decision, *Regents of the University of California v. Bakke* (see the first two selections in this chapter), the Court disallowed racial quotas in academic admission, but in a later case, *United States v. Paradise* (1987), it allowed such quotas in the hiring of state troopers. And in 1980, in *Fullilove v. Klutznick,* the Court said it was not unconstitutional to set aside a fixed number of government contracts for minorities, but in 1989, in *City of Richmond v. J. A. Crosson Company,* it said it was unconstitutional to do so.

On the other hand, the Court was generally consistent in allowing affirmative action programs that did not establish fixed numerical quotas and was also consistent in disallowing programs that would fire white workers with more seniority and retain recently hired nonwhites.

Some rulings favorable to affirmative action came when President Ronald Reagan was in office—with the Court rebuffing the militant antiaffirmative action stance of the President. The Reagan administration had provided legal assistance to parties bringing suit against affirmative action programs.

However, in the late eighties, the Court took a more conservative course, partly under the influence of new justices—appointed by Reagan and his successor, President George Bush—who were philosophically opposed to group rights having precedence over individual rights. In 1989, in *City of Richmond v. J. A. Crosson Company,* the Court ruled that a 30 percent set-aside program for minority contractors was unconstitutional. In another decision that year, the Court seemed to encourage challenges to affirmative action plans. In *Martin v. Wilks* it ruled, 5 to 4, that white firefighters could challenge a court-ordered plan that called for hiring more black firefighters, even though they had not been a party to the suit between the black firefighters and the city of Birmingham, Alabama.

However, in 1990 the Court seemed to change course again. In *Metro Broadcasting v. Federal Communication Commission*—by another 5–4 vote—the Court upheld two affirmative action programs set by Congress to increase minority ownership of broadcast licenses. This appeared to be contrary to the spirit of the 1989 Richmond decision that disallowed set-asides for minority contractors. The difference was—as the five-justice majority saw it—that Congress had greater authority than state or local governments to require affirmative action programs.

Congress itself counteracted the antiaffirmative action drive of the Reagan-Bush years by passing—over the objections of President Bush—the Civil Rights Act of 1991. The 1991 legislation amended the Civil Rights Act of 1964 by widening the scope of civil rights protections. In particular it narrowed the opportunities of whites to sue in affirmative action cases to which they had not been a party, thus offsetting the *Martin v. Wilks* decision. The Civil Rights Act of 1991 also favored affirmative action by placing on employers the burden of showing that they had not engaged in discrimination. This particularly offset a 1988 Supreme Court decision, *Ward's Cove Packing Co. v. Atonio*—not directly related to affirmative action—in which the Court had placed the burden of proving discrimination on those alleging that they had been discriminated against. At the beginning of the nineties, it seemed as if affirmative action, endangered during the Reagan and Bush years, had become newly protected by Congress.

However, in 1995 it was the Court's turn to rebuff Congress in the case of *Adarand Constructors v. Pena,* which seemed to deal a blow to affirmative action. In yet another 5–4 decision, the Court ruled that federal programs must meet the same strict standards applying to state and local programs—thus overturning the 1990 Metro Broadcasting decision.

Toward the end of the nineties, it seemed safe to predict that the fate of affirmative action would depend on the composition of the Supreme Court, which in turn would depend on the philosophical leanings of presidents appointed new justices and on the mood of the people reflected in a Congress that would ratify such appointments.

Against Set-asides: A Group of Jewish and Other White Ethnic Organizations Submit a Brief to the Supreme Court, 1977

In 1977 the U.S. Supreme Court considered the case *Regents of the University of California v. Bakke*. Alan Bakke, a white man, had been rejected twice by the University of California at Davis medical school. The Davis medical school admitted only one hundred applicants each year. Of the one hundred positions, sixteen were set aside to be filled exclusively with racial and ethnic minority students. These were admitted under a special program where academic requirements were not as high as in the regular program. Both times he applied, Bakke had better credentials than any nonwhite minority student admitted under the special program. Bakke sued the University alleging that Davis' set-aside program discriminated against him, illegally and unconstitutionally. The California State Supreme Court sided with Bakke and ordered him admitted, whereupon the University sued to reverse this decision. The Supreme Court then agreed to hear the case.

Following are excerpts from a brief submitted to the Court in the Bakke case. Any individual or group who is not a party to a legal case before the Supreme court (or any court) but has an interest in it may submit an *amicus curiae* ("friend of the court") brief—or *amicus brief* for short. It is a document arguing in favor of one of the sides, usually for the purpose of influencing the Court's ruling. It may be used to show what the position of a person or organization is on the issue being decided.

This brief was filed jointly by the American Jewish Committee, the American Jewish Congress, and several other organizations representing Greek Americans, Italian Americans, Polish Americans, and Ukrainian Americans.

Strong opposition of Jewish groups to affirmative action quotas grew in part from the fact that for many years quotas were used to discriminate against Jews in academic admission. During much of the first half of the twentieth century, many private American colleges and universities followed consciously a policy of admitting only a certain percentage of Jewish applicants. This was clearly discrimination on ethnic and religious grounds.

Restricting Jewish admission was part of a general pattern of exclusion of Jews from the social and economic life of the nation—an exclusion grounded in strong antisemitic attitudes held by great sectors of the population. Jewish exclusion would not begin to lessen in higher education and other areas until revelations about Nazi atrocities in World War II brought to Americans an awareness of the terrible consequences that antisemitism

Source: 483 U.S. 265 (1978).

might have. Such an awareness contributed to making antisemitism unpopular in the United States.

Not surprisingly, the University insists that its special admissions program should not be viewed as a "quota." Since "quota" is a painful word to many people because it is reminiscent of past injustices, it is often replaced by a euphemism such as "ratio" or "reasonable representation."

Any such semantic maneuvers to evade the trial court's explicit finding of fact, however, would be irrelevant here, since it is admitted that a fixed number, 16, of the 100 places available in each of the affected classes was reserved for those applicants who were members of certain specified racial or ethnic groups. Such a procedure, setting floor quotas for certain groups, inevitably sets ceiling quotas for other groups. The resulting injustice is palpable, particularly for the individual who would have been admitted but for his race. We submit that the principles laid down in the decisions reviewed above plainly apply to this form of discrimination.

First, there is no doubt that the Equal Protection Clause bars racial discrimination in admissions to state universities. In *Florida ex rel. Hawkins* v. *Board of Control,* 350 U.S. 413 (1956), this Court ordered the black plaintiff, who was denied admission solely because of race, admitted to the University of Florida School of Law "under the rules and regulations applicable to other qualified applicants," even though a black law school was then available to him at Florida A. & M. University. This, we believe, is the law today and, indeed, should be the law.

Second, this Court has repeatedly condemned the concept of quotas in cases dealing with employment. More than 60 years ago, it struck down state-imposed employment quotas based on alienage, holding that state action which has the effect of denying certain inhabitants the right to work for a living on grounds of race or nationality is violative of the Equal Protection Clause because it is destructive of the "very essence of the personal freedom and opportunity . . . it was the purpose of the Amendment to secure." The same result was reached 35 years later in *Hughes* v. *Superior Court of California,* 339 U.S. 460 (1950), which presented the question whether the Supreme Court of California had the right to enjoin a union from picketing which was conducted for the purpose of forcing a quota system upon an employer. This Court noted that the California court had held "that the conceded purpose of the picketing in this case—to compel the hiring of Negroes in proportion to Negro customers—was unlawful even though pursued in a peaceful manner" (at 462). The Court also quoted the part of the California decision explaining why a quota system is discriminatory, i.e., that those seeking to set up a quota system "would, to the extent of the fixed proportion, make the right to work for Lucky dependent not on fitness for the work nor on an equal right of all, regardless of race, to compete in an open market, but rather, on membership in a particular race" (at 463–464). The Court went on to say (at 464):

> To deny to California the right to ban picketing in the circumstances of this case would mean that there could be no prohibition of the pressure of picketing to secure

proportional employment on ancestral grounds of Hungarians in Cleveland, of Poles in Buffalo, of Germans in Milwaukee, of Portuguese in New Bedford, of Mexicans in San Antonio, of the numerous minority groups in New York, and so on through the whole gamut of racial and religious concentrations in various cities.

In affirming the California Supreme Court decision granting the injunction against the picketing, this Court held, in effect, that the picketing was unlawful because its purpose, to establish a quota based on race, was unlawful. In Fourteenth Amendment terms, any state action in support of a racial quota system inevitably clashes with the Equal Protection Clause.

• • • • •

Quotas can be seen as an appropriate means of dealing with a pressing public problem only if their harmful effects are ignored. We submit that [the University] is asking this court to do just that.

There are a number of reasons why racially discriminatory classifications in professional school admission practices are unsound. The most important of these is their manifest unfairness to individuals. Ineluctably they penalize innocent persons who bear no personal responsibility for historic wrongdoing. Moreover, while assuredly most people of color in this country are culturally "disadvantaged," not all are, nor are all whites by any stretch of the imagination properly to be considered "advantaged." Rarely if ever, for instance, have whites from poverty-stricken Appalachia been singled out as a group for preferential educational treatment. Nor has favoritism been bestowed on members of other ethnic groups which credibly can claim to have been subject to generalized societal discrimination—Italians, Poles, Jews, Greeks, Slavs—as a result of which at least some such persons bear the economic and cultural scars of prejudice and thus could be deemed entitled to preference as a form of restitution. As but one example, while Poles comprise 6.9% of the population in the Chicago metropolitan area, the percentage of Poles on the boards of directors of the 106 largest corporations in that area is only 0.3%. Barta, Report prepared by The Institute of Urban Life for The National Center for Urban Ethnic Affairs (1973).

On the other hand, preferential systems such as the one challenged here do confer benefits on some blacks and Hispanics who have come to this country recently—for example, from Mexico, Jamaica and Cuba—and who cannot be said to have been injured by past discrimination in this country.

Preferences also create the danger that, once race is accepted as a factor in admissions, it will progressively affect the operation of the school generally. For example, it is likely that, in the interest of demonstrating the success of the admissions policy, there will be a strong temptation to grade disadvantaged minority students on a scale less rigorous than that by which others are measured—or to reduce failure criteria for all students. If this does happen (and some believe it already has), minority students will perceive that they are beneficiaries of a double standard, which is apt to play havoc with their own self-esteem, not to mention the impact it may have on others who manage to graduate without any favoritism.

A significant adverse side effect of preferential treatment is likely to be that those minority students of high ability and accomplishment who excel strictly on merit will nevertheless carry the stigma upon graduation that they, too, were beneficiaries of a double standard.

•　•　•　•　•

Also germane to the issue of racially preferential admission to professional schools, and of artificially imposed proportional representation therein on the basis of race, are the following excerpts from the widely syndicated column by Roy Wilkins, the distinguished retired Executive Director of the National Association for the Advancement of Colored People, in the New York *Post* of March 3, 1973:

> . . .It is ridiculous for Negroes to claim that because they are 40 percent of the population, they should have 40 percent of the jobs, 40 percent of the elected offices, etc.
>
> This is self-defeating nonsense, for no person of ability wants to be limited in his horizons by an arbitrary quota or wants to endure unqualified people in positions that they fill only because of a numerical racial quota.
>
> . . .Ignoring the decades in which black college students were on a "zero quota" basis, they went into college admissions policies which on some campuses set aside a percentage of places for black applicants. In some places white applicants with excellent records have been made to stand aside for blacks with inferior records.
>
> . . .Such practices and, in fact, the whole black-tilted system are doing no favors to Negro applicants. God knows it is true that the cards have been deliberately stacked against blacks. Every feasible step, even those costing extra money, should be taken to correct this racialism.
>
> But there must not be a lowering of standards. Negroes need to insist on being among the best, not on being the best of the second- or third-raters. . . .

In his book, *Black Education, Myths and Tragedies,* Thomas Sowell, an outstanding economist who attended public school in Harlem, and is now at Stanford University in Palo Alto in California, forcefully articulated his own aversion to quotas as a remedy for past deprivation:

> . . .the actual harm done by quotas is far greater than having a few incompetent people here and there—and the harm that will actually be done will be harm primarily to the *black* population. What all the arguments and campaigns for quotas are really saying, loud and clear, is that *black people just don't have it,* and that they will have to be *given* something in order to have something. The devastating impact of this message on black people—particularly black young people—will outweigh any few extra jobs that may result from this strategy. Those black people who are already competent, and who could be instrumental in producing more competence among the rising generation, will be completely undermined, as black becomes synonymous —in the minds of black and white alike—with incompetence, and black achievement becomes synonymous with charity or payoffs.

Considerations such as these may well account for the fact that popular opposition to racial preferences is almost as strong among minority groups as it is in the general population. That is shown by a Gallup Poll taken in March, 1977. In that poll, 83% of the general population expressed opposition to preferential treatment in higher education and employment for both women and minority group members, and favored use of the criterion of ability as measured by tests, notwithstanding past discrimination. 64% of the non-white participants in this survey answered the same way (*The Gallup Opinion Index,* June 1977).

"Affirmed in part and reversed in part": The Bakke Decision, 1978

When Alan Bakke sued the University of California at Davis, he argued that the medical school's set-aside program for minorities violated the Civil Rights Act of 1964, forbidding race- and ethnic-based discrimination in programs receiving federal funds, and that the program, by setting aside positions for which he could not compete, denied him equal protection of the law under the Fourteenth Amendment. The University argued that the right to expect treatment based exclusively on color-blind individual merit was offset by the state's compelling concern for the victims of past and continuing discrimination. The California State Supreme Court ruled that the set-aside was an illegal quota, and since the University had not shown that it itself had discriminated against the same groups in the past, the quota was a denial of equal protection and was therefore unconstitutional. Bakke was ordered admitted, but the University sued to reverse the state court decision because it wanted to retain the set-aside program.

At the Supreme Court, the decision of the state court was "affirmed in part and reversed in part." By a 5–4 vote the Supreme Court agreed with the state court that the Davis program was illegal under the Civil Rights Act of 1964. On this decision, Justice Lewis Powell, who spoke for the Court, was joined by Chief Justice Warren E. Burger and justices William Rehnquist, John Paul Stevens, and Potter Stewart. Dissenting were justices Harry Blackmun, William Brennan, Thurgood Marshall, and Byron White, who essentially sided with the University's argument valuing society's needs to dismantle the effects of past discrimination over individual rights.

The four justices who sided with Powell agreed that the case could be settled by applying the Civil Rights Act without involving constitutional issues. But Powell thought that since the University had not proven previous discrimination, the Davis program was also unconstitutional. However, Powell also thought that an explicit racial classification was not unconstitutional when past discrimination could be proved.

This led Powell to side on the second issue with the four justices who had disagreed with him on the first issue. Opposing him this time were the same four justices who had sided with him on the first issue. Reversing part of the state court's decision, the Supreme Court ruled, 5 to 4, that race could be used as a criterion for admission. Powell also spoke for this major-

Source: 483 U.S. 265 (1978).

ity. However, where Powell said that race could be invoked only when past discrimination could be proved in a specific case, the other four justices agreed that past societal discrimination in general justified the use of race. Following are representative opinions of the different positions.

[I]

Mr. Justice Powell announced the judgment of the Court.

This case presents a challenge to the special admissions program of the petitioner, the Medical School of the University of California at Davis, which is designed to assure the admission of a specified number of students from certain minority groups. The Superior Court of California sustained respondent's challenge, holding that petitioner's program violated the California Constitution, Title VI of the Civil Rights Act of 1964, 42 USC §2000d [42 USCS §2000d], and the Equal Protection Clause of the Fourteenth Amendment. The court enjoined petitioner from considering respondent's race or the race of any other applicant in making admissions decisions. It refused, however, to order respondent's admission to the Medical School, holding that he had not carried his burden of proving that he would have been admitted but for the constitutional and statutory violations. The Supreme Court of California affirmed those portions of the trial court's judgment declaring the special admissions program unlawful and enjoining petitioner from considering the race of any applicant. It modified that portion of the judgment denying respondent's requested injunction and directed the trial court to order his admission.

For the reasons stated in the following opinion, I believe that so much of the judgment of the California court as holds petitioner's special admissions program unlawful and directs that respondent be admitted to the Medical School must be affirmed. For the reasons expressed in a separate opinion, my Brothers The Chief Justice, Mr. Justice Stewart, Mr. Justice Rehnquist, and Mr. Justice Stevens concur in this judgment.

I also conclude for the reasons stated in the following opinion that the portion of the court's judgment enjoining petitioner from according any consideration to race in its admissions process must be reversed. For reasons expressed in separate opinions, my Brothers Mr. Justice Brennan, Mr. Justice White, Mr. Justice Marshall, and Mr. Justice Blackmun concur in this judgment.

Affirmed in part and reversed in part.

• • • • •

The language of §601, like that of the Equal Protection Clause, is majestic in its sweep:

"No person in the United States shall, on the ground of race, color, or national origin, be excluded from participation in, be denied the benefits of, or be subjected to discrimination under any program or activity receiving Federal financial assistance."

The concept of "discrimination," like the phrase "equal protection of the laws," is susceptible to varying interpretations, for as Mr. Justice Holmes declared, "[a] word is not a crystal, transparent and unchanged, it is the skin of a living thought and may vary greatly in color and content according to the circumstances and the time in which it is used." . . . Examination of the voluminous legislative history of Title VI reveals a congressional intent to halt federal funding of entities that violate a prohibition of racial discrimination similar to that of the Constitution. Although isolated statements of various legislators, taken out of context, can be marshalled in support of the proposition that §601 enacted a purely colorblind scheme, without regard to the reach of the Equal Protection Clause, these comments must be read against the background of both the problem that Congress was addressing and the broader view of the statute that emerges from a full examination of the legislative debates.

The problem confronting Congress was discrimination against Negro citizens at the hands of recipients of federal moneys. Indeed, the colorblindness pronouncements . . . generally occur in the midst of extended remarks dealing with the evils of segregation in federally funded programs. Over and over again, proponents of the bill detailed the plight of Negroes seeking equal treatment in such programs. There simply was no reason for Congress to consider the validity of hypothetical preferences that might be accorded minority citizens; the legislators were dealing with the real and pressing problem of how to guarantee those citizens equal treatment.

In addressing that problem, supporters of Title VI repeatedly declared that the bill enacted constitutional principles. For example, Representative Celler, the Chairman of the House Judiciary Committee and floor manager of the legislation in the House, emphasized this in introducing the bill:

> "The bill would offer assurance that hospitals financed by Federal money would not deny adequate care to Negroes. It would prevent abuse of food distribution programs whereby Negroes have been known to be denied food surplus supplies when white persons were given such food. It would assure Negroes the benefits now accorded only white students in programs of higher education financed by Federal funds. It would, in short, *assure the existing right to equal treatment* in the enjoyment of Federal funds. It would not destroy any rights of private property or freedom of association." 110 Cong Rec 1519 (1964) (emphasis added).

Other sponsors shared Representative Celler's view that Title VI embodied constitutional principles.

In the Senate, Senator Humphrey declared that the purpose of Title VI was "to insure that Federal funds are spent in accordance with the Constitution and the moral sense of the Nation." Id., at 6544, Senator Ribicoff agreed that Title VI embraced the constitutional standard: "Basically, there is a constitutional restriction against discrimination in the use of federal funds; and title VI simply spells out the procedure to be used in enforcing that restriction." Id., at 13333. Other Senators expressed similar views. . . .

In view of the clear legislative intent, Title VI must be held to proscribe only those racial classifications that would violate the Equal Protection Clause or the Fifth Amendment.

[II. REGARDING THE LEGALITY OF THE SET-ASIDE]

Opinion of Mr. Justice Brennan, Mr. Justice White, Mr. Justice Marshall, and Mr. Justice Blackmun, concurring in the judgment in part and dissenting in part.

The threshold question we must decide is whether Title VI of the Civil Rights Act of 1964 bars recipients of federal funds from giving preferential consideration to disadvantaged members of racial minorities as part of a program designed to enable such individuals to surmount the obstacles imposed by racial discrimination. . . .

In our view, Title VI prohibits only those uses of racial criteria that would violate the Fourteenth Amendment if employed by a State or its agencies; it does not bar the preferential treatment of racial minorities as a means of remedying past societal discrimination to the extent that such action is consistent with the Fourteenth Amendment. The legislative history of Title VI, administrative regulations interpreting the statute, subsequent congressional and executive action, and the prior decisions of this Court compel this conclusion. None of these sources lends support to the proposition that Congress intended to bar all race conscious efforts to extend the benefits of federally financed programs to minorities who have been historically excluded from the full benefits of American life.

Mr. Justice Stevens, with whom The Chief Justice, Mr. Justice Stewart, and Mr. Justice Rehnquist join, concurring in the judgment in part and dissenting in part. . . .

The University, through its special admissions policy, excluded Bakke from participation in its program of medical education because of his race. The University also acknowledges that it was, and still is, receiving federal financial assistance. The plain language of the statute therefore requires affirmance of the judgment below. A different result cannot be justified unless that language misstates the actual intent of the Congress that enacted the statute or the statute is not enforceable in a private action. Neither conclusion is warranted.

Title VI is an integral part of the far-reaching Civil Rights Act of 1964. No doubt, when this legislation was being debated, Congress was not directly concerned with the legality of "reverse discrimination" or "affirmative action" programs. Its attention was focused on the problem at hand, "the glaring . . . discrimination against Negroes which exists throughout our Nation," and, with respect to Title VI, the federal funding of segregated facilities. The genesis of the legislation, however, did not limit the breadth of the solution adopted. Just as Congress responded to the problem of employment discrimination by enacting a provision that protects all races, . . . so too its answer to the problem of federal funding of segregated facilities stands as a broad prohibition against the exclusion of *any* individual from a federally funded program "on the ground of race." In the words of the House Report, Title VI stands for "the general principle that *no person* . . . be excluded from participation . . . on the ground of race, color, or national origin under any program or activity receiving Federal financial assistance." . . . This same broad view of Title VI and §601 was echoed throughout the congressional debate and was stressed by every one of the major spokesmen for the Act.

[III. REGARDING THE CONSTITUTIONALITY OF THE SET-ASIDE]

Opinion of Mr. Justice Powell.
. . . Racial and ethnic distinctions of any sort are inherently suspect and thus call for the most exacting judicial examination.

•   •   •   •   •

Although many of the Framers of the Fourteenth Amendment conceived of its primary function as bridging the vast distance between members of the Negro race and the white "majority," *Slaughter-House Cases,* supra, the Amendment itself was framed in universal terms, without reference to color, ethnic origin, or condition of prior servitude. . . .

Over the past 30 years, this Court has embarked upon the crucial mission of interpreting the Equal Protection Clause with the view of assuring to all persons "the protection of equal laws." . . .

Petitioner urges us to adopt for the first time a more restrictive view of the Equal Protection Clause and hold that discrimination against members of the white "majority" cannot be suspect if its purpose can be characterized as "benign." The clock of our liberties, however, cannot be turned back to 1868. . . .

Once the artificial line of a "two-class theory" of the Fourteenth Amendment is put aside, the difficulties entailed in varying the level of judicial review according to a perceived "preferred" status of a particular racial or ethnic minority are intractable. The concepts of "majority" and "minority" necessarily reflect temporary arrangements and political judgments. . . . [T]he white "majority" itself is composed of various minority groups, most of which can lay claim to a history of prior discrimination at the hands of the state and private individuals. Not all of these groups can receive preferential treatment and corresponding judicial tolerance of distinctions drawn in terms of race and nationality, for then the only "majority" left would be a new minority of White Anglo-Saxon Protestants. There is no principled basis for deciding which groups would merit "heightened judicial solicitude" and which would not. Courts would be asked to evaluate the extent of the prejudice and consequent harm suffered by various minority groups. Those whose societal injury is thought to exceed some arbitrary level of tolerability then would be entitled to preferential classifications at the expense of individuals belonging to other groups. Those classifications would be free from exacting judicial scrutiny. As these preferences began to have their desired effect, and the consequences of past discrimination were undone, new judicial rankings would be necessary. The kind of variable sociological and political analysis necessary to produce such rankings simply does not lie within the judicial competence—even if they otherwise were politically feasible and socially desirable. . . .

Opinion of Mr. Justice Brennan, Mr. Justice White, Mr. Justice Marshall, and Mr. Justice Blackmun.

The assertion of human equality is closely associated with the proposition that differences in color or creed, birth or status, are neither significant nor relevant to the way in which persons should be treated. Nonetheless, the position that such factors must be "[c]onstitutionally an irrelevance," . . . has never been adopted by this Court as the proper meaning of the Equal Protection Clause. Indeed, we have expressly rejected this proposition on a number of occasions.

Our cases have always implied that an "overriding statutory purpose," . . . could be found that would justify racial classifications. . . .

We conclude, therefore, that racial classifications are not per se invalid under the Fourteenth Amendment. Accordingly, we turn to the problem of articulating what our role should be in reviewing state action that expressly classifies by race.

Unquestionably we have held that a government practice or statute which restricts "fundamental rights" or which contains "suspect classifications" is to be subjected to "strict scrutiny" and can be justified only if it furthers a compelling government purpose and, even then, only if no less restrictive alternative is available. But no fundamental right is involved here. Nor do whites as a class have any of the "traditional indicia of suspectness: the class is not saddled with such disabilities, or subjected to such a history of purposeful unequal treatment, or relegated to such a position of political powerlessness as to command extraordinary protection from the majoritarian political process."

Moreover, if the University's representations are credited, this is not a case where racial classifications are "irrelevant and therefore prohibited." . . . Nor has anyone suggested that the University's purposes contravene the cardinal principle that racial classifications that stigmatize—because they are drawn on the presumption that one race is inferior to another or because they put the weight of government behind racial hatred and separatism—are invalid without more. . . .

On the other hand, the fact that this case does not fit neatly into our prior analytic framework for race cases does not mean that it should be analyzed by applying the very loose rational-basis standard of review that is the very least that is always applied in equal protection cases. "'[T]he mere recitation of a benign, compensatory purpose is not an automatic shield which protects against any inquiry into the actual purposes underlying a statutory scheme.'" Instead, a number of considerations—developed in gender discrimination cases but which carry even more force when applied to racial classifications—lead us to conclude that racial classifications designed to further remedial purposes "'must serve important governmental objectives and must be substantially related to achievement of those objectives.'"

First, race, like "gender-based classifications too often [has] been inexcusably utilized to stereotype and stigmatize politically powerless segments of society." . . . While a carefully tailored statute designed to remedy past discrimination could avoid these vices, we nonetheless have recognized that the line between honest and thoughtful appraisal of the effects of past discrimination and paternalistic stereotyping is not so clear and that a statute based on the latter is patently capable of stigmatizing all women with a badge of inferiority. State programs designed ostensibly to ameliorate the effects of past racial discrimination obviously create the same hazard of stigma, since they may promote racial separatism and reinforce the views of those who believe that members of racial minorities are inherently incapable of succeeding on their own.

Second, race, like gender and illegitimacy, . . . is an immutable characteristic which its possessors are powerless to escape or set aside. While a classification is not per se invalid because it divides classes on the basis of an immutable characteristic, it is nevertheless true that such divisions are contrary to our deep belief that "legal burdens should bear some relationship to individual responsibility or wrongdoing," and that advancement sanctioned, sponsored, or approved by the State should ideally be based on individual merit or achievement, or at the least on factors within the control of an individual.

Because this principle is so deeply rooted it might be supposed that it would be considered in the legislative process and weighed against the benefits of programs preferring individuals because of their race. But this is not necessarily so: The "natural consequence of our governing processes [may well be] that the most 'discrete and insular' of whites . . . will be called upon to bear the immediate, direct costs of benign discrimination." Moreover, it is clear from our cases that there are limits beyond which majorities may not go when they classify on the basis of immutable characteristics. Thus, even if the concern for individualism is weighed by the political process, that weighing cannot waive the personal rights of individuals under the Fourteenth Amendment. . . .

Affirmative Action Is not Damaging to Blacks or Unconstitutional: A Legal Scholar Refutes Objections to Affirmative Action, 1986

Randall Kennedy, professor of law at Harvard University, came to the defense of affirmative action in an article published in 1986 in *Harvard Law Review,* from which the following selection is excerpted.

Kennedy aimed to refute objections made against affirmative action. Some of these objections are not legal in nature. One is that affirmative action actually hurts rather than helps blacks. According to Kennedy, opponents of affirmative action think that preferential treatment hurts blacks in four ways: (1) by creating resentment against them, (2) by marking them as inferior because others think that they would not be able to succeed without

Source: Randall Kennedy, "Persuasion and Distrust: The Affirmative Action Debate," *Harvard Law Review* (April 1986).

affirmative action, (3) by making them feel bad because they realize they are not entitled to the position given to them, and (4) by not helping those blacks in greatest need of help, helping instead middle-class students and wealthy entrepreneurs who happen to be black. Kennedy presents arguments against each one of these objections.

Kennedy addresses also the main legal objection to affirmative action: that it is unconstitutional because it violates what is commonly referred to as the Equal Protection Clause. The latter is a part of the Fourteenth Amendment to the Constitution of the United States. Section I of the Fourteenth Amendment forbids any state in the United States from taking a number of actions. One of them is ". . . deny to any person within its jurisdiction the equal protection of the laws." It is those words that constitute the Equal Protection Clause. The Fourteenth Amendment was added to the Constitution three years after the end of the Civil War and was intended to protect the legal rights of the newly freed slaves in the South.

Opponents of affirmative action hold that hiring people for jobs or admitting them to universities on the basis of race violates the Equal Protection Clause because people of a different race are then treated as unequal. In contrast, Kennedy does not read the Equal Protection Clause as forbidding the use of the category of race in deciding how the government should act. He uses the term *Delphic proscription* to refer to what the Equal Protection Clause does. He seems to be saying that whatever the clause proscribes, that is, forbids the State to do, is as vague as the prophecies that the priestesses at Delphi issued in ancient Greece. Indeed, for Kennedy, the Equal Protection Clause is open to interpretation. His own interpretation is that the Constitution does not determine that any action by the government must be color-blind.

Affirmative action has strikingly benefited blacks as a group and the nation as a whole. It has enabled blacks to attain occupational and educational advancement in numbers and at a pace that would otherwise have been impossible. These breakthroughs engender self-perpetuating benefits: the accumulation of valuable experience, the expansion of a professional class able to pass its material advantages and elevated aspirations to subsequent generations, the eradication of debilitating stereotypes, and the inclusion of black participants in the making of consequential decisions affecting black interests. Without affirmative action, continued access for black applicants to college and professional education would be drastically narrowed. To insist, for example, upon the total exclusion of racial factors in admission decisions, especially at elite institutions, would mean classes of college, professional, and graduate students that are virtually devoid of African-American representation.

Furthermore, the benefits of affirmative action redound not only to blacks but to the nation as a whole. For example, the virtual absence of black police even in overwhelmingly black areas helped spark the ghetto rebellions of the 1960s. The integration of police forces through strong affirmative action measures has often led to better relations between minority communities and the police, a result that improves public safety for all. Positive externalities have

accompanied affirmative action programs in other contexts as well, most importantly by teaching whites that blacks, too, are capable of handling responsibility,
dispensing knowledge, and applying valued skills.

THE CLAIM THAT AFFIRMATIVE ACTION HARMS BLACKS

In the face of arguments in favor of affirmative action, opponents of the policy
frequently reply that it actually harms its ostensible beneficiaries. Various interrelated claims undergird the argument that affirmative action is detrimental to
blacks. The most weighty claim is that preferential treatment exacerbates racial
resentments, entrenches racial divisiveness, and thereby undermines the consensus necessary for effective reform. The problem with this view is that intense
white resentment has accompanied every effort to undo racial subordination no
matter how careful the attempt to anticipate and mollify the reaction. The
Supreme Court, for example, tried mightily to preempt white resistance to
school desegregation by directing that it be implemented with "all deliberate
speed." This attempt, however, to defuse white resistance may well have caused
the opposite effect and, in any event, doomed from the outset the constitutional
rights of a generation of black schoolchildren. Given the apparent inevitability
of white resistance and the uncertain efficacy of containment, proponents of
racial justice should be wary of allowing fear of white backlash to limit the range
of reforms pursued. This admonition is particularly appropriate with respect to
affirmative action insofar as it creates vital opportunities the value of which
likely outweigh their cost in social friction. A second part of the argument that
affirmative action hurts blacks is the claim that it stigmatizes them by implying
that they simply cannot compete on an equal basis with whites. Moreover, the
pall cast by preferential treatment is feared to be pervasive, hovering over blacks
who have attained positions without the aid of affirmative action as well as over
those who have been accorded preferential treatment. I do not doubt that
affirmative action causes some stigmatizing effect. It is unrealistic to think,
however, that affirmative action causes most white disparagement of the abilities
of blacks. Such disparagement, buttressed for decades by the rigid exclusion of
blacks from educational and employment opportunities, is precisely what en-
gendered the explosive crisis to which affirmative action is a response. Although
it is widely assumed that "qualified" blacks are now in great demand, with
virtually unlimited possibilities for recognition, blacks continue to encounter
prejudice that ignores or minimizes their talent. In the end, the uncertain extent
to which affirmative action diminishes the accomplishments of blacks must be
balanced against the stigmatization that occurs when blacks are virtually absent
from important institutions in the society. The presence of blacks across the
broad spectrum of institutional settings upsets conventional stereotypes about
the place of blacks and acculturates the public to the idea that blacks can and
must participate in all areas of our national life. This positive result of affirmative
action outweighs any stigma that the policy causes.

A third part of the argument against affirmative action is the claim that it
saps the internal morale of blacks. It renders them vulnerable to a dispiriting

anxiety that they have not truly earned whatever positions or honors they have attained. Moreover, it causes some blacks to lower their own expectations of themselves. Having grown accustomed to the extra boost provided by preferential treatment, some blacks simply do not try as hard as they otherwise would. There is considerable power to this claim; unaided accomplishment does give rise to a special pride felt by both the individual achiever and her community. But the suggestion that affirmative action plays a major role in undermining the internal morale of the black community is erroneous.

Although I am unaware of any systematic evidence on the self-image of beneficiaries of affirmative action, my own strong impression is that black beneficiaries do not see their attainments as tainted or undeserved—and for good reason. First, they correctly view affirmative action as rather modest compensation for the long period of racial subordination suffered by blacks as a group. Thus they do not feel that they have been merely *given* a preference; rather, they see affirmative discrimination as a form of social justice. Second, and more importantly, many black beneficiaries of affirmative action view claims of meritocracy with skepticism. They recognize that in many instances the objection that affirmative action represents a deviation from meritocratic standards is little more than disappointed nostalgia for a golden age that never really existed. Overt exclusion of blacks from public and private institutions of education and employment was one massive affront to meritocratic pretensions. Moreover, a long-standing and pervasive feature of our society is the importance of a wide range of nonobjective, nonmeritocratic factors influencing the distribution of opportunity. The significance of personal associations and informal networks is what gives durability and resonance to the adage: It's not *what* you know, it's *who* you know. As Professor Wasserstrom wryly observes, "Would anyone claim that Henry Ford II [was] head of the Ford Motor Company because he [was] the most qualified person for the job?"

Finally, and most importantly, many beneficiaries of affirmative action recognize the thoroughly political—which is to say contestable—nature of "merit"; they realize that it is a malleable concept, determined not by immanent, preexisting standards but rather by the perceived needs of society. Inasmuch as the elevation of blacks addresses pressing social needs, they rightly insist that considering a black's race as part of the bundle of traits that constitute "merit" is entirely appropriate.

A final and related objection to affirmative action is that it frequently aids those blacks who need it least and who can least plausibly claim to suffer the vestiges of past discrimination—the offspring of black middle-class parents seeking preferential treatment in admission to elite universities and black entrepreneurs seeking guaranteed set-asides for minority contractors on projects supported by the federal government. This objection, too, is unpersuasive. First, it ignores the large extent to which affirmative action has pried open opportunities for blue-collar black workers. Second, it assumes that affirmative action should be provided only to the most deprived strata of the black community or to those who can best document their victimization. In many circumstances, however, affirmative action has developed from the premise that special aid should be given to strategically important sectors of the black community—for example, those with the threshold ability to integrate the professions. Third, although affirmative action has primarily benefited the black middle class, that is no reason to condemn preferential treatment. All that fact indicates is the necessity for additional social intervention to address unmet needs in those sectors of the black community left untouched by affirmative action. One thing that proponents of affirmative action have neglected to emphasize strongly enough is that affirmative discrimination is but part—indeed a rather small part—of the needed response to the appalling crisis besetting black communities. What is so remarkable—and ominous—about the affirmative action debate is that so modest a reform calls forth such powerful resistance.

DOES AFFIRMATIVE ACTION VIOLATE THE CONSTITUTION?

The constitutional argument against affirmative action proceeds as follows: *All* governmental distinctions based on race are presumed to be illegal and can only escape that presumption by meeting the exacting requirements of "strict scrutiny." Because the typical affirmative action program cannot meet these requirements, most such programs are unconstitutional. Behind this theory lies a conviction that has attained its most passionate and oft-quoted articulation in Alexander Bickel's statement:

> The lesson of the great decisions of the Supreme Court and the lesson of contemporary history have been the same for at least a generation: discrimination on the basis of race is illegal, immoral, unconstitutional, inherently wrong, and destructive of democratic society. Now this is to be unlearned and we are told that this is not a matter of fundamental principle but only a matter of whose ox is gored.

Among the attractions of this theory are its symmetry and simplicity. It commands that the government be color blind in its treatment of persons, that it accord benefits and burdens to black and white individuals according to precisely the *same* criteria—no matter whose ox is gored. According to its proponents, this theory dispenses with manipulable sociological investigations and provides a clear *rule* that compels consistent judicial application.

In response, I would first note that the color-blind theory of the Constitution is precisely that—a "theory," one of any number of competing theories that seek to interpret the Fourteenth Amendment's Delphic proscription of state action that denies any person "the equal protection of the laws." Implicitly recognizing that neither a theory of original intent nor a theory of textual construction provides suitable guidance, Professor Bickel suggests that a proper resolution of the affirmative action dispute can be derived from "the great decisions of the Supreme Court." Certainly what Bickel had in mind were *Brown v. Board of Education* and its immediate progeny, the cases that established the foundation of our postsegregation Constitution. To opponents of affirmative action, the lesson of these cases is that, except in the narrowest, most exigent circumstances, race can play no legitimate role in governmental decision-making.

This view, however, is too abstract and ahistorical. In the forties, fifties, and early sixties, against the backdrop of laws that used racial distinctions to exclude blacks from opportunities available to white citizens, it seemed that racial subjugation could be overcome by mandating the application of race-blind law. In retrospect, however, it appears that the concept of race-blindness was simply a proxy for the fundamental demand that racial subjugation be eradicated. This demand, which matured over time in the face of myriad sorts of opposition, focused upon the *condition* of racial subjugation; its target was not only procedures that overtly excluded blacks on the basis of race, but also the self-perpetuating dynamics of subordination that had survived the demise of American apartheid. The opponents of affirmative action have stripped the historical context from the demand for race-blind law. They have fashioned this demand into a new totem and insist on deference to it no matter what its effects upon the very group the Fourteenth Amendment was created to protect. *Brown* and its progeny do not stand for the abstract principle that governmental distinctions based on race are unconstitutional. Rather, those great cases, forged by the gritty particularities of the struggle against white racism, stand for the proposition that the Constitution prohibits any arrangements imposing racial subjugation—whether such arrangements are ostensibly race neutral or even ostensibly race blind.

This interpretation, which articulates a principle of antisubjugation rather than antidiscrimination, typically encounters two closely related objections. The first objection is the claim that the constitutional injury done to a white whose chances for obtaining some scarce opportunity are diminished because of race-based allocation schemes is legally indistinguishable from that suffered by a black victim of racial exclusion. Second, others argue that affirmative discrimination based on racial distinctions cannot be satisfactorily differentiated from racial subjugation absent controversial sociological judgments that are inappropriate to the judicial role.

As to the first objection, the injury suffered by white "victims" of affirmative action does not properly give rise to a constitutional claim, because the damage does not derive from a scheme animated by racial prejudice. Whites with certain credentials may be excluded from particular opportunities they would receive if they were black. But this diminished opportunity is simply an incidental consequence of addressing a compelling societal need: undoing the subjugation of African Americans. Whites who would be admitted to professional schools in the absence of affirmative action policies are not excluded merely because of prejudice, as were countless numbers of blacks until fairly recently. Rather, whites are excluded "because of a rational calculation about the socially most beneficial use of limited resources for [professional] education."

As to the second objection, I concede that distinctions between affirmative and malign discrimination cannot be made in the absence of controversial sociological judgments. I reject the proposition, however, that drawing these distinctions is inappropriate to the judicial role. Such a proposition rests upon the assumption that there exists a judicial method wholly independent of sociological judgment. That assumption is false; to some extent, whether explicitly or implicitly, *every* judicial decision rests upon certain premises regarding the irreducibly controversial nature of social reality. The question, therefore, is not whether a court will make sociological judgments, but the content of the socio-logical judgments it must inevitably make.

Prior to *Brown*, the Supreme Court's validation of segregation statutes rested upon the premise that they did not unequally burden the black. A per-ceived difficulty in invalidating segregation statutes was that, as written, such laws were race neutral; they excluded white children from black schools just as they excluded black children from white schools. The Court finally recognized in *Brown* that racial subjugation constituted the social meaning of segregation laws. To determine that social meaning, the Court had to look past form into substance and judge the legitimacy of segregation laws given their intended and actual effects. Just as the "neutrality" of the segregation laws obfuscated racial subjugation, so, too, may the formal neutrality of race-blind policies also obfus-cate the perpetuation of racial subjugation. That issue can only be explored by an inquiry into the context of the race-blind policy at issue, an inquiry that necessarily entails judicial sociology.

Promoted Over a Male: The Diane Joyce Story, as Told by Susan Faludi, 1991

In 1991, Susan Faludi, a reporter for the *Wall Street Journal*, published *Backlash: The Undeclared War Against Women*, from which the following selection is drawn. The book's thesis is that men are reacting to advances in women's rights by attempting to bring conditions back to the way they were when the subjugation of women was the norm in the United States. Part of the backlash is manifested in male resistance to women taking jobs that men regard as their exclusive preserve.

Faludi told the story of Diane Joyce, a road maintenance worker in California who in 1980 was first denied, then given, a promotion over a male worker. The Joyce story presents aspects of the human side of the legal case known as *Johnson v. Santa Clara County*.

Two years before Joyce's promotion, her employer, the Santa Clara County Transportation Agency, had adopted voluntarily an affirmative ac-tion program that took into account the sex or race of qualified applicants for promotion within job categories traditionally open only to white men. The program did not set aside a specific number of jobs but had instead the goal of increasing annually the number of women and minorities promoted in traditionally segregated job categories. When Diane Joyce was chosen over Paul Johnson for the position of road dispatcher—which had never been held by a woman and for which she was as qualified as he—Johnson took the Transportation Agency to court. Johnson's position was that the Agency's affirmative action program was illegal under Title VII of the Civil Rights Act of 1964, which forbids discrimination in employment on the

Source: Susan Faludi, *Backlash: The Undeclared War Against American Women* (New York: Crown Publishers, 1991), pp. 388–93.

basis of sex. Johnson thought he was unfairly discriminated against because he was male.

The case reached the Supreme Court in 1986 and was decided in 1987. By a vote of 6 to 3 the Court ruled that the Santa Clara affirmative action program was legal. The Court observed that the program did not establish discriminatory quotas and required women to compete for promotion with other qualified applicants. Moreover, the program did not establish an absolute ban on promoting men. In *United Steelworkers of America v. Weber* (1979) the Court had ruled that Title VII does not prohibit voluntary race-based affirmative action when there is a need to eliminate racial imbalance in traditionally segregated lines of work. In the *Johnson* case, the Court extended that reasoning to the category of sex.

It would take Diane Joyce nearly ten years of battles to become the first female skilled crafts worker ever in Santa Clara County history. It would take another seven years of court litigation, pursued all the way to the U.S. Supreme Court, before she could actually start work. And then, the real fight would begin.

For blue-collar women, there was no honeymoon period on the job; the backlash began the first day they reported to work—and only intensified as the Reagan economy put more than a million blue-collar men out of work, reduced wages, and spread mounting fear. While the white-collar world seemed capable of absorbing countless lawyers and bankers in the '80s, the trades and crafts had no room for expansion. "Women are far more economically threatening in blue-collar work, because there are a finite number of jobs from which to choose," Mary Ellen Boyd, executive director of Non-Traditional Employment for Women, observes. "An MBA can do anything. But a plumber is only a plumber." While women never represented more than a few percentage points of the blue-collar work force, in this powder-keg situation it only took a few female faces to trigger a violent explosion.

Diane Joyce arrived in California in 1970, a thirty-three-year-old widow with four children, born and raised in Chicago. Her father was a tool-and-die maker, her mother a returned-goods clerk at a Walgreen's warehouse. At eighteen, she married Donald Joyce, a tool-and-die maker's apprentice at her father's plant. Fifteen years later, after working knee-deep in PCBs for years, he died suddenly of a rare form of liver cancer.

After her husband's death, Joyce taught herself to drive, packed her children in a 1966 Chrysler station wagon and headed west to San Jose, California, where a lone relative lived. Joyce was an experienced bookkeeper and she soon found work as a clerk in the county Office of Education, at $506 a month. A year later, she heard that the county's transportation department had a senior account clerk job vacant that paid $50 more a month. She applied in March 1972.

"You know, we wanted a man," the interviewer told her as soon as she walked through the door. But the account clerk jobs had all taken a pay cut recently, and sixteen women and no men had applied for the job. So he sent her on to the second interview. "This guy was a little politer," Joyce recalls. "First, he said, 'Nice day, isn't it?' before he tells me, 'You know, we wanted a man.' I wanted to say, 'Yeah, and where's my man? I am the man in my house.' But I'm sitting there with four kids to feed and all I can see is dollar signs, so I kept my mouth shut."

She got the job. Three months later, Joyce saw a posting for a "road maintenance man." An eighth-grade education and one year's work experience was all that was required, and the pay was $723 a month. Her current job required a high-school education, bookkeeping skills, and four years' experience—and paid $150 less a month. "I saw that flier and I said, 'Oh wow, I can do that.' Everyone in the office laughed. They thought it was a riot. . . . I let it drop."

But later that same year, every county worker got a 2 to 5 percent raise except for the 70 female account clerks. "Oh now, what do you girls need a raise for?" the director of personnel told Joyce and some other women who went before the board of supervisors to object. "All you'd do is spend the money on trips to Europe." Joyce was shocked. "Every account clerk I knew was supporting a family through death or divorce. I'd never seen Mexico, let alone Europe." Joyce decided to apply for the next better-paying "male" job that opened. In the meantime, she became active in the union; a skillful writer and one of the best-educated representatives there, Joyce wound up composing the safety language in the master contract and negotiating what became the most powerful county agreement protecting seniority rights.

In 1974, a road dispatcher retired, and both Joyce and a man named Paul Johnson, a former oil-fields roustabout, applied for the post. The supervisors told Joyce she needed to work on the road crew first and handed back her application. Johnson didn't have any road crew experience either, but his application was accepted. In the end, the job went to another man.

Joyce set out to get road crew experience. As she was filling out her application for the next road crew job that opened, in 1975, her supervisor walked in, asked what she was doing, and turned red. "You're taking a man's job away!" he shouted. Joyce sat silently for a minute, thinking. Then she said, "No, I'm not. Because a man can sit right here where I'm sitting."

In the evenings, she took courses in road maintenance and truck and light equipment operation. She came in third out of 87 applicants on the job test; there were ten openings on the road crew, and she got one of them.

For the next four years, Joyce carried tar pots on her shoulder, pulled trash from the median strip, and maneuvered trucks up the mountains to clear mud slides. "Working outdoors was great," she says. "You know, women pay fifty dollars a month to join a health club, and here I am getting paid to get in shape."

The road men didn't exactly welcome her arrival. When they trained her to drive the bobtail trucks, she says, they kept changing instructions; one gave her driving tips that nearly blew up the engine. Her supervisor wouldn't issue her a pair of coveralls; she had to file a formal grievance to get them. In the yard, the men kept the ladies' room locked, and on the road they wouldn't stop to let her use the bathroom. "You wanted a man's job, you learn to pee like a man," her supervisor told her.

Obscene graffiti about Joyce appeared on the sides of trucks. Men threw darts at union notices she posted on the bulletin board. One day, the stockroom storekeeper, Tony Laramie, who says later he liked to call her "the piglet," called a general meeting in the depot's Ready Room. "I hate the day you came here," Laramie started screaming at Joyce as the other men looked on, many nodding. "We don't want you here. You don't belong here. Why don't you go the hell away?"

Joyce's experience was typical of the forthright and often violent backlash within the blue-collar work force, an assault undisguised by decorous homages to women's "difference." At a construction site in New York, for example, where only a few female hard-hats had found work, the men took a woman's work boots and hacked them into bits. Another woman was injured by a male co-worker; he hit her on the head with a two-by-four. In Santa Clara County, where Joyce worked, the county's equal opportunity office files were stuffed with reports of ostracism, hazing, sexual harassment, threats, verbal and physical abuse. "It's pervasive in some of the shops," says John Longabaugh, the county's equal employment officer at the time. "They mess up their tools, leave pornography on their desks. Safety equipment is made difficult to get, or unavailable." A maintenance worker greeted the first woman in his department with these words: "I know someone who would break your arm or leg for a price." Another new woman was ordered to clean a transit bus by her supervisor—only to find when she climbed aboard that the men had left a little gift for her: feces smeared across the seats.

In 1980, another dispatcher job opened up. Joyce and Johnson both applied. They both got similarly high scores on the written exam. Joyce now had four years' experience on the road crew; Paul Johnson only had a year and a half. The three interviewers, one of whom later referred to Joyce in court as "rabble-rousing" and "not a lady," gave the job to Johnson. Joyce decided to complain to the county affirmative action office.

The decision fell to James Graebner, the new director of the transportation department, an engineer who believed that it was about time the county hired its first woman for its 238 skilled-crafts jobs. Graebner confronted the roads director, Ron Shields. "What's wrong with the woman?" Graebner asked. "I hate her," Shields said, according to other people in the room. "I just said I thought Johnson was more qualified," is how Shields remembers it. "She didn't have the proficiency with heavy equipment." Neither, of course, did Johnson. Not that it was relevant anyway: dispatch is an office job that doesn't require lifting anything heavier than a microphone.

Graebner told Shields he was being overruled; Joyce had the job. Later that day, Joyce recalls, her supervisor called her into the conference room. "Well, you got the job," he told her. "But you're not qualified." Johnson, meanwhile, sat by the phone, dialing up the chain of command. "I felt like tearing something up," he recalls later. He demanded a meeting with the affirmative action office. "The affirmative action man walks in," Johnson says, "and he's this big black guy. He can't tell me anything. He brings in this minority who can barely speak English. . . . I told them, 'You haven't heard the last of me.'" Within days, he had hired a lawyer and set his reverse discrimination suit in motion, contending that the county had given the job to a "less qualified" woman.

In 1987, the Supreme court ruled against Johnson. The decision was hailed by women's and civil rights groups. But victory in Washington was not the same as triumph in the transportation yard. For Joyce and the road men, the backlash was just warming up. "Something like this is going to hurt me one day," Gerald Pourroy, a foreman in Joyce's office, says of the court's ruling, his voice low and bitter. He stares at the concrete wall above his desk. "I look down the tracks and I see the train coming toward me."

The day after the Supreme Court decision, a woman in the county office sent Joyce a congratulatory bouquet, two dozen carnations. Joyce arranged the flowers in a vase on her desk. The next day they were gone. She found them finally, crushed in a garbage bin. A road foreman told her, "I drop-kicked them across the yard."

•   •   •   •   •

Several months after the court's verdict on a late summer afternoon, the county trucks groan into the depot yard, lifting the dust in slow, tired circles. The men file in, and Joyce takes their keys and signs them out. Four men in one-way sunglasses lean as far as they can over the counter.

"Well, well well. Diii-ane. How the hell are you?"

"Hey, Diane, how the fuck are you?"

"Oh, don't ask her. She don't know that."

"Yeah, Diane, she don't know nothing."

Diane Joyce continues to smile, thinly, as she collects the keys. Some of the men drift over to the Ready Room. They leaf through dog-eared copies of *Guns* magazine and kick an uncooperative snack vending machine. When asked about Diane Joyce, they respond with put-downs and bitterness.

"She thinks she is high class now that she's got her face on TV," one of the men says. "Like we are dirt or something."

"Now all a girl has got to do is say, Hey, they're discriminating, and she gets a job. You tell me how a man's supposed to get a promotion against something like that."

"She's not qualified for ninety-nine percent of the jobs, I'll tell you that right now. I bet next foreman's job opens up, she'll get it just because she's female. I've been a road maintenance worker sixteen years. Now you tell me what's fair?"

Paul Johnson has since retired to the tiny fishing town of Sequim, Washington. From there, he dispatches an "Open letter to the White Males of America" to newspaper offices across the country: "Fellow men," he writes, "I believe it is time for us to object to OUR suppression." His wife Betty, Johnson explains, helped compose and typed the letter. Her job at a bank also helped pay the bills—and underwrote much of his reverse discrimination lawsuit.

Women's numbers in the Santa Clara County's skilled-crafts jobs, after the Supreme Court ruling, increased by a paltry two to three a year. By the end of 1988, while the total number of available craft slots had grown from 238 to 468, the number of women rose only to 12. This was not because women had lost interest in these jobs. They were enrolling in union craft apprenticeship programs in the area in record numbers. And a county survey of its own female employees (who were still overwhelmingly relegated to the clerical pool) found that 85 percent of these women were interested in higher-paying "men's" jobs. Moreover, 90 percent of the women surveyed said they believed they knew the reason why they weren't getting these higher-paying positions: discrimination.

White Males as Victims: Casualties of Affirmative Action, 1991

Sociologist Frederick R. Lynch has opposed affirmative action, considering it contradictory to American legal principles. Furthermore, to Lynch, affirmative action has been imposed from above without the consent of the American people, the great majority of whom are opposed to preferential treatment based on race, ethnicity, or sex.

In 1991 Lynch published his book *Invisible Victims: White Males and the Crisis of Affirmative Action,* from which this selection is taken. According to Lynch, his book "explores how an official system of race-and-gender-preferences was imposed upon American life in spite of laws and massive public opinion against such policies."

A great part of the book deals with the actual experiences of white males who suffered the consequences of the application of affirmative action policies, which for Lynch, without exception, constitute reverse discrimination. In fact he regards *affirmative action* and *reverse discrimination* as interchangeable terms.

In providing real-life cases, Lynch wished to contrast what he saw as very negative consequences of affirmative action with what he termed its "early, airy 'ideals,'" with a view to raising the issue.

Lynch was particularly interested in studying how white men *reacted* to affirmative action. He looked at thirty-two men and divided them into five categories according to whether they (1) acquiesced quietly, (2) acquiesced but were angry, (3) acquiesced but departed, (4) were defiant and protested, or (5) circumvented affirmative action.

Lynch reported his observations partly in the shape of anecdotes. The following excerpt deals with men who were defiant and took some action.

DEFIANCE/PROTEST

Three persons interviewed for this study filed lawsuits against employers on charges of discrimination: Mike Grant, Frank Nunn, and Samuel Gray. A fourth subject, teacher David Brown, tried to seek redress through his teacher's union (to no avail) and took more colorful steps to publicly protect his fate (also to no avail).

Source: Frederick R. Lynch, *Invisible Victims: White Males and the Crisis of Affirmative Action* (New York: Praeger Publishers, 1991), pp. 63–67.

Mike Grant

Until 1983, Grant had not had a promotion in the large state administrative agency for which he had worked since 1968. In 1973, he wrote a mild letter of protest to the head of the agency, stating that, while he was sympathetic to affirmative action goals, he felt that unqualified persons were being hired and promoted. He claims to have received a "non-response response" filled with rhetoric.

Grant remained silent on the issue for the rest of the 1970s. Though he claimed that he was repeatedly bypassed for promotion in favor of less qualified minority persons, he "went along." He claimed he did not bring up the matter in private conversations unless others did. A devout Christian, he felt some sympathy for affirmative action and is sympathetic to the less fortunate.

In August 1983, Grant stated that he was asked to apply for a high-level job as aide to one of the persons overseeing the entire state division. He asked if affirmative action might be a factor and was told that the particular position fell outside of affirmative action guidelines. Besides, of the other nine similar positions, seven were filled by minority persons. In September, Grant was informally notified that he had been appointed. His superior announced the decision within the governing board. Grant completed the appropriate forms and began training assignments in mid-September.

Word was passed informally throughout the state and, as he made his rounds in his new position, Grant received many calls and notes of congratulations. But in early October, his superior called him in and told Grant that he would not have the job after all and that the supervisor had been told to hire a minority. "Let's face it, Mike, you're not the right color."

Grant filled in for his former superior, who was on vacation, then was returned to his old job. Colleagues and friends assumed Grant had somehow "screwed up" in the new job.

Grant resigned his job and filed suit in state court.

The outcome of Grant's legal actions is uncertain. Grant relocated and attempts to re-establish contact with him were unsuccessful.

Frank Nunn

By his own admission, forty-six-year-old Frank Nunn has always been a "classic Jewish liberal." He was active in the civil rights movement and suffered a back injury during a police beating, which has hospitalized him twice since that time. He believed in affirmative action and still does, though he admits he still hasn't sorted out his feelings on the matter. ("I agree with Justice Powell in the Bakke decision that race can be *a* factor, but not *the* factor.")

While involved in the civil rights movement and other social causes, Nunn obtained bachelor's and master's degrees in social science and, in the 1970s, became actively involved in the administration of a popular black mayor. Because of his background and training in public administration, Nunn obtained a rather high-level job, though he did notice that he was the only white at that level in that particular agency.

The agency for which he worked for two years was not covered by the city civil-service system until 1977, when plans were made to convert the agency positions to civil-service status. The agency employees had to take the civil service examination and be merged with civil service employees already on the list seeking promotions. Nunn claims to have been at the top of the merged list, but the next six highest scores went to persons already in city government in other agencies. There were eight new positions. Two minority administrators in Nunn's agency were not high enough on the list to retain their positions in the transformed agency, unless Nunn was removed from the list.

Therefore, according to Nunn, he was abruptly and without warning fired from his position two weeks before it was to come under civil service rules. By law, his name was automatically removed from the list, and the two minority administrators retained their positions in the "new" agency. (Nunn obtained internal memoranda detailing these intentions, and these documents were the basis of his legal proceedings.)

Nunn filed charges with the Equal Employment Opportunity Commission and the Civil Service Board. The latter voted unanimously to restore Frank to two civil service lists and he was offered another job at $8,000 a year less than he had previously earned. But city officials refused to follow through on the other recommendations of the board, and Nunn again filed charges with the Equal Employment Opportunity Commission and other federal agencies. He claimed to have been harrassed in his new position to such an extent that he was forced to seek psychiatric counseling for the first time in his life. The conflicts on the job compounded problems in his social life, and Nunn wound up taking two short disability leaves and a final long-term disability leave.

Since the EEOC had a huge backlog of cases and since the city was reneging on promises made to him, Nunn filed a reverse discrimination case against the city in 1979. Nunn reached a settlement with the city regarding the job in which he was harrassed (after the reverse discrimination event) and he enrolled in law school in another city.

Looking back on the situation in which he eventually suffered reverse discrimination, he admits

> I should have seen it coming. . . . I was the only white male at that level in the entire agency. There were various slights and slurs that I took because I wanted to work in the administration of a black mayor. So I turned the other cheek and got the shit slapped out of me. . . . It was a twenty-four-hour-a-day battle. . . . It shot my personal life to hell.

Nunn lost his reverse discrimination lawsuit against the city in 1986.

Samuel Gray

Filing reverse discrimination charges was not nearly as traumatic for Samuel Gray, a forty-nine-year-old college physics professor. Gray had been passed over for a deanship for which he'd been ranked number one through an entire process (screenings by faculty, student, and administration committees and by the president of the campus). He had remained number one until a new step was suddenly added—an interview with the head of the entire district—who was a minority and appointed "one of his own" further down the list.

"I'm mad as hell and I'm not going to take it any more," Gray quipped, when he was interviewed in 1986. "I really expected to get the position after I was first on the list. But when the chancellor's interview came up, I knew I was sunk."

He admitted the timing of his suit may have made things different for him than Bakke and others (such as Frank Nunn) who filed in the 1970s. He claimed that the entire college community had been in turmoil for years over hiring processes and that "every single hiring they've had has been a fight for years." The recently appointed Latino president of his campus, he reported, had simply been "imposed" upon the college community—over their expressed opposition —by the district administration.

"My major goal," stated Gray "is to stop this sort of hiring in the future. . . . It won't help me much. If I got the position through a lawsuit, there'd be no way of working things out anyway."

Upon hearing he had not been chosen, Gray immediately wrote to the Board of Supervisors. This action turned out to be futile and gave the faculty union an excuse to stay out of the dispute. The union claimed that by writing directly to the Board of Supervisors, he had "used up" the formal grievance process.

Gray checked out the Equal Employment Opportunity Commission, but they seemed cool and wanted to examine the matter on an individual case basis. But in contrast to EEOC's usual procedures, the agency did not want to look at past patterns of hiring and promotion in the community college district. So Gray approached a large law firm, which took his case on a contingency basis. Gray was delighted to find he had the full support of his colleagues, who donated $6,000 to cover his initial court costs.

THE FRUSTRATING COURSE OF LEGAL ACTION

I re-interviewed Gray just as this book went to production in March 1989. By that time, Gray's case had been tried before a jury in federal district court. Gray's frustrating, time-consuming experience seems typical of white males who take legal action in reverse discrimination cases.

Much to the surprise of Gray and his lawyer, they lost the charge of conspiracy and monetary damage award. An even greater frustration was the judge's refusal to allow any consideration of whether the college's affirmative action plan was constitutional. On several other aspects of the case, however, the jury remained deadlocked. Since the all-important, constitutional question had been ignored, Gray's lawyer tried to move the case directly to the federal appellate court. But the appellate court, according to Gray, had a huge backlog of reverse discrimination cases, which it appeared reluctant to confront. Gray's lawyer was told to ask for a complete retrial on all charges. In November 1988, the district judge informed Gray's lawyer that he would set a new date for retrial—but had not done so by March 1989.

The law firm conducting Gray's case was a large one and, feeling that the chances for victory were quite favorable, had accepted the case on a contingency basis. The case had cost the firm more than $300,000. Though he'd received financial contributions from fellow faculty, Gray had spent money of his own and was emotionally exhausted.

"It's really taken it out of me," he admitted. "It's been one hell of a strain on me, my family, work relationships. . . . The legal system grinds you into the ground. The courts are a real crap shoot. We were really surprised by the verdict. . . . It's going to take about five more years before this thing is settled. If anyone were to ask me to take these things to court—knowing what I do now—I think I might say 'no.'"

Gray's remarks parallel those of a potential subject whom I contacted but who refused to be interviewed for the study. He, too, had sued the public agency for which he worked. After a five-year battle, he won. His struggle, however, had taken an enormous toll on his personal life, his family relationships, and his career. He did not care to relive the ordeal through an interview.

As mentioned in Chapter 1, legal redress through administrative agencies or the courts has not been perceived as a viable option by most white males interviewed for this study. Most seemed to feel that filing a complaint with EEOC or taking action in the courts would do them little good. Legal action against current employers was seen as producing more harm than good. These attitudes of mistrust or futility toward the legal system parallel similar views among female and minority victims of discrimination interviewed by Kristen Bumiller. Her conclusions very much apply to the findings in this book.

> People who have experienced discriminatory treatment resist engagement in legal tactics because they stand in awe of the power of the law to disrupt their daily lives. At the same time, they are cynical about the power of the law actually to help them secure jobs, housing, and other opportunities they lay claim to. They fear that, if they seek a legal resolution, they will not improve their position but will lose control of a hostile situation. These respondents also feel that asserting their legal rights could not enable them to express their sense of dignity but would force them to justify their worthiness against a more powerful opponent. Injured persons reluctantly employ the label of discrimination because they shun the role of the victim. Therefore, they choose to rely on strategies for economic and personal survival that perpetuate their victimization but are seen as more desirable than submitting to the terms of legal discourse. (1988: 109)

The experiences of those white males in this study who attempted to resolve reverse discrimination through legal channels indicate that the price of justice—if obtained at all—is very high.

SUGGESTIONS FOR FURTHER READING
J. Dreyfuss and C. Lawrence III, *The Bakke Case: The Politics of Inequality*. New York: Harcourt Brace Jovanovich, 1979.

Terry Eastland and William J. Bennett, *Counting by Race: Equality from the Founding Fathers to Bakke and Weber*. New York: Basic Books, 1979.

R. K. Fullinwider, *The Reverse Discrimination Controversy*. Totowa, N.J.: Rowman & Littlefield, 1980.

A. H. Goldman, *Justice and Preferential Treatment*. Princeton, N.J.: Princeton University Press, 1979.

Kent Greenwalt, *Discrimination and Reverse Discrimination*. New York: Alfred A. Knopf, 1983.